MORESHET

Journal for the Study

of the Holocaust

and Antisemitism

Historiography of the Holocaust

Claims Conference

This publication has been supported by a grant from the Conference on Jewish Material Claims Against Germany

MORESHET

Journal for the Study

of the Holocaust

and Antisemitism

Historiography of the Holocaust

Dr. Graciela Ben Dror
Editor

Moreshet, The Mordechai Anielevich Memorial
Holocaust Study and Research Center, Givat Haviva

Alfred P. Slaner Chair in Antisemitism and Racism,
Tel Aviv University

17 | 2020

Moreshet, The Mordechai Anielevich Memorial was established in 1961 by: **Yehuda Bauer, the late Yisrael Gutman, Abba Kovner, Shalom Cholawsky, Ruzka Korczak, Akiva Nir, Yehuda Tubin, and Haika Grossman**

MORESHET
Journal for the Study of the Holocaust and Antisemitism

Editor
Dr. Graciela Ben Dror

Editorial Board
Prof. Yehuda Bauer, Dr. Graciela Ben Dror, Prof. Aviva Halamish, Dr. Ariel Hurwitz, Prof. Guy Miron, Prof. Dalia Ofer, Prof. Dina Porat, Dr. Marcos Silber, Dr. Roni Stauber, Prof. Eli Tzur, Dr. Rafi Vago, Dr. Esther Webman

Moreshet Director
Maya Van-Ech Argov

English Language Editor
Naomi Landau

Published by
Moreshet, The Mordechai Anielevich Memorial
Holocaust Study and Research Center, Givat Haviva

The Alfred P. Slaner Chair in Antisemitism and Racism
Tel Aviv University

This publication has been supported by grants from

The Havatzelet Cultural and Educational Institutions

and from the Eta and Sass Somekh Family Foundation

Design
Amy Erani www.multieducator.net

TABLE OF CONTENTS

Historiography of the Holocaust

From The Editor

We are pleased to present our readers with Issue No. 100 of *Moreshet, The Journal for the Study of the Holocaust and Antisemitism*, which has been peer-reviewed for many years. Moreshet, the Mordechai Anielevich Memorial Holocaust Study and Research Center, was founded in 1961, and its journal – *Moreshet, The Journal for the Study of the Holocaust* – published its first issue just two years later, in December 1963. The journal has been published on a regular basis ever since. In its early years it appeared biannually only in Hebrew, but it subsequently came to be published on an annual basis in both Hebrew and English. Since 2011, Professor Dina Porat, head of the Alfred P. Slaner Chair for the Study of Racism and Antisemitism at Tel Aviv University, has lent this institution's support and expertise to the undertaking, adding an important layer of academization to the journal, as well as two words, making its title: *Moreshet, The Journal for the Study of the Holocaust and Antisemitism*.

Over the years, *Moreshet Journal* has published articles authored by experts on a wide variety of topics in the field. Young scholars at the beginning of their professional careers have also been given the opportunity to publish their initial studies in the journal. *Moreshet Journal* has a number of regular sections: a main section containing articles on historical subjects that are based on primary documents; a section dealing with testimonies and documentation; and a book review section. The journal's editorial board decided to designate the journal's 100th issue strictly for articles dealing with different aspects of Holocaust historiography. As a result, the issue explores a variety of subjects related to historiography with an eye toward understanding how different scholars have reached different conclusions – which are sometimes consistent with one another and at other times completely different, sparking historiographical debate – based on exactly the same documentation: either existing documentation or new documents discovered in archives as they are opened up for public viewing. Each article focuses on a specific topic that has been researched and assigned different interpretations based on different understandings of the documents, the emphasis placed on each one, different understandings of the context, and the centrality of the events according to their analysis by different historians.

The issue begins with Professors Dalia Ofer and Dina Porat's interview with Prof. Yehuda Bauer, a recipient of the Israel Prize and one of the world's most prominent Holocaust scholars. Bauer founded *Moreshet Journal* in conjunction with Abba Kovner and Israel Gutman. To mark the journal's 100th issue, it is a great honor for us to include this interview with Prof. Bauer pertaining to the major issues of the historical scholarship on the Holocaust and genocide, which he continues to research and lecture on in international venues around the world. One of the main topics explored by the interviewers – Professors Dalia Ofer and Dina Porat – is the connection between genocide and the Holocaust as a subject of comparative research. The term "genocide," was coined by Jewish attorney Raphael Lemkin in 1946 to express the idea that the extermination of a single human group is like the extermination of humanity as a whole. He fought in international forums for "genocide" to be recognized as an "international crime" against humanity, as a means of preventing such crimes and of facilitating their punishment. In December 1948 the U.N. General Assembly decided on the matter and Lemkin was successful. Prof. Yehuda Bauer is still deeply involved in research and activity in the realm of genocide prevention. He is also active in two groups that strive to create tools to prevent genocide: the Genocide Prevention Advisory Network and the Global Action Against Mass Atrocity Crimes (GAAMAC), which is run by the government of Switzerland and seeks to create government tools for preventing these crimes in the future.

The first articles appearing in this issue address different aspects of the Holocaust itself, such as the ghettos, the concentration camps, and problems that arose during the period. Next are articles concerning the debate that emerged in the Yishuv regarding the *ma`apilim* and the Holocaust, followed by articles addressing different aspects of the debate that took place after the Holocaust and the historiography on various contexts and subjects that took form. To conclude the issue, we offer a number of articles contending with broader issues, interpretations and insights from after the war, the question of the universalism versus the uniqueness of the Holocaust, and the question of whether we can speak of an Arab historiography of the Holocaust.

Dalia Ofer's article explores the historiographic development of Jewish life in the ghettos of Eastern Europe. The first subject it considers is why, up until the 1990s, scholars preferred to discuss the organization of public life rather than discussing the individual's coping with the challenges presented by life in the ghetto. This question becomes even more intriguing in light of the fact that the historians and the researchers studying society in the ghettos focused primarily on collecting material pertaining to the coping of individuals, families, children, refugees, and others. Ofer then addresses the question of why, from the 1990s onward, the means of coping with the difficult reality in the ghetto become an important subject in the scholarship. This brings us to the method that can be used to examine these issues, which is related to the immense importance of personal materials, approaches of micro-history, and the use of terminology from the social sciences to portray the coping of the individual. The article concludes with a number of examples of new studies that have been published in Israel over the past decade and that are representative of the research method proposed in the article.

Havi Dreifuss's article deals with a subject area for which we still have little historiographical material: orthodox Jewish life during the Holocaust. In addition to a review of the academic writings on this population that have been published over the years, the author highlights the many lacunae that still exist in the scholarship on this subject and the failure to incorporate the everyday life of this population – as individuals and as communities – into the overall narrative of Holocaust research. Dreifuss examines semi-academic studies on the Holocaust written by members of the ultra-orthodox community, and highlights – in addition to the methodological challenges the orthodox historiography poses for Holocaust scholars – their importance in understanding the overall fate of the Jewish population during this period. At the end of the article, the author proposes a number of measures that could contribute to an in-depth discussion of the lives of orthodox Jews and the orthodox Jewish community during the Holocaust and their incorporation into the overall research on the period. They include expanding the documentary foundation of the subject and better linking research to the lives of Jews who lived in Europe prior to the Holocaust.

In his article on the Warsaw Ghetto and the Warsaw Ghetto Uprising in the historiography of the Holocaust and World War II, **Avinoam Patt** offers an account of historiographical phenomena in the writing on the Warsaw Ghetto, with an emphasis on the uprising. The uprising's significance as a military encounter is secondary, as it amounted to a month-long clash directed by Jewish rebels that resulted in only a small number of wounded and dead German soldiers. Nonetheless, from the perspective of Jewish history the uprising is of immense importance, as a symbol of the Jews' best-known response to the Nazis' persecution of them, and as an argument against those who argue that the Jews were led like lambs to the slaughter. Despite the many studies and non-academic texts that were written on the Warsaw Ghetto Uprising both during the war and in its aftermath, this topic sharpened the perceived dichotomy between Jewish bravery and going like lambs to the slaughter. According to Patt, the new studies also reinforce this image. However, the displays of Jewish mutual assistance and intra-Jewish solidarity that have been uncovered by the research over the years have of course imbued the topic with different nuances, in contrast to the dichotomy on the subject that used to prevail.

Nikola Zimring's article deals with the debate concerning the meaning of the report sent by two Auschwitz-Birkenau prisoners, Rudolf Vrba and Alfréd Wetzler, who escaped from that camp. They crossed the border on April 21 and immediately connected with the Jewish clandestine movement, the so-called Working Group. With the Working Group's assistance, they composed a 28-page detailed statement known today as the Vrba Wetzler Report or the Auschwitz Protocols. *The Report* reached the free world at the end of May, and caused an uproar. In June, the shorter version of the *Report* was reprinted hundreds of times in western newspapers and even broadcast by the BBC. In the early 60s Vrba undertook to share his story in a series of five articles under the title "I Warned the World of Eichmann's Murders," published in the London based *Daily Herald* and subsequently, in 1963 in the memoir *I Cannot Forgive*. The memoir's title refers to the Slovakian and primarily Hungarian-Jewish leadership who Vrba blamed for not acting more quickly and efficiently on the information they had received from him. Vrba always maintained that the main motivation for the escape from Auschwitz-Birkenau was to alert Hungarian Jewry about their impending annihilation. The specific warning for the Hungarian Jews is not present in *The Report*. Why wasn't the information included in *The Report*? Zimring's study aims to explore this debate among the protagonists, as well as historians seeking to explain the lacuna.

Aviva Halamish's article in this issue explores the representation of the *ma`apilim* in research-based texts that have been published in Hebrew by Israeli scholars in Israel, as well as other means of expression that shaped the image of the *ma`apilim* in Israeli public discourse and collective memory. The article traces the changes that have occurred in the representation of the *ma`apilim's* role in *Ha`apalah*, from the days of *Ha`apalah* itself to the second decade of the twenty-first century, as well as their transformation from objects and passive participants in the shadow of members of the Yishuv into subjects in their own right occupying center stage. Halamish reviews and analyzes the *ma`apilim's* treatment and representation against the background of the era during which each text was written, based on the consensus that historiography reflects the period in which it was written no less, and perhaps even more, than the period being researched.

Roni Stauber's article also focuses on understanding historical events after the Holocaust. In it, he extends the argument regarding Ben-Gurion's decisive influence on the Eichmann Trial, which was first articulated in Hanna Arendt's well-known book *Eichmann in Jerusalem*. According to Arendt, Ben-Gurion formulated the direction and aims of the trial ahead of time and ordered that Eichmann be abducted from Argentina and brought to Israel with the intention of taking advantage of the trial for ideological, educational, and international political purposes. Arendt's fundamental argument has been discussed in the literature on the Eichmann Trial that was published at the beginning of the 1990s. Did Ben-Gurion set the goals of the trial in advance? Did he, from the outset, present clear goals pertaining to Holocaust awareness and its lessons vis-à-vis Israeli society and the world? Was he able to estimate the trial's importance to Israeli society ahead of time? And what was his influence on the manner in which the trial was conducted? The aim of Stauber's article is to consider the different approaches to, and the disagreements regarding these questions that have emerged in the historiography.

As already noted, this issue also contains a number of articles pertaining to the historiography of specific topics that, over the years, have been disputed by different scholars.

The first of these articles, by **Graciela Ben Dror**, is situated in the realm of bystander research and provides a historiographical survey of the writings that have been produced thus far on Pius XII, with an emphasis on the conferences and the new research of the twenty-first century. Since the beginning of the 1960s, a fundamental historiographical debate involving Jewish and Christian scholars has been underway regarding Pius XII's silence, his policy on the Jews during the Holocaust, and the factors that motivated this policy. In 2003, the Vatican archives opened up documents pertaining to the tenure of Pope Pius XI, meaning the period ending in 1939, and this deepened and sharpened the work of historians on the subject. After all, Eugenio Pacelli, who was appointed Pope Pius XII in 1939, had until that time served as the Cardinal Secretary of State of his predecessor in the Holy See. Therefore, the documents from this period offered insight into Pacelli's views prior to his appointment to the papacy and the outbreak of World War II. Despite the contribution of the resulting new research, it has sharpened the initial research and highlighted conflicting interpretations, new questions, and other interpretations. In any event, historians agree that only after the archives from the period 1939-1945 are opened will it be possible to establish the new interpretations on newly discovered facts pertaining to Pope Pius XII's policies on the Jews and the motives behind them at the time of the events. The opening of the Vatican Archive began as promised on March 2, 2020, but was prompyly closed because of the coronavirus.

Judy Tydor Baumel-Schwartz's article addresses a field of research that has also been the subject of dispute in the historiography: research on women in the Holocaust from World War II until the present. In this article, the author analyzes the different waves of research on women in the Holocaust, expands on controversies on the subject that have arisen in academic frameworks and in the media, and traces the activity of the major figures who have conducted research on women in the Holocaust in recent decades.

Finally, we present a number of articles dealing with aspects of broader historiographical thinking, such as the need to take into account the whole "integrative history" in order to arrive at a comprehensive comparative picture of the Holocaust; the "uniqueness" of the Holocaust and the views of the historians Israel Gutman and Yehuda Bauer on this question; and the manner in which the Holocaust is reflected in the historiography of the Arab World.

Dan Michman writes about comparative research in Western Europe, mainly between France, Belgium and the Netherlands. He also places emphasis on the fact that during the last decades research on the Holocaust has focused on the Holocaust as the Final Solution, but the Holocaust process is much more than that. The scope of persecution before – since 1933 – and also during the implementation of the Final Solution went far beyond the murder campaign itself. In his view the volcanic outburst of "antisemitic energy was a broad undertaking which encompassed a variety of actions which have to be integrated in their entirety into the narrative." He analyses the difficulty of comparative research. His conclusion is that for a better comprehensive picture of the Shoah, it is important to include "Western Europe" and the entire extent of Nazi domination over Europe and North Africa and to integrate them into the larger picture of the research on the overall escalation of anti-Jewish policies. Moreover, it also has to be analyzed from the perspective of Jewish History and that of the history of perpetrators and from the so-called bystanders. Michman proposes an "integrative history" in order to be able to get closer to an understanding of many unsolved facets of the Holocaust.

Dina Porat writes about the uniqueness of the Holocaust and the views of Israel Gutman and Yehuda Bauer on this question. In doing so, she analyzes the tempestuous debate that has prevailed in the research over the past two decades, and that has reverberated within the public discourse, regarding the question of whether the Holocaust represented a unique historical event or, despite its extreme nature, a case of genocide that should be located on the continuum of genocides, alongside those that preceded and succeeded it. Put differently, the question is whether the Holocaust should be viewed as an event that was planned and executed solely against the Jewish People and as a national catastrophe and a Jewish tragedy alone, or as an event with repercussions extending beyond the unique experience of a specific national group of victims that bears international significance and yields universal human lessons.

In this article, Porat examines how major historians and thinkers, most of whom were active in Israel during the initial decades following the Holocaust, related to these questions, particularly to the question of the uniqueness of the Holocaust, even before the outbreak of the debate on the subject. She also considers the possible implications of their conclusions for the current research. In conclusion, she proposes a third possibility – the notion that there is no fundamental contradiction between the two approaches, as the argument between the advocates of each stems not from the core of the academic scholarship on the matter but rather from political interests and social and cultural fashion. This third approach is proposed with the utmost caution, and with consideration regarding whether a synthesis can be proposed in the case under discussion in light of the remarks of thinkers and historians, some of whom relate to such a possibility. After all, the two approaches are two sides of the same coin and complete one another, as uniqueness does not contradict the consideration of other events.

The issue concludes with **Esther Webman**'s article on the Holocaust in Arab historiography. In the West, Holocaust research stands alone in its own right in the field of historical research. In the Arab World, on the other hand, the Holocaust has not been the subject of comprehensive research, unlike the subjects of Zionism, Judaism, and Israel which have been researched extensively, although in these studies, as well, the difference between academic and polemic writing is often blurred. Webman's major argument here is that there is no Arab historiography of the Holocaust per se. Nonetheless, the narratives produced by the recurring references to the Holocaust in Arab public discourse have penetrated and become fixed in the Arab collective consciousness and in some senses constitute a type of historiography in themselves. Webman notes the change that occurred in the representation of the Holocaust in Arab public discourse in the 1990s, which paved the way for Arab scholars to engage in new topics of research that are more directly connected to the Holocaust. Her article also attempts to understand why there is no Arab historiography of the Holocaust and shows how, thanks to the information revolution in the media, reliable historical material on the Holocaust has also become available in Arabic. This, she notes, has the potential to balance out the information on the subject that is prevalent in the Arab public discourse.

I would like to thank all the members of the editorial board for their significant contribution to the production of this issue, which is the 17th issue of the English edition of *Moreshet, The Journal for the Study of the Holocaust and Antisemitism* and the 100th issue of its Hebrew edition. We hope you find interest in the diverse articles on the historiography of the Holocaust it contains.

Dr. Graciela Ben Dror
Editor

Yehuda Bauer, Dalia Ofer, Dina Porat

An Interview with Prof. Yehuda Bauer

Greetings, Prof. Bauer. Prof. Dalia Ofer and I (Prof. Dina Porat) have come to speak with you today for two reasons. The first is to congratulate you on your 93rd birthday. We wish you many more years as good as the previous ones. The second is the fact that the upcoming issue of *Moreshet: Journal for the Study of the Holocaust and Antisemitism* will be the journal's 100th issue, which is an event to celebrate. After all, you were one of the journal's founders and a member of its illustrious initial editorial staff, and you are still a member up to the present. Not every journal is lucky enough to have an editorial staff like that which has served *Moreshet Journal*. The journal's 100th issue will be devoted to the historiography of the Holocaust, and we would like to ask you a few questions regarding your broad perspective on this subject today.

Hello, Yehuda. I of course share the sentiments expressed by Dina. We are pleased to have this opportunity to interview you together. We actually share a similar history, as we wrote our doctoral dissertations in Tel Aviv and in Jerusalem at the same time. You were my advisor, and Dina's advisor was Prof. Daniel Carpi. It's nice to close the circle in this way, sitting here after so many years, chatting about the historiography of the Holocaust. Our first question pertains to the historiographical developments on Nazism and the Holocaust that have occurred in recent years. Do you think that, today, we can expect any major debates, like the debates between the functionalists and the intentionalists regarding the role of ideology in the decisions relating to the development of the Nazis' policies? Or have we passed this stage and are now heading toward a different stage of the historiographical discussion?

First of all, thank you so much for this interview, for your wishes, and for everything else. It would be difficult for me to say that I think that major fundamental discussions of this sort will develop because, to some extent, they have never ceased. With regard to the discussion on the primacy of ideology or of other factors, these are not only along the lines of Hans Mommsen or Eberhard Jaeckel, but rather deal with more complex matters, such as a geographical versus a topographical approach, a sociological approach versus one that seeks to assess what precisely ideology is, and so forth. I think that these discussions are ongoing. If a discussion develops, in my opinion, it will not arouse a major debate. Perhaps it will emerge from the approach employed by Saul Friedländer – which holds that the source of the atrocities was Germany, but that it was an all-European undertaking, as all the nations of Europe were complicit, to varying degrees, in the Nazi project of exterminating the Jews. This approach requires a much broader view, and perhaps this will be a source of debate – the question: Why the Jews? After all, the Jews are a small people whose culture is the mother of the monotheistic religions (although neither they nor Judaism are exactly monotheistic, even though they are referred to as such). Why, then, did it befall them, instead of all those with red hair or with green eyes? There is a well-known joke in Germany that goes as follows: Who is guilty of everything? The Jews and bicyclists. When the teller is asked, "Why bicyclists?" he answers, "Why the Jews?" The question of what is the cause of the matter can spark an extremely interesting and tempestuous debate – one that considers not only the distant past and the Holocaust but also the present. That is to say, this historical view cannot focus solely on the Holocaust. The Holocaust is undoubtedly at its center, but it also has a future, and I do not know when this future will end.

Your response actually brings the discussion back to antisemitism, and, if I understand you correctly, so does what you are saying about the present, that is, about what we are experiencing in the twenty-first century. Antisemitism is back on the agenda in different forms that are perhaps more varied, but also more nuanced. Do you think this is related to the matters that are the topic of discussion today?

I assume so. I am not opposed to comparisons, but every comparison must highlight not only what is similar but also what is different. Then, of course, we have continuity and change, and therefore some elements that were impossible prior to the Holocaust exist today because they stem from the Holocaust. But there is actually continuity here. The things cannot be separated, and I therefore truly think that it was the ideology (antisemitism) as opposed to the pragmatic considerations that was the major factor in the Holocaust. So, we need to clarify where the ideology (which is of course rooted in history) impacted the Nazis, and where it also influences the ideology of today, and to view it as part of the picture. I object to any monocausal approach, but we need to distinguish between matters that are of central importance and matters that are of less central importance – with regard not only to the Holocaust as a genocide of Jews but also as a cause of World War II. Antisemitism was one cause of the outbreak of war, which is something we can prove. We have documentation – an internal memo dated August 1936, in which Hitler explicitly states, in no uncertain terms, that if Germany does not go to war within four years (the Four Year Plan), the world would be controlled by Bolshevism, which aims to impose Judaism on the world as a whole. It was therefore necessary to prepare for war. I am not saying that this was the only cause, but it was an extremely significant one. Twenty-nine million non-Jews died during World War II, plus the 5.6 or 5.7 million victims of the Holocaust. The 29 million non-Jews in Europe also died primarily as a result of antisemitism.

You mentioned Friedländer, whose scholarship is based on a combination of a large number of personal testimonies (memoirs, diaries, and the like) and on documents. Its emphasis is on what is referred to today as ego-documentation. We would like to know whether this trend seems reasonable to you. Is it not moving away from the traditional work of historians, which is based on documents? Today so much is based on testimonies - there are movies all based on testimonies, memoirs, and letters. What do you think about it?

People say that this is new, but it is not true. Without testimonies, there is no history of the Holocaust. That much is completely clear. The Germans exterminated the Jews and also attempted to destroy the documentation. The documentation, produced by Jews and by non-Jews regarding Jews, are among the main sources, although we know they are not the only sources. What is a document? A document is nothing but oral testimony put down in writing.

If a German first-lieutenant reports to his commanding officer what he did in a Polish village or town during the war, this is his testimony – things that were said orally. And many oral testimonies became written testimonies. This dichotomous distinction between testimony and document was devised in its entirety by Raul Hillberg, and it is incorrect. Other scholars have relied on testimonies, not just Friedländer. For example, Christopher Browning composed two very important books based on testimonies.

That is not to say that he ignored documents. This is certainly part of the story, but I regard this distinction between testimony and non-testimony as completely unfounded. Not only is all of my work a combination of such sources, but it is also a matter of education. Today, neither older nor younger students can be provided with documents alone. It does not work. Because things happened to people, not to paper. The personal experience must also be conveyed, and personal experience means the experience of someone who was there, a person who tells someone who was not there. Here, I am referring to Jews and non-Jews alike. One example is the diary of a Pole named Kolakowski who lived in a Polish town. It was not pro-Jewish, but it is accurate, and it is one of the major sources depicting the events that occurred in a vast region.

That is true, Yehuda. But we must distinguish between contemporary testimonies – that is, the testimonies of those who lived during the Holocaust itself (the Ringelblum Archive, for example, contains testimonies that archive personnel collected from survivors of almost all the major ghettos), on the one hand, and testimonies that were collected immediately following the war and during the 1960s, 1970s, 1980s, and 1990s, on the other hand. For every testimony that assumes authority in its own right, the intention is unclear. Contemporary testimony and later testimony reflect the perspective of the time when it was given. If it was given in 1945, it reflects the perspective of 1945. You taught me that testimony does not always depict everything – it depicts the specific occurrence. And when it is given in 2010 or in 1990, it reflects completely different perspectives. The question is: How do we integrate the perspective of the time with the testimony and the historical story? I would also like to ask whether the

subsequent increased weight of the testimonies noted by Dalia is related to the survivors' increased status in society. After all, this status has become much more important than it was in the past.

First of all, I will address your addition, Dina. Yes, I think it has an impact, and it should be considered during analysis. Every testimony and every document is read with a critical eye, and the criticism is always comparative, against the background of the context of the testimony. A testimony collected in 1945 – let's say, testimonies collected in Bucharest after the Holocaust, or testimonies collected in Budapest in June 1945, or testimonies collected immediately following the Holocaust in different places in Europe – are not necessarily the most reliable. The trauma was too intense, and some of the witnesses decided not to ask themselves questions that they could not answer. This is extremely noticeable among women, for example. There are some things that women could not recount in 1945, 1948, 1949, or even 1960, but that perhaps they could recount in 1980. And then the perspective is different – subjective, but it reflects a reality that was. The opposite also occurs: immediately following the Holocaust, people recounted things bluntly and brutally and later regretted it. They did not want to hurt anyone, their own family members or others, so they changed the truth a bit – that is, their testimony regarding what they saw. The historian needs to verify the information. It sometimes turns out that an impressive testimony is actually a subjective view that does not reflect reality. On rare occasions, fraudulent testimony is given consciously, although it is usually not done intentionally. For this reason, people study a great deal in seminaries, universities, etc. to be able to analyze these aspects. I have encountered this on many occasions. For example, my book on the townships (shtetlach) is based on testimonies because the existing documentation is very weak: such and such happened on this or that date, and that's all. This is a problem, as it is necessary to distinguish where contradictions and other problems exist or do not exist. I'd also like to mention another phenomenon: There are some historians, myself included, who have tried approaching the same witness multiple times at intervals of a number of years, and the results have been very good. The testimonies can then be compared.

Dr. Sharon Kangisser Cohen's book *Testimony and Time: Survivors of the Holocaust Remember* (Jerusalem, 2015) contends with the issue of late testimonies and early testimonies.

That is true. This is one of the ways of overcoming this historiographical problem.

It is interesting to note that the conclusion of Sharon's book is that "the core story" is always the same. It's the things around it, and the overall tone, that are different.

For example, there is the well-known testimony of Eliezer Lidovsky, which is actually three testimonies given at intervals of such and such years. The late testimony does not contradict the early testimony but rather adds to it and yields a different picture. This is a favorable scenario, and there are of course also scenarios that are less favorable.

Yehuda, perhaps we can return to the matter of antisemitism. You regard it as the center of things, and you think that the question "why the Jews?" will arise and stimulate discussion. Genocide research, of which you have undoubtedly been a part for many ways, to a great extent actually pulls the rug out from under the argument that it was focused on the Jews because it first highlights the many cases of genocide in the past. We will not return to Sparta in the ancient period or other such cases, as we have examples from the more recent past in the nineteenth and the twentieth century: imperialism and imperial interests, the Soviets, the Germans, the English in Africa, and, of course, the genocides of recent years, we can almost say, such as the case of Rwanda, which is again emerging.

Why "almost?"

Because it has an historical dimension: How did the issue of genocide become so central? It raises very important points – Timothy Snyder's book *Bloodlands* and his second book, are one out of many examples.

His third book, *On Tyranny: Twenty Lessons from the Twentieth Century*, was also recently published.

How do you relate to it? And, as Dalia said, what are the implications of genocide studies today, which have expanded in their comparisons across different periods with regard to the centrality of the Holocaust?

I have written quite a bit about this. I actually belong to two groups. One is a group that strives to prevent genocide (the Genocide Prevention Advisory Network, or GPANet), which attempts to create tools for the prevention of genocide. It was established in 1998, leading up to the major 2000 assembly in Stockholm on the topic of Holocaust education. It is interesting to note that this group, which still exists today, was established following a discussion on educating about the Holocaust. The second group that was subsequently founded seeks to produce a contemporary political response, with the same idea of creating state and government tools. This group is called the GAAMAC, and it is run by the Swiss government. As a group of experts dealing with genocide in theory, we try to create the tools. We are the advisors. The last assembly of the GAAMAC was attended by representatives of 36 governments. This of course did not include the government of Israel – after all, who in Israel today is interested in genocide? It is talked about, and it is lectured about, as it is part of the business and lectures are cheap. Action is an altogether different story. However, there are governments, primarily in Africa and South America, and one European government, in addition to Switzerland, that is trying to get into the issue: Sweden. Incidentally, Israel was of course invited but has no interest. The Israeli government has no interest in genocide or the Holocaust. I am saying this explicitly. This is the connection. In contrast to what Dalia said, I believe that the distant past is important. It is central, because it explains why genocides take place today. It is ingrained in the human experience, and for this reason it is difficult to fight. The Holocaust was a genocide. This is completely clear. The term "genocide" was introduced, to a large degree and among other factors, in order to contend with the Holocaust and World War II. Therefore, the Holocaust is the most extreme and unprecedented case, as the elements that were present in the

Holocaust did not exist in any previous genocide. These features can reemerge, and therefore the Holocaust is not unique. Dina, you asked whether genocide research has influenced the perception of the Holocaust as unique: in terms of the perception of the Holocaust, the answer is yes; in terms of the perception of the Holocaust as not being unique, the answer is also yes.

The Holocaust can repeat itself, but this is not completely accurate. Nothing repeats itself in exactly the same way, but rather only approximately. It can repeat itself, and it does repeat itself. After the Holocaust, we have witnessed the reappearance of elements that did not exist prior to the Holocaust, which, to a significant extent and sometimes in a blunt manner, are based on what happened during the Holocaust. In Rwanda, for example, the intellectual leadership of the Hutus studied in Belgian and French universities; they heard about the Holocaust and World War II, and they consciously emulated the ideology of the Nazis and were put on trial for doing so. One of the central figures who engaged in the propaganda for the group that planned the murders was Ferdinand Nahimana. He was sentenced to 30 years in prison. Today he is in prison in Mali. That is to say, the connection between addressing genocide and addressing the Holocaust is a fundamental connection. I managed to convince the IHRA (International Holocaust Remembrance Alliance), for which Dina has served as an academic advisor, to provide consultations for organizations trying to prevent genocide, such as the GAAMAC. It was not difficult to do so. It will be approved as a resolution in Luxemburg in a few weeks.

You said something very pessimistic to Dalia, Yehuda. You said there would always be genocides and that you believe it is inherent in human nature to murder groups or nations.

That's right.

That is a pessimistic statement.

No. And I'll continue to say it. Like our ancestors, we are weak predators. Even strong predators can survive only in groups. Therefore, the society in which an individual lives must develop features that counter the predisposition to murder and that encourage cooperation, amity, and love.

Are these the tools that society needs?

Certainly. Tools like these.

Every society needs them in order to exist. Consider Hebrew culture, for example. The fifth of the Ten Commandments is "though shalt not murder." Murder negates society, and therefore the constant struggle is between good and evil. These terms are of course relative, and they are necessary for maintaining human society and life itself. It is therefore necessary to develop attributes that counteract the predator's predisposition to murder and displace the predisposition to genocide.

I would like to revisit two topics: your thoughts on what is referred to as "the Jerusalem School," if it at all exists; and the link to genocide that is connected to the opening of the archives in Eastern Europe and to the five year plans, in the case of the Ukrainians. How do you connect these two things? Does the Torah still emerge from Zion? That is to say, what is the status of Israeli scholarship today?

Let's begin from the second topic. The status of Israeli scholarship is on the decline. The major studies on the Holocaust today are being conducted first and foremost in Poland and Germany, as well as in the United States. A slightly smaller number are being conducted in France. I truly hope that the scholarship here [in Israel] will be revitalized.

Is research also being done in England?

Yes. Today, most people engaged in the Holocaust are not Jews, which is actually a good thing. They of course need to learn the languages of Eastern Europe so they don't have problems understanding the testimonies.

Jews also need to learn these languages.

That's right. I remember Chris Browning asking me how I handle testimonies in Polish. His solution was to hire someone to simply translate them for him. Still, most of the Jews who were murdered in the Holocaust were murdered in Eastern Europe. Therefore, those who do not know Yiddish or Polish, the basic languages that were spoken there, or at least some Slavic language – as well as English, German, and French – have difficulties.

There is a theory circulating that holds that Israel Gutman and I founded something referred to as "the Jerusalem School" of Holocaust research. This is total nonsense. A Jerusalem School does not exist. Israel Gutman and I were soulmates, in an extreme manner. But we had a completely different background, education, approach, and so on. We argued constantly, although we both believed that viewing the Holocaust from the perspective of the Jewish victim is the main thing, and that doing so does not undermine in-depth exploration of the perpetrators of the crimes and of others. But there was no school. On the topic of genocide, for example, his approach was completely different from mine.

Israel spoke of the uniqueness of the Holocaust. I oppose this approach, although it supposedly refers to the Jerusalem School. In my opinion, there is no such thing; there are scholars who worked and continue to work here [in Israel], and there are scholars who work elsewhere. It is not a school. I think it is a good thing that Holocaust research is research that is conducted by individuals. Each has his/her own approach and explores specific aspects. It is impossible to encompass everything. Today, the Yad Vashem Archive holds 220 million documents. Two hundred and twenty million? How many of them have already been reviewed by researchers? I really do not understand all this talk. I do not know who invented the Jerusalem School.

Nonetheless, Yehuda, if you think about what David Engel wrote about the approach of Jewish historians working outside of Israel regarding Jewish history during the Holocaust, as opposed to that of Jewish Israeli historians, is the difference only one of geographical location, or is there a difference in attitude?

David Engel is an Israeli who moved to the United States for family reasons. Do you regard him as an Israeli or an American? Or as a Jewish-American?

Many excellent scholars – historians who live in different places, such as Saul Friedländer, Omer Bartov, Paula Heimann, and Sam Kassow – are first and foremost individuals. They work and they research; it does not matter what their language is or where they live.

But Yehuda, David Engel is critical of Jewish historians outside of Israel who have refrained from dealing with the Holocaust for political and ideological reasons.

Yes. I do not agree with this approach, although I do greatly appreciate him.

That is your prerogative.

I do not like this idea, because in my opinion a Jewish historian pertains to the fate of the Jews and is therefore engaged in the subject, for ideological, social, or other reasons.

Cultural reasons.

Yes.

O.K.

So, this ostensibly contradicts all the research of Jewish Israeli historians on the subject. In Poland, there are historians who attack the liberals who tell us what happened in Poland. I am not at all convinced by all the generalizations and stereotypes by those who propose a general theory and then need to find explanations for exceptions. A historian is a historian is a historian. That is what I think. That is the first thing. Historians choose their subjects for personal or general reasons. I did not live through the Holocaust, and neither did you. You chose to deal with it. You were drawn to the subject, as was I. This does not invalidate those who experienced the Holocaust or are close to it for other reasons. The approach to this historiography must not be stereotypical but rather individual.

Your first book – *From Diplomacy to Resistance* – was published before Abba Kovner influenced you to move from researching Israeli state and

society to researching the Holocaust. It seems to me that the history of Zionism during the Holocaust and of the Yishuv and the Zionist leadership at that time remain a wound even today, as people still blame David Ben-Gurion, the state's founding father, for his attitude toward the Holocaust (despite Tuvia Friling's extremely important book). It is a wound in the sense that Zionism was supposed to rescue, but it did not. The question is actually how you view this dichotomy between the scholarship that better understands the ability – or inability – of the Yishuv and Zionism to rescue, and the fact that, from a public perspective, the wound and the guilt remain and are projected onto the justification for Zionism and its moral basis.

I think that Jewish Israeli society is a traumatized society, and this is understandable: one-third of the Jewish People was brutally murdered. When we consider other peoples that experienced similar things, we see that the trauma lasts a long time. For example, the trauma of the Armenians continues today, into the fourth, fifth, and sixth generations.

The trauma of the Roma also runs deep, as does that of Rwandan society. A scholar who lives in Rwanda clarified for me the traumatic foundation of Rwandan society, due to which President Paul Kagame is trying to impose a dictatorship there. But this trauma cannot be suppressed; it runs very deep, and in Israel it finds expression in the attempt to search out parties who were responsible for the Holocaust.

That's right.

OK, we know that the Germans murdered, but who is truly to blame for it? An answer must be found, and when we have no answer, we invent one. In Jewish culture, the answer is profound: all the terrible things that have befallen the Jews can be blamed on the sins of the Jews. The Jews sinned, and therefore God punished them. Who is truly to blame? We are. Well, not us, but rather those who are no longer alive. Ben-Gurion and the whole gang, and particularly the Mapai leaders, as, after all, they controlled the Yishuv at the time. So, Mapai is to blame, Ben-Gurion is to blame, and the

Yishuv is to blame; these half-a-million Jews who stood against millions of German soldiers in Europe. The British did not even allow them to establish a fighting unit until the very last moment. That is to say, they are guilty. This is clear to me from a social-psychological perspective, but I do not accept it. In my view, it is utter nonsense.

We completely agree.

I wrote a book about that as well, and since then I have written nineteen more.

Only nineteen?! Well that's not very impressive, is it?! [But seriously,] let's move on to another topic. I would prefer to not delve too deep into this discussion but rather to return to the topic of memory and history, as in any event this is related to this question. And then afterwards I will ask you about the women in Rwanda, which is interesting.

The name of the woman scholar in Rwanda is Assumpta Mugiraneza.

Yehuda, the fact that you remember these names completely…leaves us… Traumatized.

Exactly, you took the words right out of my mouth. It traumatizes us.

But let's get back on topic. What you are actually saying is that there is some kind of connection between memory and history, in terms of who is to blame and so forth. In any event, the generation that could remember what happened and translate it is no longer alive. We are talking about the second and third generations. How do you view this issue – the connection between memory and history and its impact on the generations that were born afterward?

You are talking to living proof that not all dinosaurs are extinct.

Dinosaurs like me are still around, here and there. Of course, we will eventually be gone. That is clear. If the Jews will want to forget the Holocaust, then non-Jews will remind them of it. It cannot be escaped. Memory is collective memory, and collective memory exists not only in peoples with culture but also in peoples whose cultures have not developed. Memory exists in peoples such as Jews and Germans, Poles, Russians, English, Chinese, Indian, and so on – in other cultures. This collective memory is, to a great extent, based largely on legends. You are now interviewing me before the Passover holiday, and the Exodus from Egypt is a legend. It did not occur, but it is based on something that did happen. The Children of Israel did not leave Egypt for the simple reason that they were never there. It was the Hyksos who were there – Canaanite tribes who infiltrated Egypt and so on. The Jewish People came from the north – from Aram-Naharaim, from Ur of the Chaldees, and the like. That is where the Jewish People came from. So a legend was invented that was based on history. The legend became history, and the history became legend, an epic chronicle. This is wonderful, because without the exile from Egypt there is no Jewish People. The history about which we are speaking is different: it is something that truly occurred, and it was horrible. It was shocking, and a few legends were added. For example, we tell the story of the Danish king who walked around wearing the yellow badge [of the Star of David].

Riding on his white horse.

Wearing the yellow badge, he rode his white horse to the synagogue in Copenhagen. This never happened. The Germans never introduced the yellow badge in Denmark. However, it is *based* on history, because the King of Denmark really did oppose the Nazis. He wrote this in his diary (which was published after his death). He wrote it point-black in his diary.

That's true, but he never said it to anyone. He only wrote in his diary: if the Germans seek revenge against our Jews, we may all have to wear the yellow badge – even if there was no yellow badge in Denmark. A legend was created, pure and simple. Legends are based on history, which turns back into legend. In the Holocaust, the foundation of legend is marginal. We are almost always talking about a reality that existed. However, from the mouths of those who oppose us, those who distort the Holocaust, it became a negative legend – a distorted legend. This is a danger. The historian must seek out the truth about the societies that invent such legends, about the Jews who live there and Jews in general. Here lies the complication. As scholars, we must prevent the distortion of the Holocaust.

And what is the truth? Is there an absolute truth? Certainly not. But we need to get as close as we can to the truth. That is the task of the historian.

Earlier, you raised an interesting point regarding women in Rwanda and their role in processing the trauma.

That's how it turned out.

Dalia has dealt a great deal with gender in the Holocaust. In fact, she was a pioneer in the development of this field. Hasn't there been too much focus on the question of gender in the Holocaust, or gender in history in general? This is part of the feminist revolution, but isn't it time we put gender in proportion?

I do not agree. I think that the gender approach is important because although the fate awaiting women and men was the same horrible fate, the path leading to it was different, and this needs to be emphasized. This was the case in other instances as well. For example, almost three million Polish Jews were murdered, out of the 5.6 or 5.7 million victims of the Holocaust. So, Polish Jewry is at the center, despite it all. The fate of Jewish women was different up until the point when they were murdered. It was of course integrated, and what Dalia does in her research on family, in my opinion, is very legitimate and very, very important. And again, this is not unique to the Holocaust. It also exists in other societies. So my colleagues who engage in this, in relation to the period of the Holocaust, deal with this first and foremost. In local courts in Rwanda, which are referred to as Gacaca [pronounced ga-cha-cha], it is forbidden to speak of Hutu and Tutsi – that is, about the main reasons for the genocide. They can speak about murderers and victims, yes. The murderers are directly accused. Who accuses them? In most cases, women. They also suffered differently. Almost all the women who survived were raped. Now, they are coming out and publically accusing the rapist. They have overcome their natural apprehension regarding accusing someone outside the typical boundaries and the standard morality. The accusers today of course include not only women but also many men.

However, it seems to me that the status of men has also changed in Rwanda. As we know, the status of men completely changed during the Holocaust, which is something you have written about quite a bit, Dalia, particularly with regard to the authoritative father. In Jewish communities during the Holocaust, fathers were left helpless, and such helplessness always has sexual implications. The helpless father stood powerless before his family and could no longer help. And then, in many instances, the woman would take the reins simply out of lack of choice. When you check the history of the Holocaust, I think that this is one of the most important contexts in which to work, and from this perspective I am a feminist. But I do not use such terms. I want to deal with the fate of women, men, children, and the elderly. And in each case, the context differs somewhat.

Yes, but today we can say that a feminist orientation is also developing in Holocaust studies. Zoe Waxman's book _Women in the Holocaust: A Feminist History_ (Oxford University Press, 2017) was published a few years ago. In it, the author advances a very interesting argument. Many of the stereotypes of relationships between men and women have not changed, despite the Holocaust. For this reason, there is a place for a feminist approach that emphasizes these aspects, and that does not simply describe what you just addressed, as Lenore Weizmann and I did. This approach holds significance for understanding Jewish society at the time, as well as Jewish societies after the Holocaust. I think that this is a theoretical approach whose application is interesting to observe.

Yes. I tend to agree with this approach.

As do we.

I agree because what happened during the Holocaust was an anomaly, and to a great extent they reverted to the standard traditional approaches of patriarchy. The rebellion against this reaches back to the Holocaust as a counter-example, as there – to some extent, and we should not overstate the matter – we find a change in the status of the genders vis-à-vis one another. And in places where there was full cooperation between the genders, this was less pronounced. Nowhere did the women receive the leadership. This did not occur in the Judenräte. After all, in Poland there was only one Judenrat consisting of women, and this was because all the men had been murdered. Women were not members of the Judenrat, and not only because of the gender question…

Because of the Germans.

Yes, also because of the Germans. In places where women had an influence, it was despite the Germans. We find examples of this not only in Poland but also in France, for example.

Lithuania.

Also in Holland and in other places, such as Germany.

There has recently been discussion of empathy, and empathy is not sympathy.

No, it is not.

Empathy is a fundamental element of the work of the historian. This is connected to what Dalia was trying to say, I think, about the Jerusalem School. Today you may say that this school does not exist – that Holocaust scholarship is actually international and occurs here as well, although its source is *there*. But there is also a Jerusalem school, as well as its approach in the sense of empathy for the condition of the Jews and the understanding of their situation, as opposed to blaming it and all the accusations that followed. In our profession, when we discuss Nazism and its leadership and ideologues – and today we are talking about antisemites and Holocaust deniers – there is a contradiction between the fact that empathy and understanding of the factors motivating the people who are making history are a necessary component, on the one hand, but there is this procession of people for whom we certainly have no sympathy nor empathy, on the other hand.

I think that the historian is not obligated to feel empathy for murderers. I am a member of the Israel Academy of Sciences and Humanities, and we accepted into the academy a scholar of the Mongols – a brilliant Israeli historian who deals with the history of the Mongols. Does she have empathy for Genghis Khan? No. She researches the history of the Mongols and attempts to understand them. Hitler of course is the extreme example, but let us consider empathy for other mass murderers: for Cortés in Mexico or for Pizarro in Peru. Is empathy a necessity? We need to assess what he did, why he did it, and so on. Empathy is not a necessity. In contrast, I think that empathy for the victim is extremely important. Without it, we cannot understand the feelings of the victim, although the line of separation is not entirely clear. This is because in the case of a German who came to Eastern Europe as a murderer and at the end of the day helped Jews, you will not relate to him with empathy as a murderer. But I think that in the eyes of a historian who studied to be a historian, these distinctions provide a certain level of necessary distance; otherwise, you're part of it all, which is not a good thing. It is essential to get at least a bit of distance. The empathy must exist, but only up to a certain point.

It is not a question of empathy. R.G. Collingwood wrote about this term, which he coined, I think, in the 1940s or perhaps the 1950s, and he is not talking about it in the emotional sense but rather in the sense of walking in the shoes of the historical protagonist. That is precisely the issue.

There actually is someone who will say that you or I cannot write about Hitler, because doing so is beyond our mental and emotional capacity. This is not because we identify. We do not need to identify, but it is important to try to walk in the shoes of Hitler or Göring. We had a joint student who wanted to write about Göring. I cannot remember her name at the moment.

Ravit Tzemach.

That's right. Yehuda – you remember every name. It's phenomenal. Ultimately, she did not do it. And we had misgivings about the question of empathy. But we were talking about empathy: it is far from sympathy and from identification; it is the ability to walk in the shoes of the historical protagonist.

Correct. So look, we've all reviewed Hitler's life. We've researched in order to understand the motivations, to understand this approach. From this perspective Collingwood is correct. That is to say – yes, it is empathy from this perspective. And that is what we are capable of.

One of the things that interests me a great deal – because it is how I work, and I recently spoke about it in an opening lecture I delivered in Luxemburg – is the connection between macro-history and micro-history, and the linkage between these things. How do you see it?

Well, the emphasis is on the connection between the two…

Yes.

…because without micro-history there can be no macro-history. This is clear. And if you remain only in micro-history, you get lost because you are dealing with the details. My doctoral dissertation advisor, Israel Halperin, may his memory be a blessing, would always say to me: Don't do what I did. Don't deal with the trees alone – deal with the forest. But not the forest alone – the trees *and* the forest. This is what I try to do. First of all, all of my works are a combination of these elements. Without a specific source and a specific person or a specific community, one cannot talk about the Holocaust, and certainly not about the Holocaust in its entirety – not without seeing general contexts and, ultimately, contexts that are global in both senses: in a vertical historical sense, with regard to the distant past, the recent past, the future, etc.; and in a horizontal sense – that is, in a global or a general geographic sense. As Jews fled Germany to the Philippines and to many other locations around the world, the Holocaust was a general matter. And in addition to the dispersion that already existed, more were dispersed. Therefore, this combination of micro-history and macro-history is essential. The problem is the relative weight of each, which is something about which we can argue endlessly. What exactly should be the ratio? If, for example, I now begin considering the relations between Slovakia and the Jews, is this micro-history or macro-history? It begins as micro, but micro-history must become macro – otherwise, there is no point.

On this point, the Jewish sages said that a person in his own worldstands within a full world – that is, everyone begins in his or her own world, in the micro, and must develop into a full world.

I of course agree with you, but I will offer one comment. If we look at Holocaust research and the developments within it, then certainly, we cannot achieve a general picture without specific incidents. And the goal is to achieve a general picture. Today, there is a different approach that says we need to understand the extent to which these minor specific incidents actually make the general picture more complex and interesting. It is clear that without a specific incident, without understanding ship x or person y, we cannot know. The question is: What are we striving for? It seems to me that from Carlo Ginsburg onward, all the micro approaches developed on their own, not in order to explain the Inquisition, for example, but rather to understand the people and their activities within the system that was set up by the Inquisition, about which we already know. It is my feeling that this is the state of affairs of Holocaust research today, but it definitely requires a broad discussion. This is a mere comment. It can be omitted from the protocol.

I have one last question, with your permission. Abba Kovner wrote a short, one-and-a-half-page piece titled "An Epilogue for Historians," in which he addresses the historian. The main point of these one-and-a-half pages is that the historian needs to research, explore, and leave no rock unturned. However, he must remember that Holocaust research is also located on the dark side of the moon – that there are things that will always remain unclear and unclarified, despite the faithful work of the historian. This is his message, his epilogue for historians – especially historians who are young and full of self-confidence. What is your message for young historians?

Kovner wrote these one-and-a-half pages about me. His poignant words were referring to me. The historian about whom he is speaking is me. Why? He was critical of me because, at the end of the day, I could not understand what happened there. From this perspective, he was somewhat similar to Elie Wiesel: You were not there, and therefore you understand nothing. My counter-point was that the only way I could understand was the way of the person who was not there. Because if the state of affairs remains as you (Abba) say, you will never be a historian, and you can forget about the Holocaust. Because when you go, nothing will remain. Because the historian understands nothing. In my opinion, this is incorrect. Historians do understand, although they have limitations. I cannot, and I seek not, to recreate your personal experience; but I can step into your shoes. I did not use this phrase at the time, but human suffering is general suffering, and we can understand suffering that is conveyed in descriptions of personal experience. On this basis, we can achieve the micro and macro. This was my response to him at the time, in much less of an intellectual manner than how I am presenting it now. So we did not reach agreement.

But he surely said that to you at the beginning of your path.

He said that to me because he liked me. After all, I slept in the home of the Kovner family, in a room in the Kovner's family home. I heard Abba's screams at night in a dream. It was an experience that is hard to recreate.

Thank you. Have a happy holiday.

Have a happy Passover holiday.

-- Jerusalem, April 11, 2019

Dalia Ofer

The Individual and the Public as a Subject of Research in Holocaust Historiography:
The Ghettos of Eastern Europe during the Holocaust

…while the Holocaust is truly the existential reference point for all Jews, only we, the sacrificed [victims, D.O.], are able to spiritually relive the catastrophic event as it was or fully picture it as it could be again. Let others not be prevented from empathizing. Let them contemplate a fate that yesterday could have been, and tomorrow can be theirs. Their intellectual effort will meet with our respect, but it will be a skeptical one, and in conversation with them we will soon grow silent and say to ourselves: go ahead, good people, trouble your heads as much as you want: you still sound like a blind man talking about color.[1]

Introduction

I begin with the above quote from Jean Améry out of a distinct sense of how important it is for us, as scholars seeking to comprehend the world of the victims of the Nazis and those who survived the Holocaust, to understand our limits. With a great sense of humility, however, we are obligated to try. In this article, I offer a summation of my research efforts on the life of the Jews in the ghettos of Eastern Europe on two levels: that of the individual and that of the public framework. I am hesitant to use the term "society of the ghetto," as the ghetto consisted of many diverse social groups, including youth movements, associations of Jews from one city or another, the residents of individual houses, people active in the fields of education and medicine, the police, and more. Here, I present my approach to the research on the historiography of this topic vis-à-vis the broadest category possible: all residents of the ghetto.

The first question I will attempt to answer is: Why did it take until the past two decades for the fate of the individual and society in the ghettos of Nazi-occupied Eastern Europe to assume center stage in the research? That is: Why

– despite the fact that the Jewish historians and intellectuals of Eastern Europe left behind archives containing substantial material pertaining to the everyday lives of Jews and documentation dealing with personal writing, the fate of the individual, and day-to-day coping during the era of occupation – has the research focused on issues relating to the institutional organization of life in the ghettos, the underground movements, and the Nazi policy of extermination? Ghetto documentation includes information on women and men, fathers and mothers, children and adolescents, and the ill and the healthy, both before they entered the ghetto and during their time in the ghetto itself. Moreover, many of the intellectuals who headed the documentation initiatives were historians and social scientists whose research agendas prior to the Nazi occupation focused on social issues, everyday life, and the individual as part of the public.

The second question explored below is: Who is the individual at the focus of this research? The academic research is based on materials left behind by the dead, as well as testimonies and memoirs written by survivors. Most of the documentation at our disposal takes the form of writing by those who died in the Holocaust. We can assume that many Jews wrote texts that did not survive, and that many of those who contended with everyday life in the ghetto remained anonymous. As a result, the depiction of everyday life in the ghetto is based on a small, non-representative group of people who were able to write and whose writing somehow survived. We also benefit from the documentation of survivors, who themselves are only a minority of the total Jewish ghetto population.

A third topic that will be addressed in this article is the selection of terminology for understanding daily life in the ghettos The tools of analysis for understanding everyday life belong to social science disciplines such as sociology, anthropology, and psychology. Researchers employ terminology pertaining to the role of routine in times of crisis, raising the question of the extent to which such terminology can help us understand and discuss the extreme situations with which the Jews were forced to contend during the Holocaust.

This leads us to the question of methodology, which is also addressed below. Finally, in the article's conclusion I present a number of studies that have been conducted by Israeli scholars over the past decade and that illustrate the two primary research questions presented above.

1. What delayed research on the fate of the individual and society in the ghettos?

After the war, when the scope of the extermination was realized, attention turned to political questions. Focus on the organization of Jewish public life was ostensibly an expression of Jewish political activity limited by life under occupation and the Nazis' anti-Jewish policy. This limitation made the organization of public life under the laws of the occupation regime – including the positions of the appointed or elected Jewish leadership, the organized resistance, and the underground movement – a focus of the research. Furthermore, in the years following the war, as the nations of Europe contended with the destructive impact of the conflict and the difficulties of rehabilitation in the shadow of collaboration with the Nazi regime, issues pertaining to the resistance, the underground, and the organization of public life were at the focal point of the research and the public discourse.[2]

1.a. Documentation and Research during the Holocaust

Research on the Holocaust began during the Holocaust itself, with intentional documentation conducted by intellectuals and community leaders, including professional historians who had engaged in historical research on the Jewish People prior to World War I. During the war itself, archive directors initiated surveys of various issues related to the condition of the Jews. The surveys described Jewish social phenomena from before World War II as well as the impact of Nazi policies, the life of Jews, and their concentration in the ghettos. The working methods of the historians who operated in the Warsaw Ghetto, of which Emmanuel Ringelblum's well-known enterprise was the most prominent, were reflective of the working methods of Jewish historians in Poland during the interwar period and of the research goals that were formulated by Jewish research institutions such as YIVO (*Yidisher Visnshaftlekher Institut* – the Yiddish Scientific Institute).

The Jewish historiography of Polish Jewry can be understood as belonging to two major streams of European historiography – the political national stream and the social stream, which highlights social forces, general factors, and the role of everyday people and the general public in the historical narrative and the development of society.[3]

Due to the unique nature of the Jewish People, the absence of independent political frameworks, and the lack of a territory, issues relating to community organization and to the relations between Jews on the one hand, and the government and the general public on the other hand, emerged as foci of historical research. In a certain sense, in the specific conditions of the history of the Jewish People, these topics can be understood as a manifestation of the political in the historical writing.

However, Jewish national groups – such as the Zionist movement and the Bund – and socialist social tendencies also had a significant impact on Jewish history. Historiographic approaches inspired by historical materialism and Marxism required a special sophistication when applied to the Jewish economic framework of the Pale of Settlement. The influence of Marxism was apparent in the topics selected by historians who advocated this approach, including Ignacy Schiper, Raphael Mahler, and Emanuel Ringelblum, who emphasized the importance of economic systems in the class divisions among Jews.[4]

These historians were involved in the problems of the hour of Jewish and Polish society, particularly after Poland received independence. Their intellectual world developed in the shadow of the trauma of World War I and the dissolution of the multi-national empires, and they were compelled to deal with current questions that became increasingly difficult and complex during the 1920s and the 1930s. The antisemitic charges that were levelled in independent Poland – which held that the Jews were parasites on the national economy and did not contribute to Poland's growth or welfare – constituted another challenge for the local social-economic scholars, who proved the Jews' role in the economy and in independent Poland from the middle ages through the country's partition.[5]

To a great extent, these historians were pioneers in incorporating the approaches of social history into the history of the Jewish People. In addition to their professional approach as historians, they felt obligated to a mission based on a vision for shaping the future of the Jewish People in new, modern Poland. In a study on Ringelblum, Samuel Kassow cites the following words that were written by Ringelblum in 1926:

> We are performing a task of immense social significance, a task whose goal is not just to get to know the Jewish past but also to lay the foundation for the struggle that is being conducted by the Jewish public in Poland for its national and social liberation.[6]

These words appear to reflect an optimistic view of Polish-Jewish relations and a positive outlook on the future of the Jewish People in the new Polish republic. This raises the question of whether such views could continue to guide Ringelblum and his associates in the Oyneg Shabbes documentation enterprise. In *Who Will Write Our History?*, his monumental book on Ringelblum and the Oyneg Shabbes archive, Kassow, like other scholars, estimates that this archival project was a significant manifestation of continuity in the orientation and the working methods of these historians and of Jewish intellectuals who spent time at YIVO and engaged in preserving Jewish culture and writing the history of the Jews of Poland.[7] This was the background of Ringelblum's efforts to assemble the documentation that, in retrospect, evolved into an immense archival enterprise. Warsaw, we must remember, was not the only site of an important historical archival project. Events were also recorded in an orderly manner in the Lodz Ghetto, where many issues pertaining not only to the demands of the Germans but also to the everyday lives of the Jews were noted.[8] In the Kovno Ghetto, the Judenrat initiated documentation of the ghetto in order to write its history. It assigned the task to Dr. Chaim Nachman Shapira, a docent of Semitic languages at the University of Kovno and a son of Rabbi Avraham Dobver Shapira; the result was an underground archive in the ghetto. Bibliographer and folklore scholar Abba Blosher apparently wrote the history of the ghetto (though the manuscript was lost), and the Jewish police in the Kovno Ghetto wrote its own history, through which it sought to reflect the history of the ghetto as a whole.[9]

1.b. The Turning Point and the Problem

In 1943, while in hiding, Ringelblum wrote an essay titled "*Oyneg Shabbes*" in which he explained the beginnings of the idea of the archive, the way in which its work was organized, and the collection of the material. His approach to the enterprise, and that of his partners in the project, was broad in scope. It was based on the conviction that it was important to recount the fate of the Jews in the era of Nazi occupation in different locations, and to always remember that the point of departure must be the history and the condition of the communities prior to the occupation. From that point on, it was necessary to provide a detailed description of the developments stemming from the oppressive Nazi rule. In this context, Ringelblum wrote the following:

> I began to collect contemporary documentation back in October 1939. As director of the YSA [*Yidishe Sotsyale Aleynhilf*, the Jewish Social Self-Aid Organization], I maintained live contact with the life going on around us. I received reports regarding everything that occurred among the Jews of Warsaw and its suburbs… Everything I heard during the day I wrote down in the evening, in addition to my own comments.[10]

Ringelblum and the members of the archive staff expected that the records and the collection of material would be used to write the history of the Jews during the era of Nazi occupation. Up to a certain point, they believed that, after the war, the Jews would resume living their lives in Poland, despite their terrible suffering and loss. During this period, collection focused on everyday life, the organizational efforts of the Jews, and social relations. Ringelblum and his colleagues worked hard to gather information regarding the stories of families living under the economic pressures, the closure of businesses and other places of employment, the displacement from residential neighborhoods, and the expulsion from regions of western Poland and from the country's satellite towns. They understood the importance of knowing the history of the married and single women whose husbands left for the East and never returned and the experiences of children and adolescents outside the family framework. The problems of the Jewish refugees and the frequent edicts regarding different aspects of life were recorded against the background of Nazi policy as it unfolded. So were events that occurred in different parts of Poland, in the forced-labor camps, in the prison camps and elsewhere, as well as the experiences of the Jews. These topics were selected as the foci of the research of ghetto life that was initiated at the end of 1941 by Oyneg Shabbes Archive activists, who sought to document two years of the Nazi occupation and one and a half years of the ghetto.[11]

A perusal of the catalogue of materials that were assembled within Ringelblum's archive enables us to conclude that the main priority of Ringelblum and the Oyneg Shabbes activists was the everyday life of Jews under the draconian laws of the Nazis, both before the Jews were forced into the ghetto and in the ghetto itself. Major questions that occupied Ringelblum and those involved with the archive pertained to the relations between the different social groups in the ghetto, the economic disparities that emerged, and the organization of the ghetto economy – all of which are distinct topics of social history.

The chief study of the life of the Jews in the Warsaw Ghetto, titled "Two Years of Occupation and One and a Half Years of the Ghetto," was interrupted by the major deportation of its inhabitants. However, the documentation enterprise was not. Although the chances of remaining alive had decreased, the archive activists made a feverish effort to finish collecting and burying the material. While in hiding, Ringelblum himself wrote the monograph on Jewish-Polish relations, as well as biographies of different public leaders and their activities in the ghetto. These figures included individuals such as Yitzhak Gitterman, a leader of Jewish Self-Help; Shakhne Zagan, a leader of Poalei Zion Left in the ghetto; and the historians Ignacy Schiper and Meir Balaban. Ringelblum also produced short biographies of intellectuals, artists, and social activists.

After the war, however, Holocaust research focused not on social history but rather on what I refer to above as "political history." Many explored the political developments pertaining to Nazi Germany, its allies, its satellite states, and the policies of the democracies before and during the war. They explored the ghetto and its institutions, the organization of the underground and the armed resistance, and the deportations to the forced-labor camps and death camps.

It is interesting to note that the above repositioning of topics within the research agenda was also observable in the approach of Ringelblum himself. In 1943, while in hiding in Warsaw, Ringelblum wrote a letter articulating his views on the agenda for future research after the war. He now wrote in light of the total destruction of the ghetto, when only a minority of Poland's three million Jews remained alive in forced-labor camps. This letter can be regarded as his last will and testament, and its subject was the national and universal priorities of research.[12] Ringelblum estimated that achieving a comprehensive account would require interviewing survivors in order to complete the documentation that had been collected by the Oyneg Shabbes archive.

The first priority was information about the deportations, the principles of the selections that were conducted by the Nazis, and the community's attitude toward the deportees. This was followed by other priorities, such as:

- Self-defense and passive defense, including the fate of the fighters, the structure of the bunkers, and how they were liquidated.
- The death camps, including everything that was known about camps such as Sobibor and Treblinka.
- The Poles' attitude toward the Jews.
- The fate of the refugees during the deportations.

Only after these topics did Ringelblum list subjects pertaining to the nature and structure of the ghetto itself, such as employment in the ghetto, the activity of aid organizations and their relationship to the community (Judenrat), the mood of the ghetto residents, religious and cultural life in the ghetto, and those responsible for the ghettos.

These guidelines reflected a genuine change in the documentation enterprise envisioned by Ringelblum. As a result of the total destruction, Ringelblum thought it necessary to emphasize subjects that the Germans and their collaborators would seek to cover up. To this end, he regarded it as imperative to complete the Jewish documentation of the deportations and the murders by asking explicit questions, including as much detail as possible, providing the names of the individuals involved in the murders, and specifying their precise locations and dates.

The research revolved around political history and subjects related to Germans, Poles, and the organizations and institutions that were established by the Jews. The documentation assembled by the historical committees that were established immediately following the war in Poland, and subsequently in the displaced persons camps in Germany and Austria, indicates that Ringelblum's assessment had been correct. The witnesses wished to recount the destruction and describe the atrocities and the cruelty that were part and parcel of the fate of the Jews. In his article on historian and researcher Philip Friedman who survived in Lwów, to which he fled in 1939, Roni Stauber explains that these subjects also became the focus of Friedman's work. Friedman was one of the founders of the historical commissions in Poland and in the DP camps and one of the shapers of their work. Although we do not know if he read Ringelblum's letter, his work reflects similar motivations.[13]

In the survivors' testimonies, the period from the beginning of the Nazi occupation until the deportations is swallowed up by an intense desire to describe that which was most urgent for them and that which they could not contain: the cruelty and brutality, the deportations, the murders, and the suffering they had experienced from deportation to liberation. Compared to the overall destruction, the stages that preceded the deportations –the hardships of life in the ghetto, family life, the organization of social life, and the problems of hunger and livelihood – appeared trivial. Ringelblum articulated this notion from his hiding place in Warsaw.[14] "As a result of all this," I have maintained, "it is almost 'natural' for topics relating to what I refer to as 'political' to be made the focus of historical research."[15]

1.c. Holocaust Research and Research on the Nazis

The research on Nazism and Nazi Germany, including on issues relating to society and government, had a major impact on Holocaust research. These topics were discussed in the political and ideological realm. Nazi rule abruptly interrupted long-term social developments pertaining not only to Jews but to the countries of Europe as a whole. After the war, historians explored issues such as resistance to and warfare against Nazi rule, collaborators, fascist and semi-fascist parties, and the governments of satellite states. In the context of Germany, the prevailing discourse pertained to the country's "special path" (*Sonderweg*) to unity and the modernization processes of the final third of the nineteenth century.

During the 1950s and 1960s, the murder of the Jews did not constitute the core of the research on Nazism, although the issue was present in the historiographical discourse. Raul Hilberg's classic study *The Destruction of the European Jews* supplied road signs for the research and focused on the political-organizational realm: that is, the German bureaucracy. British historian Gerald Reitlinger's study also focused on the political system, as did the first studies on the death camps that were written by former camp inmates.[16] Only in the 1980s did the research expand into a discussion of the social and cultural roots of the Third Reich and its policies. This change was related to the development of local history in Germany and to new trends in historiography that emphasized individuals and their circles of social activity.[17]

Research on the Jews remained the domain of Jewish historians. They too dealt primarily with the different explanations for the Nazis' policy of murder, the Final Solution, and the organization of occupation - Jewish institutions such as the Judenrat, the Jewish police, and other bodies that continued to function (for example, the Jews' social self-help institutions), although their modes of operation changed.

Another topic that occupied many researchers was Jewish resistance to Nazi rule. The different definitions of resistance reflect development in the understanding of the fate of European Jewry among survivors, including leaders of the uprisings in the ghettos and the forests, and among members of the Jewish public living outside of Europe. As in the countries of occupied Europe, this topic served both personal and national interests and proved particularly helpful in coping with the inconsolability that remained in the wake of the massive destruction. Research on the resistance incorporated many social elements, such as youth movements and movement activists, and distinctions between the young men and women who were willing to join the underground and engage in armed struggle on the one hand, and the older population, who were caring for families, children, and the like, on the other hand. But this line of inquiry also did not develop into general social research on the Jews in the ghettos; discussion focused on the armed uprising, dying with dignity, and the historiographical controversy surrounding the Jewish leadership as reflected in the relations between the underground movement and the Judenrat.[18]

I regard these topics as substitutes for the "political" history of the Holocaust. In this context, the term "political history" must be understood in light of the Jewish reality of lack of political power in the customary sense. However, in the lives of Jews during the Holocaust, these topics reflected the struggle over internal authority, with all its limitations; over leadership and influence; and over management of the order of public life. Manifestations of this dynamic can be found in the documentation pertaining to the Judenrat in the different ghettos, the Chronicle of the Lodz Ghetto, the history of the Jewish police in the Kovno Ghetto, and other such sources. The debate in the research that evolved regarding the definition of resistance and use of the term "Jewish steadfastness" (amida in Hebrew) presents an opportunity to take a closer look at the different social groups, at the individual (mother and father), and at the family.[19]

The change occurred in the 1990s, when history "from below" and studies dealing with German society and Nazism aroused interest in the lives of Jews not from the perspective of public organization but rather from the perspective of the everyday life of the individual and the development of different social groups within the Jewish public. These studies focused on the lives of Jews up until the mass deportations and helped develop discussion of issues of gender and the fate of women in the Holocaust. These issues, in turn, placed questions pertaining to family and the everyday lives of Jews (including children, youth, etc.) on the agenda.

One might say that the very issues that Ringelblum pushed aside due to his awareness of the scope of the extermination and the destruction have reemerged and that we are now returning to them. By investigating everyday life, can we learn how the Jews read the reality around them? Can research of how families organized the lives the of their families in the ghetto illuminate their faith or desperation regarding the future and their own survival? Was the historical experience of Jews reflected in individual and group efforts to live and to survive? All of these issues were documented in the archives, the organizers of which regarded them as extremely important as long as they believed that, despite the destruction and the devastation, the Jewish People would continue to exist, even in Eastern Europe.

The study of social issues and the life of the individual was based on a foundation laid by the authors of the important monographs on the major ghettos, including Warsaw, Vilna, Kovno, Bialystok, Lwow, and Kielce, and of the comprehensive studies on the Judenräte, the Jewish police, and the resistance.[20] These historians sketched the outline of public life under occupation and in the ghettos and the connection with Jewish organizational efforts and leadership (to which I refer to above as "the political").

This work produced a foundation on which the empirical research could continue and focus on the life of the individual. The research then turned to issues pertaining to the small circles of the individual, including the immediate and the extended family; the home, with its many residents; services (such as medical); and education as it pertained to the family, youth, and children. In this way, it helped us depict the physical and mental space of the inhabitants of the ghettos. The challenge facing historians is to present readers not only with personal stories but also with a broader, more comprehensive, and more in-depth picture of the life of Jews up until the point that they were sent to their deaths. However, it is also important to draw attention to questions of methodology.

2. Who is the individual?

The documentation present in the writings of men, women, and children from the Holocaust era is substantial, and historians have difficulty contending with the large quantity of material at their disposal. Still, this documentation is eclectic and only infrequently enables us to systematically trace changes and transitions in the lives of the men, women, children, youth, and families living under Nazi occupation, both before the Jews entered the ghettos and in the ghettos themselves. As noted above, the bias present in this important type of documentation stems from its authors, as those who left behind personal documentation of some kind – letters, questionnaires, diaries, reports, or articles from the underground press or the ghetto archives – were intellectuals, social and political leaders, and youth movement members. On numerous occasions documentation was produced with the intention of highlighting a particular perspective in the hope that future historians and researchers would read and study the texts. As historians, therefore, we need to remember that much of our research is based on the writings of skilled individuals who, to some extent, were part of a social group, and that as readers and researchers we are employing the interpretations of the authors from those days.

We can sometimes learn the biography and worldview of the authors. A good example is the case of Emmanuel Ringelblum, about whom many have written. However, in *Who Will Write Our History?*, Kassow emphasizes the

political and social views of Ringelblum himself, as well as his effort, and that
of his fellow archive organizers and partners, to represent the different political
and social views that he and his close friends espoused. This is an instructive
example of wise usage of the early information available regarding the man and
his partners in setting up the archive, their political and social outlooks prior to
the Holocaust, and their activity in different realms.[21]

On the other hand, there are documenters about whom we know very little.
For example, we possess no biographical information on Stanisław Różycki, who left
behind impressive essays on the street in the ghetto, the Soviet occupation of Lwow,
and Jewish-Ukrainian relations; all we know about this author is what he mentions
in his writings in Polish. Kassow's conclusions regarding Różycki's intellectual world
is based on his own interpretation of the texts that he read.[22]

Here, it is important to distinguish between writings with clear aims, such
as the writings of the Oyneg Shabbes archive that proceeded in accordance with
the questionnaires and goals set by those involved in the archive, and the texts
that were written by people in discussion with themselves and that somehow
made it to the archive or were preserved in other ways. In any event, these texts
were typically not written by "everyday Jews," as Jabotinsky characterized them,
and researchers must keep in mind that they already contain interpretations
reflecting the ethical world of the writer.

As a result, we can also conclude that the research methods employed must
be qualitative as opposed to quantitative. In addition to what we refer to as
official documentation, such as the minutes of Judenrat meetings (Bialystok and
Lublin), reports of the Jewish self-help organizations, JDC reports, newspapers
of the ghetto and newspapers of the underground, the personal documentation
regarding such issues is also important. Diaries and memoirs that were written
during the war, personal letters that were sent to friends and relatives in
different ghettos and outside the areas of Nazi rule, and oral documentation
collected during different periods all serve as foundation stones of the research.
Personal documentation is subjective by nature and requires treatment that is
personal and limited in its potential for generalization, whereas we aspire to
achieve an element of generalization with regard to the lives of individuals and
families. The challenge of this research, therefore, is to combine macro-history

and micro-history, in which the story of the individual is neither an example nor a test case but rather an account that offers a glimpse into the experience of a population characterized by the same social, economic, and cultural attributes as the individual being documented.[23]

Due to the small number of sources available, it is more difficult to learn about the experiences and the way of life of Jews from small places. Many more sources are available regarding the major ghettos in which archives that survived the destruction were kept. For example, we possess a large quantity of material on the Lodz Ghetto, and Ringelblum's archive provides us with significant material on Warsaw and the surrounding area.[24]

3. The Challenge of Depicting Everyday Life: The Terms of Analysis

3.a. Banality

How is it possible to describe "everyday life" or "daily routine" when the predominant usage of these terms pertains to regular life in which banality reigns: everyday matters such as work, earning a livelihood, social life, celebrations, love, food, arguments, jealousy, compassion, and many other things that are important for maintaining normalcy? Normalcy, as defined by Emile Durkheim, is a manifestation of everyday life that is entrenched in the value system of society. Such systems have a number of major components. One is work and its financial remuneration, the source of livelihood and life for the family unit that expresses emotions, solidarity, mutual relationships, and social arrangements; another is the ability to expect that activity in everyday life will have predictable results.[25]

Life in the ghetto was far from such a reality. For this reason, the use of terminology pertaining to the extreme reality of the ghetto may be interpreted incorrectly, as in it we encounter not only banal terms but also terms that distort the modes of survival of ghetto inhabitants. With regard to the quick pace of changes in the lives of Jews in the ghetto, Ringelblum wrote the following:

> The war caused rapid change in the lives of Jews in the cities of Poland. Each day differed from the last, and images changed at the speed of a film at the cinema. The days of the ghetto seem

like heaven to the Warsaw Jew imprisoned within his shop – and the days that preceded the ghetto are truly ideal. Each month has ushered in profound changes that completely transformed the lives of the Jews. It is therefore also extremely important to photograph every event in the life of the Jews the moment it occurs, while it is still alive and fluttering. The shop before the deportation is as far from the shop after the deportation as east is from west. The same is true of smuggling and of social and cultural life – even the way in which the Jews dress has differed from period to period.[26]

Can such a pace be contended with without losing one's head? The above quote leads us to the next problem: that of containment and generalization.

3.b. Containment and Generalization

Ringelblum broached the topic of generalization in Warsaw itself when the ghetto was still in existence. This, however, raises the question of whether, and in what way, we can apply generalizations based on such a complex and diverse reality to everyday life in the different ghettos of Eastern Europe. After all, there were open and closed ghettos; small, medium, and large ghettos; ghettos established before or hand-in-hand with the mass murders; ghettos in which Jews suffered from the difficult times faced by the local population prior to its establishment (Kovno); ghettos in which the majority of the population and its leadership consisted of locals (Kovno, Vilna, and Lodz); ghettos in Transnistria that contained many Jewish deportees from the same country or a different country (Warsaw); and ghettos (such as Transnistria) in which local Jews were the minority.

In addition to the challenge posed by this multiplicity of ghetto types, how can we compare places in which the Jews' historical experience and memory were different, resulting in the different interpretations of reality and the Nazi occupation that are recorded in the diaries and the letters that remain at our disposal?

3.c. Ways of Writing and Producing a Narrative

We can also ask whether we possess the tools required to simultaneously write both empathetically and critically about the individual, the public, and society in extreme situations. Such situations lasted for long periods of time, as one tragedy followed another and uncertainty and terror prevailed.

Historians are committed to writing that achieves both distance and closeness, to which philosopher Robin Collingwood has referred as historical empathy. This does not denote identification or sympathy with the historical protagonists but rather an attempt to "walk in their shoes" down the paths and along the routes they traveled. This raises the question of whether we are capable of building a bridge we can walk over, heel to toe, to get from here to there, as proposed by Sam Wineburg in the context of teaching history.[27]

This approach applies to the history of the murderers and the victims alike, as well as to the history of all those who were not murderers but nonetheless belonged to an abusive group. The intellectual effort required to create empathy exists in every writing of history. However, when the historian aspires to represent the world of individuals in the public and social framework in which they lived and were active, the task becomes even more daunting due to the extreme situations and the eclectic sources noted above.

4. Methodology and the Questions that Need to be Asked

As noted above, describing the everyday life of the complex and diverse reality of the ghettos of Eastern Europe requires us to consult a variety of types of personal documentation, such as diaries, personal letters, testimonies and memoirs. Most importantly, the researcher must be open to the methodology of qualitative narrative analysis.[28] A number of research projects on everyday life under Nazi occupation, beginning with everyday life in Nazi Germany, made use of personal documentation about which many historians had reservations from the outset. However, since the 1990s, the usage of personal documentation, referred to as "ego documentation," has been widespread and acceptable, not only as an illustration.

Personal documentation calls for wide-ranging familiarity with the authors, their families, the social groups to which they belonged, their places of employment or other sources of livelihood, and other such aspects (which we often do not know, as mentioned above). The personal is connected to the external reality in which the individual lives and is active, yielding a linkage between the personal and the public.[29]

In addition to this approach, to which we can refer as historical, social and cultural, the historian can examine the reality of Jewish life in the ghettos through the eyes of the anthropologist. Clifford Geertz's approach to thick description, and to the system of images and terms that were used in the ghettos and by the diverse Jewish public prior to the Holocaust and during the Nazi occupation, directs the historian to gather as much information as possible about the ghettos from a multiplicity of sources, personal and official alike.[30] This enables learning about the diverse phenomena, events, feelings and thoughts of the ghetto public. However, alongside the attempt to understand the approach, the way of thinking and the inner world of the historical protagonists, Geertz calls for understanding the influences of our own cultural system and our political and ideological views on the interpretation that we as researchers propose. He highlights the importance of recognizing that our questions as researchers and our ways of thinking are meaningful components of the manner in which we interpret the behavior of historical protagonists.[31]

In addition to the above, we must also think about the fields of psychology and social psychology as they apply to the individual and the public. How does the individual act in states of uncertainty? How does a society operate in situations of uncertainty? How do they react to terror and violence? And can they contain questions pertaining to post-trauma, including the contest between collapse and resilience within those who remained in the ghetto after the murders and the transports and continued to live their personal and collective lives after one-third or one-half of the ghetto's residents had already been sent to the killing zone?[32]

At times, the documentation reveals contradictory behaviors by the same people, ostensibly indicating states of collapse alongside efforts to act based on an existing normative framework. And at times, we find another sliver of faith that the world will eventually revert to functioning according to an orderly system of values. How is it possible to 'package' the cultural heritage of our historical experience and memory and at the same time try to learn from the past?

Understanding these views helps us rely on cultural history, which provides us with the symbols, images, and intellectual apparatus with which the residents of the ghetto interpreted their reality. Moshe Rosman defines cultural history as history of the meanings that people ascribe to the reality in which they live. These meanings are produced by personal biography, historical experience as preserved in the collective memory, and the emotional world that forms within the individual and society vis-à-vis phenomena or behavior of the individual.[33]

This brings us back to thinking about "normalcy" and everyday life in extreme situations. I am not referring here to the abovementioned link between normalcy and banality but rather to the ability, in severe states of crisis, to continue to maintain the organization of life, including its overall experience and its way of thinking regarding the future – when values will once again serve as guides for the individual and society. To contend with these questions, we can use the approach advanced by sociologists Peter Berger and Thomas Luckman in their book on the shaping of reality and the sociology of knowledge.[34]

According to Berger and Luckman, most individual behavior is the product of common sense, which is how individuals behave in the social system. Using common sense, the individual interprets information and the knowledge that he or she needs in everyday life. Berger and Luckman define this kind of knowledge, which is a basis for useful action, as "recipe knowledge." The individual needs it when executing everyday tasks at work, at home, in social life, and in other contexts. To better understand the use of common sense, they compare it to a beam of light produced by a flashlight used by someone walking through a dark forest to clear a path for himself through the darkness. In their view, this useful knowledge enables normalcy (the prevailing situation) and the ability to contend with events that deviate from normalcy, such as a crisis at work, a strike at a factory, or a crisis in a couple's relationship. In this way, the individual produces an objectification of reality and manages to view it coherently and to identify its internal logic. He is also able to assess it in terms of "here" and "now," as his system of knowledge also contains memory relating to the biographical and historical past. Using these, individuals create mutual relations with their surroundings, including the different and the similar, and strengthen their ability to understand the temporality of the crisis. Temporality is the other important element in Berger and Luckman's approach. It is the temporality of human existence and of good and evil alike.

Berger and Luckman's approach highlights the tools that people use to cope with crises. But we still need to ask whether we can conclude that this is how people will react in unprecedented extreme situations.

Researchers of the individual and the public in the ghettos need to contend with a reality of extreme situations. Although Berger and Lackman did not envision such situations in their research, I maintain that by using these categories, we can examine the contemporary writing and learn how the individual copes (or fails to cope), in thought and in action, with an extreme reality. When we read diaries, letters, jokes, images, and rumors that were prevalent in the ghetto, and we consider them in the context of the question of continuity or change, we possess tools that help us understand the way in which the residents of the ghetto interpreted their situation. We can achieve a more in depth understanding of how the individual and the public understood the transition from one situation to the next, as well as the extent to which images related to the concrete events were interpreted using terms from the world of Jewish tradition and culture, such as "mysticism, "Gematria," and references to the historical past.

Historians are not sociologists, psychologists, or anthropologists, and they must therefore read the sources with an open mind and as few preconceived notions as possible, and only then begin an ongoing dialogue with the sources. This dialogue must be dynamic: the more historians learn about and get to know the sources and the more they feel that the reconstruction of the historical reality as a whole is clear, the more direct and precise – yet also tentative – their questions will be. This, in my opinion, is the stage at which we can and should make use of categories from the different disciplines mentioned above to enhance our analysis.

We must remember that the reality of the ghettos was dynamic. Many of the reasons for this had to do with external factors, such as the changing German policy, the unfolding of the war and the figures controlling the ghetto, as well as what the people themselves experienced in the ghetto and the changes that occurred in their consciousness and their understanding of themselves. This dynamic nature must be contained in the historical description. It was given expression by Ringelblum in his hiding place in Warsaw, as reflected in the above-cited quote regarding the rapid pace of change in the ghetto.

Ringelblum's ability to see his initial time in the ghetto as good days, as he himself wrote, is reflective of insight resulting from the major deportation. During the early days of the ghetto, no one imagined the total destruction that would follow. The rapid pace at which things changed created mental chaos and a fragmented interpretation of reality, and accepting what was acceptable in everyday life became increasingly difficult and almost impossible. The following was written by the authors of the history of the Jewish police in the Kovno Ghetto, when only a third of the ghetto's population was still alive:

> There is no concern for what is permitted and what is prohibited. It is all the same, it is all insignificant. As long as they allow us to live, we might as well at least enjoy ourselves as much as possible. In this way, boundaries are erased, and people hop over fences which, in normal times, we kept well-guarded.[35]

On the other hand, immediately after the ghetto's establishment, Chaim Aron Kaplan wrote: "Even abnormal living becomes normal when it becomes constant. But our nerves are working hard."[36]

Both texts relate to adaptation, on the one hand, and an awareness of the twisted nature of adaptation, on the other hand. And thus, the term "normalcy" assumes different meanings, raising the question of whether normalcy in a state of constant change is actually normalcy.

Still, the different aspects of daily routine prevailed in the ghetto. Diaries carry frequent reports of events of "changing routine." For example, Kaplan mentions the tension between those calling for speaking in Hebrew and those advocating the use of Yiddish in 1941, the year in which the number of dead skyrocketed. In the Kovno Ghetto, the Jewish police documented its implementation of an oath of allegiance ceremony that made use of prominent features of ceremonies that were customary within the social frameworks in which the Jews had functioned prior to the war, including the Zionist movements, as well as a deep sense of national identity. In religious ceremonies in the Telšiai Ghetto, Jewish women replaced men, who were no longer among the living.[37]

This duality finds distinct expression in two quotes from the writing of Oskar Rosenfeld, a Jew from Prague who was deported to Lodz where he helped write the chronicles of the ghetto. The first quote was written immediately following the "Sperre," the major deportation of September 1942:

Here in the ghetto, after three years of war, the concept of family –
with few exceptions – has been struck from the dictionary. And if
any illusions on the matter still remained, they vanished after the
deportation and no longer exist.

It was a terrible time, with scenes of horror in which children were
forcibly separated from their mothers and vice-versa. And still, a certain
apathy was noticeable immediately following the action, and even more
so two days later. The apathy of the masses, the direct return to regular
everyday activities, and the denseness of thought – if we can refer to it
in this manner – are all indicative of an indescribable dullness of the
senses and a complete paralysis of normal thinking…

Most people have returned to routine after the tragedy.
And after three years of war, this dullness is nothing to marvel at.
It is difficult to be critical of people for having a sense of apathy
regarding the fate of others.

Approximately one year later, in 1943, Rosenfeld wrote as follows:

On the Sabbath of Yom Kippur there were all the signs of respect and formality.
People moved through the streets quietly, dressed in holiday attire. Everyone who
could get their hands on them wore clothes of better quality…Once again, after a
long time, the entire family gathered together. Parents walked with their children,
holding their hands. On that day, work in the Resorts did not separate husband
from wife and from child. Here and there, a Polish Jew could even be seen openly
carrying a Torah scroll in the streets of the ghetto to bring it to the house where
prayers were being conducted… If we were to sum up the prevailing atmosphere
at home and in the street, we could say that on Yom Kippur of 1943, the ghetto
became a "shtetl" in the full sense of the word.[38]

Toward Conclusion

At the beginning of this article, I asked what delayed research on the individual and
the public in the ghettos of Eastern Europe, even though the subject was central to
the documentation effort of the Jews of the ghetto during the Holocaust itself. The

answer I proposed is rooted in the historical experience of total annihilation, the need to document and give testimony about it after the war, and historiographical development pertaining to the reaction to the Nazis and to the Final Solution in the various countries of Europe. The preference for the "political" (as I define it) as opposed to the social, I explained, reflected the understanding reached by the survivors, which was consistent with the feelings of Ringelblum while he was in hiding and engaged in organizing his writings. I also discussed the change that has occurred over the past two decades as a manifestation of the impact of historiography's call for engaging in history "from below," and of the impact of gender research on the historiography of Nazi Germany and women during the Holocaust. The change in status of personal documentation (ego documents) in the historical writing both stemmed from and contributed to these factors. Moreover, the discussion of personal documentation focused attention on the narrative analysis of changes in linguistic terms (see the Encyclopedia of the Ghetto in the diary of Oskar Rosenfeld[39]) and on the reading of diaries, memoirs, and testimonies as expressions of the context of the writer and the reader, as well as of the personality and the inner world of the individual. I sought to emphasize that we could engage in an in-depth discussion of the public and the individual only after the production of the research literature on the organizational frameworks of the Jews in the ghetto.

This resulted in the raising of methodical questions pertaining to the definition of the individual: Does the documentation that remains at our disposal represent the individual in the sense of "everyman" or, alternatively, individuals belonging to a writing elite? What is the conceptual terminology with which we can achieve a deep understanding of the behavior of individuals in the dynamic and extreme reality which the ghetto summoned?

Recent decades has witnessed a proliferation of studies dealing with the life of Jews in the ghetto based on an analytical approach that implements the above presented principles in terms of the use of sources, the use of a systematic approach and approaches of micro-history, and the extensive use of terminology borrowed from other disciplines in the humanities and the social sciences.[40] Relevant to this context is Gustavo Corni's book *Hitler's Ghettos* – one of the first texts to contend with the fundamental problems that were characteristic of all of the ghettos. Corni devoted two of the book's 11 chapters to issues of the individual and society: "Life in the Ghettos" and "Ghetto Society: All Equal?" Both of these chapters engage in discussion that is extremely important.[41]

Here, I would like to briefly expand on a number of Israeli scholars who have published books in recent years. Amos Goldberg's book *Trauma in First Person* revolves around the concept of "trauma," which it uses to analyze the condition of its major protagonists – Victor Klemperer and Chaim Aron Kaplan – and their diaries, after providing an extensive explanation in the first part of the book for his reasons for adopting this approach.[42] In her book *White Coats inside the Ghetto*, which deals with medicine during the Holocaust with a focus on the organizational system of the Warsaw Ghetto, Miriam Ofer combines the use of routine archival documentation with personal documentation. In its concluding chapter – while contending with the physicians' dilemmas, during the days of the deportations, between their oath as physicians to save lives and the taking of lives of patients in order to prevent them from suffering at the hands of the Nazi murderers – she considers issues pertaining to ethics and turns to the field of philosophy to illuminate her proposed analysis.[43] In a discussion of deportees and refugees in *Displaced Persons at Home: Refugees in the Fabric of Jewish Life in Warsaw*, Lea Prais makes use of substantial literature on refugees and immigration, and, in a depiction of the everyday life of the refugees, she relates extensively to relations between the public (the *landsmannschaft* aid organizations) on the one hand and the individual and the family on the other. Using these perspectives, she succeeds in contending with the stereotype of the refugees as passive and discusses their survival efforts and class differences.[44] In the third chapter of *Warsaw Ghetto: The End (April 1942-June 1943)*,[45] Havi Dreifuss (Ben-Sasson) writes about those who remained in the Warsaw Ghetto after the major deportation. In a chapter titled, "An Abandoned, Beaten Remnant in a Painful Awakening," and in the final section of this chapter, titled "Abnormal Routine," Dreifuss addresses the social and consciousness-related situations of the few Jews who remained in the ghetto after the deportation and the mass murders and tries to understand how they continued their everyday life in conditions of complete uncertainty, in constant fear of deporetation and murder, and in a state of total mistrust in the promises of the Germans. In addition, she discusses the renewed coping with mutual aid, with different services in the realms of health and education, and with the effort to create life – even if only disrupted and fragmented – in the shops. This brings us to the usage of the contradictory terms "routine" and "abnormal" in the analaysis of the situation of the Jews during this period. We can also expand this question and ask whether the term "abnormal routine" may also be applied to previous periods in the life of the ghetto which Dreifuss does not address.

In her book *A Remote Region*, Sara Rosen explores the everyday life of the ghettos in northern Transnistria under Romanian rule.[46] In this study, Rosen highlights the distinctions between deportees and refugees, between the local Jewish population and the local Ukrainian population, and between the means of organization of the different groups. Here too, in addition to the use of personal and other materials, the trajectories of discussion are between the public-social and the private-personal. Rosen applies sociologist Edward Shils' terminology of "center" and "periphery" to the social sphere,[47] exploring the networks of connection that were created within and among the different ghettos and contending with the terms of normalcy in the organization of everyday life by following the different patterns that took form in the public space of the ghettos. Rosen considers the organizational framework and the leadership, or whoever headed the ghetto, in light of the personal framework of family and its importance to survival.

The abovementioned scholars, including the authors of the anthologies dealing with life in the ghetto, struggle with these questions and propose different insights that open a door to the continuation of research on this important subject.

Recent years have also witnessed an expansion of the discussion that compares other cases of genocide to the Holocaust. Although the rich literature pertaining to genocide deals primarily with the murderers and those who set the murders in motion, I hold that the studies on the life of Jews under Nazi occupation, in the shadow of death and the mass murders, have the potential to serve as a model for learning about and understanding the victims of other instances of genocide.

Endnotes

1   Jean Améry, *At the Mind's Limits: Contemplations by a Survivor on Auschwitz and Its Realities*, translated by Sidney Rosenfeld and Stella P. Rosenfeld (Indiana University Press, 1980), p. 93.

2   Dalia Ofer, "Three Lines in History: Modes of Jewish Resistance in East European Ghettos," in Patrick Henry (ed.), *Jewish Resistance against the* Nazis (The Catholic University of America Press, 2014), pp. 366-392. See also Havi Dreifuss, "Jewish Historiography of the Holocaust in Eastern Europe," *Polin: Studies in Polish Jewry* 29 (2017), pp. 217-245.

3   Artur Eisenbach, "Jewish Historiography in Poland between the Two World Wars," in Israel Bartal and Israel Gutman (ed.), *The Broken Chain: Polish Jewry through the Ages* (Jerusalem, 2001), pp. 669-695 (Hebrew).

4   Ibid. See also Emanuel Ringelblum, "Dr. Ignacy Schiper: Builder of the New Jewish Historiography" and "Meir Balaban" A Praiseworthy Historian of Polish Jewry," *Last Writings: Polish–Jewish Relations, January 1943–April 1944* (Hebrew) (Jerusalem, 1994), pp. 86-99 (Hebrew). See also David Engel's approach to Jewish historiography in Poland during the interwar period and his attitude toward the major historians, in David Engel, "The Writing of History as a National Mission: The Jews of Poland and Their Historiographic Traditions," in Israel Gutman (ed.), *Emanuel Ringelblum: The Man and the Historian* (Jerusalem, 2010), pp. 117-140.

5   Roni Stauber, "Philip Friedman and the Beginning of Holocaust Studies," *Gilad* 21 (2007), pp. 77-114 (Hebrew).

6   Samuel Kassow, "Politics and History: Emmanuel Ringelblum and the Oneg Shabes Archive," *Michael: on the History of the Jews in the Diaspora* 16 (2004), pp. 51-80: 3-4.

7   Samuel Kassow, *Who Will Write Our History? Rediscovering a Hidden Archive from the Warsaw Ghetto* (Indiana University Press, 2007); Gutman, *Emanuel Ringelblum*.

8   *A Chronical of the Lodz Ghetto*, translated and annotated by Arieh Ben-Menachem and Joseph Rab (Jerusalem, 1996-1998) (Hebrew).

9   Dalia Ofer (ed.), *The Clandestine History of the Kovno Jewish Ghetto Police* (Jerusalem, 2016) (Hebrew). For the English version of this source see *The Clandestine History of the Kovno Jewish Ghetto Police*, translated and edited by Samuel Kassow (Indiana University Press, 2014). Page numbers listed in these notes apply to the Hebrew version. See also Leib Garfunkel, *Jewish Kovno Destroyed* (Jerusalem, 1959), p. 237 (Hebrew).

10   Ringelblum, *Last Writings*, p. 4. The Jewish Social Self-Help Organization (*Jüdische Soziale Selbsthilfe*, or JSS, in German; *Żydowska Samopomoc Społeczna*, or ŻSS, in Polish; *Yidishe Sotsyale Aleynhilf*, or YSA, in Yiddish) was a Jewish relief organization set up by JDC personnel that provided support for masses of needy Jews during the

Holocaust. Representatives of the Jewish public arena participated in the enterprise and rose above their ideological disagreements with the aim of easing the difficulties of Jews. The organization had different departments that sought to contend with the different hardships. Among other things, it established soup kitchens that provided people with a portion of soup and a slice of bread.

11 Kassow, *Who Will Write Our History?*, pp. 14-28. Many of the materials from Ringelblum's archives, and many articles based on studies that were conducted, appear in Joseph Kermish's book *To Live with Honor and Die with Honor: Selected Documents from the Warsaw Underground Archive O.S.* (Jerusalem, 1986).

12 I would like to thank the late Prof. Israel Gutman for providing me with this letter, which bears no date and no markings and appears to be from the Ghetto Fighters' House Archive. Based on its content, it appears to have been written at the end, or at least the second half of 1943.

13 Roni Stauber, *Laying the Foundations for Holocaust Research: The Impact of the Historian Philip* Friedman (Jerusalem, 2009). See also Natalia Aleksiun, "Polish Historiography of the Holocaust: Between Silence and Public Debate," *German History* 22(3) (2004), pp. 406-432, especially pp. 412-418.

14 Ringelblum, *Last Writings*, p. 11.

15 Dalia Ofer, "The Community and the Individual: Different Narratives of Early and Late Testimonies and their Significance for Historians," in David Bankier and Dan Michman, (eds.), *Holocaust Historiography in Context: Emergence, Challenges, Polemics and Achievements* (Jerusalem, 2008), pp. 519-535.

16 Gerald Reitlinger, *The Final Solution: The Attempt to Exterminate the Jews of Europe, 1939-1945* (New York, 1953); Raul Hilberg, *The Destruction of the European Jews* (Yale University Press, 1961). For an interesting article on the historiography of the Holocaust from the perspective of paradigms for understanding the murder of the Jews, see Marina Cattaruzza, "The Historiography of the Holocaust: An Attempt at a Bibliographical Synthesis," *Totalitrismus und Demokratie* 3 (2006), pp. 285-321.

17 Detlev J. K. Peukert, *Inside Nazi Germany: Conformity, Opposition and Racism in Everyday Life* (London, 1986). See also Martin Broszat et al. (eds.), *Bayern in der NS-Zeit*, 4 vols. (Munich/Vienna, 1977-1983). For an article that summarizes the development of the German research on the genocide and the development of Nazi policy, see Herbert Ulrich, "A Policy of Extermination: New Answers and Questions on the History of the Holocaust," *History of the Holocaust*, https://www.yadvashem.org/odot_pdf/Microsoft%20Word%20-%201137.pdf (Hebrew) (last accessed on September 5, 2019). It is interesting to note that Gustavo Corni's book on the ghetto allocates more space to issues of everyday life. Gustavo Corni, *Hitler's Ghettos: Voices from a Beleaguered Society, 1939-1944* (Oxford University Press, 2002), pp. 48-61, 168-226.

18 Michael Marrus's *The Holocaust in History* can be viewed as an expression of this assessment. This 1983 book, which addresses the historiography of the Holocaust, contains two chapters on the Jews that do not deal with social history at all. The first considers the victims of the ghettos of Eastern and Central Europe and the Jews of the West, and the second explores the resistance in different parts of Europe. Michael R. Marrus, *The Holocaust in History* (University Press of New England, 1987), pp.108-133. The papers presented at a conference on the historiography of the Holocaust that was held at Yad Vashem, which were published in 2005, said nothing about the everyday life of the Jews, gender, or the social relations within the Jewish communities in the ghettos and in other parts of Europe. Dan Michman (ed.), *The Holocaust in Jewish History: Historiography, Consciousness, and Interpretation* (Jerusalem, 2005) (Hebrew). Also see Michman's article "One Subject, Several Voices: Language and Culture in Holocaust Research," in Shmuel Almog, Daniel Blatman, David Bankier, and Dalia Ofer (eds.), *The Holocaust: The Unique and the Universal* (Jerusalem, 2002), pp. 8-37 (Hebrew).

19 Nachman Blumenthal, *Conducts and Actions of a Judenrat: Documents from the Białystok Ghetto* (Jerusalem, 1962) (Hebrew); Nachman Blumenthal, *Judenrat without Direction: Documents from the Lublin Ghetto* (Jerusalem, 1967); and Lucjan Dobroszycki (ed.), *The Chronicle of the Lodz Ghetto, 1941-1944* (Yale University Press, 1987).

20 Isaiah Trunk, *Judenrat: The Jewish Councils in Eastern Europe under Nazi Occupation* (New York, 1972); Israel Gutman, *The Jews of Warsaw, 1939-1943: Ghetto, Underground, Revolt* (Indiana University Press, 1982); Yael Peled (Margolin), *Jewish Krakow, 1939–1943: Resistance, Underground, Struggle* (Ghetto Fighters' House, 1993) (Hebrew); Michal Unger (ed.), *The Last Ghetto: Life in the Lodz Ghetto, 1940-1944* (Jerusalem, 2005) (Hebrew); Sarah Bender, *The Jews of Białystok during World War II and the Holocaust* (Brandeis University Press, 2008); Sarah Bender, *In Enemy Land: The Jews of Kielce and the Region, 1939-1946* (Boston, 2018); Tikva Fatal-Knaani, *Grodno is Not the Same: The Jewish Community of Grodno and its Surroundings* (Jerusalem, 2001) (Hebrew); Aharon Weiss, "The Jewish Police in the General Government and Upper Silesia during the Holocaust," doctoral dissertation, The Hebrew University of Jerusalem, 1974 (Hebrew); Aharon Weiss, "The Relationship between the Judenrat and the Jewish Police in Occupied Poland," in Israel Gutman (ed.), *Patterns of Jewish Leadership in Nazi Europe, 1933-1945: Proceedings of the Third Yad Vashem International Historical Conference, Jerusalem, April 4-7, 1977* (Jerusalem, 1979), pp. 201-217.

21 Kassow, *Who Will Write Our History?* pp. 163-224.

22 Ibid., pp. 164, 266-268. See excerpts from Różycki's memoirs in Lea Prais (ed.), *In the Fog of Wanderings: A Collection of Testimonies of Jewish Refugees from the Oyneg Shabbes Archive, 1939-1942* (Jerusalem, 2014), pp. 534-577 (Hebrew); Dalia Ofer, "The Ghetto as a Forced and Changing Society in the Shadow of Death: Methodological Comments," in Roni Stauber, Aviva Halamish, and Esther Webman (eds.), *Holocaust and Anti-Semitism: Research and Public Discourse: Essays Presented in Honor of Dina Porat* (Tel Aviv and Jerusalem, 2015), pp. 43-70 (Hebrew).

23 On microhistory, see "Microhistory Today: A Roundtable Discussion," in *Journal of Medieval and Early Modern Studies* 47(1) (January 2017), pp. 7-51. See also Claire Zalc and Tal Bruttmann (eds.), *Microhistories of the Holocaust* (New York and Oxford, 2017).

24 Over the past few years, the research has expanded to include a discussion of rural areas and small ghettos, which, after all, is where most of the Jews were located. This research has been conducted primarily by Polish historians. See Aleksiun, "Polish Historiography of the Holocaust"; Barbara Engelking, *Such a Beautiful Summer Day: Jews Seeking Refuge in the Polish Countryside, 1942-1944* (Jerusalem, 2016); Jan Grabowski, *Hunt for Jews: Betrayal and Murder in German Occupied Europe* (Indiana University Press, 2013).

25 Emile Durkheim, *Rules of the Sociological Method* (New York, 1968), pp. 46-47.

26 Ringelblum, *Last Writings*, p 11.

27 Robin George Collingwood, *The Idea of History* (Oxford University Press, 1956); Sam Wineburg, *Historical Thinking and Other Unnatural Acts: Charting the Future of Teaching the Past* (Temple University Press, 2001); Sam Wineburg, "Historical Thinking and Other Unnatural Acts", *The Phi Delta Kappan* 80(7) (March 1999), pp. 488-499.

28 Narrative analysis, which is characteristic of qualitative analysis, has been the topic of many studies. In Israel, this approach has been employed by the various studies of Amia Lieblich, who explains it in Amia Lieblich, Rivka Tuval-Mashiach, and Tamar Zilber, *Narrative Research: Reading, Analysis and Interpretation* (Thousand Oaks, CA, 1998). See also Asher Shkedi's book *Words of Meaning: Qualitative Research – Theory and Practice* (Tel Aviv, 2004) (Hebrew).

29 Prof. Tatjana Tönsmeyer, *World War II: Everyday Life under German Occupation*, https://www.buw-output.de/en/archive/edition9/world-war-ii-everyday-life-under-german-occupation; Societies under German Occupation – Experiences and Everyday Life in World War II, http://www.societiesunder-german-occupation.com/#project-description; Tatjana Tönsmeyer, Peter Haslinger, and Agnes Laba (eds.), *Coping with Hunger and Shortage under German Occupation in World War II* (Cham, Switzerland, 2018); Natalia Alexuin, "Food, Money and Barter in the Lvov Ghetto, Eastern Galicia," in Tönsmeyer, Haslinger, and Laba, *Coping with Hunger*, pp. 243-247.

30 Clifford Geertz, *The Interpretation of Cultures: Selected Essays by Clifford Geertz* (New York, 1973), pp. 3-30.

31 Ibid., p. 14: "Understanding a people's culture exposes their normalness without reducing their particularity...It renders them accessible: setting them in the frame of their own banalities, it dissolves their opacity." Ibid., p. 28: "A good interpretation of anything – a poem, a person, a history, a ritual, an institution, a society – takes us into the heart of that of which it is the interpretation."

32 On post-trauma, see Judith Lewis Herman, *Trauma and Recovery: The Aftermath of Violence – From Domestic Abuse to Political Terror* (New York, 1992); Amos Goldberg, *Trauma in First Person: Diary Writing during the Holocaust* (Ben-Gurion University of the Negev, 2012), pp. 153-155 (Hebrew).

33 Cultural history can be summed up as "a history of meaning and feelings broadly defined, as embedded in expressive practices widely observed." See Moshe Rosman, "Prolegomenon to the Study of Jewish Cultural History," in *How Jewish is Jewish History?* (Oxford and Portland, 2007), p. 131. Also interesting is Alon Konfino's view on the importance of culture and the history of mentality in Alon Konfino, "A World without Jews: Interpreting the Holocaust," in *German History* 27(4) (2009), pp. 531-559.
    Goldberg's book *Trauma in First Person* is an instructive example of the approach that prioritizes the trauma and the cultural system within the actions of the historical protagonist. The book's discussion of the biographies of Victor Klemperer and Chaim Aron Kaplan is reflective of the broad approach of analyzing their personalities and their actions, their thinking, and their consciousness, which are anchored in their life experiences and the public life in which they lived and acted. The discussion of each of the characters – and their writing and modes of expression in light of the rise of the Nazis, following the outbreak of the war and the anti-Jewish policy at its various stages – enables the reader to enter the spiritual, day-to-day, practical worlds of the historical protagonists. See Amos Goldberg, "The History of the Jews in the Ghettos: A Cultural Perspective," in Dan Stone (ed.), *The Holocaust and Historical Methodology* (New York, 2012), pp. 79-100.

34 Peter Berger and Thomas Luckmann, *The Social Construction of Reality: A Treatise in the Sociology of Knowledge* (New York, 1966).

35 Ofer, *The Clandestine History of the Kovno Jewish Ghetto Police*, p. 276.

36 Chaim Aron Kaplan, *Scroll of Agony: The Warsaw Diary of Chaim A. Kaplan*, translated and edited by Abraham I. Katsch (Indiana University Press, 1965), p. 21.

37 Ofer, *The Clandestine History of the Kovno Jewish Ghetto Police*, pp. 450-457; Anat Volenberger, "The Final Solution of the Jewish Problem in the Telšiai Ghetto: A Test Case?" master's thesis, Hebrew University of Jerusalem, 2005, p. 60 (Hebrew).

38 Dobrosyzcki, The *Chronicle of the Lodz Ghetto*, pp. 395-396.

39 Oskar Rosenfeld, *In the Beginning was the Ghetto: Notebooks from Lodz* (Northwestern University Press, 2002), pp. 229-231.

40 Eric J. Sterling (ed.), *Life in the Ghettos during the Holocaust* (Syracuse University Press, 2005); Imke Hansen, Katrin Steffen, and Joachim Tauber (eds), *Lebenswelt Ghetto: Altag und sociale Unfeld während der nationalsocialistischen Verlolgung* (Wiesbaden, 2013); Thomas Kuehne and Tom Lawson, (eds.), *The Holocaust and Local History* (London, 2011); Claire Zalc and Tal Bruttmann (eds.), *Microhistories*

of the Holocaust (New York, 2017); Dalia Ofer, "The Ghettos in Transnistria and Ghettos under German Occupation in Eastern Europe A Comparative Approach," in Christoph Dieckmann and Babette Quinkert (eds.), *Im Ghetto 1939-1945, Neue Froschungen zu Alltag und Umfeld* (Göttingen, 2009), pp. 30-53.

41　Corni, *Hitler's Ghettos*, especially chapters 6 and 7, pp. 119-226.

42　Goldberg, *Trauma in First Person*, note 32.

43　Miriam Ofer, *White Coats Inside the Ghetto: Jewish Medicine in Poland During the Holocaust* (Jerusalem, 2015) (Hebrew).

44　Lea Prais, *Displaced Persons at Home: Refugees in the Fabric of Jewish Life in Warsaw, September 1939 – July 1942* (Jerusalem, 2015).

45　Havi Dreifuss (Ben-Sasson), *Warsaw Ghetto: The End (April 1942-June 1943)* (Jerusalem, 2017); "Christians in the Ghetto: All Saint's Church, Birth of the Holy Virgin Mary Church and the Jews of the Warsaw Ghetto," *Yad Vashem Studies* 31 (2003), pp. 153-17.

46　Sara Rosen, *In a Remote Region: The Jews of Bessarabia, Bucovina, and the District of Dorohoi – The Ghettos of Northern Transnistria, 1941-1944* (Jerusalem, 2020) (Hebrew); Sara Rosen, "Surviving in the Murafa Ghetto: A Case Study of One Ghetto in Transnistria," in Thomas Kuehne and Tom Lawson (eds.), *The Holocaust and Local History* (London, 2011), pp. 143-160.

47　Edward Albert Shils, *Center and Periphery: Essays in Macrosociology* (University of Chicago Press, 1975).

Havi Dreifuss

Orthodox Jews during the Holocaust: An Ongoing Lacuna of Research

Orthodox Jewry[1] has never been the focus of Holocaust research. Despite the substantial research that has been undertaken on the Holocaust, analysis of the patterns of life of Orthodox Jews during World War II – as individuals and as part of communities – has remained marginal and has not actually been integrated into the overall research on the period. Although recent years have witnessed some development in this area, and although this lacuna of research was identified years ago, the diverse Orthodox Jewish community has yet to be the subject of in-depth treatment by Holocaust research.

Academic Writing on Orthodox Jewry during the Holocaust

The first researcher to view the religious world as a subject of research in its own right was Meir (Mark) Dworzecki (1908-1975), a physician and Holocaust survivor from Vilna who held the Chair in Holocaust Research at Bar-Ilan University from 1960 onward. In his articles, Dworzecki began analyzing select aspects of the everyday life of religious Jews during the Holocaust, emphasizing the risk and the sense of mission involved in observing the Jewish commandments during this period.[2] Although a number of scholars who came later devoted time to researching religious life during the Holocaust, this subject ultimately never became a focal point of research in its own right, by them or by others.[3]

The scholar who returned to this issue and made it the focus of his interest was Dan Michman, who replaced Dworzecki at Bar-Ilan University and assumed direction of the Arnold and Leona Finkler Institute of Holocaust Research. On a number of occasions, Michman observed the lack of systematic research on religious Jews during the Holocaust and noted the potential of research on the subject. In the 1980s, Michman addressed this lacuna and maintained that the increased engagement with the theological questions that emerged as a result of the Holocaust[4] and the ideological affiliations of the researchers had influenced the research from the outset and served to limit it ex post facto.[5] Ten years later, Michman again noted the ongoing lack of research on Jewish religious life during the Holocaust, placed it in broad context, and argued that the failure to engage in research on the everyday life of Jews in the Holocaust had resulted in a reality devoid of systematic research on religious Jews.[6] In his book *Holocaust Historiography: A Jewish Perspective: Conceptualizations, Terminology, Approaches, and Fundamental Issues*, Michman devoted an entire chapter to "Religious Jewry and the Jewish Religion"[7] and defined the main focal points of the everyday life of religious Jews, which underwent fundamental change during the Holocaust. These focal points included the synagogue, the rabbi, study and education, prayer, Sabbath and holidays, kosher diet, matrimony, faith, and interpreting reality. Michman's research highlighted the changes to these focal points that occurred; as an example, it considered the central role that the synagogue began to play as a place of expression of Jewish identity, as well as the importance of prayer as a tool of religious expression in light of the horrors of the era. Michman's studies addressed the vast religious diversity that existed within the Jewish population and offered initial guidelines for systematic in-depth research of religious life in the Holocaust.[8] However, because he himself began taking an interest in other subjects, this preliminary work has yet to manifest itself in a substantial and fundamental manner.

Alongside Michman, and at times under his influence, other scholars began to research specific religious issues. For example, Judy Tydor Baumel-Schwartz, also from Bar-Ilan University, explored prayer during the Holocaust and assembled prayers that were written during the war in occupied Europe and beyond.[9] In addition, Bar-Ilan University's Finkler Institute of Holocaust Research has conducted a number of initial research projects to identify sources for the study of religious life during the Holocaust.[10] At the same time, other scholars assembled a collection of religious sources along with a partial analysis of major phenomena, although their writings for the most part did not result in in-depth comprehensive research.[11] A number of scholars have attempted to explore the "religious" aspect of questions that lie at the heart of historiographical debates regarding the Holocaust and have explored the actions of the rabbinical leadership during the Holocaust[12] and the religious youth movements' role in rescue, education, and rebellion.[13] Others who grew up in the religious world and were pained by the lack of engagement in it began to publish texts on religious life. One of the most important of these authors was Avraham Fuchs, who sought to provide his readers with the valuable historical information that can be gleaned from religious sources, such as rabbinical sermons, responsa, and religious legal rulings.[14]

These studies illuminated select topics from the broad fabric of religious life during the Holocaust, with an emphasis on the observance of commandments and the fate of select figures from this community. They did not, however, serve to consolidate research on religious life as a subject that stands alone; they also did not produce systematic in-depth research on the subject. It is important to remember that, at that point in time, research on the Jewish religious population during the Holocaust had not been incorporated into the general research that was being conducted in Israel on the subject. For example, even texts dealing with communities in which orthodox Jewry constituted a significant percentage of the Jewish population often excluded the religious population from the stories they presented. Important fundamental monographs say nothing about the experience of the devout Jewish population, and an examination of these studies indicate that many that present a complex reality of the everyday life of the Jewish individual and community do not address religious life and do not interweave the orthodox population.[15] Nonetheless, recent years appear to be witnessing a growing awareness of the importance of this world, and a number of new monographs reflect an integration of the religious and the general narratives, as well as entire pages devoted to religious life during the Holocaust.[16] In addition, a number of scholars (including some young scholars) have recently published studies focusing on the orthodox Jewish population and the religious way of life.[17] We can only hope that this trend of addressing religious life and the religious world as an aspect of everyday life during the Holocaust will expand to encompass other subjects, and that researchers will not be overly hesitant about incorporating religious sources into their studies.

In addition to the religious narrative's integration with the general narrative on the one hand, and the initial studies on the life of the orthodox Jewish population on the other hand, one can identify a burgeoning interest on the part of Israeli researchers – historians and sociologists included – in the manner in which the Ultra-Orthodox community relates to the Holocaust and its memory/commemoration. In a series of studies, Menachem Friedman[18] and Kimmy Caplan[19] have examined the Holocaust's central role in the private and public lives of Ultra-Orthodox Jews in Israel and analyzed the way in which, in their view, the memory of the Holocaust has been shaped by the Ultra-Orthodox as a tool to promote their contemporary ideological goals. Other researchers have focused on the Ultra-Orthodox public's polemical discourse with Zionism and its approach to the Holocaust.[20] And still others have considered the evolving patterns of commemoration and the memory of the Holocaust in the Ultra-Orthodox community.[21] Also relevant in this context is Michal Shaul, whose significant book highlights the Holocaust's central role in the rehabilitation of Ultra-Orthodox society in Israel and in the shaping of the local Ultra-Orthodox identity.[22] In this way, the Ultra-Orthodox view of the Holocaust and its impact[23] has been, and continues to be, the subject of intensive and comprehensive exploration. At the same time, although it is important to emphasize that these studies have contributed significantly to the understanding of the Holocaust's role in Ultra-Orthodox society, they do not deal directly with religious life as it existed during the war itself.

Another thematic focus that overlaps with orthodox historiography and the Holocaust and that has been the subject of heightened interest in recent years is the role that was played by religious organizations and individuals in rescue and relief activities during the Holocaust. For example, Efraim Zuroff has explored the American orthodox Jewish community's awareness of the events in occupied Europe as reflected in its treatment of the rescue and relief efforts of the Haredi Rescue Committee;[24] Haim Shalem has analyzed the activity of the Yishuv's Ultra-Orthodox political party Agudas Yisroel in light of the Holocaust;[25] and David Kranzler has examined a variety of rescue initiatives by orthodox figures.[26] These studies make a substantial contribution to the historical research, but, like other studies, ultimately focus on individuals and bodies that resided outside of Nazi occupied Europe and confronted the reality of the Holocaust only indirectly.[27]

Examination of the texts exploring religious life that have been published primarily in recent years indicates that interest in the subject is growing and beginning to percolate into the general research on the Holocaust, even if the results have not always been sufficient. At the same time, a significant portion of this research has dealt with topics that interface with Holocaust research or research on the Ultra-Orthodox population but do not necessarily combine the two. As a result, despite the substantial research on the fate of the Jews during World War II on the one hand and research on the Ultra-Orthodox community on the other hand, we still lack penetrating studies on most of the elements that comprised the worlds of those who belonged to the Ultra-Orthodox Jewish community under Nazi rule and in the satellite countries.

Orthodox Historiography

Alongside the lacunae that exist in the academic research on this subject, it is important to emphasize that the orthodox community itself has devoted, and continues to devote, significant attention to the subject of religious life during the Holocaust. In fact, the Holocaust remains consistently on its agenda, and the immense corpus of sources that has emerged is indicative of the changes that have occurred and continue to occur in Holocaust memory. These changes have found expression not only in semi-academic books and articles but also in weekly Torah portion texts, rabbinic sermons, the Ultra-Orthodox press, and internet websites.[28] However, most of the Ultra-Orthodox population's writing on the Holocaust differs from that which is written in the academic world and constitutes an Orthodox Historiography with its own unique attributes.[29]

A considerable portion of the Ultra-Orthodox writing on the Holocaust has focused on two primary issues: blaming the Zionist leadership for frustrating attempts to save European Jewry during the Holocaust,[30] and representing the preservation of religious life as an alternative and loftier type of heroism than that of the ghetto fighters.[31] In addition to esoteric texts that make no concrete contribution to the research on orthodox Jewish public life during the Holocaust, a number of prominent Ultra-Orthodox authors have also contributed to the research on the subject. And whereas their writings possess distinct semi-academic features that pose a complicated challenge for researchers, their role in the documentation of a variety of major issues in religious life and initial attempts to characterize them cannot be ignored. For example, Yehuda Leib

Levin's monumental *Book of Poland* offers a unique historical survey of Nazism and the Jewish world that was lost in the Holocaust.[32] In addition, the Ultra-Orthodox press – in Hebrew, English, and Yiddish – contains hundreds of texts on the World War II period, providing a detailed description of various figures, communities, and events from the era of the war.[33] Despite the important role played by these many contributors,[34] I relate here only briefly to three of the most productive Ultra-Orthodox Holocaust researchers: Moshe Prager, Yechiel Granatstein, and Yehoshua Eibeshitz.

Moshe Prager (1909-1984),[35] a Gerer Hasid who was involved in the efforts to rescue the Gerer Rebbe (great rabbi) from the area of Nazi occupation during the Holocaust, is rightfully considered to be a figure who has contributed significantly to making the Holocaust present in the Ultra-Orthodox discourse. In September 1941, Prager authored the first text on the Holocaust published in Mandatory Palestine: *The New Yeven Metsula [Abyss of Despair]: Polish Jewry in the Clutches of the Nazis.*[36] In 1964, following his fundamental criticism of the handling of the Eichmann trial and of what he regarded as the intentional silencing of episodes that were of central importance to the Ultra-Orthodox public, he established the "Genzach Kiddush Hashem" – an Ultra-Orthodox documentation, research, and commemoration institute that is still operating today. The archive's explicit aim is to commemorate the Jewish world that was destroyed and to publicize the "heroic Jewish spirit." Over the years, it has amassed many writings and photographs that document religious life in the Holocaust, though a significant number of them have already been published (in the print media and research literature).[37] The Genzach Kiddush Hashem Archive maintains one of the most impressive collections of memory literature of the Ultra-Orthodox population, as well as a significant number of texts on the Holocaust from the Orthodox Historiographic genre. One of Prager's most influential books was *Those Who Never Yielded.* This text, first published in 1963 and since then reissued in numerous editions,[38] has served as a resource for some Holocaust researchers.[39] The first part of the book tells the story of a Hasidic underground movement whose members engaged in Torah study and in maintaining a Hasidic way of life during the war; the second part deals with different acts of observance of the Jewish commandments during the Holocaust. Prager presents dozens of testimonies reflecting that, even during the Holocaust, young Jews throughout Poland succeeded in observing minor and major commandments and, in doing so, defeated the Nazi enemy. At the beginning of the book, he writes:

> I have no doubt that once you learn all the details of the history of this Hasidic spiritual underground, which was established and operated in the ghettos and the camps, you will appreciate who is worthy of the crown of spiritual heroism in contending with the corrupting Nazi devil.[40]

A similar goal was pursued in the impressive three-volume *Mikadshei Hashem* encyclopedia, written by Yechiel Granatstein (1913-2008).[41] Granatstein, born in Lublin, fled the Slonim Ghetto during the Holocaust and joined a partisan unit. His first book unfolded his own memories from this horror-ridden period.[42] After the war, Granatstein worked with Prager for years on setting up the Genzach Kiddush Hashem Archive, served as a member of Yad Vashem's World Council, and was considered as someone who was familiar with the "other world" but who clearly represented the views of orthodox Jewish society. A distinct expression of this role can be found in his all-encompassing *Mikadshei Hashem* encyclopedia – an impressive project of Orthodox Historiography that highlights an alternative heroism. In this project, Granatstein assembled information on hundreds of Jews – rabbis, students of sages, devout women, and everyday Jews – whose actions he regarded as *kiddush hashem* (the sanctification of God's name). In addition to observing commandments, these actions included acts of self-sacrifice and providing aid to others. At the beginning of the text, Granatstein states that his work "was not conducted according to the rules of standard university research" and that his goal was to depict the world of the religious Jew that had been neglected by academic research. Indeed, an examination of the different entries reveals the work's polemic nature. For example, its first entry is devoted to Rabbi David Avigdor, a figure who is unknown but impressive in his own right. However, omitted from Avigdor's history is the fact that he was a member of the religious Zionist movement Hamizrachi.[43] Still, it is difficult to ignore this impressive enterprise, which includes not only information found in the memory books but also some valuable primary sources (many of which are found in the Genzach).[44]

Another prominent researcher was Yehoshua Eibeshitz, a native of Wielun, Poland (1916-2019). During the war, Eibeshitz wandered from the Warsaw region to the Lodz region and was caught and sent to concentration camps where he remained until liberation. He put down his story in writing in his autobiographical work *The Uprooted*.[45] In Israel, in parallel to his work in the Kfar Ata municipal library, Eibeshitz worked energetically on documenting and researching the Holocaust. He established the Hedva Eibeshitz Institute of Holocaust Studies in Haifa,[46] was among the founders of the "Zachor" organization, and for years served as the editor of *Zachor*, its journal. Eibeshitz was also a pioneer of research on women in the Holocaust, publishing the book series *Women in the Holocaust: A Documentary Collection of the Steadfastness of Women during the Holocaust*.[47] Over the years, he wrote texts about the Holocaust, authoring more than ten books on the subject.[48] He also did not refrain from criticizing Holocaust researchers and Yad Vashem and argued that they had not only ignored the orthodox population during the Holocaust but that they had also been overly judgmental of Jews during the period, including those who served within Judenrats and as kapos.[49] At the same time, he spoke out against attempts in Ultra-Orthodox society to conceal various aspects of this charged period, and maintained on behalf of his rabbi, Yehoshua Moshe Aharonson, that those engaging with the arena of the Holocaust must present the material as it is – "…not to beautify it and under no circumstances to exaggerate descriptions of the horror and the bereavement. Not to add and not to diminish, as the events of the Holocaust are so horrific that any addition or diminishment represents an unforgivable transgression."[50]

These researchers wrote first and foremost for the Ultra-Orthodox public, based their work on its writings and memoirs, and provided comprehensive information on orthodox Jewish life during the Holocaust that is completely unknown to many Holocaust scholars. Nonetheless, an examination of their abovementioned writings – and other texts, such as *Sparks of Glory, The Other Heroism* and *With Sanctity and Heroism*[51] – demonstrates the tendency in the Ultra-Orthodox historiography to highlight alternative religious heroism. At the same time, it should be emphasized that although the Ultra-Orthodox historiographic discourse was aimed at the religiously observant public, it appears to have been shaped by an ongoing confrontation with the general discourse underway in Israeli society. In contrast to the narrative of physical heroism of the 1960s, the Ultra-Orthodox proposed an alternative heroism; and when rabbis were accused of abandoning the devout Jewish population of occupied Europe and thwarting the call to immigrate to *Eretz Israel* prior to the Holocaust, the orthodox population maintained that it was the Zionist leadership that had frustrated rescue attempts. Moreover, today, at a time when the general emphasis is on the personal and human story of the victims and survivors, the Ultra-Orthodox community has also found a way to give expression to these voices. Indeed, beginning in the early 1990s, we can discern an expansion of a phenomenon that had previously been absent from the Ultra-Orthodox public: the publication of hundreds of memory books composed by Ultra-Orthodox Holocaust survivors.[52] Indeed, the titles and contents of these books reflect that many were written in an attempt to prove that, even during the Holocaust, they had felt the benevolence of heaven and remained devout Jews. In this respect, however, the Ultra-Orthodox survivors of the Holocaust are not exceptional. In recent years, efforts of Holocaust survivors to give testimony regarding their experiences during the Holocaust have been on the rise, and many of the texts produced have sought to give meaning to the lives and actions of their authors during and following the war.[53]

An examination of the orthodox historiography of the Holocaust reveals not only the extensive publication of memory literature but also concrete development in the writing of history among the Ultra-Orthodox public in Israel. In recent years, research on the life of the religious Jewish population during the Holocaust has been enriched by the work of researchers belonging to the orthodox community who write academic studies and are publicized in the academic arena. The most important scholar of this kind is Esther Farbstein, an Ultra-Orthodox historian who engages in Holocaust research and holds the Chair for Holocaust Studies at Jerusalem College for Women. Farbstein, who has an academic education and grew up in the heart of the Ultra-Orthodox world and continues to belong to it, has brought about a true revolution in research on the life of the orthodox Jewish population during the Holocaust. Her intimate knowledge of the world and unique language of her coreligionists, her familiarity with the internal writings of this public, and her broad knowledge regarding other historical subjects endow her with a perspective that is both important and unique. Farbstein's many writings examine different issues pertaining to the life of Ultra-Orthodox individuals and communities during the Holocaust, including rabbinic leadership, religious and Halakhic norms contending with everyday life, and the rehabilitation of the Ultra-Orthodox world after the war. Farbstein's findings are based on a broad foundation of research and reflection, in part facilitated by her belonging to the Ultra-Orthodox community, and are published in religious and academic journals alike.[54] In addition to the significant studies she has conducted, Farbstein has also revealed valuable internal documents of the orthodox community that were hitherto unknown by researchers.[55] In the gaping vacuum in the scholarship on the subject, these documents highlight the great potential contribution of research on the orthodox community in Poland during the Holocaust. At the same time, these internal writings, more than others, reflect the tension and complexity that characterized religious life during this period. Their examination underlines the fact that Ultra-Orthodox researchers' focus on exceptional exemplary accounts on the one hand, and their advancement of an alternative narrative for public debate on the other hand, have resulted, in retrospect, in the neglect of research on the fate of hundreds of thousands of religious Jews during the Holocaust.

Looking toward the Future

Despite the important developments of recent years, it is clear that vast lacunae still exist in the study of Jewish religious life during the Holocaust and its incorporation into the general research on the period. Still, the changes that have gotten underway in the past few years may be heralding a significant change in the importance assigned to the subject and its role in our general understanding of Jewish life in the Holocaust. Below, I suggest a number of points that could bring about an expansion and a deepening of the discussion.

Holocaust researchers who need to engage religious life tend to focus on a few select aspects, beginning with the question of the observance or non-observance of the commandments in the ghettos, in the camps, and in hiding.[56] However, the religious obligations and worldview of Jews, and orthodox Jews in particular, influenced all realms of Jewish life: from daily schedule, dress, and diet; to economic, family, and social life; to overall expectations and fears.

Glimpses of this lost world appear in the diverse memory literature that has been written by orthodox Holocaust survivors. These sources are written differently to those familiar to researchers who work with documents from the Holocaust era, and they frequently include elements of glorification and hagiography in addition to intentional and unintentional obfuscation and concealment. However, disregarding the texts of the orthodox Jewish population necessarily results in deception and blindness regarding major phenomena among the Jews of Europe during this period. As scholars engaged in Holocaust research, it is our obligation to acquire better knowledge about this documentary wealth, which is currently absent from most of the professional libraries on the subject, and to glean from them the relevant historical information while contending with their methodological limitations.[57] Ultimately, just as it is impossible to research the Jewish population during the Holocaust without testimonies,[58] the fate of the orthodox population in the Holocaust cannot be understood without the broad usage of such sources.

But examination of the orthodox Jewish population during the Holocaust is important not only for the limited discussion of Jewish religious life but also for an understanding of Jewish society as a whole. The different shades of religion and the different forms of Jewish community had an impact on religious and non-religious Jews alike, especially in the Jewish communities of Eastern Europe. Many Jews used the services of the community for specific religious purposes (marriage, burial, etc.), either by choice or due to lack of another option, and others had social ties to some of its institutions (synagogues, prominent rabbis, etc.). There were also Jews who defined their lives as contrary to those of the Jewish community (for example, Jews belonging to liberal communities or those of the Zionist movements and the Bund). In this manner, association with the orthodox community was solidly incorporated into the life of European Jewry between the two world wars and influenced many others in a direct and indirect manner.

Despite the greater representation of the orthodox community in Eastern Europe, it is important to emphasize that the Jewish religion also had significant influence on Jewish communities in Western and Central Europe. This is of particular importance because these communities account for only a minor portion of the Ultra-Orthodox discourse. This imbalance should also serve as a warning sign regarding the attempt to apply the current living patterns of Ultra-Orthodox society to the orthodox world that existed prior to and during the war. That world differed from today's Ultra-Orthodox world in many ways and should be associated with the research on Jewish life prior to the Holocaust to a much greater extent than to Ultra-Orthodox society in Israel and in the world today.

Indeed, one of the major challenges currently facing researchers interested in the life of the religious Jewish population during the Holocaust is the need to trace the trends of disruption and continuity that existed among this population between the pre-war period and the Holocaust. For example, in his book *Rabbi and Community in the Pale*, which portrays the complex world of rabbis in the nineteenth century,[59] Mordechai Zalkin considers not only the rabbinical training track but also the tensions that characterized their activity in communities and the many forces influencing the way they operated, for better or for worse. However, most of the research that has been conducted on rabbis during the Holocaust has focused on a small number of well-known rabbis,[60] leaving thousands of rabbis and other religious figures who served small and medium sized communities unexplored.[61] For example, the volumes of *Pinkas Hekehilot* and other encyclopedic enterprises dealing with the Holocaust contain descriptions of the rabbis, the yeshivas, and the religious activists of the pre-war Jewish community, but moving into the Holocaust years these figures and institutions go virtually unmentioned.

Expanding our scope by considering orthodox public life during the years that preceded the war can help us segue into a discussion of this population during the Holocaust. For example, Ben-Tsiyon Klibansky has researched the *Tifaeres Bachurim* organization which operated in Lithuania (and elsewhere) between the two world wars[62]; Moria Herman has investigated the youth-related activity of five prominent rabbis;[63] and other researchers have considered the immense variety within the Hasidic world of pre-war Europe, including dozens of small and medium sized Hasidic communities.[64] What happened to these figures, institutions, and activities during the war? What befell the different streams of the Hasidic movement, the religious leaders and their families, and the students of the yeshivas of Lithuania? Did they try to remain in existence? To what extent were they able to preserve past patterns, and to what extent can their actions be considered new? When did they cease to exist, and what happened to their survivors over the years? Conducting a concrete discussion regarding these questions necessarily requires broadening the documentary and research foundation at the disposal of Holocaust researchers.

However, in the discussion of religious life during the Holocaust, the research world has a tendency to rely entirely on the impressive writings of Rabbi Shimon Huberband (1909-1942) of the Oyneg Shabbes Archive project, and of Rabbi Kalonymus Kalman Shapira, the Rebbe of Piaseczno (1889-1943).[65] Despite the importance of these individuals and the documents they left behind, we must remember that they are not reflective of the rich hues of the orthodox public in Warsaw or throughout Europe. Hubberband documented and collected valuable information but ultimately remained a single man with certain connections and his own inclinations – a refugee in the Warsaw Ghetto who revealed only a limited segment of the rich religious life that existed in practice.[66] We must also remember that although the Rebbe of Piaseczno was an exemplary and wise scholar, an outstanding teacher, and a man of great influence relative to his age, he was not necessarily the most prominent or well-known rabbi living in Warsaw during the war. Dozens of prominent rabbis were active in the Warsaw Ghetto, including Rabbi Yitzchak Menachem Mendel Dancyger, the Alexander Rebbe; Rabbi Moshe Bezalel Alter, brother of the Gerer Rebbe; and Rabbi Dovid Bornstein, the Sochatchover Rebbe – none of whom are typically mentioned in the research.[67] While it is true that the absence of orderly writings by most of these figures means that tracing their activities during the Holocaust requires careful and comprehensive investigation, disregarding these sources creates a significant aberration in the research of orthodox public life during the Holocaust, as they – and others – were among the most important figures in the Hasidic world in the Warsaw ghetto and elsewhere.

Indeed, one of the major challenges we currently face is the need to expand the documentary foundation serving researchers interested in exploring the internal life of the Jewish public in a manner that also integrates the range of voices of the orthodox community. In addition to the above-mentioned memoirs of orthodox individuals, we must also intensify our usage of published sources,[68] archival sources,[69] rabbinical sermons delivered during the Holocaust,[70] and responsa literature. Although some of the relevant responsa literature appears to have been written after the Holocaust and should therefore be considered mainly as memory literature as opposed to primary source material,[71] we can also find responsa addressed to rabbis during the Holocaust, some of which were answered.[72] Moreover, after the war, an immense volume of halakhic literature emerged surrounding the problem of *hatarat agunot* (the release of abandoned wives from marriage).[73] These writings contained numerous testimonies of life during and following the Holocaust. The halakhic process of *hatarat agunot* requires a meticulous account of the information collected, and the resulting halakhic literature provides a plethora of information regarding the fate of individuals and communities during the Holocaust.[74]

As already noted, the names of witnesses and valuable documentation with which researchers from academic circles are not necessarily familiar can be found in the Genzach Kiddush Hashem Archive, within the framework of other Ultra-Orthodox documentary and research enterprises such as Ruth Lichtenstein's "Project Witness,"[75] and in texts of the orthodox historiography. Although some of these writings lack footnotes and organized references, they contain primary sources that cannot be found elsewhere.[76] Moreover, a careful reading of these studies, notwithstanding their limitations, also raises major issues and weighty subjects that have not yet received proper academic treatment. One example, in which the author of the present article also failed, is the description of the secret Hasidic underground that was first depicted in Prager's *Those Who Never Yielded*. This text received cold reviews from the academic community when it was published and was ultimately almost completely ignored.[77] It is typically considered an interesting expression of the genre of Orthodox Historiographical writing and an attempt by its Ultra-Orthodox authors to propose alternative heroes.[78] However, a look at the world of Gerer Hasidism during the interwar period reveals that during this time, the group established a youth apparatus, consisting of groups led by *Kommandants*, as an alternative to the sweeping draw of the youth movements. This initiative continued to function to some extent during the war; and even if Prager's account contains some exaggerations and inaccuracies, they too – like youth movements during the Holocaust, but also in a different manner – operated in underground frameworks during the war.[79] By disregarding the orthodox texts and the internal sources of these groups, the research world excluded this population from the broad discussion of youth movements during the Holocaust. As a result, their usage stands to increase knowledge about these groups and to help produce a fuller account of the activities of Jews during the war.

Thus, using the orthodox historiography in a controlled manner and carefully examining the internal sources of this population, in conjunction with a closer linkage to the pre-war Jewish world, could add a great deal to our understanding of the subtle diversities that existed within the orthodox populations in different geographical centers. A study that succeeds in substantively incorporating the lives of these Jews, as individuals and as part of communities and a society, into the overall story of the Jews during the Holocaust will benefit not only by providing better knowledge of a large population within European Jewry between the world wars, but also by facilitating a better understanding of the period of the Holocaust and the terrors it involved.

Endnotes

1   *This research was supported by the Israel Science Foundation (grant No. 155/16).
I am grateful for the comments of Rabbi Yehuda Aryeh Markson, my devoted
research assistant on this project, and to Mrs. Adaya Klin, who helped prepare the
English version of this article.

The research literature contains a number of definitions of an Orthodox
community. According to Yaacov Katz, an Orthodox community is a traditional
Jewish community that adapts to modernity by defending itself against it. A similar
definition is offered by Eliezer Schweid, who defines it as a movement that resolutely
and blatantly prefers the traditional past to the modern present, despite its own
belonging to the very present it rejects. Schweid, *From Destruction to Salvation* (Tel
Aviv, 1994), p. 9 (Hebrew).

2   Meir Dworzecki, "Religious Life in the Vilna Ghetto," *Sinai* 47 (1959/60)
(Hebrew). Online, see also: http://www.daat.ac.il/daat/kitveyet/sinay/vilna-2.htm
(last accessed on November 27, 2019). "On Talmud Torah during the Holocaust,"
Bar Ilan 4-5 (1966/67), pp. 289-298 (Hebrew); "Steadfastness in Everyday Life
in the Ghettos and the Camps," in Israel Gutman and Livia Rotkirchen (eds.),
The Catastrophe of European Jewry – Antecedents, History, Reflections: Selected Papers
(Jerusalem, 1973), pp. 269-283 (Hebrew). See also Isaiah Wolfsberg-Aviad,
"Devout Jewry during the War," in Gutman and Rotkirchen, *The Catastrophe of
European Jewry*, pp. 504-514 (Hebrew). See also the essays published in *Keshev: A
Collection of Studies, Sources, and News Items from the Holocaust Research Institute*
(Bar Ilan University) (Hebrew).

3   Joseph Nedava, "The Problem of Halakha in the Ghettos," *Dapim: Studies on the
Holocaust* 1 (1975), pp. 44-56 (Hebrew); Haim Strauss, "The Sabbath and Holidays
in the Ghettos of the Generalgouvernement in Poland," master's thesis, Bar-Ilan
University, 1974/75 (Hebrew); Yosef Walk, "The Final Month of the Talmud Torah
School in Hamburg," *Basadeh Hemed* 5 (1971/72), pp. 117-120 (Hebrew). See also
the details in the following notes.

4   See, for example, Zvi Bachrach, "Man, Providence and Auschwitz," *Zmanim
Quartenly* 6 (1981), pp. 93-97; Uriel Tal, "The Historical and Spiritual Significance
of the Holocaust," *Yalkut Moreshet* 40 (1985), pp. 7-13; Rabbi Yisrael Lau, "Faith
and Jewish Steadfastness in the Holocaust," *Yalkut Moreshet* 76 (2003), pp. 63-
80 (Hebrew); Dan Michman, "The Holocaust's Impact on Religious Jewry," in
Tmurot Yesod, pp. 613-656 (Hebrew); Schweid, *From Destruction to Salvation*. See
also the extensive writings of Gershon Greenberg, including for example: Gershon
Greenberg, "Shlomo Zalman Unsdorfer: With God Through the Holocaust," *Yad
Vashem Studies* 31 (2003), pp. 61-95; Gershon Greenberg and Assaf Yedidia (eds.),
Mishpatecha Tehom Raba: Orthodox Meditative Responses to the Holocaust (Jerusalem,
2016) (Hebrew); Gershon Greenberg, "The Holocaust Apocalypse of Ya'akov

Moshe Harlap," *Jewish Studies* 41 (2002), pp. 1-5; Gershon Greenberg, "Yehuda Leb Gerst's Religious 'Ascent' Through the Holocaust," *Holocaust and Genocide Studies* 13(1) (Spring 1999), pp. 62–89.

5 Dan Michman, "The Research on the Way of Life of the Religious Population under Nazi Rule," in Israel Gutman and Gideon Greif (eds.), *The Historiography of the Holocaust* (Jerusalem, 1987), p. 605 (Hebrew).

6 Dan Michman, *The Holocaust and Holocaust Research: Conceptualization, Terminology, and Basic Issues* (Tel Aviv, 1998), p. 194 (Hebrew). Although this text is based on previously published articles and a significant amount of time has passed since it was first published, Michman's assertion remains accurate today.

7 Ibid., pp. 193-235.

8 For example, Michman analyzes the holidays as moments of Jewish unity – for religious and secular Jews alike – and enumerates the spectrum of responses ranging from belief in God, to the blaming of God, to secularism.

9 Judith Tydor Baumel, *A Voice of Lament: The Holocaust and Prayer* (Jerusalem, 1992) (Hebrew).

10 See, for example: Gershon Greenberg (ed.), *She'erit Ha'peleta Confronting the Holocaust: A Listing of Articles and Books Reflecting the Jewish Religious Responses to the Holocaust in Its Immediate Aftermath (1944-1949)* (Bar-Ilan University, 1994) (Hebrew); Josef Karniel (ed.), *A Listing of Articles on Orthodox Jewry in Austria, Published in the Austrian Orthodox Jewish Press, 1918-1938* (Bar-Ilan University, 1996) (Hebrew); Pnina Meislish (ed.), *Religious Life in the Holocaust according to Community Memorial Books* (Bar-Ilan University, 1990) (Hebrew). Following this book, Meislish later published *Rabbis who Perished in the Holocaust: Biographies of Rabbis and Grand Rabbis from Poland and the Other Countries of Eastern Europe Who Died in the Holocaust* (Jerusalem, 2006) (Hebrew). A database regarding the rabbis can also be found online at: http://horabis.blogspot.com/ (last accessed on November 27, 2019).

11 Nathaniel Katzburg (ed.), *Pedut: Rescue in the Holocaust* (Jerusalem, 1984) (Hebrew); Itamar Levin, *Letters of Fire: Testimonies from the Holocaust Period in Halakhic Literature* (Tel-Aviv, 2002) (Hebrew).

12 Joseph Walk, "The Religious Leadership during the Holocaust," in Israel Gutman (ed.), *Patterns of Jewish Leadership in Nazi Europe: Proceedings of the 3rd International Conference of Holocaust Researchers* (Jerusalem, 1979), pp. 325-335 (Hebrew); Judith Tydor Baumel, "Sacred Fire: The Piasecner Rebbe's Book and Its Role in Understanding Religious Life in the Warsaw Ghetto," *Yalkut Moreshet* 29 (Spring 1980), pp. 173-187 (Hebrew); Dan Michman, "Rabbinical Leadership in the Netherlands during the Holocaust," *Dapim: Studies on the Holocaust* 7 (1989), pp. 81-106 (Hebrew); Yehuda Ben-Avner, "Description of the Activity of the Devout

Rabbis in Germany," *Sinai* 91(3-4) (1982), pp. 140-155 (Hebrew); Yehuda Ben-Avner, "One Rabbinic Area during the Nazis' Rise to Power," *Sinai* 102 (1988), pp. 72-85 (Hebrew).

13 Haim Genizi and Naomi Blank, "Rescue Efforts of Bnei Akiva in Hungary," *Yad Vashem Studies* 23 (1993), pp. 143-212; Yael Peled, "The Activity and Responsibility of Hashomer Hadati in the Krakow Ghetto, 1942-1943," *Yalkut Moreshet* 63 (1997), pp. 77-82; Pnina Meislish, "Bnei Akiva and Hashomer Hadati in Poland and Lithuania during the Holocaust," *Dapim: Studies on the Holocaust* 9 (1991), pp. 165-189 (Hebrew); Judith Tydor Baumel, "The Ultra-Orthodox Response to the Armed Uprising," *Dapim: Studies on the Holocaust* 12 (1995), pp. 289-308 (Hebrew).

14 Abraham Fuchs, *The Holocaust in Rabbinical Sources* (Jerusalem, 1995) (Hebrew).

15 Michman, "The Research on the Way of Life of the Religious Population," p. 609. See also Israel Gutman, *Resistance: The Warsaw Ghetto Uprising* (Boston and New York, 1994), pp. 51-52, 146-147; Yitzhak Arad, *Ghetto in Flames: The Struggle and Destruction of the Jews in Vilna in the Holocaust* (New York, 1980); Yael Peled, *Jewish Krakow, 1939-1945: Steadfastness, Underground, and Struggle* (Israel, 1993), pp. 56, 79-80, 87, 130 (Hebrew); Tikva Fatal-Cnaani, *It's Not The Same Grodno: The Jewish Community in Grodno and Its Vicinity during the Second World War and the Holocaust* (Jerusalem, 2001), pp. 31-39 (Hebrew). A different description can be found only among those survivor-researchers who espoused a perspective similar to that of the religious world and wrote semi-academic texts about their communities. Most prominent among these were Leib Garfunkel, *The Destruction of Kovno's Jewry* (Jerusalem, 1959) (Hebrew); Meir Dworzecki, *Lithuanian Jewry* (Tel Aviv, 1951) (Hebrew).

16 See David Silberklang, *Gates of Tears: The Holocaust in the Lublin District* (Jerusalem, 2013); Sarah Bender, *The Jews of Białystok During World War II, 1939-1943* (Tel Aviv, 2008), pp. 11-13, 31-33, 37-38, 67-68; (Hebrew); Sarah Bender, Religious Life in the Pulcery Labor Camp in Częstochowa, 1942-1945," *Shem Olam* 15 (September 2016), pp. 8-15 (Hebrew). Particularly extensive treatment can be found in Michal Unger's detailed monograph on the Lodz Ghetto, in which she devoted specific chapters to religious life and, among other things, addressed the following topics: the character of religious life, prayer, traditional Jewish dress and the growing of beards, purification of the dead and customs of mourning, the rabbinate, and the rabbis' position on the deportations from the ghetto. Michal Unger, *The Last Ghetto: Life in the Lodz Ghetto* (Jerusalem, 2005), pp. 440-469 (Hebrew).

    Another example of this can be found in Yizhak Arad's comprehensive study of the camps of Operation Reinhard, in which he deals not only with questions of faith in the camps but rather also the existence of religious activity in these camps as an integral part of the historical description. Yizhak Arad, *Belzec, Sobibor, Treblinka: The Operation Reinhard* (Indiana University Press, 1987), pp 170-174.

17 Gershon Greenberg, "Out of the Shadows: The Haredi Religious Realities of Holocaust History," *Yad Vashem Studies* 41(1) (2013), pp. 263-275; Alan Rosen, "Tracking Jewish Time in Auschwitz," *Yad Vashem Studies* 42(2) (2014), pp. 11-46. See also the following four articles that appeared in *Yad Vashem Studies* 47(1) (2016): Moshe Tarshansky, "The Writings of Rabbi Ephraim Oshry of the Kovno Ghetto: Orthodox Historiography?" (59-104); David Deutsch, "Religious and Halakhic Observance in View of Deconstruction Processes in the Holocaust" (105-142); Tehila Darmon Malka, "'Our Unfortunate Sisters, the Daughters of Israel': Holocaust-Survivor Rabbis Confront the Problem of Post-Holocaust `Agunot" (143-173); Miriam Schulz, "From *Kiddush Hashem* to the Rise of Heroines in Soviet Yiddish Literature of the 1940s." (175-208) See Shmuel Zanvil Kehana, *Burning Scrolls and Ascending Letters: Unpublished Writings on the Holocaust*, edited by Zohar Maor (Bar-Ilan University, 2018) (Hebrew); Jacob Borut (ed.), *Religious Practice of German Jews under Nazi Rule (1933-1938) and Its Reflection in the German Jewish Press* (Jerusalem, 2017) (Hebrew); Kiril Feferman, "Save Your Souls : Jewish Conversion and Survival in the Occupied Soviet Territories during the Holocaust," *Modern Judaism* 39(2) (2019), pp. 184-204.

18 Menachem Friedman, "Why did God do that? Ultra-Orthodox Coping with the Holocaust," in Dan Michman (ed.), *The Holocaust in Jewish History: Historiography, Consciousness, Interpretations* (Jerusalem, 2005), pp. 579-607 (Hebrew); Menachem Friedman, "The Haredim and the Holocaust," *Jerusalem Quarterly* 53 (1990), pp. 86-114.

19 Kimmy Caplan, "Have 'Many Lies Accumulated in History Books'?: The Holocaust in Ashkenazi Haredi Historical Consciousness in Israel," *Yad Vashem Studies* 29 (2001), pp. 321-376; Kimmy Caplan, "Haredi Society in Israel and Its Attitude toward the Holocaust," *Alpayim* 17 (1999), pp. 176–208 (Hebrew); Kimmy Caplan, *In the Secret of Haredi Discourse* (Jerusalem, 2007), pp. 138-196 (Hebrew).

20 Dina Porat, "'Amalek's Accomplices': Blaming Zionism for the Holocaust: Anti-Zionist Ultra Orthodoxy in Israel during the 1980's," *Journal of Contemporary History* 27 (October 1992), pp. 695-729; Haim Nirel, *The Haredim and the Holocaust: Ultra-Orthodox Accusations of Zionist Responsibility for the Holocaust* (Jerusalem, 1997), pp. 72–108 (Hebrew); Meir Sompolinsky, "Jewish Institutions in the World and the Yishuv as Reflected in the Holocaust Historiography of the Ultra-Orthodox," in Gutman and Greif, *The Historiography of the Holocaust*, pp. 497-516 (Hebrew).

21 In addition to the studies mentioned above, see also: Amos Goldberg, "The Holocaust in the Ultra-Orthodox Press: Between Memory and Repression," *Contemporary Jewry* 11-12 (1997/98), pp. 155-206 (Hebrew); Leah Langleben, "The Holocaust as a Subject of Study at the Beit Yaakov Seminary," *Hagigei Giva* 8 (1999/2000), pp. 1090-132 (Hebrew); Michal Zemer-Shaul, "The Holocaust between Public Memory and Private Memory," master's thesis, Hebrew University of Jerusalem, 2003 (Hebrew); Ruth Ebenstein, *Marking through Rejection: Yom*

Hashoah as Seen through the Ashkenazi Haredi Daily Press, 1950-2000 (Jerusalem, 2002); Arye Edrei, "Holocaust Memorial: A Paradigm of Competing Memories in the Religious and Secular Societies in Israel," in Doron Mendels (ed.), *On Memory: An Interdisciplinary Approach* (Bern, 2007), pp. 37-100.

22 Michal Shaul, *Beauty for Ashes: Holocaust Memory and the Rehabilitation of Ashkenazi Haredi Society in Israel, 1945-1961* (Jerusalem, 2014) (Hebrew).

23 Yossef Fund, *Movement in Ruins: Agudat Israel's leadership confronting the Holocaust* (Jerusalem, 2008) (Hebrew).

24 Efraim Zurrof, "American Orthodox Jewry's Response to the Holocaust: The Activities of the *Vaad Ha-Hatzala* Rescue Committee, 1939-1945," doctoral dissertation, Hebrew University of Jerusalem, 1997 (Hebrew).

25 Haim Shalem, *A Time to Take Action to Rescue Jews: Agudat Israel in Eretz Israel Confronting the Holocaust, 1942-1945* (Jerusalem, 2007). See also Shalem's article on the rescue efforts of Chaim Yisroel Eiss: Haim Shalem, "'Remember, there are not many Eisses now in the Swiss market': Assistance and Rescue Endeavors of Chaim Yisrael Eiss in Switzerland," *Yad Vashem Studies* 33 (2005), pp. 347-379.

26 See, for example, David Kranzler and Joseph Friedenson, *For how can I bear to see the calamity awaiting my people? And how can I bear to see the destruction of my kindred?* (Jerusalem, 2012) (Hebrew); David Kranzler, *Thy Brother's Blood: The Orthodox Jewish Response during the Holocaust* (New York, 1987); David Kranzler, *Holocaust Hero: The Untold Story and Vignettes of Solomon Schonfeld* (Jersey City, NJ, 2004).

27 Meir Sompolinsky, "The Rescue Policy of the Chief Rabbi's Emergency Religious Council in Britain," in Katzburg, *Pedut*, pp. 149-180 (Hebrew); Judith Tydor Baumel, "Religious Life of the Jewish Refugee Children in Britain, 1938-1945," in Katzburg, *Pedut*, pp. 185-201 (Hebrew).

28 Shmaryahu Ben-Pazi, "Germany's Image in the Ultra-Orthodox Press and Historiography," in Moshe Zimmerman, *Germany and the Land of Israel: A Cultural Encounter* (Jerusalem, 2004), pp. 169-187 (Hebrew); Kimmy Caplan, "The Holocaust's Role in Ultra-Orthodox Popular Religion in Israel," in Michman, *The Holocaust in Jewish History*, pp. 595-596 (Hebrew). Articles by Rabbi Avraham Krieger of the Shem Olam Institute also relate to this issue to a certain extent. See: "The Religious Public and Leadership in the Lodz Ghetto," http://www.shemolam.org.il/fullnews.asp?id=35 (last accessed on November 27, 2019) (Hebrew); "Rabbinic Leadership in the Holocaust: The Intermediate Layers," http://www.shemolam.org.il/fullnews.asp?id=8 (last accessed on November 28, 2019) (Hebrew); "Prayer in the Extermination Camps," *Shem Olam* 1 (2011), pp. 8-11 (Hebrew); "The Dignity of the Dead," *Shem Olam* 6 (2013), pp. 7-13 (Hebrew). "Shem Olam: Faith & the Holocaust Institute for Education, Documentation & Research" is a Jewish orthodox research center that

does not belong to Ultra-Orthodox circles but that also differs from the academic institutes. Despite its importance, this institute lies beyond the scope of this study. Shem Olam focuses on the religious world in the Holocaust and defines its role as "researching – through the use of historical academic tools and by bringing unknown documents and sources to light – the world of values, faith, religious life and spirit, and especially coping during the Holocaust." Over the years, this organization has succeeded in collecting documents on religious life, including sources that are absent from other archives. Nonetheless, and despite the financial support it has received from various sources, its collections are not substantially accessible to researchers who are not affiliated with the institute.

29 David Assaf, "Kvod Elokim Haster Davar: A New Chapter in the Historiography of Hasidism in Eretz Israel," *Cathedra* 68 (June 1993), p. 58 (Hebrew). In recent years, a significant number of articles have been published on orthodox historiography. See, for example Nachum Karlinsky, "Between Biography and Hagiography: *Bays Rabi* and the Beginning of Hasidic-Orthodox Historiography," *Proceedings of the World Congress of Jewish Studies* 11 (1993), Division C, Vol. 2, pp. 162-168 (Hebrew); Israel Bartal, "True Knowledge and Wisdom: On Orthodox Historiography," *Studies in Contemporary Jewry* 10 (1994), pp. 178-192; Jacob Katz, "Orthodoxy in Historical Perspective," *Studies in Contemporary Jewry* 2 (1986), pp. 3-17; Ada Rapoport-Albert, "Hagiography with Footnotes: Edifying Tales and the Writing of History in Hasidism," *History and Theory* 27 (1988), pp. 119-159; Israel Bartal, "True Knowledge and Wisdom: On Orthodox Historiography," *Studies in Contemporary Jewry* 10 (1994), pp. 178-192. On the principles of orthodox historiography in the context of the Holocaust, see Kimmy Caplan's book *In the Secret of Haredi Discourse*, pp. 140-166.

30 Moshe Shenfeld, *Those Burned in the Furnaces Accuse* (Bnei Brak, 1975), no page number indicated. This text marks the beginning of a series that would subsequently be published in a number of editions. Shalom Shalmon, *The Crimes of Zionism in the Extermination of the Diaspora* (Bnei Brak, 1988) (expanded fourth release) (Hebrew); Menachem Vazelman, *Sign of Cain: On the Zionist Movement and Jewish Agency's Omissions during the Holocaust, 1939-1945* (Tel Aviv, 1988) (Hebrew). For an analysis of these phenomena in addition to the abovementioned texts, see Yeshayahu Jelinek, "Rabbi Weissmandl and the Rabbis' plan: An anti-Zionist plot?" *Yalkut Moreshet* 58 (1994), pp. 83-92 (Hebrew).

31 For an analysis of these phenomena, see Goldberg, "The Holocaust in the Ultra-Orthodox Press," pp. 160, 167, 176-178; Friedman, "Why did God do that?" pp. 595-596, 600; Dalia Ofer, "50 Years of Israeli Discourse on the Holocaust: Features and Dilemmas," in Michman, *The Holocaust in Jewish History*, p. 320 (Hebrew).

32 Yehuda Leib Levin, *Book of Poland* I (Jerusalem and New York, 1961) (Hebrew). See also Shaul, *Beauty for Ashes*, pp. 311-316.

33 Joseph Friedenson, son of Eliezer Gershon Friedenson and editor of *Dos Yidishe Vort*, wrote prodigiously in the press, as did thinker and author Yehuda Leib Gerst, a Holocaust survivor from Lodz.

34 See the discussion of a number of major writers in Shaul, *Beauty for Ashes*, pp. 317-405.

35 On the image and the writing of Moshe Prager during the Holocaust see: Mali Eisenberg, "Witness, Crier, Documenter, and Commentator: Rabbi Moshe Prager and the Holocaust, 1940-1984," master's thesis, Bar-Ilan University, 2004 (Hebrew).

36 Moshe Prager, *The New Yeven Metsula [Abyss of Despair]: Polish Jewry in the Clutches of the Nazis* (Tel Aviv, 1941) (Hebrew).

37 In the 1990s, the Kiddush Hashem Archive devoted itself to collecting testimonies of Ultra-Orthodox Holocaust survivors and in so doing achieved the documentation of many voices that had not been heard in the past. In addition, the archive has served female students and teachers, primarily (though not exclusively) from the Ultra-Orthodox education system, in its engagement with the Holocaust and its involvement in publishing programs of study on the subject. Those affiliated with it have published a number of texts dealing with religious life in the Holocaust and different acts of Jewish heroism. For more details, see: http://www.ganzach.org.il/ (last accessed on November 27, 2019).

38 Moshe Prager, *Those Who Did Not Surrender: History of the Hassidic Resistance Movement in the Ghettos* (Bnei Brak, 1997) (Hebrew). All references provided in the present article relate to the third expanded edition. Prager's book was "dedicated with love and is dear to those who carry on the heroic lives of 'those who did not surrender' – members of the Talmud teaching institution of the Gerrer Hasids, Bnei Brak [the Gerrer Hasids' first Kolel in Eretz Israel, established in 1956 on a lot owned by Prager, who was one of its founders], who carry on the Hasidic Torah heritage of glorified Polish Jewry." With these words, Prager commemorated his view that the Hasidic students were the successors of the Hasidic rebels – that is, the true rebels. The Kiddush Hashem Archive was established above this Kolel, which today is considered one of the largest of all the kolels of Gerrer Hasidism and is attended by some 400 young Gerrer Hasid students

39 See, for example, Peled, *Jewish Krakow, 1939-1945*, pp. 79-80, 111, 130; Aaron Weiss, "The Jewish Police in the Generalgouvernement and Upper Silesia during the Period of the Holocaust," doctoral dissertation, Hebrew University of Jerusalem, 1972/73, p. 172, notes 13 and 14 (Hebrew). As a result of his writing during and following the Holocaust, Prager was considered to be an expert on the subject, especially in the 1950s and the 1960s. For example, he took part in a conference held at Yad Vashem on Jewish steadfastness during the Holocaust, and he wrote and edited the entry for "Auschwitz" in Encyclopedia Hebraica. See Israel Gutman

(ed.), *Jewish Steadfastness during the Holocaust* (Jerusalem, 1971), pp. 118-119, 345; Moshe Prager, "Auschwitz," *Encyclopedia Hebraica*, II, lines 331-332 (Jerusalem, 1953) (Hebrew); Moshe Prager, "Anti-Semitism," *Encyclopedia Hebraica*, IV, lines 528-568 (Jerusalem, 1953) (Hebrew).

40   Prager, *Those Who Did Not Surrender*, I, p. 12.

41   Yechiel Granatstein, *Mikadshei Hashem: An Encyclopedia*, I-III (Bnei Brak, 2006) (Hebrew). See also Yechiel Granatstein, *One Jew's Power One Jew's Glory: The Life of Rav Yitzchak Shumuel Eliyahu Finkler the Rebbe of Radoschitz in the Ghetto and Concentration Camps* (Jerusalem and New York, 1991).

42   Yechiel Granatstein, *The War of a Jewish Partisan: A Youth Imperiled by his Russian Comrades and Nazi Conquerors* (Brooklyn, 1986). For a detailed discussion of his writings, see Shaul, *Beauty for Ashes*, pp. 348-362 (Hebrew).

43   Granatstein, *Mikadshei Hashem*, I, p. 49. Another example is found in the partial quote from the emotionally moving last will and testament of a teenage girl named Fania Barbakov. Compare *Mikadshei Hashem*, I, pp. 153-154 with Mordechai Neistadt (ed.), *The Book of Druya and the Miur, Dravisk and Leonopol Jewish Communnities* (Ramat Gan, 1973), pp. 95-100 (Hebrew). Although this comprehensive text requires broader discussion than permitted by the present article, it is worth noting that the assembly of encyclopedic information about people and institutions, without the presentation of general historical insights, is a familiar genre of the religious writing.

44   See, for example, *Mikadshei Hashem*, I, p. 227 (the Alexander Rebbe – Rebbe Yitzchak Menachem Mendel Dancyger); II, p. 418 (the Gaon Kelmė –Rabbi Arieh Zeev Levine); and III, pp. 70-74 (the Kossonye Rebbe – Rabbi Israel Zvi Halevi Rottenberg).

45   Yehoshua Eibeshitz, *The Uprooted: A Survivor Autobiography* (Haifa, 2002).

46   This center was established in memory of his wife, who was a Holocaust survivor. After her death, Eibeshitz married Hannah Eilenberg Eibeshitz, also a Holocaust survivor who dedicated her life to Holocaust documentation. See, for example: Anna Eilenberg Eibeshitz, ⊠hildren in the Holocaust (Haifa, 2013); Anna Eilenberg Eibeshitz, *Sisters in the Storm* (New York and Jerusalem, 1992).

47   Yehoshua Eibeshitz (ed.), *Women in the Holocaust: A Documentary Collection of the Steadfastness of Women during the Holocaust*, I-VII (Jerusalem, 1986-1991) (Hebrew). The first volume addresses a variety of subjects, and subsequent volumes focus on defined issues: Vol. II – Family; Vol. III – Helping others in the ghetto; Vol. IV – Helping others in the camps; Vol. V – Girls and female adolescents under false Christian identities; Vol. VI – At the time, Volume VI marked the first publication of the diary of Ruthka Leiblich – *"The Diary of Ruthka Leiblich: The History of the Holocaust through the Eyes of a 13-Year-Old Girl,"* in Yehoshua Eibeshitz (assembled

and edited), *Women in the Holocaust: A Documentary Collection of the Heroism of the Woman* (Jerusalem, 1991). Vol. VII – Consolidated the Holocaust memoirs of Anna Eilenberg Eibeshitz.

48　See also other references to his work below.

49　Eibeshitz remained alive and active for many years. In 2017-2018, he was invited to a series of lectures by the Holocaust Research Center in Poland at the international Research Institute at Yad Vashem. He died childless in 2019 at the age of 103.

50　Yehoshua Eibeshitz, *Remarks and Writings: Personalities and Figures* (Haifa, 2015), p. 296 (Hebrew). These words pertained to the omission of an instance of rape from the publication of the diary of Rabbi Aharonson: "And I dare to ask…How were the hands that committed such a foolish and evil act not trembling? Let us assume that the diary was not that of a righteous rabbi who was publicly known for acting with caution and clear judgement. And let us assume that we were dealing with a reliable testimony of a 'common' Jew…who left behind an authentic diary documenting the malicious abuse (even if it contains details of the horror)…Such a diary is the equivalent of the last will and testament of a deathly ill person. It is of immeasurable importance on every scale, and every detail in such a diary is worth more than its weight in gold. Is there anyone in the world who is permitted to make changes or revisions to, or omissions from, such a document? The answer is: under no circumstances, absolutely not!" (Eibeshitz, *Remarks and Writings*, p. 297).

51　In addition to the abovementioned books, see Moshe Prager, *Sparks of Glory* (New York, 1974) (Hebrew). This book has been published in a number of editions. Yechiel Granatstein, *The Other Heroism: The Religious Jew in the Heroic Struggle and Rebellion against the Nazi Decrees during the Holocaust* (Jerusalem, 1989) (Hebrew); Yehoshua Eibeshitz, *On Matzah and Bitter Herbs: Acts of Heroism and Sacrifice for the Observance of the Passover Commandments in the Ghettos and the Camps during the Holocaust* (Kiryat Ata, 1974) (Hebrew); Yehoshua Eibeshitz, *With Sanctity and Heroism: Cases of Martyrdom and Self-Sacrifice: A Documentary Collection on Faith as an Influencing Factor during the Holocaust* (Tel Aviv, 1975/76) (Hebrew); Yehoshua Eibeshitz, *Among Those Who Approach Me I Will Be Proved Holy: A Collection of Deeds of Martyrdom and Self-Sacrifice in the Days of Destruction of Our Era* (Haifa, 2004/05) (Hebrew); No author indicated, *93: In Memory of 93 of our Sisters in Poland Who Chose Death* (Haifa, 1942/43). For a characterization of this phenomenon, see also Ofer, "50 Years of Israeli Discourse," p. 320.

52　One of the first memory books to be published was Yehezkel Parnas's *The Pocket of a Sling: A Diary from the Extermination Camps* (Bnei Brak, 1980/81). A great many texts were published from the early 1990s onward, including Pearl Benish, *To Vanquish the Dragon* (Nanuet, NY, 1991); Yonah ʿImanuʾel, *Dignity to Survive: One Family's Story of Faith in the Holocaust* (Nanuet, NY, 1998); Hadassa Levin, *Bat Ami: The Path of Anguish and Faith of a Daughter of Lithuanian Jewry during the Holocaust* (Bnei Brak, 1996) (Hebrew).

53 Anat Livne, "The Shaping of the Holocaust Memories of Survivors under the Influence of their Encounter with Israel: A Study Based on Holocaust Memoirs Published in Israel between 1945 and 1961," doctoral dissertation, Tel Aviv University, 2006 (Hebrew). On the characteristics of the writing and testimony of the Ultra-Orthodox public, see also Michal Zemer-Shaul, "The Holocaust between Public Memory and Private Memory." Also see Ofer, "50 Years of Israeli Discourse," p. 310.

54 For a selection of her studies, see Esther Farbstein, *Hidden In Thunder: Perspectives on Faith, Halakhah and Leadership during the Holocaust* (New York, 2007); *Hidden In the Heights: Orthodox Jewry In Hungary During The Holocaust* (New York, 2014); "Diaries and Memoirs as a Historical Source: The Diary and Memoir of a Rabbi at the 'Konin House of Bondage'," *Yad Vashem Studies* 26 (1998), 87-128; "The Halakhic Coping of women in the Holocaust," *Sinai* 144 (2011/12), pp. 41-73 (Hebrew); "The Four Cubits of Halakha—In the Company of Writings of a Community Rabbi in the Holocaust Era: Rabbinical Rulings and Halakha in the Writings of Rabbi Aharonson," *Sinai* 117 (1996), pp. 235–260 (Hebrew), and 118 (1996), pp. 43-70 (Hebrew); "'It is for your sake that we are slain…': Intention in the Act of Martyrdom in the Holocaust," *Mikhlol: Studies in Judaism, Education, and Science* 16 (1998), pp. 42-80 (Hebrew); "Rabbis in the Holocaust: Captains of a Sinking Ship," *Nativ* 16(3-4) (2004), pp. 31-36 (Hebrew); "Sermons Speak History: Rabbinic Dilemmas in Internment between Metz and Auschwitz," *Modern Judaism* 27(2) (2007), pp. 146-172. Farbstein is the most prominent reflection of these trends, though she is not the only one. For example, see also Sarah Kaplan, "Halakhic Discussions concerning the Slaughter Edict in Nazi Germany: Historical Aspects," *Mikhlol* 19 (1999), pp. 55-68 (Hebrew); Leah Langleben, "Always Remain a Decent Human Being: Torah Life in the Kovno Ghetto, 1941-1944," *Hagigei Giva* 4 (1995/96), pp. 227-266 (Hebrew).

55 Database: *Holocaust History in Prefaces to Rabbinic Literature* as well as Esther Farbstein, *The Forgotten Memories: Moving Personal Accounts from Rabbis who Survived the Holocaust*, (New-York, 2011). See Ibid., "Rabbis' Prefaces as a Historical Text of the Holocaust: An Introduction," *Dapim Studies on the Holocaust* 20 (2006), pp. 81-84 (Hebrew). See also Assaf Yedidya, Nathan Cohen, and Esther Farbstein (eds.), *Memory in a Book: Holocaust History in the Prefaces to Rabbinical Literature* (Jerusalem, 2008) (Hebrew). These prefaces, which were written as introductions to the Halakhic and philosophical literature, also contain the histories of the authors prior to the book's publication, including during the Holocaust. These multiple sources disprove claims regarding the silence of Holocaust survivors in general and Ultra-Orthodox survivors in particular. Moreover, as a large portion of these prefaces were written a few years after the war and were meant for the internal Ultra-Orthodox audience, they contain testimonies regarding topics that the Ultra-Orthodox public did place at the forefront of its engagement with the Holocaust. In these writings, we find explicit expression of the unbearable situations in which

rabbis and religious people found themselves, and of the difficult dilemmas stemming from their inability to preserve the world of Halakha as they had previously known it. In this manner, the authors show how everyday men and women, and rabbis and public leaders, coped with their constant inability to observe the commandments, including observance of the Sabbath and praying in a *minyan*.

56 In addition to the above-mentioned studies see Thomas Rahe, *"Höre Israel": Jüdische Religiosität in nationalsozialistischen Konzentrationslagern* (Göttingen, 1999).

57 In addition to the items already cited, see, for example, *Ephraim Londner, Bridge to a Bygone World: Conversations with Reb Ephraim Londner*, compiled by Rabbi Shmuel Albert (Ashdod, 2012/13) (Hebrew); Ben-Zion Klugman, *Tablets and Fragments of Tablets* (Bnei Brak, 1990/91) (Hebrew); Hanoch Simcha Bressler, *Sefer Yechi Reuven: Ma`agalei Haim shel Gvurah Yehudit* (Jerusalem, 2002/03) (Hebrew).

58 See, for example, Christopher R. Browning, *Remembering Survival: Memories of a Nazi Forced Labor Camp* (New York, 2011); Omer Bartov, "Wartime Lies and Other Testimonies: Jewish-Christian Relationships in Buczacz, 1939-1944," *East European Politics and Societies* 25(3) (August 2011), pp. 486-511.

59 Mordechai Zalkin, *Mara Deatra?: Rabbi and Community in the Pale of Settlement* (Jerusalem, 2017) (Hebrew).

60 See, for example, Mendel Piekarz, *Polish Hasidism: Between the Wars (The Holocaust)* (Jerusalem, 1977), pp. 412-4343 (Hebrew); Mendel Piekarz, *The Literature of Testimony as a Historical Source of the Holocaust and Three Hasidic Reflections of the Holocaust* (Jerusalem, 2003) (Hebrew); Moshe [Prager] Yehezkeli, *The Saving of the Rebbe of Belz from the Valley of Death in Poland, Told by Eye Witnesses* (Jerusalem, 1961) (Hebrew); Moshe [Prager] Yehezkeli, *The Miracle of the Saving of the Gerrer Rebbe* (Jerusalem, 1959) (Hebrew); Esther Farbstein, "Eyes of the Community: The Rescue of Hasidic Leaders," in *Hidden in Thunder*, pp. 67-154; Isaac Hershkowitz, "'This Enormous Offense to the Torah': New Discoveries About the Controversy over the Escape of the Rabbis from Budapest, 1943-1944," *Yad Vashem Studies* 37(1) (2009), pp. 109-136.

61 For an initial discussion of this topic, see my article: Havi Dreifuss, "'Like a Sheep without a Shepherd'? The Status of Rabbis in the Holocaust," in Yedidya, Cohen, and Farbstein, *Memory in a Book*, pp. 143-167 (Hebrew).

62 Ben-Tsiyon Klibansky, "'Tiferes Bachurim': A Large-Scale Torah Study Movement for Proletarian Youngsters in Interwar Lithuania," *Zion* (2017), pp. 439-488 (Hebrew).

63 Moriah Herman, "Attitudes and Policies pertaining to Youth in the Hasidic Movement during the Interwar Period in Poland, 1914-1939: Responses to the Abandonment of Religion," doctoral dissertation, Bar-Ilan University, 2014 (Hebrew).

64 David Biale et al., *Hasidism: A New History* (Princeton University Press, 2017), chapter 26, especially pp. 652–658; Marcin Wodziński, *Historical Atlas of Hasidism* (Princeton University Press, 2018), pp. 168–176.

65 Shimon Hubberband, *Kiddush Hashem: Jewish Religious and Cultural Life in Poland during the Holocaust* (Hoboken, NJ, 1987); Kalonymus Kalman Shapira, *Sermons from the Years of Rage: The Sermons of the Piaseczno Rebbe from the Warsaw Ghetto, 1939-1942*, edited by Daniel Resier (Jerusalem, 2017) (Hebrew). On the sermons of the Piaseczno Rebbe and their connection to the reality of life in the ghetto, see Henry Abramson, *Torah from the Years of Wrath, 1939-1943: The Historical Context of the Aish Kodesh* (North Charleston, SC, 2017).

66 An examination of Hubberband's writings are indicative of some tendencies that cannot be discussed in detail here. One of the most important is a bias in his description of the activity of Gerrer Hasidism, which may stem from his close relationship with Alexander Hasidism of Piotrkow, or for other reasons.

67 For other figures, see "The works of my hands are drowning in the sea and you would offer me song?!": Orthodox Behavior and Leadership in Warsaw during the Holocaust," in Glenn Dynner and Francois Guesnet (eds.), *Warsaw, the Jewish Metropolis: Essays in Honor of the 75th Birthday of Professor Antony Polonsky* (Liden and Boston, 2015), pp. 467-495, especially p. 477.

68 See the scope of publications in recent years: Leib Rochman, *And in Your Blood You Shall Live* (Jerusalem, 1961) (Hebrew); Moshe Flinker, *Young Moshe's Diary: The Spiritual Torment of a Jewish Boy in Nazi Europe* (Jerusalem, 1965); Rabbi Yehoshua Moshe Aaronson, *Leaves of Bitterness* (Bnei Brak, 1996) (Hebrew); David Kahana, *Lvov Ghetto Diary* (University of Massachusetts Press, 1991); Rosa Jacobs, *Diary of a Girl in Hiding during the Holocaust, 1942-1944* (Israel, 2001/02) (Hebrew); Alexander Klein and Haim Shalem (eds.), *Walking with Our Heads Held High: Spiritual Steadfastness in France during the Holocaust as Reflected in the Documentation* (Jerusalem, 2011/12) (Hebrew); Esther Farbstein (ed.), *From Telshe to Telshe: The Diary of Rabbi Chaim Stein, 1939-1944* (Jerusalem, 2015) (Hebrew); Leah Langleben, *To Live and to Study: Jewish Education in Poland and Lithuania during the Holocaust: A Collection of Documents* (Jerusalem, 2014/15) (Hebrew); Esther Farbstein, Michal Unger, and Hadasa Halamish (eds.), *To Write Forever: The Diary of Rivka Lifshitz, a Girl from the Lodz Ghetto* (Jerusalem, 2018) (Hebrew); Esther Farbstein and Havi Dreifuss (eds.), *A Spiritual Candle Burns within Me: The Diary of Josph Guzik, A Wise Student from Dukla* (Jerusalem, 2018/19) (Hebrew); Chaim Yitzchok Wolgelernter, *The Unfinished Diary: A Chronicle of Tears* (Lakewood, NJ, 2015).

69 For selected examples, see the diaries of: Hinda Schwartz of Lesko, Yad Vashem Archive (hereinafter, YVA), 033.755; Sarah Fishman of Rubieżewicze, YVA 033.2222 (a portion of this diary was published in Yalkut Moreshet 2(4) (July

1965), pp, 21-35 (Hebrew); and an anonymous religious Jew from Piotrków Trybunalski, YVA 302.147.

70 Rabbi Yissachar Shlomo Teichtal, *Faith Refined in the Furnace of the Holocaust* (no date of publication indicated) (Hebrew); Sermons of Rabbi Moïse Kahlenberg, *Yad Moshe: Sermons in a Detention Camp in France during the Holocaust*, edited by Esther Farbstein (Jerusalem, 2004/05) (Hebrew); Rabbi Shlomo Zalman Unsdorfer, *Sfati Shlema* (Montreal, 1971/72) (Hebrew); Rabbi Mordechai Brisk, *Sermons of Maharam Brisk* (Brooklyn, NY, 1986/87) (Hebrew); Rabbi Shlomo Zalman Ehrenreich, *Lechem Shlomo Sermons* (Brooklyn, NY, 1975/76) (Hebrew); Rabbi Gavriel Gestetner, *Sefer Sfatei Gavriel* (Brooklyn, 1962/63) (Hebrew); Rabbi Avraham Yosef Lichtenstein, *Sefer She`arit Yekutiel* (Brooklyn, 1978/79) (Hebrew).

71 See Tarshansky, "The Writings of Rabbi Ephraim Oshry." Rabbi Ephraim Oshry, *Responsa from the Depths: Responsa and Issues That Were Relevant in the Era of Killing and Destruction of 1940/41-1944/45 in the Kovno Ghetto*, 5 Volumes (New York, 1958/59-1978/9) (Hebrew); Rabbi Ephraim Oshry, *Responsa from the Holocaust*, edited by B. Goldman and translated by Y. Leiman (New York, 2001); Rabbi Shimon Efrati, *From the Killing Ravine* (Responsa) (Jerusalem, 1960/61) (Hebrew); Rabbi Shimon Efrati, *From the Valley of Tears* (Jerusalem, 1947/48) (Hebrew); Rabbi Tzvi Hirsch Meizlish, *The Binyan Tzvi Responsa*, Part II (New York, 1955/56); Rabbi Tzvi Hirsch Meizlish, *The Mikadshei Hashem Responsa*, 2 Volumes (Chicago, 1954/55-1966/67) (Hebrew).

72 Examples of such responsa can be found in the following books: Rabbi Mordechai Brisk, *Sefer Brit Eitanim* (Netanya, 2001/02) (Hebrew); Rabbi Yitzchak Tzvi Sofer, *Misaper Hasofer* (Jerusalem, 2001/02) (Hebrew); Rabbi Yehoshua Greenwald, *Responsa Hesed Yehoshua* (New York, 1947/48) (Hebrew); Rabbi Shmuel Shmelke Segal Litch, *These Are Shmuel's Words* (New York, 1982/83) (Hebrew); Rabbi Yonasan Steif, *Responsa and Additions of Rabbi Yonasan Steif on the Four Sections of Shulchan Aruch* (Brooklyn, 1967/68) (Hebrew).

73 Judaism prohibits a woman from being married to two husbands. Therefore, in cases when a husband is not present, but his fate is unknown, his wife remains bound to her marriage ("*aguna*") until the ruling of a certified court, based on clear evidence that the husband is not alive. In the aftermath of the Holocaust, there were thousands of women whose husbands' fates were unknown and whose tracks the courts and rabbis attempted to trace.

74 In addition to the above-mentioned texts, see Rabbi Yitzchok Yaakov Weiss, *Responsa Minchat Yitzchok*, 10 Volumes (London, 1957/58 – Jerusalem, 1989/90) (Hebrew); Rabbi Meshulam Rata, *Kol Mevaser Responsa* (Jerusalem, 1972/73) (Hebrew).

75 An impressive expression of Mrs. Lichtenstein's extensive research and documentation activity can be found in Ruth Lichtenstein (ed.), *Witness to History* (New York, 2009).

76 Texts that have been published in the past few years contain photos of documents from the period that cannot be found elsewhere. For an especially impressive example, see Hanoch Tzvi Rubinstein, *V'emunatcha Balaylot* (Bnei Brak, 2014/15) (Hebrew). See also Shoshana Shenkar (Chen), *"You Are Staying There": Letters to a Sister I Never Knew* (Bnei Brak, 2013/14) (Hebrew).

77 Nathan Eck, "Religious Experience or Resistance," *Yediot Yad Vashem* 21/22 (December 1959), p. 15 (Hebrew). Located in the Kiddush Hashem Archive, Doc. 37 in the list Moshe Prager, His Works and Writings, File No. 72 on Prager.

78 Havi Ben-Sasson (Dreifuss), "L'historiographie orthodoxe et la Shoah: ses repercussions dans le monde universitaire," *Revue d'histoire de la Shoah* 188 (January/June 2008), pp. 453-477.

79 Havi Dreifuss, "Gerer Hasidic Youth during the Sho'ah: A Representative Blind Spot in Holocaust Research," *Polin* [forthcoming]; Ibid., "Matys Gelman: nieznany przywódca nieznanego ruchu chasydzkiego w czasie Zagłady," *Zagłada **Żydów*** (forthcoming).

Avinoam Patt

Martyrs and Fighters: The Historiography of the Warsaw Ghetto and the Warsaw Ghetto Uprising

In historical writing on the Holocaust, the Warsaw Ghetto and the Warsaw Ghetto Uprising have captured a disproportionate amount of scholarly attention. What accounts for the centrality of Warsaw in historical writing on the Holocaust? Is it the size of Warsaw, which in 1939 was the second largest Jewish city in the world? Or the population of the ghetto itself, which with nearly 500,000 inhabitants easily made it the largest ghetto in German-occupied Europe? Or is it perhaps the Warsaw Ghetto Uprising, which rapidly became the focal point of commemorative activities organized around the anniversary of the revolt on April 19, 1943? Was it the dedicated activity of underground archivists associated with the Oneg Shabbes Archive of Emanuel Ringelblum, who successfully preserved the memory of a destroyed Jewish community? Or the thousands of diaries written by Jews, some who perished and others who survived, which accounted for the voluminous literature on the city? Surely all these factors account for the fact that Warsaw still stands in the center of historical writing on the Shoah, although such patterns have clearly shifted in recent years, particularly as other topics have surpassed Warsaw as areas of focus. This chapter will trace historiographical patterns in writing on the Warsaw Ghetto, with a particular focus on the Warsaw Ghetto Uprising. What accounts for the past scholarly attention to this event, and what has been the impact of this specific focus on Holocaust historiography in general? Despite a great deal of literature on the Warsaw ghetto in general, the wartime and early postwar focus on the "last battle of Warsaw's Jews," has paradoxically reinforced a dichotomy between ghetto fighters who chose to die with dignity and Jewish martyrs who went passively like "lambs to the slaughter" in the 75 years since the end of the war.

The Centrality of Warsaw

In 1939, Warsaw was the second largest Jewish city in the world; only New York had a larger Jewish population at the time. While Jewish settlement in Warsaw dated back to the 15th century, the Jewish community experienced its greatest growth in the 19th century, increasing from 6,750 Jews in Warsaw in 1792 (8.3 percent of the population), to an astonishing 320,030 Jews in 1918 (or 42.4 percent of a total population of approximately 750,000).[1] Rapid industrialization and urbanization in the 19th century helped turn Warsaw into a major Jewish center, making it the largest Jewish city in Europe (Warsaw's population of 337,000 Jews in 1914 was equal to the Jewish population of France).[2] Warsaw became the capital of an independent Poland after World War I, and Jews from parts of the newly created Poland that had formerly been part of the Austro-Hungarian empire (like Galicia) or the Russian empire, streamed towards the new capital, eager to partake in the economic, educational, and political opportunities it offered. Jews in Warsaw played a central role in the growth of industry and trade in the city, especially in textiles, clothing, and tobacco. At the same time, an increasing number of Jews entered the liberal professions, with more and more adopting Polish as their first language.[3] As the population of Warsaw grew in the interwar period, so did its Jewish population, although the number of Jews as a percentage of the overall population declined (by 1938, the 368,394 Jews in Warsaw constituted 29.1 percent of the total population of 1.265 million).[4]

With the outbreak of war on September 1, 1939, Jews and non-Jews alike suffered from the indiscriminate bombing of the *Luftwaffe*. A JDC (American Jewish Joint Distribution Committee) report in Warsaw estimated that 20,000 Jews were killed in the first month of the war, with 7,000 Jews killed in Warsaw alone in September 1939.[5] Thousands of Jewish homes, businesses, factories and shops were also destroyed in the bombings. In the first weeks of the war, Warsaw's Jewish population fluctuated as a result of mobilization, flight to the East, and the arrival of refugees fleeing the advancing German army; by early 1940, the Jewish population of Warsaw swelled to some 400,000 as Jews from areas annexed to the Reich were deported to the Generalgouvernement, and refugees crowded into Warsaw.[6] This only further compounded the scarcity of housing, food, and medical supplies in the city. On November 15, 1940 German authorities ordered the Warsaw ghetto in the General Government sealed off, creating the largest ghetto in both area and population in Poland. Over 350,000 Jews, approximately

30 percent of the city's population, were confined to about 2.4 percent of Warsaw's total area. Over 120,000 additional refugees would later be sent to the ghetto, bringing the total population of the ghetto to nearly 500,000.[7] With a population of nearly half a million Jews by the spring of 1941, it is unsurprising that the Warsaw Ghetto would occupy such a central place in historical writing on the Holocaust, both because of the size of the Jewish population crowded there, the subsequently stunning and rapid decimation of that population, deported to Treblinka in the summer of 1942, and as a result of the revolt which would break out in Warsaw on April 19, 1943 and seize the attention of the world outside occupied Europe.

Historical Writing on the Warsaw Ghetto Uprising

The Warsaw Ghetto Uprising has occupied a central place in the history of the Holocaust and of the Second World War; as a military encounter, its significance may seem relatively minor, resulting in a small number of German dead and wounded over the course of the month that the Jewish resistance fighters managed to battle German forces in the ghetto. Nonetheless, the revolt in the Warsaw ghetto had a major impact on Jewish communities elsewhere in Eastern Europe and on German procedures in the aftermath of the uprising as well, and this impact has been well-documented in historical writing on the war.[8] And, from the perspective of Jewish history, its significance has been tremendous, representing perhaps the most well-known Jewish response to Nazi persecution during the war, serving both as the counterargument to the myth that the Jews of Europe had been "led like lambs to the slaughter" and conversely, reinforcing the mistaken view that the Warsaw Ghetto uprising represented the only case of armed Jewish resistance in Europe.

Recent literature on the subject reinforces a continued fascination with the topic of Jewish resistance, while also suggesting a perceived need to continue arguing against the stereotype of Jewish passivity and for an expanded definition of what constituted "resistance" and "defiance."[9] For example, Nechama Tec, *Resistance: Jews and Christians who Defied the Nazi Terror*, sets out to refute the notion that "Jews marched like lambs to the slaughter" by demonstrating acts of resistance (large and small) in the ghettos, camps, and forests. A 2014 volume edited by Patrick Henry on *Jewish Resistance Against the Nazis* begins with a chapter titled "The Myth of Jewish Passivity" by Richard Middleton Kaplan that explores the origins and enduring power of the stereotype of Jewish passivity, explaining that "one aim of our volume is to demonstrate definitively that Jews during the Holocaust did not go to their deaths passively like sheep. One might ask why such a project is necessary given the voluminous evidence attesting to the fact that Jews resisted the Nazis whenever, wherever, and however it was possible. The compelling evidence has simply done little to change a nearly universal perception."[10] While scholars frequently critique Raul Hilberg's argument that "Preventive attack, armed resistance, and revenge were almost completely absent in Jewish exilic history,"[11] a review of early commemorations and historical treatments of the war reveals that the poles of passivity and resistance cited by Tec and others were established very early – in fact, they were fixed even before the war.[12]

Historical writing on the Warsaw Ghetto and the Uprising developed rapidly both during and after the war. While testimonies were received and published in the "free world" already in 1944, we know they were not the first testimonies from occupied Europe to be shared publicly during the war: for example, *Letters from the Ghettoes*, compiled by Bracha Habas, appeared in the Yishuv in 1943. Likewise, portions of Jan Karski's *Story of a Secret State* appeared earlier in 1944 (selections were published in *Colliers* in January 1944). Selections from the Diary of Mary Watten(Berg) were also published in American newspapers in 1944 after her arrival in the United States in March 1944.[13]

Historical frameworks, in place before the war, also influenced writing and documentation projects during the war. Journalists, historians, surviving participants, writers of fiction and non-fiction and others began to create historical accounts of the "battle of Warsaw's Jews" almost immediately after it occurred.[14] Document collections that presented eyewitness testimony, underground reports and other tantalizing details on the event were already published in 1944; examples include the Bund's *Ghetto in Flames*, the publication of Shloyme Mendelson's 1944 lecture at YIVO, and *Warsaw Ghetto Rising*, written by Melech Neustadt and published by Poalei Zion.[15] Melech Neustadt also compiled one of the first document collections on the revolt, published in the Yishuv in 1946 as *Churban ve-Mered shel Yehudei Varsha* (Destruction and

Rising: The Epic of the Jews of Warsaw, Tel Aviv, 1946). The testimonies of surviving ghetto fighters (like Marek Edelman, Feygele Peltel (Vladka Meed), Zivia Lubetkin, Tuvia Borzykowski, Yitzhak Zuckerman, Stefan Grajek and others) also found a broad audience soon after the war, as did one of the earliest popular historical treatments of Jewish resistance during the war, American writer Marie Syrkin's *Blessed is the Match* (published in 1947), which situated the Warsaw Ghetto Uprising within a decidedly Zionist interpretation of the origins of the resistance.

In 1944, the American representation of the General Jewish Workers Union in Poland (the Bund) published *Geto in Flamen* (Ghetto in Flames), a volume including chapters providing background history on "the Jewish-German war" (L. Hodes), the "Underground Bund" (by S. Hertz), "the Miracle of Uprising" (by Jacob Pat), a chapter on Szmuel Zygielbojm (by Emanuel Novogrodzki), portraits of the ghetto heroes (by S. Hertz), and messages delivered by luminaries at the first anniversary of the Warsaw Ghetto Uprising on April 19, 1944 (Einstein, Eleanor Roosevelt, LaGuardia, Lehman, etc.), as well as poetry and stories by Z. Shneur (*Plitim Kinder*), "Jewish Balad" by Avrom Glanz-Leyles and "On the 19th of April" by Josef Opatoshu. The volume, perhaps the first anthology to be published in the United States dedicated specifically to the Warsaw Ghetto Uprising, highlighted a distinctly Bundist perspective on the uprising, featuring the Jewish workers' underground reports smuggled out of Warsaw, as well as essays and background by prominent figures in the Bund and Jewish Labor Committee (including Hodes, Hertz, Pat, Novogrodzki and Mendelson). From the Bundist perspective, the revolt was a popular uprising, the reflection of a spirit that emanated from a broad swath of the surviving population in Warsaw and was a continuation of the Jewish workers struggle throughout the war.[16] Melech Neustadt (Noy), who had been so active compiling information sent to the Yishuv by the Jewish National Committee (and would be the author/editor of *Destruction and Revolt in the Warsaw Ghetto* published in 1946), responded to the Bundist claims of credit for the revolt and the publication of the Jewish Labor Underground's reports by the Bund with the publication of *The Warsaw Ghetto Rising* (as told by the insurgents).[17] Neustadt set out to demonstrate that Zionist groups played the leading role in the revolt (contrary to Bundist claims) and dominated the Jewish Fighting Organization numerically and militarily. Such early competing claims of credit for leadership in the revolt have remained a consistent theme in writing on the revolt in the 75 years since 1943.

In a review of literature on the "Jewish Catastrophe" by Philip Friedman and Koppel Pinson published in *Jewish Social Studies* in January 1950, the scholars argued that over 300 books, memoirs, and document collections dealing with the Warsaw ghetto and the ghetto uprising had been published in less than five years after the war, including what they identified as "the first serious study of the uprising in the Warsaw ghetto" by Dr. Josef Kermisz, *Der Oyfshtand in varshever geto* (translated from the Polish by Shloyme Lastik. Buenos Aires: Zentral Farband fun Poylishe Yidn in Argentine, 1948).[18] Other early treatments of the revolt included Ber Mark, *Dos bukh fun gevure. Vol. I, Oyfshtand fun varshever geto* (Lodz: Dos Naye Lebn. 1947); Rokhl Auerbach, *Der yidisher oyfshtand in varshe 1943* (Warsaw: Zentral Komitet fun Poylishe Yidn, 1948); and Jonas Turkow, *Azoy is es geven. Khurbn varshe* (Buenos Aires: Zentral Farband fun Poylishe Yidn in Argentine, 1948). Published memoirs by ghetto fighters and underground members included Wladke's [Feigele Peltel-Miedzyrzecki], *Fun beyde zaytn getomoyer* (*On Both Sides of the Wall*) (New York: Arbeter Ring, 1948. Pp. 358); Tuvia Bozykowski, *Tsvishn falendike vent* (*Bein Kirot Noflim*) (Warsaw: Hechalutz, 1949. Pp. 353); and Bernard Goldstein, *Finf yor in varshever geto*, edited by Viktor Shulman (New York: Unzer Tsait, 1947) into English by Leonard Shatzkin under the title of *The Stars Bear Witness*. New York: Viking Press, 1949. Pp. 295.)

Postwar travelogues by writers, journalists, and Jewish leaders who visited destroyed European Jewish communities also reached a broad Jewish audience. Yakov Pat traveled to Poland for two months in 1946, sent by the Jewish Labor Committee to distribute aid to the surviving Jewish communities there. In his travelogue, *Ash un Fayer: Iber di Hurves fun Poylen* (*Ashes and Fire: On the Ruins of Poland*), Pat detailed his 60 days in Poland for an American reading audience, writing both to describe the destruction of Polish Jewry and to inspire support for the "remnant of Israel" that he found in Poland – help for the homeless, the children, the youth, help for Jewish culture, for the working people, those "rescued from the ovens" striving to build a productive life, help for the tens of thousands of Jews who returned from Soviet Russia.[19] While Pat sought to detail all aspects of what he witnessed in Poland over those 60 days and his encounters in Oświęcim, his birthplace of Białystok, Lublin, Częstochowa, Tarnów, and Treblinka (among other places) – he framed his wrenching account beginning and ending in the ruins of the destroyed Warsaw ghetto. In Hal Lehrman's review in *Commentary* this aspect stood out as well, for "*Ashes and Fire* confirms with fresh detail the already well-authenticated fact that the Jews of the Warsaw Ghetto and the partisan forests merit a chapter all their own in the epic of hopeless resistance which the world has been writing since Thermopylae."[20]

As a rich historical literature on the revolt developed in the first decade after 1943 (in Yiddish, Polish, English and Hebrew) several key patterns in the historiography began to emerge. All reinforced the centrality of the Warsaw Ghetto Uprising as the *key* focal point of Jewish collective memory of the war – but also as an event sufficiently flexible as to be incorporated into multiple postwar Jewish political and historical frameworks. Likewise, the focus on the revolt reinforced a dichotomy in assessments of Jewish behavior in the war, a division captured by the two sides of Natan Rapaport's famous monument in Warsaw dedicated on the 5th anniversary of the revolt on April 19, 1948: ghetto fighters bursting forth as actors in history on one side, passive ghetto Jews being led to their deaths at the umschlagplatz on the other.

The 1954 publication of Philip Friedman's *Martyrs and Fighters: The Epic of the Warsaw Ghetto* captured this duality – both the division of Jewish responses between an emphasis on martyrdom or heroism, and the bifurcation of the Jewish world between Israel and America. By dedicating the book to the struggle which took place in the Warsaw Ghetto, the Club of Polish Jews hoped to demonstrate that the genocide was unable to destroy the "faith, ideas, and traditions" of Polish Jews. Although Polish Jews were "slain by the millions in the gas chambers of the Nazis," a small group survived. "Some of these survivors have settled in Israel, where they are helping to build the foundations of a new state. Another group of survivors made their homes in the free land of Washington and Jefferson where they try to continue the finest traditions of Polish Jewry." (8).

As a response to Nazi persecution, the revolt symbolized the determination of the Jewish people to endure, persevere and preserve their faith and traditions, whether in Israel or America. The revolt symbolized the defense of freedom and democracy *and* the collective ethos of the Jewish people. The editor of the anthology was Dr. Philip Friedman (1901-1960), a Polish Jewish historian who trained in Vienna and taught in Warsaw, Lodz, and Vilna before the war. Friedman survived the war in hiding in Poland and became the director of the Central Jewish Historical Commission in Poland after the war, later testifying at the Nuremberg Trials before directing the educational department of the JDC in Germany. Friedman would serve as a lecturer at Columbia University from 1951 until his death in 1960. In his introduction to the anthology, Friedman argued that the "Jewish revolt in Warsaw is almost unique in its historical significance," demonstrating that "moral factors prove stronger than brute force and terror."

Ten years have elapsed since the Warsaw ghetto uprising; yet the great historical issue symbolized by this heroic battle is still real. More than ever the world is in need of a warning reminder of the ruthless and coldly calculated crimes, including genocide, of which the totalitarian regimes are capable. Whatever their color – black or brown, red or white – they inevitably bring havoc and destruction when they run rampant in our troubled, twisted world and when they are unchecked by the vigorous will of free men. (12).

For Friedman, writing and teaching in English in New York in December 1953, the connections were clear: the Warsaw Ghetto Uprising symbolized the ability of free men to stand up to the evil power of totalitarian regimes whether represented by Nazi Germany or the Soviet Union. Friedman, who had published a detailed "Bibliography of the Warsaw Ghetto" in *The Jewish Book Annual* (vol. XI, 1952-53)[21] based his selection in the anthology on a wide range of sources in Yiddish, Polish, German and French, which included testimonies of eyewitnesses, ghetto fighters, members of the Jewish Fighting Organization, and reports written by Rachel Auerbach, Adolf Berman, Tuvia Borzykowski, Marek Edelman, Bernard Goldstein, Zivia Lubetkin, Vladka Meed, Simcha Rathayzer (Kazik), Emanuel Ringelblum, Hillel Seidman, Wladyslaw Szpilman, David Wdowinski, Szmuel Zygielbojm and others, along with reports by SS general Jurgen Stroop and the Polish Underground courier

Jan Karski (from *Story of a Secret State*, published in 1944), that reflected a broad array of viewpoints translated into English for an American audience. Approximately two-thirds of the volume focused on accounts of life before the revolt, and Friedman made clear that his goal was to use primary sources as "records of human sufferings, as well as documents of revolt against slavery and oppression" in order to "plunge the reader directly into the day-by-day life and strife of the ghetto, into the whirlpool of feelings and emotions, into the maze of various, sometimes contradictory, currents and problems which moved and stirred the inhabitants of the ghetto." (12). Even though a broad range of sources was already available (with some translated into English and Hebrew) on Jewish life in the Warsaw Ghetto, the revolt and the subject of death in the ghetto remained the primary focus. *Martyrs and Fighters* – the two poles of Jewish behavior in the ghetto – would be reinforced repeatedly in representations of the uprising and in historical literature on the war.

In Israel in the 1950s, too, the two poles of Jewish behavior also seemed fixed, determined by a pre-WWII Zionist worldview predicated on the negation of the passive Diaspora Jewish mentality. As Roni Stauber's research on *The Holocaust in Israeli Public Debate in the 1950s* argues, with few exceptions, the "maladies of the Diaspora" (as opposed to independent autonomous life in Israel) had determined the standard Jewish response in the face of destruction, define by a complete lack of self-defense and armed struggle.[22] The Ghetto Fighters House, founded on April 19, 1949, worked to counteract the myth of Jewish passivity during the war by focusing on specific examples of Jewish resistance and Jewish heroism. The main goal of the Ghetto Fighters House was to expose the population to the special aspects and broad scope of active Jewish self-defense during the Holocaust. As Havi Dreifuss argues, however, "Although there were several institutions in Israel that proclaimed the Jewish triumph over the Holocaust, including the Ghetto Fighters' House and Yad Vashem itself, research was not high on their list of their priorities," and academic research on the Holocaust was quite limited in Israel in the 1950s.[23] Nonetheless, those publications that dealt with the Holocaust tended to focus on Jewish involvement in armed resistance to the Germans. These included the publication of diaries and memoirs of M. Tannenbaum Tamaroff, *Dapim min hadelekah* (Lohamei Hagetaot, 1948); R. Korczak, *Lehavot ba'efer* (Merhavia, 1946); C. Lazar Litai, *Hurban umered*

(Tel Aviv, 1950); C. Grossman, *Anshei hamahteret* (Merhavia, 1950) G. Davidson, *Yomanah shel yustinah* (Tel Aviv, 1953); M. Kahanowic, *Milhemet hapartizanim hayehudim bemizrah eiropah* (Tel Aviv A. Kovner et al., *Sefer hapartizanim hayehudim* (Merhavia, 1954); A. Karmi and C. Frimer, *Min hadelekah hahi* (Lohamei Hagetaot, 1961); T. Borzykowski, *Bein kirot nofelim* (Lohamei Hagetaot, 1964). Even so, the political context in Israel led each movement to emphasize the role of its own members in the struggle against German oppression, while critiquing what was seen as the collaboration of the Judenrate.[24]

Sefer Milhamot Ha-Getaot (1954) edited by Yitzhak Zuckerman and Moshe Basok and published by the Ghetto Fighters House, argued in its introduction that "Jewish historiography has a duty to historical truth to the legacy our generation has to leave to the next, a duty to make known in addition to the loss which was one side of the life in the ghetto the full extent of the people's heroic struggle individually and as a group during the days and places of annihilation themselves." The *Book of the Ghetto Wars* contained more than 150 testimonies and parts of original sources from the GFH archives, although more than 40% of the book was devoted to the Warsaw ghetto, especially its underground activity and rebellion.[25] Apart from resistance in Warsaw, the book documented the underground in Kraków, Będzin, Białystok, and Wilno (Vilna), with most of the reports and sources dealing with the large ghettos coming from members of the pioneering youth movements. Testimonies by members of the Jewish Socialist (non-Zionist) Bund and the Revisionist Zionist youth movement Betar were largely excluded (with the exception of a brief excerpt from the Bundist Marek Edelman) and the *Book of the Ghetto Wars* devoted very little space to the activity of the partisans.[26] The introduction to the volume explained.

> ghetto wars means fighting for life, if only to die with honor, to die a death different from that the enemy has decreed. Fighting means every action taken against the interests of the suffering is caused by a violent invader, actions taken in public and in secret, by groups of people and by individuals, organized and planned or suddenly at the last moment, armed and even by taking a daring stance by protesting in a brave voice. (p. vii)

Although the *Book of the Ghetto Wars* offered an expanded definition of resistance – defining ghetto wars as fighting against the decrees of the invaders (in a form similar to Bauer's later use of the term *amidah*), the volume reinforced a divide that had existed between the ghetto fighters themselves, the leaders of the Jewish councils, and the rest of the ghetto population as a whole. The book focused primarily on physical struggle as the supreme form of Jewish rebellion and highlighted calls by the underground for the Jewish population to not go passively to their deaths, while also stressing the alienation felt by the underground from the rest of the ghetto population, which they perceived as helpless and passive.[27] In this sense, two factors seemed to influence the historiography of the Warsaw Ghetto in the first two decades after the war: 1) a tendency to minimize experiences of Jews not affiliated with the underground that would later fall under the category of *Amidah* or spiritual resistance, but which came to be seen as obstacles to resistance and 2) political factors, which led political parties to emphasize their own members' experiences at the expense of minimizing the role of others.

In his 1961 opus *The Destruction of the European Jews* (a second edition was published in 1985 and a third edition in 2003), Raul Hilberg focused almost exclusively on how the Germans organized the Final Solution, generally ignoring Jewish responses and Jewish source material. In his treatment of the Warsaw Ghetto Uprising, Hilberg used the report of SS General Jurgen Stroop as a main source, offering a table with the comparative strength of each force in the revolt. Hilberg estimated 1500 Jewish fighters combined between the ZOB and the ZZW (which he labeled *Irgun Zwai Leumi* or National Military Organization, the name of a Revisionist Zionist paramilitary organization operating in Palestine before 1948, *not* in Warsaw during WWII) vs. approximately 2000-3000 Germans; Hilberg's table also presented the battle in military terms as a struggle between Jews and Germans listing each side's commander (Anielewicz vs. Stroop); manpower (the ZOB's 22 platoon-sized battle groups vs. the forces of the Waffen SS, Order Police, Security Police, Army, and Ukrainian collaborators) and equipment (the ZOB's 2-3 light machine guns, one hundred rifles, hundreds of revolvers and pistols, Molotov cocktails, and improvised explosives vs. tanks, armored cars, anti-aircraft guns, howitzers, flamethrowers, etc). Finally, Hilberg compared each group's objective: Jews (to hold out as long as possible) vs. the Germans (to clear the ghetto in three days).[28] Hilberg presented the uneven confrontation as a military battle in the chapter on Deportations. He based his evidence largely on the Stroop report, while also relying on the ZOB report reprinted in Friedman, *Martyrs and Fighters*, as well as testimonies by Edelman, Goldstein, and others that had been printed in English.

All the same, Hilberg's assessment of the Warsaw Ghetto Uprising measured its significance from the perspective of the history of the development of the Final Solution:

> the largest single clash between Jews and Germans occurred in the ghetto of Warsaw. For the further development of the destruction process, this armed encounter was without consequence. In Jewish history, however, the battle is literally a revolution, for after two thousand years of a policy of submission the wheel had been turned and once again Jews were using force.[29]

For Hilberg, the Jewish councils were part of the machinery of destruction, part of the Jewish tendency to submit to the power of the oppressor, "composed of precisely those elements of the community that had staked everything on a course of complete cooperation with the German administration" while the resistance was organized by "a new hierarchy that was strong enough to challenge the council successfully in a bid for control over the Jewish community" formed from the political parties that had been "represented in the prewar Jewish community machinery", had managed to survive in the ghetto by looking out for their members and "now banded together into a resistance bloc."[30] For Hilberg, the revolution in Jewish history was as much a manifestation of resistance against Nazi oppression as it was a determination to throw off the yoke of 2000 years of Jewish submission to passivity and compliance. Still, studying the Holocaust solely through the lens of German history and the Final Solution rendered the diversity of Jewish responses to persecution largely irrelevant, as these responses had no impact on the final outcome of the destruction of European Jewry. Likewise, Hilberg only covered armed resistance briefly, focusing almost exclusively on the Warsaw ghetto because it did nothing to alter the fate of Poland's Jews or the outcome of the Final Solution.

In the same year that Hilberg published *The Destruction of European Jewry*, the trial of Adolf Eichmann commenced in Jerusalem on April 12, 1961 (the day before Yom HaShoah vehaGevurah). Just a week later, on April 17, Gideon Hausner, the Israel Attorney General, read the indictment on behalf of the "six million accusers."[31] Surviving ghetto fighters like Yitzhak Zuckerman, Zivia Lubetkin, and Abba Kovner testified at the trial in May 1961, again seeking to offset the notion that Jews had gone passively to their deaths. Adolf Berman and Rachel Auerbach also testified, offering evidence on education and social welfare efforts in the Warsaw Ghetto. Auerbach, who had been part of the Oneg Shabbat underground archive project and then an important figure in the postwar Historical Commission before emigrating to Israel and founding the oral history department at Yad Vashem, also played a central role in convincing the prosecution to incorporate the voices of so many survivors in the case. This decision would greatly expand awareness of the vast array of Jewish experiences during the war and raise general awareness of the Holocaust among broad audiences that had not existed before.

Reporting on the Eichmann Trial, Hannah Arendt singled out this "contrast between Israeli heroism and the submissive meekness with which Jews went to their death" as a telling point of the trial, noting that in his cross-examination of witnesses, Hausner seemed to emphasize the behavior of Jewish victims "arriving on time at the transportation points, walking under their own power to the places of execution, digging their own graves, undressing and making neat piles of their clothing, and lying down side by side to be shot" as he asked witness after witness, "Why did you not protest?"; "Why did you board the train?"; "Fifteen thousand people were standing there and hundreds of guards facing you—why didn't you revolt and charge and attack these guards?" harping on it for all it was worth. Nonetheless, Arendt concluded,

> …the deliberate attempt in Jerusalem to tell only the Jewish side
> of the story distorted the truth, even the Jewish truth. The glory
> of the uprising in the Warsaw ghetto and the heroism of the few
> others who fought back lay precisely in their having refused the
> comparatively easy death that the Nazis offered them—before the
> firing squad or in the gas chamber. And the witnesses in Jerusalem

who testified to resistance and rebellion, to 'the small place the uprising had in this history of the holocaust,' confirmed the known fact that only the very young had been capable of taking the 'decision that we cannot go and be slaughtered like sheep.'[32]

Twenty years after the revolt, despite the prominence accorded to members of the underground affiliated with Zionist youth movements who testified at the Eichmann Trial (most notably Yitzhak Zuckerman, Zivia Lubetkin, and Abba Kovner), Hashomer Hatzair still felt that their members (Kovner and Mordecai Anielewicz notwithstanding) had not received their due in the historiography. The movement felt that both the Ghetto Fighters House and Yad Vashem marginalized Hashomer Hatzair and its members as participants and members of the underground. Therefore, in 1963, Abba Kovner and other members established Moreshet (the Heritage Circle) which sought to transcend the politicization of Holocaust research.[33]

Moreshet would end up playing an instrumental role in developing projects that explored Jewish experiences beyond armed resistance, in particular through the work of Yehuda Bauer, who would go on to become the leading Holocaust scholar at the Hebrew University, and Yisrael Gutman, himself a survivor who fought in Warsaw and began his academic career after the Eichmann Trial; his *Revolt of the Besieged: Mordecai Anielewicz and the Uprising of the Warsaw Ghetto* (Hebrew, 1963) can be seen in the context of restoring Hashomer Hatzair to a more prominent role in leading the revolt. Although, as Dreifuss suggests, this early work "is based almost exclusively on Jewish sources, lacks certain historical contexts, and inserts reconstructed excerpts of Gutman's own diary along with other testimonies," Gutman's "focus on the lives of Jews in the Holocaust on the basis of their own sources and the ability to reconstruct and explain personal dilemmas as well as complex social interactions," would become a defining feature of his research and writing, and make a major contribution to the historiography of the Holocaust in general, and of the Warsaw Ghetto in particular.[34]

Despite increasing evidence of a broad range of Jewish responses to persecution during the war, however, most published historical literature on Warsaw and the Uprising itself continued to reinforce the view that the revolt in Warsaw served as the counterpoint to a history of Jewish passivity. Yuri Suhl's *They Fought Back: The Story of Jewish Resistance in Nazi Europe* was published in 1967 to counteract the notion that "too long there has been an unchallenged myth that European Jews went passively to their deaths." Suhl's volume, which provided details on revolts in Białystok, Łachwa, Tuczyn, Minsk, Vilna, Sobibor, Treblinka, Auschwitz, and elsewhere sought specifically to correct the idea that the world knows little or nothing about the other side of the Holocaust picture: Jewish resistance – how the Jews struck back at their tormentors. The epic Warsaw Ghetto uprising is famous, but it is not generally known that in practically every ghetto and in every labor and concentration camp there existed a Jewish underground organization that kept up the prisoners morale, reduced their physical sufferings, committed acts of sabotage, organized escapes, collected arms, planned revolts, and in many instances, carried them out. (1)

As Suhl argued, the disproportionate focus on the Warsaw Ghetto Uprising as the prism of Jewish memory and the focal point of historical writing on the war had obscured most other aspects of Jewish experiences during the war (and if it had overshadowed all other cases of armed resistance, it had most certainly obscured almost all other forms of Jewish experience during the war).

Speaking at a conference at Yad Vashem dedicated to the subject of "Jewish Resistance during the Holocaust" convened on the 25th anniversary of the revolt in Warsaw to present a much broader array of resistance activities (including Jewish education, underground political work, the role of youth movements, Jewish partisans, documentation projects in ghettos, the struggle for daily life, Jewish involvement in allied resistance movements, rescue work, and more), Dr. Yosef Burg (Minister of Social Welfare for the State of Israel) brought greetings on behalf of the State, less than a year after the momentous turning point in Israel's history, the Six Day War. Burg, one of the founders of the National Religious Party in Israel and an Orthodox Jew, presented the choice to engage in resistance as a major transformation in Jewish self-understanding.

I am certain that this conference will show how large a role the individual, isolated Jew, as well as the Jews organized in group frameworks, played in the struggle against the demonic oppressor. We must remember that this struggle marked a departure from the *traditional passive martyrdom and Kiddush Hashem* to a new active "sanctification of the name" – a process which involved a difficult spiritual revolution. It was a departure from the historical passivity of the believing Jew, but only a Jew who believed profoundly in the future of the Jewish people could make the transition in our generation from self-sacrificing Kiddush Hashem to the Kiddush Hashem of armed resistance. Thus our generation is a direct continuation of all the previous generations who believed in, and suffered for, the eternity of the Jewish people.[35]

Yitzhak Zuckerman, one of the leaders of the Jewish Fighting Organization, who had been stationed outside the ghetto to secure weapons when the revolt began, also spoke at the conference, offering reflections twenty-five years after the Warsaw Ghetto Revolt. While great armies engaged one another on the battlefield and mass revolts in European cities would erupt later in the war, the "Jewish revolt (in Warsaw) took place far from the great historic events, thousands of miles from the titanic battles, and many months before these other uprisings. The revolt was dictated by the existing conditions of the Jews, by the fact that they had only two alternatives – death in Treblinka, or battle." And yet, as Zuckerman explained, most of the Jews in the ghetto before the summer of 1942 did not comprehend the gravity of their predicament and "the call of the young people to resistance and armed struggle was only seen as a provocation that endangered the many." According to Zuckerman, the Zionist pioneering underground called for defense of the ghetto in terms that could be understood by the Jewish masses. Citing the words of Mordecai Tenenbaum-Tamaroff, Zuckerman noted the revolt was "the last stand of an isolated people on the precipice of destruction…fortress under siege…The spirit in which we act each day must be that of Masada. All other matters must be set aside for the sake of this one over-riding question: life or death."[36]

According to Zuckerman, "it is not remarkable that it was the Zionist pioneering youth who rejected the Diaspora, who had no faith in Jewish survival in a foreign land, who had left their homes to prepare themselves for a new life in the Eretz Yisrael – that it was precisely these young people who upheld the case for struggle within the ghettos and clung to the ghetto walls?"[37] Such arguments were not the product of 25 years of historical research on armed resistance by Jewish groups in occupied Europe, however. The opposing viewpoints on armed resistance, which focused almost exclusively on the role of Zionist youth affiliated with the Labor Zionist movements (and excluded members of the Bund, Communists, and the Revisionist Zionists) were the products of pre-war and wartime debates that colored the writing of the history of armed resistance in Warsaw at the time, in the immediate aftermath of the revolt. As a matter of historical interpretation, the inability to understand the grave danger facing the Jewish masses in Warsaw, which would erupt into bitter rivalry between Zionist groups in the ghetto who would argue that they called for the organization of armed resistance in the spring of 1942, and the Bund, who argued that lack of weaponry and outside support made the call to revolt premature, would influence the manner in which historians wrote about Jewish experiences in Warsaw before the revolt for decades after the war.

৶ ৶ ৶

Historical writing on the Holocaust, which continued to develop in the decades after the war, has not questioned the centrality of the Warsaw Ghetto Uprising as an event deserving unique focus in broader histories of the war. Lucy Dawidowicz (nee Schildkret, 1915-1990), born and raised in New York, briefly trained at Columbia University before studying and working at YIVO in Vilna before the outbreak of the war. News of the revolt in Warsaw had a profound impact on her in 1943 back in New York, where she recalled attending the memorial service at Carnegie Hall on June 19, 1943: "The events of the Warsaw ghetto burned into my consciousness…The Warsaw ghetto became a constant part of my internal life. I used to imagine myself there, test myself as to how I would have behaved. Would I have had the courage to fight? Would I have had the stamina against despair?"[38] She would dedicate her major work on the history of the Holocaust, *The War Against the Jews,* to the relatives of her husband Szymon Dawidowicz, including Toba (Tobcie) Dawidowicz, who died fighting with the Bund and the ZOB in the Warsaw ghetto, and Zarek Dawidowicz, killed at Treblinka in 1942, "two of the six million," a dedication that again reflected the duality of "heroes and martyrs." The book was divided into two parts, *The Final Solution* (focused primarily on German plans for the extermination of European Jewry) and *The Holocaust* (based primarily on Jewish responses). The penultimate chapter (and culmination point) of Dawidowicz's highly popular historical treatment was the Warsaw Ghetto Uprising (essentially concluding the book in 1943, even though the volume covered the years 1933-1945). Explaining the armed resistance organized by the youth in the Jewish political movements, Dawidowicz argued that "the young people in the Zionist and Bundist movements, reared in the ideals of secular modernity, rejected the traditionalist values and modes of behavior that had sustained Diaspora existence for centuries. Contemptuous of the long tradition of Jewish accommodation, they sought ways – whether nationalist or socialist – to combat Jewish powerlessness."[39] For both Zionists and Bundists, according to Dawidowicz (and in contrast to Yosef Burg), "the Jewish tradition of martyrdom, Kiddush-hashem, was the epitome of the Diaspora fate against which they rebelled. To them, nonbelievers, martyrdom did not mean bearing witness to God, but merely signified Jewish helplessness, passivity in the face of destruction." United by a drive for revenge against the Germans, all members of the Jewish underground engaged in resistance, not merely as a form of self-defense, according to Dawidowicz, but as "an act of desperation, whose Jewish paradigm was the suicidal stand of the zealots at Masada against Rome's imperial legions. Masada had been incorporated into modern Zionist myth under the influence of Yitzhak Lamdan's epic poem: "We have one treasure left – the daring after despair. Since hope for survival had been abandoned, one must die gloriously." (313). Concluding her account of the Warsaw Ghetto uprising with the final gassing of the ZOB headquarters on Mila 18, Dawidowicz notes "they began to kill themselves and each other, in a scene that must have rivaled the mass suicide at Masada. Mordecai Anielewicz was among them." (339.) Thus, while the Warsaw Ghetto uprising reflected the end point of the Jewish experience of the war, the final act of the Holocaust, whose participants saw it as throwing off the yoke of centuries of Jewish passivity, the destruction of the Warsaw Ghetto also marked the end of one historical time period: "there were no Jewish communities anymore, no synagogues, no Jewish schools, no Jewish life to sustain. Blood-soaked debris of Yiddish and Hebrew books at the banks of the Vistula were all that remained of the thousand-year-old civilization of Jews in Poland" (340).

Dawidowicz also sought to incorporate Jewish responses into her analysis, an implicit critique of the work of Raul Hilberg, which had relied primarily on German sources. This approach included an analysis of Jewish responses in Germany, life and death in the ghettos, the response of the official and unofficial Jewish leadership (the Judenräte and the underground), and the organization of self-help. Even so, by presenting the Warsaw Ghetto uprising as the final act of the Jews in Europe that "must have rivaled the mass suicide at Masada," Dawidowicz reinforced a tendency in the literature to present armed resistance, and specifically the case of the Warsaw Ghetto uprising, as the counterargument to Hilberg's notion that "preventive attack, armed resistance, and revenge were almost completely absent in Jewish exilic history" and "the Jewish reactions to force have always been alleviation and compliance."[40]

Scholars in Israel in the 1970s and 1980s also sought to refute what was seen as the tendency to dismiss Jewish resistance in the general historical literature as insignificant, not only by emphasizing lesser known cases of armed resistance that took place beyond Warsaw, but by expanding the definition of the term "resistance" to encompass a much broader spectrum of Jewish responses to persecution. In his study of the development of resistance in Warsaw, Yisrael Gutman sought to provide a comprehensive overview of the development of armed resistance within the context of life in the ghetto from 1939-1943. As he noted in the preface to the book (adapted from his dissertation completed at Hebrew University in 1975):

> The purpose of this work is to examine the character and conduct of the Jewish community of Warsaw in face of the persecutive tactics of the Nazi occupation regime; to throw light on the means that were adopted to cope, both intellectually and psychologically, with the grave problems of the period; and to analyze the development of the armed resistance movement and the armed struggle of the Jews of Warsaw. During the preliminary research for this book, it became clear that one cannot detach the acts of resistance and the armed uprising from the broader character of Jewish public life as it took shape during the periods of the occupation and the ghetto. I have therefore chosen to describe the growth and development of the resistance movement and the armed struggle against the wider background of ghetto life and clandestine communal activities. It is impossible to understand the significance of the resistance and the

uprising without appreciating the tensions and human and social conditions that existed during the Holocaust.[41]

Gutman made use of the materials collected by Ringelblum and the Oneg Shabbat archive to place the development of armed resistance against the broader context of the Jewish struggle to survive in the ghetto. Rather than focus merely on the underground reports or the testimonies of surviving ghetto fighters or the report of Jurgen Stroop, Gutman's comprehensive study offered a synthesis of the available source material in German, Polish, Yiddish, and Hebrew, to overcome the challenge of relying on only one viewpoint or the tendency to overlook the broad range of Jewish responses before revolt. Still, by largely overlooking the experiences of those not affiliated with the ZOB (both the ZZW and the majority of Jews who endured the final battle in the ghetto on their own) and by making the revolt the endpoint of his study, Gutman did not question how and why the Warsaw Ghetto Uprising became the turning point in history that it did, or the ways in which the collective memory of the revolt was shaped by those who survived it. Nonetheless, along with Yehuda Bauer, Gutman's work helped broaden the scope of research on Jewish responses to persecution among Holocaust historians in Israel, who began to broaden the definition of "resistance" beyond armed combat.

Yehuda Bauer defined *Amidah* as including "smuggling food into ghettos; mutual self-sacrifice within the family to avoid starvation or worse; cultural, educational, religious, and political activities taken to strengthen morale; the work of doctors, nurses, and educators to consciously maintain health and moral fiber to enable individual and group survival; and, of course, armed rebellion or the use of force (with bare hands or with 'cold' weapons) against the Germans and their collaborators."[42] Bauer also cautioned against over-emphasizing the degree of resistance, both armed and unarmed, physical and spiritual, that took place under German occupation.

A reader might get the impression that while there was suffering, the majority of the Jews were busy educating, learning, putting on plays or making music or painting, giving or listening to lectures, publishing illegal newspapers, and so on. Let me state therefore, in unmistakable language, that life was hell, the people were starving to death, and that when survivors tell us that inmates of the Łódź or Warsaw ghetto made attempts to educate their children, for instance, these attempts were heroic, but they did not encompass all or even most of the children, and they were part of a constant struggle against impossible odds.[43]

While acknowledging that armed resistance was not massive, and quantitatively speaking "was marginal," Bauer argued that nonetheless, Jewish resistance was "qualitatively an important series of events and is an important component of collective Jewish memory-quite rightly so."[44] The impact of resistance should not be measured according to the effect it had on German policies, but according to its effect on those Jews who fought and on postwar Jewish consciousness. Nonetheless, as Bauer argued, "the motivations of the rebels were several" and included the desire for revenge, escape, a drive to participate in the fight against a murderous regime for the liberation of a common homeland, or to "make a moral and political statement as Jews by taking up arms against the murders of Jews." Finally, Bauer noted, some fought in the defense of Jewish honor to convey a message to Jews in the free world, "as in the famous words of Dolek Liebeskind of the Zionist underground in Kraków; for three lines in history that will be written about the youth who fought and did not go like lambs to the slaughter it is even worth dying."[45]

In his definitive history of the Warsaw Ghetto Uprising, *Resistance* (1994), Yisrael Gutman concluded that "The Uprising was literally a revolution in Jewish history." Citing the last letter of Anielewicz, Gutman notes "Its importance was understood all too well by those who fought."[46] Gutman framed the revolt in Jewish terms writing in Introduction:

> No act of Jewish resistance during the Holocaust fired the imagination
> quite as much as the Warsaw Ghetto Uprising of April 1943. It was an
> event of epic proportions, pitting a few poorly armed, starving Jews
> against the might of the Nazi power. The ghetto Uprising was the first
> urban rebellion of consequence in any of the Nazi-occupied countries
> and was a significant point in Jewish history. The Uprising represents
> defiance and great sacrifice in a world characterized by destruction and

> death…The Warsaw Ghetto Uprising is a historical event, but it also has become a symbol of Jewish resistance and determination, a moment in history that has transformed the self-perception of the Jewish people from passivity to active armed struggle. The Uprising has shaped Israel's national self-understanding. It is viewed as the first Jewish rebellion since the heroic days of the Bar Kochba revolt in 135 CE. The Uprising has become a universal symbol of resistance and courage.[47]

In his detailed popular history of the uprising, *The Bravest Battle*, Dan Kurzman writes that the "military encounter" in the Warsaw ghetto was one of the most stirring, impossible, and important battles in history. Seldom, if ever, before has a single armed conflict produced greater heroism or more explosive political consequences. Indeed, this conflict, an enduring symbol of man's inhumanity to man, reverberated far beyond the pale that enclosed it.

> Although groups of Jews have at various times revolted against their persecutors, the Warsaw Ghetto uprising, more than any other event, symbolically ended two thousand years of Jewish submission to discrimination, oppression, and finally, genocide. It signaled the beginning of an iron militancy rooted in the will to survive, a militancy that was to be given form and direction by the creation of the state of Israel.[48]

In this sense, we have the historiographical parameters within which the Warsaw Ghetto Uprising has generally been interpreted – from the perspective of World War II history, while understood as the last, desperate act of a doomed people, it was an event that had little impact on the course of the war. From the perspective of Jewish history, however, the event came to be explained as the most significant event since the Bar Kochba Revolt of 135 CE, celebrated as a revolution in Jewish history, as the counterproof to the myth that Jews did not fight back, and generally linked to the struggle for the creation of the Jewish state after the war.

In responding to the notion that the Warsaw Ghetto Uprising was rooted in an iron militancy that was given form by the creation of the State of Israel, more recent literature in Israel has questioned the role of the Jewish state in shaping a particular Zionist memory of the Holocaust. This approach analyzes the role of the state and social/cultural structures in shaping collective memory, thereby influencing the way in which history is written and remembered.[49] The re-examination of the early years of postwar commemoration and history writing has employed the critical construct of collective memory defined by Yael Zerubavel in *Recovered Roots* "continuously negotiat(ing) between available historical records and current social and political agendas." As Zerubavel's study of the shaping of Israel's national tradition, which focuses on how the defense of Masada, the Bar Kochba Revolt, and the defense of Tel Hai were interpreted and reinterpreted, demonstrates, "Modern societies continue to develop their shared memories of their past in spite of the upsurge of historical research and writing."[50] According to Zerubavel, in the shaping of collective memory, "the master commemorative narrative thus presents these events as *turning points* that changed the course of the group's historical development and hence are commemorated in great emphasis and elaboration. In turn, the selection of certain events as turning points highlights the ideological principles underlying the master commemorative narrative by dramatizing the transitions between periods." In this sense, the Warsaw Ghetto Uprising is presented within the Zionist master commemorative narrative as a turning point in Jewish history, which changed the course of the Jewish nation's historical development.[51] In the case of the Warsaw Ghetto Uprising, the actors who participated in the uprising, the ghetto fighters who lived to tell the tale, the writers, journalists, politicians and historians all played a role in shaping a particular collective memory of the revolt. The process of shaping a particular memory of the war did not take place in the decades after the war; instead this process began contemporaneously, as events unfolded in the ghetto.

Thus, several more recent works have argued that the Labor Zionist master narrative excluded the Revisionist Zionist members of the Jewish Military Union from their rightful place in the history of the Warsaw Ghetto Uprising, including most notably Moshe Arens in *Flags Over the Ghetto: The Untold Story of the Warsaw Ghetto Uprising* (Gefen Publishing House, 2011).[52]

This re-examination not only applies to the ways in which the Holocaust has been re-interpreted in the shaping of Israeli national tradition. This approach goes hand in hand with the notion that we must also re-examine the ways in which Holocaust history, memory, and awareness developed in the United States, especially among Jews, and the timing of these developments.[53]

In response to Peter Novick's argument that American Jews paid little attention to the Holocaust until the 1960s, Hasia Diner categorically refutes the myth of silence, demonstrating that American Jews publicly and privately commemorated the Shoah in a multitude of ways between 1945-1962; and while she notes that the Warsaw Ghetto Uprising became the prism through which American Jews "performed the memory of the six million" she leaves as an open question why this might have been:

Why did the Warsaw Ghetto become the prism through which American Jews performed the memory of the six million? Did the heroism of the ghetto fighters offer them something to be proud of rather than something that caused shame? Did they use the Warsaw Ghetto as a magnet for the community mourning because other images of the Holocaust inspired in them embarrassment and discomfort?[54]

Diner clearly counters Novick's thesis that the Holocaust was marginalized in early postwar years, demonstrating the early and frequent invoking of the Holocaust in American Jewish life, but still leaves open the question of why it is that the Warsaw Ghetto Uprising became the focal point of Jewish commemorations both during and after the war.[55] Certainly, as the proliferation of survivor testimony has developed since the 1980s, offering a much broader spectrum of Jewish experiences during the war, the field of history has focused on the diverse range of experiences. This has found its way into popular culture, with a broad range of books and films. And yet, martyrs and fighters, passivity and resistance, still hold a powerful place in delineating the spectrum of response. The result has been that over several generations of research on the Holocaust, historians have continued to construct the paradigm of victims' responses between the binary poles of passivity and resistance, viewing the victims only as passive objects of the perpetrators' ferocity or as heroic ghetto fighters.

More recent works on the history of the Holocaust, such as Saul Friedlander's *The Years of Extermination* seek to correct some of the oversights of previous generations of historiography by writing an "integrated history" of the Holocaust which should, according to Friedlander, "include the reactions (and at times the initiatives) of the surrounding world and the attitudes of the victims, for the fundamental reason that the events we call the Holocaust represent a totality defined by this very convergence of distinct elements."[56] Friedlander's assessment provides a more balanced assessment of the meaning and impact of the revolt in Warsaw, too, which he interprets in light of Yehoshua Perle's harsh judgment of the Warsaw ghetto population in *Khurbn Varshe*. Perle, a Polish-Jewish novelist active in the Yiddish underground cultural organization in the Warsaw Ghetto, YIKOR, wrote *Khurbn Varshe* for the Oneg Shabbes archive in October 1942 after the horrible deportations to Treblinka, and condemned Jewish behavior, and especially Jewish leadership in the ghetto, writing that "each one (in Warsaw) was out to save his own skin. Each one was ready to sacrifice even his own father, his own mother, his own wife and children."[57]

According to Friedlander, then:

> The events of April 1943 introduced a new perspective. Of course the Warsaw fighters did not seek even a minimal success in military terms. Whether they wanted to redeem the image of Jews facing death, and to erase, so to speak, Perle's terrible verdict, is not certain, either. They knew that most of a leaderless, hungry, and utterly desperate mass could not but passively submit to unbridled violence, before the uprising and no less so in its wake. Not all of them meant to send a message to their own political movements in Eretz Israel or to the socialist community: For a long time already, many had given up on the active solidarity of their comrades outside Europe. They just wanted, as they had proclaimed, to die with dignity.[58]

The context matters – in the aftermath of the horrific devastation and shame wrought both by the great deportation and Jewish behavior at the time, the actions of those who fought back in the ghetto must be seen as a choice to "die with dignity" – in the formulation of the Oneg Shabbes: "to live with honor, and die with honor." And yet, while such assessments offer the benefit of contextual understanding of Jewish behavior and the meaning of resistance, it is clear that as it occurred and in its aftermath, both participants and observers sought to interpret and impose a political meaning onto the event.

All the same, Friedlander's work does raise a question – if the war and the relentless persecution led to a complete breakdown of Jewish social structures and any notion of Jewish solidarity; if in fact Yehoshua Perle was correct in his assessment that "each was out to save his own skin" then what was revolutionary about the revolt was not the fact that it represented a throwing off of the yoke of Jewish passivity in the ghetto; instead the uprising literally represented a revolt not against Nazi oppression, but a revolt against patterns of Jewish behavior and Jewish leadership that had developed under three years of Nazi rule. In *The Years of Extermination*, Saul Friedlander notes the impact of increasing persecution on Jewish solidarity: "one of the most basic aspects of the dramatically changing Jewish condition appears to be the ongoing disintegration of overall Jewish solidarity—insofar as it ever existed…." In Germany, Poland and France, groups of Jews made distinctions among one another on the basis of class, religious affiliation, country of origin, political background, and more. And as Friedlander also suggests, "obversely, a strengthening of bonds appeared within small groups sharing a specific political or religious background. Such was typically the case in political youth groups in the ghettos, among Jewish scouts in France, and of course, among this or that group of Orthodox Jews. Such developments should not lead to disregarding the widespread welfare efforts, or the education or cultural activities open to all; yet a trend was becoming apparent: It would greatly intensify with the growth of the external threat."[59]

And indeed, studies of smaller groups of Jews in the ghetto reveal such strengthening of bonds. One of the most significant additions to the literature on the Warsaw Ghetto in recent years, which adds to a broader definition of "resistance" in the ghetto – not only as armed resistance, but including forms of defiance like the Oyneg Shabbes documentation project, is Samuel Kassow's *Who Will Write Our History?: Emanuel Ringelblum, the Warsaw Ghetto, and the Oyneg Shabes Archive* (Bloomington: Indiana University Press, 2007). Kassow demonstrates convincingly that to understand Jewish responses to persecution in Warsaw, such responses must be placed in the context of prewar and wartime experiences and examined through the lens of those groups in the ghetto that had contact with the greatest number of Jews in the ghetto. While most research and writing had focused on either the role of the Jewish Council or the resistance organizations, "it was precisely the(se) intermediate organizations that had the closest daily contact with ordinary Jews in certain ghettos. The Oyneg Shabbes was embedded in, and grew out of, the single most important of these "intermediate organization(s)," the Aleynhilf (literally,

"Self-Help") that Ringelblum took part in organizing in the Warsaw Ghetto." (p. 14) Kassow demonstrates the value in studying Jewish experiences in the ghetto through organizations like the Aleynhilf and the Oyneg Shabbes, which were aligned with a broader social base in the ghetto and provide a lens onto a much wider range of social activities in the ghetto, which include but are not limited to relations with the Jewish councils and the development of armed resistance. Other newer projects which expand on diverse responses of Jews in the Warsaw Ghetto include Gunnar Paulsson, *Secret City: The Hidden Jews of Warsaw, 1940-1945* (New Haven: Yale University Press, 2002. Engelking and Leociak, *The Warsaw Ghetto: A Guide to the Perished City* (Yale University Press, 2009) and David Roskies, ed., *Voices from the Warsaw Ghetto: Writing Our History* (Yale University, 2019).

Most recently, Havi Dreifuss' work, which expands on the experiences of thousands of Jews who remained in the ghetto until its final destruction (and were not affiliated with the Jewish Fighting Organization, which counted fewer than 500 members) adds to a broader understanding of the final weeks and months of the ghetto. The book points to the need to broaden the focus beyond the underground and the Jewish council, to write a history of the ghetto that includes the Jewish masses.[60] Dreifuss has identified a critical gap – what were the experiences of the 40,000 Jews left in the Warsaw Ghetto after the deportations to Treblinka – those Jews who constituted the vast majority of the surviving Jewish population in Warsaw but were not members of the Jewish Fighting Organization (ZOB) or Jewish Military Union (ZZW)?

During and after the war, surviving ghetto fighters played a prominent role in distinguishing their actions from the Jewish masses who "refused to believe" information of Nazi plans for extermination and boarded the deportation trains, marching like "lambs to the slaughter." Dreifuss' new analysis challenges the distinction between "fighters" and "lambs to the slaughter" by offering a much broader context for resistance activities, challenging the notion of an armed underground who led the revolt (because for the revolt to succeed it needed the participation of the Jewish masses – the revolt did not succeed despite the Jewish masses), and instead reinforcing a point that actually emerged in early reports about the revolt in Warsaw – that it was distinguished by the fact it was a broad popular uprising. The Warsaw Ghetto Uprising was not a revolt of several hundred armed fighters who battled German soldiers, SS troops, and Ukrainian auxiliaries despite the presence of thousands of unarmed civilians in the ghetto; on the contrary, the revolt must be understood as the determined resistance of those thousands of unarmed Jews in the ghetto who resolved to go into hiding, defy deportation orders, and force the Germans to round up each and every Jew in the ghetto to complete the liquidation. Turning the historiography on its head, Dreifuss' book makes the convincing case that we have misunderstood the significance of the revolt for generations: it was not the battle of the armed fighters that made this such a unique historical event; as she argues: "There were those who emphasized that next to the armed struggle there was another struggle, the struggle of the masses of tens of thousands of Jews who hid in hiding places in the burning ghetto. Nonetheless the masses of the Jewish public - who in their lives and deaths gave the revolt its popular character - have never stood at the center of research and their fate has been ignored."[61]

Despite such progress in historical writing on the Warsaw ghetto and the revolt, it is clear that the topic remains politically fraught, and that interpretations of the meaning and significance of this history are colored by current events. In his remarks at the 75th anniversary ceremony to commemorate the Warsaw Ghetto Uprising on April 19, 2018, President of Poland Andrzej Duda, emphasized that the fighters in the Warsaw ghetto were Polish citizens, that they had "flown both the Jewish blue-and-white flag, as well as the Polish red-and-white flag," over the walls of the ghetto during the revolt, that they received "rifles and machine guns" from the Polish underground, and that the news of the revolt that was broadcast by the BBC had been delivered by the Polish government-in-exile in London. With a nod to Poland's recent Holocaust law, Duda said that "those who talk about Polish co-responsibility for the genocide of the Jews hurt both of us." What was the meaning of the revolt 75 years later, according to the President of Poland? The Warsaw Ghetto Uprising, he seemed to suggest, was a battle of Polish Jews, determined to fight to preserve what little dignity they had managed to maintain, in order to defend freedom and the Polish nation. Likewise, recent controversies over the Museum of the Warsaw Ghetto and its chief historian, Daniel Blatman, who numerous Polish and Israeli Holocaust scholars say is being used by the Polish government and/or is a willing participant in historical distortions, suggest that historical writing on the Warsaw Ghetto and the Uprising will continue to command disproportionate attention both in the field of Holocaust Studies and in popular memory of the Shoah.

Endnotes

1   Michael Meng, *Shattered Spaces: Jewish Sites in Germany and Poland after 1945* (Ph.D. Dissertation, UNC-Chapel Hill, 2008), p. 107; see also Artur Eisenbach, "The Jewish Population in Warsaw at the End of the Nineteenth Century," in Władysław Bartoszewski and Antony Polonsky, eds., The Jews in Warsaw: A History (Cambridge, Mass.: Blackwell, 1991), 108; Zalewska, Ludność, pp. 49-53.)

2   Antony Polonsky, "Warsaw" *YIVO Encyclopedia,* http://www.yivoencyclopedia.org/article.aspx/Warsaw.

3   See statistics in Ezra Mendelsohn, *The Jews of East Central Europe Between the Two World Wars.*

4   Barbara Engelking and Jacek Leociak, *The Warsaw Ghetto: A Guide to the Perished City* (New Haven: Yale University Press, 2009), p. 15.

5   See as cited in Garbarini, Kerenji, Lambertz, and Patt, *Jewish Responses to Persecution, 1938-1940* (USHMM/AltaMira Press, 2011), p. 121.

6   Barbara Engelking and Jacek Leociak, *The Warsaw Ghetto: A Guide to the Perished City* (New Haven: Yale University Press, 2009), pp. 47-48.

7   Gutman, pp. 60-61. It is impossible to provide accurate numbers of Jewish refugees and ghetto inhabitants in Warsaw for this chaotic period. Israel Gutman cites 130,000 Jewish refugees in Warsaw by April 1941, while Yehuda Bauer estimates the number of Jewish refugees in the city at 150,000 after September 1940. Yisrael Gutman, *The Jews of Warsaw, 1939-1943: Ghetto, Underground, Revolt* (Bloomington: Indiana University Press, 1982), p. 63; Bauer, *American Jewry,* p. 69. Barbara Engelking and Jacek Leociak estimate the peak number of inhabitants of the Warsaw ghetto at 460,000 in March 1941 (15,000 more than Gutman's number for the same month), and quote Nazi documents that put the number as high as 490,000, p. 49.

8   Gerhard Weinberg, "The Final Solution and the War in 1943," in *Revolt Amid the Darkness* (Washington, DC: United States Holocaust Memorial Museum, 1993), p. 6.

9   Nechama Tec, *Resistance: Jews and Christians Who Defied the Nazi Terror,* (Oxford: Oxford University Press, 2013) p. 15.

10 Richard Kaplan, "The Myth of Jewish Passivity" in Patrick Henry, ed., *Jewish Resistance Against the Nazis* (Washington, D.C., Catholic University Press, 2014).

11 See in Hilberg, "The Destruction of the European Jews: Precedents" in Omer Bartov, ed., *The Holocaust: Origins, Implementation, Aftermath* (New York: Routledge, 2000), pp. 39-40.

12 For a through and fascinating analysis of the history of the term "sheep to the slaughter," see Yael S. Feldman, "'Not as Sheep Led to Slaughter'? On Trauma, Selective Memory, and the Making of Historical Consciousness," *Jewish Social Studies: History, Culture, Society* n.s. 19, no. 5 (Spring/Summer 2013), pp. 159-169.

13 See https://www.nytimes.com/2014/11/11/arts/survivor-who-hated-the-spotlight.html?_r=0)

14 See Avinoam Patt, "The Jewish Heroes of Warsaw: The Meaning of the Revolt in the First Year after the Uprising," in *American Jewish History* (Volume 103, Issue 2, April 2019), 147-175.

15 Shlomo Mendelsohn, *The Battle of the Warsaw Ghetto* (New York: Jewish Scientific Institute-YIVO, 1944). The paper was also published in Yiddish in Yivo bleter 13 (January/February 1944).

16 The Bund also published the *Zygielbojm Bukh* (New York: Farlag Unser Tsait, 1947), which chronicled the history of the ghetto through the lens of Szmuel Zygielbojm, the Bundist activist who committed suicide in May 1943, following news of the death of his family during the Warsaw Ghetto Uprising.

17 *The Warsaw Ghetto Rising*, published by The World Union Poale-Zion (Z.S.) – Hitachduth (Tel Aviv, publication date February 1944; Dated November 1944).

18 Philip Freidman and Koppel S. Pinson, "Some Books on the Jewish Catastrophe," *Jewish Social Studies*, Vol. 12, No. 1 (Jan., 1950), pp. 83-94. See also the dissertation of Mark Smith, "The Yiddish Historians and the Struggle for a Jewish History of the Holocaust." (UCLA, 2016).

19 Published in Yiddish in 1946 by the Central Yiddish Culture Organization and in 1947, *Ashes and Fire: On the Ruins of Poland*, (New York: International Universities Press, 1947). See Pat, *Ash un Fayer*, p. 385.

20 Lehrman, Review of Ashes and Fire, by Jacob Pat. https://www.commentarymagazine.com/articles/ashes-and-fire-by-jacob-pat/

21 Friedman also published a summary of "The European Jewish Research on the Recent Jewish Catastrophe in 1939-1945," in the *Proceedings of the American Academy for Jewish Research*, Vol. 18 (1948 - 1949), pp. 179-211. For a list of publications just on Warsaw by 1948, see Z. Szajkowski (YIVO-Bleter, vol. XXX, #2 pp. 2).

22 Roni Stauber, *The Holocaust in Israeli Public Debate in the 1950s: Ideology and Memory. (Portland: Valentine Mitchell, 2007).*

23 Havi Dreifuss, "Jewish Historiography of the Holocaust in Eastern Europe", *POLIN: Studies in Polish Jewry, vol 29, Writing Jewish History in Eastern Europe*, Natalia Aleksiun, Brian Horowitz, and Antony Polonsky, eds, (Oxford: Littman Library of Jewish Civilization, 2017), p. 228.

24 See Dreifuss, p. 229.

25 See Stauber, p. 169.

26 As Stauber points out, this may have reflected the debate over whether to stay in the ghetto or go to the forests amongst the underground movements in some of the larger ghettos.

27 Stauber, pp. 174-175.

28 Hilberg, *The Destruction of the European Jews, p.* 324. (Chicago: Quadrangle Books, 1961.

29 *Raul Hilberg, Destruction of European Jews*, p. 318.

30 Ibid.

31 Gideon Hausner, "Six Million Accusers," excerpt reprinted in Paul Mendes-Flohr and Jehuda Reinharz, eds., *The Jew in the Modern World: A Documentary History,* Third Edition, (New York: Oxford University Press, 2011), p. 788. See also Anita Shapira, "The Eichmann Trial: Changing Perspectives," *Journal of Israeli History Politics, Society, Culture,* Volume 23, 2004, p. 18-39.

32 Hannah Arendt, "Eichmann in Jerusalem, I), *The New Yorker*, February 16, 1963) https://www.newyorker.com/magazine/1963/02/16/eichmann-in-jerusalem-i

33 Dreifuss, "Jewish Historiography of the Holocaust in Eastern Europe", p. 232-33.

34 For the gradual entrance of Gutman into Holocaust research, see H. Dreifuss, "'They are so alive inside me': Israel Gutman (1923-2013): Holocaust Survivor, Ghetto Fighter, and Jewish Historian", *Yad Vashem Studies*, 41 (2014), pp. 23-53.

35 "Greetings on Behalf of the State of Israel by his excellency the Minister of Social Welfare, Dr. Yosef Burg," in *Jewish Resistance during the Holocaust,* April 1968 (Jerusalem, 1971), pp. 15-16.

36 Mordecai Tenenbaum-Tamaroff, *Yediot* (Warsaw Ghetto Underground publication), June 9, 1942, cited by Yitzhak Zuckerman, in *Jewish Resistance during the Holocaust*, 24.

37 Ibid. Zuckerman, p. 27.

38 Dawidowicz, Lucy S. *From That Place and Time: A Memoir, 1938-1947.* (New York, 1989), See also: http://motlc.wiesenthal.com/site/pp.asp?c=ivKVLcMVIsG&b=476149

39 Dawidowicz, *The War Against the Jews*, p. 312.

40 See in Hilberg, *Destruction of European Jews*, p. 14 (Chicago, 1961) and reprinted in "The Destruction of the European Jews: Precedents" in Omer Bartov, ed., *The Holocaust: Origins, Implementation, Aftermath* (New York: Routledge, 2000), pp. 39-40.

41 Israel Gutman, *The Jews of Warsaw, 1939-1943: Ghetto, Underground, Revolt*, ix.

42 Bauer, *Rethinking the Holocaust* (New Haven and London: Yale University Press, 2001), p. 120.

43 Bauer, *Rethinking the Holocaust*, p. 127.

44 Ibid., p. 136.

45 Ibid., p. 141.

46 Israel Gutman, *Resistance: The Warsaw Ghetto Uprising* (New York: Houghton Mifflin, in association with USHMM, 1994), xx.

47 Gutman, *Resistance*, p. xi. My emphasis.

48 Dan Kurzman, *The Bravest Battle: The Twenty-Eight Days of the Warsaw Ghetto Uprising* (Da Capo Press, 1993), 17.

49 See for example, Ofer, Dalia. "The Past That Does Not Pass: Israelis and Holocaust Memory." *Israeli Studies* 14, no. 1 (2009); pp. 1–35; Ofer, Dalia. "The Strength of Remembrance: Commemorating the Holocaust During the First Decade of Israel." *Jewish Social Studies* 6, no. 2 (2000), pp. 24–55; Segev, Tom. *The Seventh Million: The Israelis and the Holocaust* (New York: Hill and Wang, 1993); Stauber, Roni. *The Holocaust in Israeli Public Debate in the 1950s: Ideology and Memory.* (Valentine Mitchell, 2007); Zertal, Idith. *Israel's Holocaust and the Politics of Nationhood.* (Cambridge: Cambridge University Press, 2005). For an earlier example of the post-Zionist trend, see Shabtai B. Beit-Tzvi, *Hatzionut Hapost-Ugandit Bemashber Hashoah (Post-Uganda Zionism in face of the Holocaust Crisis)*, Tel Aviv 1977).

50 Zerubavel, p. 5

51 Ibid., p. 9. See also, for example: Zerubavel, 'The Death of Memory and the Memory of Death: Masada and the Holocaust as Historical Metaphors". Author(s): Yael Zerubavel Source: *Representations*, No. 45 (Winter, 1994), 72-100.

52 See also Arens, "The Jewish Military Organization in the Warsaw Ghetto," *Holocaust and Genocide Studies,* vol. 19 (2), Fall 2005, pp. 201-225 and Dariusz Libionka and Laurence Weinbaum, "Deconstructing Memory and History: The Jewish Military Union (ZZW) and the Warsaw Ghetto Uprising," *Jewish Political Studies Review* 18:1-2 (Spring 2006). The history of the Warsaw Ghetto Uprising has also been a central point in debates over Polish-Jewish relations during the war. As Joshua Zimmerman notes in *The Polish Underground and the Jews, 1939-1945* "The Warsaw Ghetto Uprising is in many ways the axis around which the problem of wartime Polish-Jewish relations is discussed." Zimmerman also highlights the degree to which the sources of Jewish histories of revolt influence the perception of Polish assistance – fighters affiliated with Bundist groups,

Labor Zionist groups, Revisionist Zionist groups, Communists, and other all had differing perception of the degree to which they could expect or received assistance from the Polish Underground.

53 Peter Novick, *The Holocaust in American Life* (New York, 1999).

54 Hasia Diner, *We Remember with Reverence and Love: American Jews and the Myth of Silence after the Holocaust*, (New York: NYU Press, 2010), p. 74.

55 David Slucki, "A Community of Suffering: Jewish Holocaust Survivor Networks in Postwar America," *Jewish Social Studies: History, Culture, Society* n.s. 22, no. 2 (Winter 2017): pp. 116–145 also argues against the "myth of silence" highlighting the active role played by survivor organizations, especially the Katsetler Farband in emphasizing Jewish resistance in the creation of a "community of memory" and focuses on the group's work in the early postwar period.

56 Friedländer, *Years of Extermination, (xv)*.

57 Ibid., p. 528.

58 Ibid.

59 Ibid., p. 192.

60 Likewise, more encyclopedic approaches to the history of the ghetto as a whole, such as Barbara Engelking and Jacek Leociak, *The Warsaw Ghetto: A Guide to the Perished City* (Yale University Press, 2009) provide a much broader "collection of studies on various issues connected with the sealed district." Their guide, "also an atlas of the Warsaw Ghetto" replete with maps which form "an integral part of the guide," covers geography, institutions, administration, economic life, spiritual resistance in the form of culture, arts, religion, the Ringelblum Archive, the Great Deportation, the Uprising, and finally the period in the ghetto after the Uprising until Liberation. As such, the *Warsaw Ghetto* guide encompasses a much broader examination of the life and death of the ghetto than a study of the revolt itself, reflecting a broader historiographic appreciation for the life and death of Jewish Warsaw as a whole.

61 Havi Dreifuss, *Geto Varsha – Sof* (*The Warsaw Ghetto – The End*, April 1942-June 1943), (Jerusalem: Yad Vashem, 2018), p. 11.

Nikola Zimring

The Controversy of the Missing Warning for Hungarian Jews in the Vrba-Wetzler Report[1]

It was Monday, April 10, 1944, late afternoon. For three days, Rudolf Vrba and Alfréd Wetzler, two Auschwitz-Birkenau prisoners, had been cowering under the planks in a tiny bunker in the camp's construction site, outside the heavily guarded inner perimeter where the prisoners slept. They were at the final stage of their escape. Because secrecy was essential for the smooth running of the Birkenau death factory, the camp was heavily guarded and any attempt to escape was severely punished. But Vrba and Wetzler had learned from their observations that there was a flaw in the elaborate mechanism set in place to prevent escapes. Whenever a prisoner was reported missing, the camp and its immediate surroundings were meticulously searched for three days, after which time it was assumed that the prisoner had escaped and the search was abandoned. Vrba and Wetzler reasoned that if they could hide for those critical three days, they would have a fair chance to slip out of the camp unobserved after the search was called off.

For two years they had planned and awaited this moment when they would leave Birkenau, expose the terrible crimes committed there to the outside world, and spur the world to take action to liberate the camp and warn potential victims about the true purpose of Birkenau. They collected all available data, including verifiable information, carefully, painstakingly, and responsibly in order to make their testimony credible so their warning would be taken seriously.

Finally, they heard the sound of the sirens announcing the halt of the search. They waited just a little more, then they quietly snuck out of the bunker, carefully rearranged the planks so that the hiding place could be used again, and disappeared into the darkness in the direction of their native Slovakia.[2] They crossed the border on April 21 and immediately connected with the Jewish clandestine movement, the so-called Working Group. With the Working

Group's assistance, they composed a 28-page detailed statement known today as the Vrba Wetzler Report or the Auschwitz Protocols.[3] *The Report* reached the free world at the end of May, and caused an uproar. In June, the shorter version of the *Report* was reprinted hundreds of times in western newspapers[4] and even broadcast by the BBC.[5] The impact of Vrba and Wetzler's efforts was crucial to what was described by Martin Gilbert as the largest single rescue of Jews in WWII.[6] The revelations about the true purpose of Birkenau played a significant role in the decisions of the American president Franklin D. Roosevelt, as well as of Pope Pius XII and King Gustav of Sweden, to compel Hungarian leader Miklós Horthy to stop the outgoing transports of Hungarian Jewry to Auschwitz-Birkenau. He submitted to their demands on July 7, 1944, saving approximately 200,000 Jews in central Hungary from death in the Auschwitz gas chambers.[7] Unfortunately, however, between May 15 and July 9, 1944 (two days after Horthy's order) 437,000 Hungarian Jews were deported to Auschwitz, and most of them perished there.

In the early 60s Vrba, who was living in England at that time, undertook to share his story for the first time since the end of the war in a series of five articles under the title "I Warned the World of Eichmann's Murders," published in the London based *Daily Herald* and subsequently, in 1963 in the memoir *I Cannot Forgive.*[8] The memoir's title did not refer to the Nazis but rather to the Slovakian and primarily Hungarian-Jewish leadership who Vrba blamed for not acting more quickly and efficiently on the information they had received from him. During his life Vrba published many articles in various journals, gave countless interviews, and participated in several documentary movies in which he reiterated his stance.[9]

Vrba always maintained that the main motivation for the escape from Auschwitz-Birkenau was to alert Hungarian Jewry about their impending annihilation. Curiously, the specific warning for the Hungarian Jews is not present in *The Report*, which does, however, contain speculations about the expected arrival of Greece's Jewish transports. This missing warning in *The Report* about the fate of the Hungarian Jews set off a discussion among historians regarding whether Vrba and Wetzler could even have known - before their escape - about the impending fate of Hungarians. Assuming they could have, and did, why wasn't the information included in *The Report*? The present study aims to review this debate. I will first briefly introduce Vrba and Wetzler and their whereabouts before and in Auschwitz, the circumstances of the escape and creation of the Vrba Wetzler Report. I will then introduce the debate among the protagonists as well as historians seeking to explain the lacuna.

Vrba and Wetzler in Slovakia

Rudolf Vrba was born Walter Rosenberg (he adopted the name Rudolf Vrba after his escape from Auschwitz), in 1924, in Topolčany in the Slovakian part of what was then Czechoslovakia. His mother was widowed when he was four, and they (eventually) relocated to Trnava, where she remarried and "built up a small dress-making business from more or less nothing."[10] Alfred Wetzler, who was six years older than Vrba, was born and grew up in Trnava, and because neither he nor his family could afford to finance further studies, he worked there as a laborer after completing high school.[11] Vrba and Wetzler knew each other casually from Trnava.

The Slovaks, led by Catholic priest Jozef Tiso[12] and his "People's Party," desperately wanted to preserve this historical first instance of independence, that was declared on March 14, 1939 and to restore the territories annexed by Hungary on November 2, 1938.[13] For that they needed to secure Germany's patronage. On March 23, 1939, the Treaty of Protection (*Schutzvertrag*) signed by the Germans and the Slovak state guaranteed to the Germans the subordination of Slovakian foreign policy and essentially transformed the Slovak state into a satellite of the Reich.[14]

The Slovak state almost immediately adopted a number of antisemitic laws - the first one as early as one month after the establishment of independent Slovakia – in part to satisfy its own antisemitism and in part to pander to their German allies. Slovak soldiers participated in the invasion of Poland, which made them the first foreign soldiers to participate in Nazi aggression. Wetzler, too, was summoned to compulsory military service, where he as a non-Aryan served for two years in a military forced labor camp.[15] Vrba, who was fifteen at that time, was forced to leave high school and was prohibited from work other than as a laborer for reduced wages due to the new antisemitic legislation.[16]

The anti-Jewish policies gradually stripped the Jews of their property and means to make money. This posed a problem for the government, which was unwilling to put effort into finding a solution to the resulting fallout and certainly was unwilling to support the disenfranchised Jews financially. The Slovakian officials thus welcomed the opportunity to "relocate" the Jews to the territories in the east with relief. It is not clear whether the idea of this "solution" originated in Berlin or in Bratislava.[17] Between March and October 1942, 58,000 of the 89,000 Slovakian Jews were deported to either Auschwitz, Lublin (Majdanek), or Sobibor; —Wetzler and Vrba among them. Only a handful of the deported ever returned.[18]

Wetzler was detained upon his return home from military service on April 9, 1942, at his parents' house by the Hlinka Guard[19] and sent through the Sered transit camp to Auschwitz.[20]

Vrba's arrival in Auschwitz was more convoluted. He very much wanted to contribute in the fight against the Nazis and join the forces of the Czechoslovak exiled government. He managed to cross the border to Hungary illegally, reach Budapest, and meet Jewish activists who promised him false papers. For mysterious reasons, Vrba was to pick up the false papers in Slovakia. While crossing the border back home, Vrba was caught by the Hungarian border guards and handed over to the Slovakian authorities. He was sent to the Nováky transit camp, from which he managed to escape, if only for a few days. Deemed a troublemaker, upon his capture he was immediately added to the next transport "to the east" to Majdanek, where he stayed for 12 days, after which, on June 27th 1942, he was transferred to Auschwitz.[21]

Vrba and Wetzler in Auschwitz

When Wetzler first arrived in Auschwitz, in April, 1942, Birkenau (Auschwitz II) – which today is an iconic symbol of the Holocaust and destruction of European Jewry - consisted of only three buildings and a kitchen. Wetzler was incorporated into the working unit that constructed the barracks in the camp. He subsequently toiled in the German armament factories at the Auschwitz complex.[22]

Approximately three months after his arrival, Wetzler obtained an administrative position as a *Schreiber*[23] – first at the "French block" in Birkenau section B-I-b, then in the same section, in the "Hospital" at block 7. On the one hand, it was a huge improvement, since he was now sheltered and avoided hard physical labor; on the other hand, the hospital aroused horror in the inmates, including Wetzler. It was nicknamed "the waiting room for death;" all the patients, including the ones who recovered, were sent to the gas chambers. During Wetzler's time in the "hospital," more than 50,000 inmates were murdered.[24] It is my belief that Wetzler's "hospital" assignment scarred him for his entire life.

Beginning in January 1943 Wetzler worked as a *Schreiber* in the mortuary in Birkenau's block B-I-b. Before cremation, whenever prisoners died of "natural causes," or were "selected" for death or otherwise killed, they were first processed in the morgue. Wetzler's task was to record the day, the deceased prisoner's number, and the block or kommando to which the prisoner belonged. The purpose of his job was to track the numbers of the deceased prisoners and to ensure that no one was unaccounted for, for example a possible escapee. Wetzler also kept track of the gold teeth extracted from the deceased.[25] From June 1943, Wetzler worked as a clerk in different blocks of the B-II-d area of Birkenau.[26]

Vrba's first assignment was in Auschwitz's main camp, in an SS food storeroom. His job was to unload the food supplies from railway wagons and stack them neatly. He was able occasionally to steal food and to stay clean, which latter opportunity was crucial in Auschwitz since the place was rife with diseases, and the unsanitary conditions in the camp were dangerous to the prisoners. Unfortunately, Vrba's Kapo was caught stealing, and, as punishment, Vrba was transferred to Buna Kommando, which built factories for I.G. Farben.[27] The conditions there were so horrible that the average life expectancy of the prisoners was 3-4 months.[28] Vrba was there for five weeks. Then, circumstances tilted in Vrba's favor. A terrible typhus epidemic broke out and all the prisoners were ordered to undergo a selection. Vrba was able to obtain a newly opened position in the *Aufräumungskommando* unit. His new job consisted of meeting the newly arrived deportees to Birkenau at the ramp, collecting their property, and then hiding all signs of the "human cargo" from the freight cars so the next "cargo" would see no clues about what awaited them.[29] He also sorted the property in a storage area nicknamed Kanada by the prisoners for the vast resources they imagined Canada had. From this position, he was able to observe the transports, where they came from, their numbers and dates; and he also learned how unaware the newly arrived were about the place they now found themselves.[30] Vrba worked there until June 1943. Upon his arrival to the camp, Vrba was housed in block 4 in Auschwitz I; however, on January 15th, 1943, his whole working kommando was transferred to Birkenau, section B-I-b, block 16. His assignment did not change in the transfer.[31]

On June 8, 1943, Vrba was appointed registrar in the quarantine camp for men, in section B-II-a. The newcomers who were selected for labor (approximately 10-15%) were all initially brought to the quarantine camp, where they were registered.[32] This position allowed Vrba to collect additional information and verify his previous estimates.

I have detailed Vrba and Wetzler's positions in order to clarify their ability to observe the camp modus operandi and to gather data on the victims as well as the perpetrators. These details are also important for determining whether or not Wetzler and Vrba could have known about the coming mass deportation of the Hungarian Jews.

Both Vrba and Wetzler were relatively fortunate. They were not compromised by hunger, grief over the loss of family, and fatigue from slave labor. Only a small fraction of the prisoners – for the most part, those who came to the camp relatively early, the "old-timers," or prisoners with connections - were able to obtain jobs that enabled them a relatively better quality of life, such as the work in "Kanada" or as a *Schreiber*. They were sheltered from the bad weather and they could occasionally "organize"[33] food, medicine, warmer clothes or other valuables for themselves or for exchange. Their positions also provided them with relative freedom of movement. Additionally, they would regularly meet fellow old-timer prisoners after work, which allowed them to comfort and encourage each other as well as to exchange information that would be otherwise out of reach of Vrba and Wetzler (namely, the information they could not witness). The most notable among these old-timers was Filip Müller,[34] a Slovakian who worked in the crematoria. Müller was a member of the *Sonderkommando*, a "special work unit," whose task it was to dispose of the bodies of the gas chamber victims as well as prisoners who died in the camp from "natural causes."

Unique Situation of Hungarian Jewish Community

At the time of Vrba and Wetzler's escape, Hungary had the sole remaining large intact Jewish community in Nazi-dominated Europe. The Hungarians, aching to reclaim territories lost after WWI in the 1920 Treaty of Trianon, became Germany's ally. With Germany's backing, between 1938 and 1941, Hungary gradually regained parts of southern Slovakia and Carpathian Ruthenia (both formerly portions of Czechoslovakia), Northern Transylvania (Romania), and parts of Northern Yugoslavia. With the annexation Hungary's size doubled and its Jewish population reached 825,000.[35]

Despite the numerous anti-Jewish laws[36] and the Nazi rampage in Europe, Hungarian Jews remained relatively untouched and "survived the first four-and-one-half years of the Second World War almost oblivious to what was happening to the other Jewish communities in Nazi-dominated Europe."[37] The exception were young Jews who were conscripted to the forced labor service units and who were treated with the utmost abuse and brutality (which caused the death of approximately 42,000 of them), and Jews who were defined as non-Hungarian citizens - around 18,000 mostly Polish and Russian refugees were murdered in the Kamenetz-Podolsk Massacre in Ukraine in the summer of 1941, and around 1,000 were murdered in the Újvidék Massacre (Novi Sad raid) in the regained part of Yugoslavia at the beginning of 1942.[38]

On March 19, 1944, the Germans invaded Hungary in order to thwart attempts to break from the alliance. Adolf Eichmann, too, arrived with his tiny team of "final solution" experts - Dieter Wisliceny,[39] Hermann Krumey and Otto Hunsche.[40] They were eager to implement what Horthy – a self-proclaimed antisemite – had stubbornly resisted and what they had cultivated to perfection.

Escape and Creation of *The Report*

Vrba and Wetzler escaped Birkenau approximately three weeks after the German invasion of Hungary. From the beginning they planned to flee to their native Slovakia, since even though it was a Nazi satellite state and the locals were hostile to Jews, it was still their best chance to go unnoticed, as they knew the language and the realities there. In addition, they also hoped to be able to warn or receive help from some of their family members, friends or acquaintances. The distance between Auschwitz-Birkenau and the Slovakian border was 130 km in a straight line through mountainous and unfriendly terrain. They traveled during the night and rested in hiding during the day. Despite their careful measures, they frequently became lost and at one point they were spotted by a German patrol and shot at.

In the meantime, restrictions were being imposed in rapid succession on Hungarian Jews with the aim to isolate and impoverish the community. They were prohibited from traveling, and they were not allowed to keep private vehicles. Phone lines were disconnected, bank accounts were blocked. Apartments, jewelry, radios, bicycles and other property were confiscated; all employment of Jews was terminated, Jewish businesses were closed, and food rations were decreased. All Jews were required to wear the yellow Star of David for easy identification. By the middle of April the process of ghettoization had begun.[41]

On April 21, 1944, Vrba and Wetzler reached Slovakia. A week later, they were putting the finishing touches on their 28-page report in the basement of a Jewish retirement home in Žilina, assisted by the key members of the Jewish clandestine organization Working Group: Oscar Krasniansky[42] and Oskar Neumann. The final version of their report was typed on April 27, 1944,[43] almost six weeks after the German invasion of Hungary.

Krasniansky swiftly translated *The Report* from Slovak to German (the original Slovak version is lost), added to it a short foreword wherein he vouched for the authenticity of *The Report* and its authors (whose identities were withheld) and immediately distributed it to his international as well as domestic contacts, which he as a seasoned activist had cultivated over the years. The copies were dispatched to the following contacts: through Mikus (Mikuláš) Sternfeld – a Jewish businessman based in Bratislava - to Giuseppe Burzio, the Papal Apostolic Delegate in Slovakia; to Nathan Schwalb of the Hechalutz Movement in Geneva; the Yeshuv Rescue Mission in Constantinople; and to Rudolf Kasztner a bold member of the Budapest Aid and Rescue Committee in Hungary.[44]

Michael Dov Weissmandel (an important member of Working Group, who was not present when *The Report* was created) translated *The Report* into Yiddish. He also provided a five-page summary and added a cover letter providing an update of recent developments with respect to the Hungarian Jews as well as suggestions for how to avert the catastrophe, such as calling on the Allies to bomb the death camp and the railways. He sent the letters to his contacts, among them his student Rabbi Solomon Schönfeld in London,[45] and Füllöp Freudiger, his cousin and the head of Orthodox Jewry in Hungary.[46]

On May 15, two and half weeks after the completion of the Vrba Wetzler Report, the mass deportations of Hungarian Jews to Auschwitz started,[47] beginning with Carpathian Ruthenia and Northern Transylvania, the territories annexed outside the Trianon Treaty borders of Hungary. From May 15 onward, 12,000 Hungarian Jews were shipped to Auschwitz daily.[48]

Six weeks after Vrba and Wetzler's escape, two other prisoners, Czesław Mordowicz and Arnošt Rosin (who was a good friend of both Vrba and Wetzler) escaped from Birkenau and through an unbelievable chain of events reached the same members of the Working Group. They fully corroborated Vrba and Wetzler's account and added details of their observations of the events at the camp subsequent to Vrba and Wetzler's escape, specifically the mass murder (mass even in Birkenau terms – 12,000 victims a day) of Hungarian Jews.[49]

Rosin and Mordowicz estimated that between May 15 and their escape on May 27, 1944, over 100,000 Hungarian Jews were transported to Birkenau, where most of them were immediately murdered in the gas chambers.[50] The Slovakian Jewish leaders swiftly drafted a seven-page report focusing on the events that took place after Vrba and Wetzler's escape, attached it to Vrba and Wetzler's report, and distributed it to their contacts. The report is today known as the Mordowicz-Rosin Report, or Second Auschwitz Protocol, and it is part of the so-called Auschwitz Protocols -- it never stands by itself.

On July 7, 1944, Horthy succumbed to the pressure of important personages who had learned of *The Report* and who either pleaded with or threatened Horthy in an effort to stop the deportations. Horthy ordered the deportations to cease via an order that became effective by July 9.[51]

The Debate over the Missing Warning

After the war, Vrba accused Hungarian Jewish leaders - including particularly scathing words directed at Rudolf Kasztner[52] - of betraying their people when they kept this warning to themselves.[53] He argued that had the Jewish leadership acted faster and more efficiently on the information he had provided, had they tried to warn the Jewish communities and urge people to disobey their German and Hungarian oppressors, or go into hiding, many of the 437,000 Hungarian Jews could have been saved. "No Jewish mothers and fathers would bring their children to their sordid execution in the gas chambers in Auschwitz had they known," Vrba claimed.[54]

Vrba was in turn met with criticism, including accusations that he had fabricated the intention of warning the Hungarian Jews as a motive for his escape, since there is not even a single reference to Hungary in The Vrba Wetzler Report, which does however include speculation regarding the expected arrival of Greek Jews.[55]

Vrba's clarifications

Vrba identified several motivations for the escape in addition to the obvious desire to flee the death camp. He had hoped to damage the Nazis' plans, tell the world what was really happening in Auschwitz-Birkenau, warn those who were still to come, and report and prevent the crimes committed there.[56] But he also always maintained that he had escaped Auschwitz-Birkenau with the intention of alerting Hungarian Jewry about their impending annihilation.[57] As a reaction to the doubts raised by the historian community regarding whether he knew about the upcoming fate of the Hungarians Jews, Vrba published the article "The Preparations for the Holocaust in Hungary: An Eyewitness Account," in 1989 in which he added many clarifying details in order to resolve misunderstandings that had led to his being criticized.

In January 1944, Vrba observed extensive technical preparations in the camp being made in the anticipation of the arrival of the Hungarian Jews. The purpose of the renovations was twofold: to make the killing process quicker and more efficient, and to increase its capacity for killing.

On January 15, 1944, Vrba saw an unusual commotion outside his "office," between blocks B-I-a and B-II-a (his block). Curious, he approached the fence and saw "Kapo Yup," a political prisoner from Berlin whom Vrba knew from his stay in Auschwitz I and with whom he had previously been on friendly terms, overseeing a working unit comprised of Polish prisoners. At that time, Vrba had already been in Birkenau for a year, so Yup was pleasantly surprised to see him "looking well," and they engaged in conversation. Yup confided to Vrba that his unit was constructing a new railway ramp that was to lead straight to crematoria.[58] At that time, the newly arrived victims who were not selected for work (between 85-90% of each transport) had to either walk 3 km or be transported by truck to the gas chambers, which demanded logistical planning and resources – one truck could take a maximum of 100 souls.[59]

In addition, Yup revealed to Vrba that he had overheard the SS talking about the imminent arrival of up to a million Hungarian Jews. The new ramp was a necessary improvement to be able to "handle such masses of people with sufficient speed."[60]

The purpose of building a new ramp was obvious to Birkenau prisoners, according to Vrba, and the expected arrival of Hungarian Jews was an open secret. Vrba explained that secrecy was not strictly kept in Auschwitz-Birkenau, because no one was ever expected to leave the "premises;" for example, prisoners in Birkenau knew that most of the arrivals were immediately killed in the gas chambers.[61] The prisoners were aware that the Hungarian Jewish community was the last large community that had not yet arrived at the camp. In addition, two SS officers in the quarantine camp in Birkenau, the SS-*Unterscharführers* Buntrock and Kurpanick,[62] both thieves, murderers and alcoholics who were talkative when drunk, boasted of the "Hungarian salami" that would soon arrive.[63]

Vrba claimed to have observed additional changes that affirmed his conclusion that Birkenau was preparing for a large influx. The old trenches that had been used to burn bodies before the crematoria were constructed were being restored, while new trenches were being dug. Moreover, a new subsection to the camp was being developed, in an area parallel to the "Czech Family Camp", and it was this building site, called "Mexiko" in the camp's jargon, that provided Vrba and Wetzler with the hiding place needed for their escape.

It is curious that in their report, Vrba and Wetzler did not mention any of these ongoing "improvements" designed to increase the murderous capacity of Birkenau, especially if their motivations were to warn the world; even more odd is that they mentioned the building site twice with a comment that the "purpose of this extensive planning is not known to us."[64] This raises even more questions about to what extent Vrba and Wetzler were aware of the realities in Auschwitz at the time of their imprisonment there and to what extent they reconstructed the events they observed retrospectively with their post-war knowledge.

Wetzler's perspective

Wetzler was quieter, partly because he was living in communist Czechoslovakia, and partly because his experience in the camp was more arduous, and he needed to distance himself more from the past. Just as Vrba, Wetzler provided a myriad of reasons for the escape. Some of his expressions of the motives for escape are located in his fictionalized accounts of the events surrounding the escape, however, and this needs to be kept in mind when evaluating the veracity of those claims. In *Oswiecim, hrobka styroch milionov ludi (Auschwitz, Tomb of Four Million People)* -- the Slovakian version of both the Vrba Wetzler and Mordowicz Rosin Reports, which Wetzler edited (and to which he added many details that were not included in the original *Report*) -- Wetzler expressed the desire to expose the great crimes of the Nazis (in fact, Wetzler claimed that every prisoner in Birkenau dreamed to be the first to do so).[65] According to his fictional short story *Smrť býva na druhej strane (Death Lives on the Other Side)*, Wetzler's motivation was to liberate the camp and to pass on a warning to the Hungarians.[66] Like Vrba, Wetzler too maintained, in his fictional as well as non-fictional accounts, that the approaching arrival of Hungarian Jews was no secret in Auschwitz-Birkenau.[67]

Meeting the Slovakian Jewish Underground – The Working Group

Vrba and Wetzler both insisted that upon meeting the representatives of the Slovak Jewish community, they immediately and clearly articulated the imminent jeopardy that the Hungarian Jewish community faced.[68]

According to Vrba, Krasniansky and Neumann reassured them that they were in "daily contact with the Hungarian Jewish leaders" and *The Report* would "be in their hands tomorrow."[69] In particular, they identified Rudolf Kasztner as a man of "vast experience who knew how to respond to the situation," and they assured Vrba and Wetzler that Kasztner could be relied upon to "take the right action at the right time."[70]

Vrba's version of the events is further corroborated by the fact that *The Report* was, according to both Krasniansky and Neumann, immediately dispatched to Hungary.[71] Krasniansky emphasized that he personally handed *The Report* to Kasztner in Bratislava before the end of April. Furthermore, Ida Steiner, who typed out *The Report*, recalled, when interviewed in 1965, how shaken Krasniansky was by *The Report* and how he immediately started to contemplate how to warn the Hungarian Jews, since he had been unable to rescue his own (Slovakian) Jews.[72]

The Letter

There is one significant document that seems to support all of Vrba's claims. It is a cover letter sent by Rabbi Weissmandel and Gisi Fleischmann, the leader of the Working Group, to Rabbi Schoenfeld, a former student of Weissmandel's who at the time lived in London. The letter was sent on May 22, 1944,[73] which was *before* Mordowicz and Rosin escaped from Auschwitz-Birkenau. It was included with the Vrba Wetzler and the Polish Major Reports, and it reached Jaromir Kopecký, the representative of the Czechoslovak exiled government in Switzerland. The letter - more specifically paragraph "l" - contained the following item: "a special railway line [in Birkenau] has already been built leading into the extermination halls, in order to prepare the new work of annihilation of Hungarian Jews. That was said by knowledgeable people there in that hell; it is discussed there without scruples, without suspecting that someone outside might learn about it."[74]

Obviously, Weissmandel and Fleischmann received the information about the deportations of Hungarians Jews from other sources as well, since they provided the accurate figure of 12,000 daily deported Jews (paragraph "b" and "m"), as well as a detailed route of the transports (paragraph "d"). But the other information, namely that the line was extended to the "extermination halls" and that this was done to prepare for the Hungarians as the next victims and that this was an open secret in Birkenau could not possibly have been known to Weissmandel and Fleischmann without their having been told this by Vrba or Wetzler. This unique information is entirely consistent with all of Vrba's claims.

Perspective of the Historians

The historian Dina Porat took a skeptical position with respect to Vrba and Wetzler's foreknowledge of the threat to Hungarian Jews. In her article "A Holocaust and Wartime Triangle: 'The Protocols of Auschwitz' Reach Chaim Barlas, Angelo G. Roncalli, and Pius XII," it was important to her to emphasize that the warning about the upcoming annihilation of Hungarian Jews and the information of the preparations being made in their anticipation "is only found in Vrba's book and his later oral testimonies."[75] The Vrba Wetzler Report is significant to her as the first reliable insider account that exposed Birkenau as an extermination center rather than the slave center that "was believed by many until then."[76] Nevertheless, when disseminating *The Report* (either in its entirety or summarized), the Jewish activists provided their contacts with additional information about the ongoing deportations of Hungarian Jewry, which created a powerful warning.

For his part, the prominent historian of the Hungarian Holocaust, Randolph L. Braham, was also skeptical regarding Vrba's knowledge about the upcoming destruction of Hungarian Jewry: "Clearly isolated from the outside world in the hermetically closed death camp, Rudi [Vrba] could not possibly have been acquainted with the sinister plans of the top Nazis, plans that were probably unknown even to the low-ranked SS camp guards."[77] The plans to invade Hungary were being developed from autumn 1943 when Germans caught wind of Hungarian negotiations with the Western Allies and their intention to break free from the Axis alliance. However, these plans, which also included the "Jewish Solution," were only finalized by Hitler in February, 1944.[78]

Braham made an important observation regarding the timing of Vrba's first publication of his unique story. It was shortly after Kasztner's libel trials were concluded in Israel. In the early 1950s, the state of Israel took legal action against Malkiel Gruenwald for his continuous accusations against Kasztner, a senior government official and member of the leading Mapai party at that time, of collaboration with the Nazis in the extermination of Hungarian Jews, plunder of Jewish property, and support of a Nazi war criminal after the war.[79] The trial turned, quite unexpectedly, into a political spectacle that stirred the whole nation into discussions about the controversial Hungarian tragedy (and led to the collapse of Moshe Sharett's government). Gruenwald was acquitted and Kasztner emerged from the trial accused of "selling his soul to the devil."[80] The verdict was immediately appealed, however before being officially cleared by the Supreme Court in 1958 of the stigma of collaboration, Kastner was assassinated by extreme-right activist Ze'ev Eckstein.[81] Coincidentally, Vrba lived in Israel between 1958-1960, and Braham thought that the debates surrounding the trials were reflected in Vrba's depiction of his story - the escape occurred in order to warn Hungarian Jews against the mortal danger of Birkenau and it was thwarted by Hungarian Jewish leaders, Kasztner in particular. To Braham, Vrba's narrative was a recollection "of a non-historian survivor of the Holocaust 17 years later." [82]

Interviewing Rosin, Erich Kulka asked directly whether Vrba and Wetzler could have known about the upcoming transports of Hungarians at the time of their escape. Rosin gave Kulka this unequivocal answer: "It is no coincidence the warning is missing from *The Report*. They could not have known. We often discussed in camp that the Hungarian, Romanian and Bulgarian Jews haven't arrived yet and we were waiting for them. The crematoria were being expanded and perfected and the SS man would tell us that after the Jews, Poles and Czechs will be the next [victims]."[83] Kulka never directly addressed the missing warning in his studies.

In his studies, Yehuda Bauer frequently dealt with the Auschwitz Protocols and Rudolf Vrba. Bauer deeply disapproved of Vrba's "preposterous" accusations against Hungarian and Slovakian Jewish leaders, which he explained in his works.[84] However, Bauer never doubted Vrba's genuine desire to inform the world about Auschwitz and his intention to warn the Hungarian Jews about what awaited them. Bauer praised *The Report* as the first authentic account giving credible and detailed information on what was happening in Auschwitz, although he found the victim statistics exaggerated.[85] Bauer valued Vrba's testimony about Auschwitz, but considered his attempts to analyze the developments subsequent to his escape historically as very problematic and simply wrong.[86]

Of the historians writing on this topic, Miroslav Kárný confronted the issue of the missing warning most extensively. The Czech historian sharply disagreed with what according to him was the widely accepted belief that there was, at the time of Vrba and Wetzler's escape, general knowledge among the Auschwitz prisoners that prospective victims would be Hungarians. According to Kárný, Vrba and Wetzler "did not know about the imminent Hungarian *Endlösung*,"[87] which is why the specific warning for Hungarian Jews was missing from *The Report*. The fact that *The Report* included a warning for Greek Jewry was, according to Kárný, further proof of how unaware Vrba and Wetzler were about the Nazi plans.[88]

In personal correspondence with historian John S. Conway, [89] Kárný explained further why he believed Vrba and Wetzler did not know about the imminent danger of Hungarian Jewry. He studied the Auschwitz underground correspondence from 1944. In the hundreds of messages held in the Auschwitz Museum that were sent from Auschwitz to Krakow by the camp underground organization, there is no indication that the authors of these messages, who were probably the best informed of all the prisoners, knew anything in advance about the upcoming Hungarian transports. If the underground did not know about it, then certainly Vrba and Wetzler did not know either.[90] In one letter to Conway, Kárný went so far as to accuse Vrba of using his post-war knowledge to "build up his legend."[91] Kárný instead preferred Wetzler's alleged motivation for the escape, namely "to warn the world, and to appeal for the salvation of hundreds of thousands of people who were in prisons in Auschwitz and other death camps."[92]

Kárný failed to note, however, that he took this quote from a manuscript of a fictional account of the events that diverged considerably from what actually happened. Reading Wetzler's novel, no one would, without making the connection to what is known about Auschwitz-Birkenau, guess that Jews were the targets of the industrialized murder. The word "Jew" appeared in the manuscript only a very few times. Instead, the reader would likely conclude that the Nazi rage was aimed at Communists or Soviets. Wetzler actually claimed that the Nazis did not build Auschwitz "for the Jews," but that, rather: "they kill everything that is burdensome for them and is in their way, mainly Communists."[93] Consistent with that general interpretation of the purpose of Auschwitz, "Mexiko" was, according to this novel, being prepared for the anticipated influx of tens of thousands of Soviet POWs. And the fictional escapees, when they met with the anti-Nazi underground movement in Slovakia, were concerned foremost with delivering a report to Moscow.[94] With that narrative established, Wetzler could not suddenly identify the reason for his escape as wanting to warn the Hungarian Jews.

Interestingly, the escapees in Wetzler's story became very frustrated with how much time the underground movement members were taking and begged the underground workers to hurry up since 500,000 "Hungarians will come to the camp any day now." When asked how they could know, they answered that it was widely known in the camp and there were even jokes about Hungarian salami.[95]

Kárný and Wetzler corresponded for a number of years, and it is safe to say they formed a kind of friendship. Nevertheless, it seems (based on the correspondence) that Kárný never directly asked Wetzler about his own motivations for escape, and he never specifically asked what Wetzler knew about the Hungarians. Instead, Kárný based the conclusions of his influential article, that had been widely cited in both popular and scholarly works, on a fictional account that was obviously (too obviously for it to go unnoticed by a historian who spent time as a prisoner in Auschwitz) adjusted to the *Zeitgeist* and intended to appease the Communist regime in Czechoslovakia.

Vrba's explanation for the lacuna

Vrba offered an explanation why the warning was missing. He insisted that he wanted to include the specific warning in *The Report*, but Krasniansky believed that "only murders in Auschwitz that already had occurred should be recorded [and] the final report should be a record of facts, not weakened by 'forecasts' and 'prophecies.'"[96] Since Krasniansky insisted on having an "advisory vote" in the final editing, and since he was literally Vrba's only link to Hungarian Jewry, and who, in addition, grasped the urgency of the message and had the means to deliver *The Report* without delay, Vrba decided not to antagonize him and accepted his conditions. His intention was to get the news published quickly.[97] Moreover, it is known that the original *Report* in Slovak was swiftly translated by Krasniansky into German and rushed to Hungary. Vrba suggested that as opposed to the translated version, the lost original Slovak version may have contained the specific warning to Hungarian Jews. In a letter to historian David S. Wyman from February 17, 1977, Vrba wrote that, "It is conspicuous that our report about the impending fate of Hungarian Jewry is missing there. We both knew well about the preparations made for the murder... everybody in Auschwitz knew.... Neither Wetzler nor I made any secrets of anything we knew about Auschwitz – and we did know."[98]

Conclusion

The Auschwitz-Birkenau prisoners and SS personnel were well aware that the Hungarian Jews had not yet been brought to the camp, and rumors regarding their possible arrival circulated in the camp widely and openly, which is obvious by the commonly used cynical remark of "Hungarian salami." But we can only speculate to what degree the SS personnel (and from them the prisoners) could have known about the future plans of the Wehrmacht or Eichmann's team and to what degree these rumors were just accurate educated guesses.

When compiling *The Report*, Vrba and Wetzler must have known about the recent occupation of Hungary – either from Auschwitz-Birkenau or from the members of the well-informed Working Group. They also learned about the still intact Hungarian Jewish community. Even if Vrba and Wetzler were not absolutely sure Hungarian Jews were to be the next prospective group of victims, they must have suspected as much.

The information Vrba and Wetzler brought to the world was of the most serious nature. It was about an extermination center for Jews that operated smoothly and consistently for over two years and was now opening its jaws even wider. It is clear that Vrba and Wetzler collected information with great care for the purpose of informing the outside world. There can be doubts about what exactly they knew, but there need be no doubts whatsoever about their intent to warn any potential victims. The missing warning will probably just remain unresolved.

Endnotes

1   This article is based on the second chapter of my MA Thesis: "The Men Who Knew Too Much: Reflections on the Historiography of Rudolf Vrba and Alfred Wetzler's Escape from Auschwitz-Birkenau and their Attempt to Warn the World," (Tel Aviv University, 2018). I would like to thank my advisor Dr. Roni Stauber for his valuable comments, helpful advice, and limitless encouragement.

2   For the approximate position, see appendix.

3   The Vrba Wetzler Report was part of the so-called *Auschwitz Protocols*, or Auschwitz Reports, which is a collection of reports by Jerzy Tabeau (because of whom it is often referred to as the "Polish Major Report"), Vrba, Wetzler, Arnošt Rosin and Czesław Mordowicz, who were all Auschwitz prisoners who escaped Auschwitz in this chronological order. Jerzy Tabeau was as non-Jew imprisoned in Auschwitz's main camp (Auschwitz I) and his report was created independently of the reports of the Jewish prisoners. Vrba, Wetzler, Mordowicz and Rosin were imprisoned for the most part in Birkenau (Auschwitz II) and compiled their reports with the help of "Working Group," Slovakian Jewish underground organization. Because Vrba and Wetzler's report is by far the most comprehensive, it is sometimes referred to as the Auschwitz Protocols.

4   David Kranzler, *The Man Who Stopped the Trains to Auschwitz: George Mantello, El Salvador, and, Switzerland's Finest Hour* (New York: Syracuse University Press, 2000), p. 123.

5   Martin Gilbert, *Auschwitz and the Allies* (New York, 1982), p. 234.

6   Escape from Auschwitz (motion picture), Alexander Dunlop (Director), PBS, 2008.

7   Randolph L. Braham, *The Politics of Genocide: The Holocaust in Hungary* (New York, 1981), p. 714.

8   In later editions the book was retitled to *44070: The Conspiracy of the Twentieth Century* (Washington, 1989) and *I escaped Auschwitz* (New Jersey, 2002). The latter versions also included translation of the Vrba-Wetzler Report, Vrba's article: "The Role of Holocaust in German Economy and Military Strategy During 1941-1945" and John S. Conway article: "The Significance of the Vrba-Wetzler Report on Auschwitz-Birkenau". The newest edition of the book is scheduled to be released in 2020 under the name *I escaped Auschwitz: The Story of a Man Whose Actions Led to the Largest Single Rescue of Jews in World War II*. Robin Vrba, Rudolf Vrba's widow, and I updated the book with many details, corrected a few minor mistakes and added maps for bigger clarity.

9   Most detailed article is "The Preparations for the Holocaust in Hungary: An Eyewitness Account," in *The Nazis' last victims: The Holocaust in Hungary* (eds. Randolph L. Braham and Scott Miller) (Detroit: Wayne State University Press, 1998). The best known of the documentary movies is Claude Lanzmann's "Shoa" (1985) where

Vrba's testimony was central, as Lanzmann believed it was crucial for understanding the Holocaust; other documentaries are "Genocide" (1973), by Michael Darlow, and "Auschwitz and the Allies" (1982), by Rex Bloomstein and Martin Gilbert.

10 Rudolf Vrba and Alan Bestic, *44070: The Conspiracy of the Twentieth Century* (Washington, 1989), p. 22.

11 Affidavit of Dr. Vrba in the Matter of the Immigration and Nationality Act, Franklin D. Roosevelt Library, Hyde Park, New York (FDRPL), Vrba's Collection, box 25.

12 After the war Tiso, a Catholic priest, was tried as a war criminal, condemned to death and hanged. Today he is celebrated by some as a victim of struggle for political power between Czechs and Slovaks and perceived as one of the founding fathers of the Slovak Nation. See for example Gila Fatran, "Holocaust and collaboration in Slovakia in the postwar discourse," in *Collaboration with the Nazis: Public Discourse after the Holocaust* (ed. Roni Stauber), (Routledge, 2010), pp. 197-206.

13 On November 8, 1938 Slovakia (at that time still part of Czechoslovakia) lost part of its territory – rich fertile lands - to Hungary as part of so-called Vienna Award, which was revision of the Trianon Treaty. Slovaks swiftly blamed the Jews for this loss (they accused them of dissemination of Hungarian culture) and the Jews who were born at these territories were forcefully sent there and their property was confiscated.

14 Livia Rothkirchen, *The Destruction of Slovakian Jewry: A Documentary History* (in Hebrew with English Introduction), (Jerusalem, 1961), pp. XI-XII.

15 Ivan Kamenec, "Nechcený autor, nechcený hrdina…," in Alfréd Wetzler, *Čo Dante Nevidel* (Bratislava, 2009), p. 258.

16 Affidavit of Dr. Vrba in the Matter of the Immigration and Nationality Act.

17 Hans Safrian, *Eichmann's Men* (Cambridge University Press, 2009), p. 144. According to Ivan Kamenec, prominent historian of Slovakian Holocaust, the initiative came from the Slovaks.

18 Rothkirchen, p. XXIII-XXVI. The very first transport consisting of 999 young Slovakian girls on March 26, 1942 was also the first transport that arrived in Auschwitz through RSHA IV B 4.

19 The Hlinka Guard were paramilitary forces, created and modeled on the Nazi SA by Tiso's predecessor Andrej Hlinka. Andrej Hlinka (1864-1938) was a Catholic priest and politician, founder of the Slovak People's Party and the Hlinka Guard. Today, he is openly celebrated as one of the founding fathers of Slovakia, and virtually every Slovakian city has either a street or square named after him, including Sered. Rothkirchen, pp. VIII-X.

20 Wetzler's testimony at Vašek's Trial, Slovak National Archives (SNA), Bratislava, National Tribunal Collection, Onľud 17/46.

21 *The Auschwitz Protocols* (under the original title The Extermination Camps of Auschwitz and Birkenau in Upper Silesia), FRDPL, General Correspondence, Box 7, pp. 21-24.

22 Ibid., pp. 4-6.

23 The administrative "right hand" to the Blockführer (i.e. the Blockleader).

24 The German extermination camps Auschwitz and Birkenau, pp. 7-8.

25 Rudolf Vrba, "The Preparations," p. 72.

26 Arnošt Rosin's interview with Erich Kulka from 1965-66, Yad Vashem Archives (YVA), Jerusalem, P. 25/21.

27 Vrba, "The Conspiracy", pp. 86-122.

28 In 1961 together with few other survivors, Vrba sued the I.G. Farben conglomerate for lost wages owed them for their slave labor while Auschwitz prisoners at the Buna Chemical Plant. Vrba was awarded 2500 marcs, but the German court refused to award the families of those who lost their lives there. Ironically, after the war Vrba was offered a job with I.G. Farben as a chemical Engineer, which he of course refused. Rudolf Vrba, *Utekl jsem z Osvětimi* (Praha, 1998), p. 418.

29 Vrba, "The Preparation," pp. 58-59.

30 Their luggage contained clothing for all seasons and cooking and working utensils that proved they were preparing themselves for "resettling." Ibid., pp. 64-65.

31 Ibid., p. 59.

32 Ibid., pp. 66-67.

33 Camps slang for stealing.

34 Filip Müller survived Auschwitz and recorded a horrifying account of the events in the book *Eyewitness Auschwitz, Three Years in the Gas Chambers* (Chicago, 1999).

35 Randolph L. Braham, "Rescue Operations in Hungary: Myths and Realities," in *Yad Vashem Studies* 32 (2004), p. 22. According to the census of 1941, Hungary then had a Jewish population of 725,007, as well as approximately 100,000 converts and Christians who were identified as Jews under the racial laws then in effect.

36 Numerus Clausus – law that limited the number of Jewish students at the national universities, was legislated in Hungary in 1920 – it was the first anti-Jewish legislation in post-World War I Europe, Braham, Rescue, p. 26.

37 Randolph L. Braham, "Hungary: The Controversial chapter of the Holocaust," in *The Auschwitz Reports and the Holocaust in Hungary* (eds. Randolph L. Braham and William J. vanden Huevel) (Boulder: Social Science Monographs; New

York: Rosenthal Institute for Holocaust Studies Graduate Center/City University of New York, 2011), p. 29.

38 Ibid., p. 33.

39 Wisliceny was previously an "advisor for Jewish affairs" in Slovakia and Greece. He was able to manipulate the Slovakian Jewish clandestine movement "Working Group" to give him a letter of recommendation that would encourage the Hungarian Jewish leaders to pursue a "business" with him. Working Group falsely believed Wisliceny was bribable since their bribe to him ($25,000, which he pocketed for himself) coincided with the (temporary) halt of deportation of Jews from Slovakia for reasons unrelated to Wisliceny. His testimony during the Nuremberg trials proved important in the prosecution of Eichmann and in understanding the process of the "Final Solution." He was tried in Bratislava, condemned to death, and hanged in 1946.

40 Hunsche and Krumey were tried for their crimes in Frankfurt in 1960's. Initially, Krumey received five years, and Hunsche was acquitted. An appeal by the public prosecutor led to a second trial, which found both guilty. Krumey was sentenced to life imprisonment and Hunsche to twelve years. Rudolf Vrba was a witness for the prosecution in both trials.

41 István Deák, "The Hungarian-Jewish Historical Context Leading to the Creation of the OMIKE Művészakció and Its Aftermath, 1848–1945," in Jenő Lévai and Frederick Bondy, *The Writers, Artists, Singers, and Musicians of the National Hungarian Jewish Cultural Association* (OMIKE), 1939–1944 (Expanded English edition ed.) (West Lafayette: Purdue University Press, 2016), pp. 8-9.

42 Oscar Krasniansky – whose name is spelled in slightly different ways in various documents, e.g., Krasnanski, Krasnyansky, Krasnansky, Krasnyanski or Krasznyansky – immigrated to Israel after the war and changed his name to Karmiel and worked in diplomatic services.

43 Vrba, "The Preparations," pp. 77-79, Wetzler's interview with Erich Kulka from 1964, YVA P.25/21. Erich Kulka, "Attempts by Jewish Escapees to Stop Mass Extermination," in *Jewish Social Studies* 47, 3/4 (1985), p. 300.

44 Krasniansky's interview with Erich Kukla, YVA, O.3/3366, Gilbert, p. 204, Miroslav Kárný, "The Vrba and Wetzler Report," in *Anatomy of the Auschwitz Death Camp* (eds. Yisrael Gutman and Michael Berenbaum) (Bloomington: Indiana University Press, 1994), p. 556.

45 Richard Lichtheim, Aktenvermerkbetreffend Birkenau und Auschwitz, June 23, 1944, Czech National Archive, Prague (CNA), Kárný Collection, box 10.

46 Braham, *The Politics*, pp. 711-12.

47 There were two pre-transports on April 28, 1944 that passed through Žilina, Yehuda Bauer, *Jews for Sale, Nazi-Jewish Negotiations, 1933-1945* (New Haven: Yale University Press, 1994), p. 156.

48 Braham, *The Politics,* p. 714.

49 For more details about Mordowicz and Rosin escape see Nikola Zimring, "A Tale of Dakness: Story of the Mordowicz-Rosin Report," in Rudolf Vrba, *I escaped Auschwitz: The Story of a Man Whose Actions Led to the Largest Single Rescue of Jews in World War II* (New York, 2020).

50 *The Auschwitz Protocols,* p. 30.

51 Horthy's order was difficult for Eichmann to accept. With fanatical stubbornness, he managed to trick the remains of the Jewish community and organized two additional transports to Auschwitz: 1,200 Jews from Kistarcsa on July 19, 1944; and 1,500 Jews from the Sarvan camp on July 24. Safrian, pp. 204-205.

52 Vrba described Kasztner as a skillful diplomat who knew the value of silence and who intentionally withheld (from the victims) information regarding the true purpose of Auschwitz-Birkenau in order to protect his negotiations with Adolf Eichmann and secure the rescue of 1684 prominent Jews on his famous train. There is a much larger ongoing stormy debate among historians about the role of Kasztner, Vaada, and the Working Group and no consensus on the matter seems to be reached.

53 Vrba, "The Conspiracy", pp. 262-269.

54 Vrba, "Preparations," p. 70.

55 *The Auschwitz Protocols,* p. 17.

56 Vrba, "The Conspiracy", p. 147 and 198.

57 Vrba, "The Preparations," p. 56.

58 Ibid., pp. 68 - 69.

59 Ibid., p. 68.

60 Ibid., pp. 56-68.

61 Ibid., p. 70.

62 After the war both Buntrock and Kurpanick were tried in Krakow for war crimes, found guilty and hanged. Ibid., p. 97, n. 16.

63 Ibid., pp. 68-70, also Vrba's letter to Gilbert, August 12, 1980, FDRPL, Vrba's Collection, box 2. (Almost every country was characterized by country-specific edible product, that was found and stolen immediately at the arrival, for example Jews from Protectorate brought ham (!), Jews from France Sardines, and Greek Jews halva and olives).

64 *The Auschwitz Protocols,* p. 5 and 22.

65 Jozef Lánik (Alfréd Wetzler), *Oswiecim, hrobka styroch milionov ludi* (Košice: Wiko, 1946), p. 21. Wetzler wrote about his war experience under the pseudonym Jozef (Jožko) Lánik, which was the false identity the Working Group provided him after the escape in order to protect him and his family.

66 Jozef Lánik (Alfréd Wetzler), *Smrť býva na druhej strane* (Unpublished, 1958), CNA, Archive of the Union of the Antifascist Fighters, "Competition 774" file.

67 Lanik (Wetzler), *Oswencim*, p. 63, Josef Lanik (Alfréd Wetzler), *Pruhované Karavány* (Unpublished, 1963), CNA, Archive of the Union of the Antifascist Fighters, "Competition 774" file, p. 289.

68 Vrba, "The Preparations," p. 79; Wetzler's interview with Erich Kulka from 1964, YVA P.25/21, p. 5.

69 Vrba, "The Conspiracy" p. 251.

70 Ibid., p. 250.

71 Krasniansky's interview with Erich Kukla, YVA, O.3/3366; Gilbert, p. 204; Jirmejahu Oskar Neumann, Im Schatten Des Todes: Ein Tatsachenbericht Vom Schicksalskampf Des Slovakischen Judentums (Tel-Aviv, 1956), p. 181. There are two possible versions on when and how Kasztner received The Report. Krasniansky claimed he personally handed The Report to Kasztner in Bratislava before the end of April, which was disputed by Hansi Brand, Kasztner's confidant at that time. The other version is that The Report was sent to Kasztner in Budapest. Either way, it is agreed that Kasztner was at least familiar with the main points of The Report in early May.

72 Steiner's interview with Kulka, conducted in 1965, YVA, K25/21.

73 The letter was dated May 22, 1944, but Weissmandel probably started composing it by May 16, 1944 and kept adding information that was coming to him. The letter opens with: "Yesterday began the deportation of the Hungarian Jews," which led all the activists to believe the deportations started on May 21, 1944.

74 CNA, Kárný Collection, box 10. The letter and The Reports were translated into English and given to Roswell McClelland, a representative of the War Refugee Board in Switzerland. The paragraph "m" includes a translator's note (probably Kopecký's): "The above statement is more understandable if read in correlation with the [a] forementioned twenty-nine page report [i.e., the Vrba Wetzler Report]. This explains that these two men are the only ones who succeeded in escaping." FRDPL, General Correspondence of Roswell D. McClelland: January 1944-July 1945, box 65.

75 Dina Porat, "A Holocaust and Wartime Triangle: 'The Protocols of Auschwitz' Reach Chaim Barlas, Angelo G. Roncalli and Pius XII", in *Roncalli and the Jews during the Holocaust: Concern and Efforts to Help* (eds. Dina Porat and David Bankier) (Jerusalem, 2014), p. 30.

76 Ibid., p. 32.

77 Braham, "Hungary," pp. 47-48.

78 Ibid., p. 37.

79 Yechiam Weitz, *The Man Who Was Murdered Twice: The Life, Trial and Death of Israel Kasztner* (Jerusalem, 2011), pp. 84-85.

80 Ibid., p.219

81 Ibid., p. 310. Eckstein served seven years for the murder.

82 Braham, "Hungary," p. 47.

83 Rosin's interview with Erich Kulka from 1965-66, YVA P.25/21, p. 10.

84 Yehuda Bauer, *Rethinking the Holocaust* (Yale University Press: New Haven and London, 2001), p. 230.

85 Ibid., p. 229.

86 Yehuda Bauer, "Anmerkungen zum 'Auschwitz-Bericht' von Rudolf Vrba," in Vierteljahrshefte für Zeitgeschichte. 45 (2) (1997), pp. 297- 307.

87 Kárný, p. 560.

88 Ibid.

89 Conway was Vrba's friend and colleague at the University of British Columbia, Canada.

90 Letter from Kárný to Conway, February 28, 1984, CNA, Kárný Collection, box 10.

91 Letter from Kárný to Conway, December 7, 1983, CNA, Kárný Collection, box 10.

92 Kárný, "The Vrba and Wetzler Report," p.560. Kárný cited from Josef Lánik (Wetzler), Pruhované Karavány, (Unpublished, 1963), CNA, Archive of the Union of the Antifascist Fighters, "Competition 774" file p. 143 and 147.

93 Lánik (Wetzler), Pruhované Karavány, p. 289.

94 Ibid., p. 161 and 273.

95 Ibid., p. 289.

96 Vrba, "The Preparations," pp. 88-89.

97 Letter from Conway to Kárný, January 11, 1984, CNA, Kárný Collection, box 10.

98 Vrba's letter to David S. Wyman, February 17, 1977, FDRPL, Vrba's Collection, box 7.

Aviva Halamish

The Ma'apilim of 1945–48 in Israeli Historiography (1945–2019)

Between 1945 and 1948, *Ha'apalah* – the prevailing Hebrew term used to refer to the clandestine Jewish immigration to Mandatory Palestine (Eretz Israel) – was a human and political drama that cannot be understood without insight into these two mutually complementary primary aspects. During the years in question, this immigration was both one of a number of channels of the Zionist struggle for the establishment of a Jewish state in Palestine, and one of the immigration routes of Jews who survived the Holocaust.[1] Ha'apalah began during the period that preceded World War II as one of the methods of illegal Jewish immigration to British controlled Palestine. However, not all forms of illegal Jewish immigration can be considered Ha'apalah, which differed from other types of illegal immigration in that its goal and fundamental essence were not only, or even primarily, to bring additional Jews to Palestine in contravention of the laws of the authorities. Rather, Ha'apalah was also ascribed political goals either in the internal Zionist realm or on the forefront of the struggle against the decrees of the British regime, as well as in the effort to influence world public opinion and decision makers in Britain and other countries. According to this definition, Ha'apalah began at the onset of the 1930s and is typically broken down into three periods: the period prior to World War II (approximately 20,000 people), during the war (16,500 people), and from the end of the war until the establishment of the state of Israel (70,000 people).

The Israeli historiography of Ha'apalah between the end of World War II and the establishment of the state of Israel deals primarily with four topics. The first two topics – the role which it was assigned by the Zionist leadership and its contribution to the establishment of the state – also pertain to the British and other international parties. The third topic is implementation (the acquisition and preparation of ships, the journey to Palestine, and the arrival to

Palestine or capture at sea).[2] The fourth topic is the people involved: the Zionist leadership, agents of the Mossad Le'Aliyah Bet, members of the Palmach, the American volunteers, and the immigrants – the "*ma'apilim*" (plural of ma'apil, the prevalent Hebrew term used to refer to these immigrants) themselves. It is no coincidence that the ma'apilim are the last subject listed above, as will be explained in this article of which they are the focus. The article addresses the manner in which Israeli historiography has portrayed the ma'apilim, their motivations, their aspirations and their conduct, from the period during which the events themselves occurred through the second decade of the twenty-first century. It surveys and analyzes the ma'apilim's major characteristics and orientations, and the changes in the manner in which they have been represented in remarks made during Ha'apalah and in what has been written about it since the establishment of the state.

Overall, some 70,000 ma'apilim set sail for the shores of Palestine from European ports (two ships actually set sail from North Africa) on 65 ships of the Mossad Le'Aliyah Bet (and one ship organized by the Revisionist movement). The customary breakdown of ma'apilim into sub-groups has been based on their experiences during the journey.[3] Approximately 3,000 arrived in ships that evaded the British blockade and sailed directly to the shores of Palestine, whereas some 9,500 arrived in ships that the British intercepted at sea and were taken ashore at the port of Haifa and held for a time in a detention camp at Atlit. An additional 4,500, the ma'apilim of the *Exodus*, were returned by Britain to France in three deportation ships and were ultimately deported to Germany, and 52,000 were jailed for a period (of between a few months and more than a year) in detention camps in Cyprus. Most of the Cyprus detainees had been aboard ships that were intercepted at sea by the British, and approximately 15,000 had been aboard the *Kibbutz Galuyot* and the *Atzmaut* (often referred to as the "Pans," due to their original names: the *Pan York* and the *Pan Crescent*), which sailed from the port of Burgas, Bulgaria directly to Cyprus according to an agreement between Britain and the Jewish Agency. These ma'apilim, whose origins were in Romania, differed from most of the others in their wartime histories and in the fact that they set out on their voyage to Palestine not from temporary displaced persons' (DP) centers but from their homes. The total count of ma'apilim, therefore, does not include only those who resided in Nazi-occupied Europe during the Holocaust or spent the war inside the Soviet Union and returned westward at the end of the war (the repatriates). Rather, it also includes some 15,000 from Romania and some 5,000 from Bulgaria (who are also not included in the classic definition of *She'erit Hapleta* – the "surviving remnant" of European Jewry),[4] and approximately 2,500 ma'apilim of North African origin.[5]

The ma'apilim who set out for Palestine from the DP camps and other centers in Western Europe (including Italy) were the flesh and blood of She'erit Hapleta, and in many senses can serve as a case study for issues pertaining to this group as a whole. An article published approximately 12 years ago contains an expanded and in-depth review and analysis of the historiography of She'erit Hapleta, though its author, Dalia Ofer, has explicitly clarified that her discussion of the subject does not include the writing on Ha'apalah. This article is therefore another link in this discussion and is meant to complete it, due to the need to address what Ofer's article does not contain and the years that have passed since its publication.[6]

This article explores the representation of the ma'apilim in the Israeli historiography – "historiography" in its broad sense, meaning that the article relies not only on essays based on academic research but also on other means of expression that have shaped the image of the ma'apilim in Israeli public discourse and collective memory. At the same time, because the article is concerned with public material it does not address memoirs that have been published here and there over the years and that may have been read by only a few people, if by anyone at all. "Israeli historiography" refers to texts written by Israeli scholars that were published in Israel and in Hebrew.

This article employs two chronological frameworks. The first is the period under research: from the end of World War II to the establishment of the state of Israel. This demarcation is also indicative of what the article does *not* address – namely the immigrants' absorption and integration into Israeli society. The second chronological framework is the period during which the essays were written, which begins at the time of the events themselves and continues until the present day. The discussion pertaining to the ma'apilim and their portrayal is conducted against the background of the period in which they were written, based on the prevailing view that – in the spirit of Italian historian and philosopher Benedetto Croce's epigram, "all history is contemporary history" – historiography says no less, and perhaps even more, about the period in which it was written than about the period under research. Our discussion proceeds along a chronological axis divided into five periods, the limits of which are not entirely rigid:

1. The period of Ha'apalah, 1945-1948

2. From the establishment of the state until the end of the 1970s

3. From the 1980s until the beginning of the 1990s

4. The 1990s

5. The first two decades of the twenty-first century

I. 1945-1948: The ma'apilim are being carried on the backs of our boys, and their shoulders are weak.

In the first phase of the resumption of Ha'apalah after the end of World War II, between August and December 1945, eight small ships reached the shores of Palestine carrying 1,040 passengers, all of whom remained undetected by the British and succeeded in entering the country. On shore they were met by members of the Palmach (including personnel of the Palyam, the Palmach's "sea companies," who for the sake of discussion here are considered as the same entity) and others from the "Yishuv" (the organized Jewish community in Palestine). At the time, the Yishuv regarded Ha'apalah as extending a helping hand to Holocaust survivors; from its perspective, the Yishuv's emissaries in Europe, on the ships, and on shore were the active parties, whereas the role of the ma'apilim was passive. Verbal or written remarks by inhabitants of the Yishuv referred to the ma'apilim in the third person. Their experience of meeting the ma'apilim, the impressions the ma'apilim made on them, and the manner in which they related to them found public expression in a text that became a formative text on the subject: "My

Sister on the Beach," by Yitzhak Sadeh, the commander of the Palmach. The text was published in October 1945 under Sadeh's pseudonym Y. Noded in his regular column "Around the Campfire" in *Alon Hapalmach* (the Palmach bulletin). It was also later published in other venues.[7]

On the beach, the author meets a "sister," who is "filthy, tattered, wild haired." Who is she? A young woman who survived the Holocaust by virtue of her role as a sex object for German officers. "Her flesh is branded: 'For officers only'…Evil people have tortured her and made her barren." And how did she reach the shore? She was brought there by members of the Yishuv. She "weeps and says: Friend, why am I here? **Why was I brought** here? Am I worthy that young healthy boys risk their lives for me?" Sadeh responds as follows – not to her, but to his public:

> Before these sisters I kneel, I prostrate myself in the dust at their feet. And when I rise to my feet; straighten my body, raise my head upwards, I sense and I know:
> For these sisters – I am strong.
> For these sisters – I am brave.
> For these sisters – I will also be cruel.
> For you – everything, everything.

Sadeh articulates a sense of empathy for and camaraderie and identification with the woman. Her words are not conveyed directly from her own mouth but rather are mediated by the author. The ma'apila is mute. Sadeh's words contain an echo of the guilt feelings that were the lot of the inhabitants of the Yishuv, originating in the days of helplessness during the war (this is not to say that they were guilty of anything, but rather that this was how they felt).[8]

A few weeks later, on Christmas Eve, 1945, the immigrant ship the *Hannah Senesz* arrived off the shore near Naharia, and the ma'apilim (with the exception of two) were taken ashore and blended into the Yishuv. Following the celebration held in honor of the ship's Italian captain, Nathan Alterman wrote one of his "Seventh Column" (*Hatur Hashvi'i*) poems bearing the lengthy headline: "Reply to an Italian Captain after Landing Night."[9] The poems of Alterman's "Seventh Column," which were published on Fridays in *Davar*, the Yishuv's most widely circulated newspaper at the time, reflected the period in which they were written and also helped shape the image of the ma'apilim in the eyes of their contemporaries and Israelis of later periods. But whom does the poet laud in this poem? The night, the danger, the grueling toil, the ships en route, "our boys," and the captain. He says nothing about the ma'apilim. And when Alterman informs the captain what the future holds – "For the gates they are open, / A while they've been open" – he also declares who opened them: "'tis the party of youth / That stood that night in the waters." [10]

The ma'apilim are also absent from the names of the Ha'apalah ships. The names assigned to the ships were usually internal in orientation, with the goal of raising the morale and unity surrounding the struggle. The names of the ships derived from the events of the period (*Birya, Yagur, Latrun, Rafiah*) or conveyed slogans of encouragement and morale, such as "You Won't Frighten Us," "To Victory," and "Despite It All" (in response to the deportation to Hamburg of the ma'apilim of the *Exodus*). Some of the ships' names commemorated the founding fathers of the Zionist Movement as well as its leaders and friends. Others commemorated the young men and women of the Yishuv who died in World War II (Hanna Senesz, Enzo Sereni, Haviva Reick, Katriel Yafeh, the 23 Seamen, and Amiram Shochat) and members of the Yishuv who took part in the Ha'apalah enterprise (for example, the *Bracha Fuld*, named after the Palmach fighter killed in a clash with the British army on "Wingate Night" in 1946, and the *Shabtai Luzhinski*, named after a Ha'apalah emissary who died in a car accident in Italy). A dozen people – eleven ma'apilim and one American volunteer – were killed in the fighting with the British along the shores of Palestine, and eight ma'apilim of *The Rafiah* drowned at sea. However, only one ship bore a name containing the word "ma'apil." In February 1947, an immigrant bound for Palestine was killed in a battle aboard the *La-Negev*. As his name was initially not known, announcements were posted in Haifa for the funeral of "the unknown ma'apil," and this name was assigned to a ship which was then on its way to Palestine.[11]

Between January and July 1946, 11 immigrant ships made their way to Palestine carrying a total of 10,500 passengers. Two of these ships – the *Eliyahu*

Golomb and the *Dov Hoz* – arrived with British authorization at the conclusion of the La Spezia affair (Italy);[12] the others were apprehended, and the ma'apilim were jailed at the Atlit camp and released after a short quarantine period, their number being deducted from the certificate quota of 1,500 per month that had been set by the British. The inhabitants of the Yishuv did not encounter the ma'apilim as a defined group, and if they made their acquaintance with them, it was typically via the impressions of the Yishuv's emissaries in the DP camps in Europe, where they met with the potential ma'apilim. What most interested the emissaries was the camp residents' suitability for the Zionist struggle and for building the country.[13]

In August 1946, Britain began to implement a new policy in its efforts to curb illegal immigration, and ma'apilim who were apprehended were now deported to Cyprus. At this stage, the Yishuv's observations and impressions of the ma'apilim were those of the ships' escorts and its emissaries in the detention camps in Cyprus. Some emissaries expressed negative views of the ma'apilim, whereas others believed it necessary to refute such views, which were widespread in the Yishuv. Both approaches offer insight into the way in which the Yishuv inhabitants viewed the ma'apilim.[14] Yishuv inhabitants harbored a negative image of the survivors, including those detained in Cyprus, and the Cyprus detainees were aware of it.[15]

Simultaneous with the onset of the deportations to Cyprus, the Zionist leadership decided on a tactical change in the struggle against the British. In the summer of 1946, the Yishuv's armed struggle reached its peak with the "Night of the Bridges" (June) and the bombing of the King David Hotel (July). Ha'apalah gained momentum, and the ships grew increasingly larger and arrived more frequently. However, on the political front of the struggle for statehood, no progress was being made. The Anglo-American Committee did not recommend the establishment of a Jewish state (or an Arab state), and the Morrison Grady Plan, which emerged in its wake and revolved around regional autonomy in Palestine, served to push back the Jewish struggle for statehood. At that point the Zionist leadership decided to curtail the various manifestations of the armed struggle and to shift the center of gravity to the political front. Accordingly, it was decided to cease the "continuous struggle" (*ma'avak ratzuf*) and instead to engage in a more focused struggle (*ma'avak tzamud*) that was limited to defending the rights to Jewish immigration, settlement, and self-defense, and to concentrate the effort on the political-diplomatic arena. The ma'apilim, who were initially viewed as war refugees in need of urgent rescue, now became the almost exclusive bearers of the struggle. From being carried on the backs of "our boys," the ma'apilim, to paraphrase the line from Alterman's "Seventh Column," became those shouldering the struggle of their People.

Many discerned the change that had occurred, and in addition to the words of admonishment for the Yishuv for remaining on the sidelines and the pangs of conscience for leaving the ma'apilim alone on the front, concern was growing that the effort would be too much for their "weak shoulders," which would not be able to endure the burden. The escorts aboard the Ha'apalah ships reported incidents in which instructions were issued to resist the British forces' seizure of ships, but the ma'apilim displayed only weak resistance "out of fear of shooting."[16] This is what occurred on the *Mordei Hagetaot* in May 1947, and the incident was addressed in Haaretz as follows: "The Yishuv and all those bearing good will welcome this decision…Whatever the forms of resistance to the government decrees, they, the ma'apilim, must not be charged with the obligation to actualize them. They have already done their part through their Ha'apalah."[17] On the other hand, there were also cases in which ma'apilim were instructed to restrain themselves but insisted on resisting.[18]

In the struggle against the British aboard the *Knesset Israel* at Haifa port in November 1946, three ma'apilim were killed. Alterman placed the issue on the public agenda in a column titled "Division of Duties."[19] This text has a young girl representing the ma'apilim and rearticulates the theme of a struggle resting on the shoulders of the ma'apilim (alone), and the author's concern that their weak shoulders might not be able to bear the load. According to Alterman, the "division of duties" that had been delineated between the ma'apilim and the Yishuv was "not in accordance with the division of strength." The column, which in essence constituted fundamental criticism of the conduct of the Yishuv as a bystander, reflects a lack of trust in the ma'apilim's ability to fulfill the mission with which they had been charged. In addition, the ships' escorts and others repeatedly depicted the ma'apilim using the words "difficult human material," and the Palmach members encountered what they regarded as the ma'apilim's incomprehensible and repellant behavior as they prepared them for their maritime voyages and during the journeys themselves.[20]

Expressions conveyed at the time portray a complex attitude toward the ma'apilim: an appreciation for them on the one hand, diluted with criticism and concern regarding their character and their endurance on the other. Concern regarding the ma'apilim's weakness, and a lack of faith in their ability to bear the burden of the struggle that accompanied the various stages of the Exodus affair, gradually dissipated and ultimately evolved into appreciation bordering on veneration and self-deprecation. Usually, the ma'apilim's maritime voyage was short. The only ones whose journey lasted a long time and included a number of stages were the 4,500 ma'apilim of the *Exodus*, who took part in a three-stage odyssey that lasted more than two months. The first stage was the battle against ships of the British Navy and the soldiers that tried to seize their ship on the open sea. The second stage was the deportation ships' anchoring for three weeks off the coast of France in the blistering August heat, and the ma'apilim's refusal to come ashore despite the French government's invitation to do so. And the third stage was the ma'apilim's disembarkment from the deportation ships at the port of Hamburg.

When the deportation ships reached France carrying the ma'apilim of the *Exodus*, the Yishuv emissaries – the on-board escorts and those awaiting them on shore – were pleasantly surprised by their conduct. They spoke with an air of amazement: "The steadfastness of the masses of ma'apilim – that was the greatest revelation for us. We asked ourselves: Where did these people get the strength to live and persevere in the horrific conditions in which they lived?" The Yishuv's emissary was astonished: "After all, we were told that we would encounter a certain type of people – people who were – "'especially difficult.'"[21] The emissary of the Hechalutz movement in southern France wrote the following to his friends in Palestine immediately after the ships departed Port de Bouc on their way to Hamburg: "We had no faith in these people… We were trembling in anticipation of the ships. What shape would the people be in? How desperate were they? What did they want for the future?... And we were surprised anew."[22] The conduct of the ma'apilim in the *Exodus* affair resulted in a positive change to their image, and the Yishuv was swept up in a collective catharsis of veneration. The intensity of the enthusiastic response and the pleasant surprise was reflective of the low assessment of the ma'apilim that had been widespread in the Yishuv until that point.

The Exodus affair provided background and inspiration for three of Alterman's columns.[23] The first, titled "The War of Europe, 1947," makes no mention of the ma'apilim, but rather relates only to the political aspect of the affair and briefly mentions a youth from the Yishuv who was engaged in bringing over ma'apilim ships.[24] The second column, titled "The People and its Envoy," was inspired by a newspaper report: "A baby born on one of the deportation ships after setting sail died en route. He was buried at sea in a tin box off the Bay of Biscay." The poem's message is as follows: "For we summoned him for this mission - I, you, all of you!" and his "small body … / was recruited for a political and military mission / even before he could stand or speak." Alterman expresses feelings of guilt for placing the burden of the mission on "such an envoy," and he is "questioning whether the nation was pursuing to its limit / a life of boundless and immeasurable sacrifice, / setting its shoulders to the time and their yoke?"[25] While in his column titled "Knesset Israel" the ma'apilim are represented by a young girl, here the heroic ma'apil is an infant. The third column, titled "What is a National Holiday?," is devoted to the *Exodus* and glorifies the ma'apilim – this time, the adults whom the army was forced to drag ashore in Hamburg by their arms and legs: according to the column, a national holiday is "a day on which five English / will need to grasp each man and woman / if they wish to tear them from the state of the Jews."[26]

But of all the poems of "The Seventh Column" that Alterman wrote about Ha'apalah, that praise the heroism of the ma'apilim and are critical of the Yishuv's and the American Jewish community's indifference toward the struggle, the poem that was ingrained in the selective collective memory was actually a poem about "our boys" from Eretz Israel, members of the Palmach, who are "carrying their People on their backs." And for a time, the role of the ma'apilim in the Ha'apalah saga was played down and vanished.

II. From the Establishment of the State to the End of the 1970s: Ha'apalah Devoid of Ma'apilim

During the initial phase of the writing of the history of Ha'apalah between 1945 and 1948, it was devoid of ma'apilim, and the ma'apilim vanished from the public agenda of the newborn state.[27] The heroes of the story being told then are the operatives of the Mossad Le'Aliyah Bet and the Palmach, and the ma'apilim themselves are ignored. If mentioned at all, the ma'apilim are portrayed as a passive factor.

The pioneering text published during this phase of the historiography was *The Ship That Won*, written and edited by the journalist Bracha Habas.[28] This book, which was first published in 1949, recounts the story of the *Exodus* in chapters. The chapter titled "The Plot according to Its Executors" presents the account of Mossad Le'Aliyah Bet operatives and Palmach members, words of one of the American volunteers, and the account of one ma'apil, titled "In the Eyes of a 77 Year Old," who concludes his account as follows: "Had the Jewish Agency and the Haganah not helped us, the refugees, we would have become a horde. *Half* of us would not have remained."[29] The chapter titled "They Were with Us" begins with words of admiration for the "boys from Eretz Israel" who "issued instructions to the ma'apilim," and the latter "entrusted their fate to these comrades and relied on them like children clinging to their mother in the face of danger."[30] This chapter then presents correspondences of the Yishuv emissaries. In one letter, "Gad," who is actually Micha Perry, writes: "It seems that you do not sufficiently appreciate the question of food in terms of steadfastness and the possibility of maintaining a regime that would be suitable for our situation. Just remember that the large majority of the people were former camp inmates, families with children and babies, and a great deal of pregnant women."[31] Many of the letters raised the issue of the ma'apilim's steadfastness in the event that their time on the ships off Port de Bouc was extended. The emissary on one of the deportation ships estimated that "95% of the people are strong and are willing to fight to the end and not to disembark. But the remaining 5% may cause significant difficulties."[32]

A chapter titled "The Anonymous Letter" offers excerpts from letters that were written by the ma'apilim on the deportation ships at Port de Bouc. The letters are signed properly, but then the ma'apilim are anonymous. Moreover, many if not all of the letters that appear in *The Ship That Won* never reached their intended recipients. Mossad Le'Aliyah Bet operatives and other Yishuv emissaries permitted themselves to use these letters as a propaganda tool, prioritizing propaganda over the privacy of the authors.[33]

The Ship That Won exhibits a notable tendency to glorify the boys from the Yishuv while playing down the role of the ma'apilim (and also venerating the Mossad Le'Aliyah Bet at the expense of other parties). The beginning of the book lists the instigators of the "fire of the Hebrew rebellion," including "its **heroes** – the 4,500 people, Jewish refugees, teenage boys and girls, young mothers and 60 babies who fought and went hungry and who became one in their cry: We will not disembark!" However, it goes on to state that "Its **soul** was a small number of young men and women from Eretz Israel, emissaries of the Haganah who carried out its instructions, from which they emerged and which guided their actions and whose spark ignited in their [the ma'apilim's] hearts the torch of sacrifice that is magnificent in sanctifying the name of Israel."[34] Discernible in the book are the fingerprints of Mossad Le'Aliyah Bet chief Shaul Avigur (previously Meirov), who also left his mark on the writing of *History of the Haganah* (noted below). According to Avigur's biographer Arieh Boaz, *The Ship That Won* is an authentic testimony to Avigur's custodianship of the historical writing on issues he regarded as critical, such as Ha'apalah. Indeed, he provided Habas with documents and information, intervened in the content of the book and the manner in which it portrayed the events, and wrote a preface for it.[35]

Another book in the first phase of writing, *The Palmach Book* (1953), highlighted the role of Palmach members in conducting the resistance to the British seizure of ships with a patronizing tone toward the ma'apilim. According to this source, the Palmach members were full of "desire to set out with them – with these ma'apilim fighters, to truly protect them with their bodies, and to pave a path of redemption for them."[36] In the essay "Orientations and Action," which begins the book's section titled "Third Act / Struggle," Yigal Alon writes: "It should be remembered that the resistance to deportation naturally rested on the ma'apilim themselves, and even more so on the Palmach members."[37] And in his summation of the arrival of the *Shabtai Luzhinski* in March 1947, he writes that the operation "was successful thanks to the courage of those who carried out the undertaking...These were the seamen of the Fourth Battalion and the infantrymen of the Second Battalion [of the Palmach]."[38] But where are the 823 ma'apilim?

Approximately 20 years later the second section of Vol. 3 of *History of the Haganah*, which deals with the period of the struggle following World War II, was published. Like *The Ship That Won*, this book also reflects a perceptible tendency to venerate the Mossad Le'Aliyah Bet at the expense of other parties and to glorify the boys of the Yishuv while playing down the role of the ma'apilim.[39] Although the book was published relatively late, in 1972, it is permeated with the spirit of the writing of the 1950s and 1960s, as reflected in the following characteristic examples. The ma'apilim, referred to here as "refugees," are defined as "the grey soldiers" of Ha'apalah.[40] However, the "grey army of Ha'apalah" is in need of protection, and this role is played by the Haganah.[41] The ma'apilim are passive: "The Jewish ma'apil **was brought [to Palestine]** in old, rickety ships."[42] They are also portrayed as passive in the book's account of the La Spezia affair,[43] and the chapter (53) titled "The Ma'apilim Force Their Way to Eretz Israel" speaks of the ships and of Mossad Le'Aliyah Bet operatives, but not of the ma'apilim. The same is true of the chapter (55) titled "Exodus out of Europe, 1947," in which Mordechai Roseman, the leader of the ma'apilim, is characterized simply as "one of the ma'apilim."[44] The chapter is based on testimonies of the Yishuv operatives who took part in Ha'apalah, and when the words of ma'apilim are quoted, they amount to words of praise for their Yishuv escorts.[45]

How can we explain the fact that, during the initial decades following the establishment of the state of Israel, the picture that emerged is one of "Ha'apalah devoid of ma'apilim?" The fundamental explanation lies in the fact that this historiographical phase was a direct extension of the clashes that divided the Yishuv during the period in question (1945-1948). Moreover, the writing was intended to add validity, in retrospect, to the view of one side or the other in the disputes that were dividing the Yishuv at the time, and to strengthen it in the political struggle that was underway within the state of Israel at the time and toward the future. As Avigur had worked to memorialize the role of the Mossad Le'Aliyah Bet that was under his direction, the editor of *The Palmach Book* wrote the following: "The book before us not only fulfills its role as a chronicle of the events it contains and as a monument to the magnificence of an adventurous generation of youth; it also serves as an educational tool and a weapon for ***what lies ahead***."[46] The myth of Ha'apalah, which began to evolve according to the needs of Yishuv society toward the end of the British Mandate, was nurtured with even greater vigor during the initial years of statehood as part of the formation of Israeli society and the struggles that were underway within it.

Four leitmotifs that characterized the first phase of writing contributed to the disappearance and the silencing of the ma'apilim:

1. The first wave of writing of the history of the struggle for the establishment of the state was, for all intents and purposes, history written, officially and semi-officially, on behalf of a national liberation movement for the purpose of creating a national myth for itself and highlighting that it was the master of its own fate and victorious in the struggle against foreign rule. Such writing obviously emphasizes the role of the Yishuv's struggle in the establishment of the state and plays down the importance of international processes and global economic and strategic considerations.

2. In the context of the debate over "who expelled the British from Palestine?" the official and semi-official historiography during the period of Mapai rule emphasized the contribution of Ha'apalah – the Yishuv's mode of struggling, under the direction of the Zionist leadership – to the success of the struggle, while playing down the role of the dissident organizations (whose political legacy was in the opposition) and denouncing the terrorist activities they perpetrated.

3. The Ha'apalah enterprise was also an arena of struggle among forces within the organized Yishuv itself. The Mossad Le'Aliyah Bet, as a stronghold of Mapai, and the Palmach, which was dominated by members of Mapam (which between 1948 and 1954 served to unify Hakibbutz Hameuchad and the Ahdut Ha'avoda movement with Hakibbutz Ha'artzi and the Hashomer Hatzair party) competed with one another regarding their respective contributions to the Ha'apalah enterprise. This period, which witnessed the dismantling of the

Palmach, marked the height of tensions between Ben-Gurion and Mapai on the one hand, and Mapam, which remained in the parliamentary opposition, on the other hand.

4. Just as they exaggerated the description of Ha'apala's centrality to the history of the Yishuv between 1945 and 1948 and the extent of the Yishuv members' participation in the enterprise, they understated the role of the ma'apilim. How did this occur? First, the ma'apilim played no role in the internal Yishuv struggle that guided not only the actions of the period but also the writing of its history. Second, they lacked the free time required to commemorate their role, as their minds at the time were focused on their very existence and on efforts to integrate into their new country. Moreover, the ma'apilim were not yet sufficiently connected within Israel's social, cultural, and political systems. It is common practice to say that history belongs to the victors; however, to an equal extent, it is also the domain of the commemorators; and although they were on the victorious side, the ma'apilim at this stage did not take part in the work of commemoration, and as a result their role in what is commemorated is lacking. Thus, the ma'apilim were relegated to a passive role – not to mention one of "statistics" – in the internal Yishuv struggle that guided not only the actions of the period but also the writing of its history.

In the texts written during the period surveyed in this section, the ma'apilim are portrayed as objects as opposed to subjects. They are discussed as people fulfilling the purpose they were assigned by the leadership and considered in terms of the extent to which they fulfilled their task. The premise of these texts is that the ma'apilim were devoted Zionists. However, alongside this assertion, doubt regarding their resolve also emerges, creating the impression that they were led by members of the Yishuv. For example, Avigur explains the Ha'apalah enterprise as "making use of the unyielding strength of the ma'apilim. We were faced with a stychic force, at some times in a more latent manner and at

other times more explicitly, [people] that had no other choice. And in the final
account, we banked on the existence of such an unyielding force."[47]

Alterman, whose columns between 1945 and 1948 influenced the shaping
of the image of the ma'apilim, returned to Ha'apalah in the 1950s in his poetry
book *City of the Dove*, published in 1957.[48] The book's first section, "Poems of
City of the Dove," contains 30 poems, half of which are devoted to Ha'apalah.
They correspond with and complement poems of "The Seventh Column" from
the period in question, and they deal with the ma'apilim themselves more than
in the past. In "Poem of a Voyage," Alterman's words regarding the ma'apilim
can be understood as maintaining that they were acting on their own free will
and were unified around the aim of reaching Eretz Israel. However, the final line
of the poem returns to "our boys": "And on the shore between Jaffa and Tyre
/ Boys have already pulled a cable to the ship."[49] It is no simple undertaking
to interpret "Sea Canopy," a poem written in the first person plural consisting
of ma'apilim introducing themselves: "And we are just a cramped and desperate
group / having no human face or the image of a woman." Later, they recount a
rebellion that took place on deck: "Horrified / We demanded to divert the ship
from its route / to call for the help of a pursuer from Rhodes or Crete / even if it
diminishes the dignity of the underground." After a description of the Haganah
men seizing the ship, he writes in the name of the ma'apilim: "Against our will we
are intertwined with one another / and not in vain we were called one against the
other this night."[50] Whether or not this description pertains to an event that did
in fact occur, the ma'apilim are not portrayed in a positive manner. In "Poem of
the Elderly," the aged speakers describe the youths' view "that we are an obstacle
to the voyage / and we are millstones weighing down the battle."[51] One of the
poems describes the difficulties of the voyage: not the struggle with the British but
rather the more prosaic difficulties, such as the moldy food, the murky water, and
the meagre clothing. It is a description that arouses identification with the misery
of the ma'apilim.[52] As in the past, the poet gives voice to the weaker among the
ma'apilim: the elderly described above and the children, to whom four out of the
five poems in the cycle "The Woman Born"[53] are devoted.

In the poem "Michael's Page," Alterman returns to the night of disembarkment
from "Reply to an Italian Captain after Landing Night" (January 1946) and shares

the words of Michael, of the Yishuv, that describe the ma'apilim with compassion and returns to the theme of their being carried on the shoulders of his comrades: "As we shoulder those who arrive in the dark, as we carry their lives on our backs / We sense the fear in their breathing and the moaning of their tortured and outcast bodies / But also their hands closing around our throats."[54]

There is no real difference between the view and portrayal of the ma'apilim in the poems of "The Seventh Column," which were written during the period of Ha'apalah, and the "Poems of City of the Dove" that were written during the first decade of Israeli statehood. Alterman wrote the Ha'apalah poems of the 1950s against the background of the mass immigration of the first few years of statehood. He sought to glorify this formative event by linking it to Ha'apalah, which preceded it, and in doing so he also painted the image of the ma'apilim as viewed by members of the Yishuv. Although publication of *City of the Dove* was a widely resonating event in Israeli literary life,[55] it is difficult to estimate its impact on the image of the ma'apilim in Israeli discourse and collective memory.

At the beginning of the 1960s, the Israeli arena witnessed the entry of two powerful forces that helped shape the memory of the Ha'apalah and the role played by the ma'apilim: the book *Exodus*, by Leon Uris, and, even more influential, the Hollywood movie that was based on the book, directed by Otto Preminger and starring Paul Newman. The movie opened in Israeli cinemas in June 1961 (approximately half a year after its release in the United States on Christmas 1960).[56] The film's influence on the historiography of the period that preceded the establishment of the state – including Ha'apalah, the period's representation in the eyes of later generations, and the film's role in shaping private and collective memory in Israel – were all, to a great extent, a product of timing. While the movie was being filmed in Israel the country was rocked by Prime Minister David Ben-Gurion's dramatic announcement before the Knesset (on May 23, 1960) that Adolf Eichmann had been apprehended and was being held in Israel. The film's Israeli premiere in the summer of 1961 (June 21) took place when the Eichmann trial was underway in Jerusalem (beginning on April 11).

The movie was among the experiences of many Israelis for whom the Eichmann trial was a formative experience and a milestone in the development of their Jewish and Israeli identity. To understand the powerful impact of the movie *Exodus*, we need to remember that this was Israel's pre-television era and the golden age of the portable radio. For Israelis in 1961, the Eichmann trial consisted primarily of voices emerging from radio receivers at every turn and brief items on newsreels preceding the main feature in the movie theaters. The scenes in *Exodus* recreating the experiences of the ma'apilim during the Holocaust, the detailed description of the selections in Auschwitz, and the minute, almost technical details of the extermination process provided by Dov Landau during his interview for acceptance into the Etzel were some of the first visual images of the Holocaust seen by Israelis. A picture is worth a thousand words, and *Exodus*, which was more than 200 minutes in length, overshadowed the written material, which at the time was relatively meagre, due to still the pre-historiographic state of the end of the British Mandate. The movie burst into the Israeli reality at a time when the public was thirsty for knowledge on the history of the struggle of 1945-1948 but had few sources of information at its disposal. This was before Israelis were provided academic studies on the period in question, and long before they would see documentary footage of the period.

Uris wrote *Exodus* based on the written material that existed at the time, as well as on interviews that he conducted with countless individuals. Since the beginning of the 1960s, through a process of feedback, the movie has influenced the way in which the people who took part in the events thought they remembered the period.[57] It is well known that the ship and the movie that bore its name had very little in common, if at all. Nonetheless, it influenced the writing about Ha'apalah in the years that followed. For example, the movie contains messages such as "Let me die with the Philistines" and the Masada syndrome. In the midst of the ma'apilim's hunger strike, Ari Ben-Canaan (Paul Newman) tells Kitty Fremont (Eva Marie Saint), who tries to convince him to end the strike and to surrender: "Each person on board this ship is a soldier. The only weapon we have to fight with is our willingness to die." However, such things did not occur during the Ha'apalah enterprise in actuality, and certainly not in the blunt and extreme way it does in the movie. On the contrary: explicit instructions were issued to avoid casualties, Jewish and British alike. On *Exodus*, the ship, children were forbidden to take part in the battle against the British,[58] and they were exempt from the 24-hour hunger strike which the Ma'apilim declared off the coast of France.[59] Still, items from the third phase of the historiography (the 1990s) contain accounts and interpretations that characterize the ma'apilim of the *Exodus* as "sacrificed and sanctified" and integrate them as a link in the chain of Zionist martyrology.

Not only has the movie disrupted memories of the past, it has also served to influence present and future. It positioned Ha'apalah at the apex of public attention in the first half of the 1960s, and 1964 was declared the "year of Ha'apalah." Ostensibly, it was observed to mark the 30th anniversary of the arrival of the first ma'apilim ship, the *Vellos*. However, how can we explain the decision to celebrate the event's 30th anniversary rather than its 25th (a frequently celebrated anniversary referred to in Hebrew as "*hatzi yovel*," or "half jubilee")? This may have resulted from a combination of the impact of *Exodus*, the movie, and processes that had gotten underway in Israeli society. Just as the state of Israel was only freed up to engage with the Holocaust on the state level beginning in the early 1960s, after years of war, mass immigration, and establishing itself economically and in the realm of security – dealing with the milestones of the struggle for statehood was also delayed. The Eichmann trial paved the way and created the need for addressing the period that followed the Holocaust: 1945-1948. And when steps were finally taken to do so, first in the institutional realm and then in academia, *Exodus*, the movie, had already cast its shadow over and influenced the portrayal of the period in question.

One of the major events of the Year of Ha'apalah was a state ceremony held in honor of *Exodus 1947*, which highlighted the role of the Yishuv and members of Mapai. The ma'apilim, who felt they had not been sufficiently represented, erupted in shouts of "Let us have Mordechai Roseman!" and "Get Mordechai on stage!"[60] The same year, the Israeli Information [*hasbara*] Center released a booklet titled *Stories of Ha'apalah: A Collection* that, according to its own description, contained "things that had been said or written during or after the period of Ha'apalah regarding various episodes pertaining to the enterprise. The collection is meant for reading and for the planning of parties and reading evenings and contains excerpts from articles, speeches, memoirs, poems, and more."[61] However, it contains no words articulated by the ma'apilim themselves, as the accounts are primarily those of emissaries, members of the Yishuv, and leaders. The ma'apilim are still mute.

Later on in the period defined here as the first phase of writing about Ha'apalah, a number of books were written and published by Yishuv members who took part in the undertaking. *The Ulua: Arthur's Story*, by Aryeh (Lova) Eliav, is a memoir written with 20 years of perspective on the events and, as indicated by the title, from the viewpoint of the ship's commander from the Yishuv.[62] In general, the ma'apilim are portrayed in a positive manner in the book, which, however, is not devoid of traces of Yishuv condescension.[63] Eliav describes the ma'apilim's conduct during the battle as being "as if by order,"[64] giving the reader the impression that they behaved as they should have, but without addressing the question of whether there was leadership from within their ranks. Ada Sereni's book *Ships with No Flag* on the Ha'apalah from Italy, published a few years later, was also written from a distinctly Yishuv perspective.

Also relevant in this context is Jacques Derogy's 1972 book *A New Light on The Exodus Affair*, which was initially published in French under the title *The Law of Return*. In this book, "new light" is shed primarily on the French involvement, as its protagonists are Mossad operatives and French citizens and statesmen. Although it contains the story of two ma'apilim, "Mordechai" (Roseman) and "Norbert" (Noah Kliger), the ma'apilim still remain in the shadows as relatively mute objects.

In *Ships or a State*, a book published some ten years later (at the beginning of the 1980s), the ma'apilim still play a passive role.[65] The question of how they would conduct themselves, the book states, was a "major unknown,"[66] giving the reader the feeling that the Yishuv's attitude toward this group ranged from condescension to alienation.[67] In general, the ma'apilim's role was written about from the outside and not based on their own accounts.[68] The book was the product of cooperation between a person who took part in the history (Zeev Hadari of the Mossad Le'Aliyah Bet) and a historian (Zeev Tzahor) and was an initial bud of the academic research on Ha'apalah that was published during the period following World War II.

III. The 1980s and the Early 1990s: Returning the Ma'apilim to the story of Ha'apalah

The second historiographical phase of the Ha'apalah, which began at the end of the 1970s, was forced (to use phrasing borrowed from Ahad Ha'am)[69] to contend not only with "the archeological truth" – the events that occurred during the 1940s – but also with the layers of "the historical truth" – meaning, the historiography that had accumulated since then: books, anthologies, articles, films, and public discourse.

The starting point of the second phase of writing is commonly attributed to the opening up of the relevant files in the British archives, which are released 30 years after the date of the events. Thus, from 1976 onward, access was gradually afforded to the files pertaining to the period under discussion here. The declassification of the files of the British (and US) archives has been of paramount importance to research on the political aspects of the period, and the fruits of the research that could be harvested as a result of the opening of the archives also helped shed light on the human aspect of the story of Ha'apalah. Ha'apalah research was also pushed forward by the establishment of the Shaul Avigur (who died in 1978) Interuniversity Project for Research of Ha'apalah in the early 1980s. The project assisted researchers with the provision of scholarships and grants, by making material that was being stored outside of Israel more accessible, and by funding the publication of the products of research as a series of books.[70]

Even before the initial fruits of the Ha'apalah project began to see the light of day (1990), Zeev Hadari's *Refugees Defeating an Empire* appeared. This book, which, like his above mentioned book *Ships or a State*, can be considered a transitional link between the different phases of the Israeli historiography of Ha'apalah. Indeed, Hadari defined his book as "the beginning of a discussion."[71] The book's name gives the impression that it revolves around the ma'apilim, but this is not the case; in fact, it deals primarily with issues of policy and organization. Indeed, it appears to be indecisive, discussing the ma'apilim but offering no words attributed directly to them, and expressing awe at their conduct.[72]

The subtitle of the first book published as part of the Ha'apalah project – *Ha'apalah: Studies of the History of the Rescue, Flight [B'richa], Illegal Immigration and She'erit Hapleta*[73] – accurately reflects its content, and only two articles actually deal with Ha'apalah from Europe following World War II, but not necessarily with the ma'apilim. Only few of the books that were published as part of the project dealt with the ma'apilim's role in Ha'apalah[74] or considered their wants, their desires, their conduct, and the social dynamics among them. Quite a few articles reflecting this approach were also published. Although during this phase of the writing the ma'apilim were portrayed as having had no choice – as all other paths of immigration were closed to them and they did not want to remain in Europe – the picture it paints is that they had not been facing a matter of life and death. To paraphrase an adage taken from a different conceptual world, the ma'apilim and the Jewish survivors as a whole are portrayed not as proletarians with nothing to lose but their chains, but rather as a population with a national consciousness who, under the circumstances of the time and place, chose to take this path and not another. These studies, which are based on sources of the time, show that the Zionist leadership indeed recruited the ma'apilim into the struggle it was leading, but that the ma'apilim identified with it. The ma'apilim were not forced to board the immigrant ships, and the demand to do so outstripped the supply of spaces aboard the ships of the Mossad Le'Aliyah Bet.

The next book published after the *Ha'apalah* volume was a study of the immigrant ship *Exodus 1947* by the author of the present article. Its major innovation was the positioning of the ma'apilim themselves at the heart of the drama,[75] and its major claim was that the Exodus affair was a victory from the Zionist perspective because of the ma'apilim. Flung into a campaign for which they were unprepared, they fulfilled their role in the undertaking beyond all expectations. The book provides a detailed account of the ma'apilim's conduct at each stage of the affair. It shows how ma'apilim who did not take part in the battle off the shores of Palestine were determined in their refusal to disembark in France and how, once they recognized the importance of the task with which they were faced, the importance of their own contribution to it, and their ability to play this role, they did so with distinction. When it came time to disembark in Hamburg following the joint test endured by the ma'apilim off the coast of Port de Bouc, many ma'apilim who had not participated in the battle off the coast of Palestine engaged in passive and even active resistance to leaving the ship. The book also clarifies that the ma'apilim's decision to not leave the ship ("We will not disembark!") on French shores had taken form before instructions along these lines reached the deportation ships orally (via speakers on boats circling the ships) and in writing: "Do not disembark!" We must also address the fact that in the accounts of the Yishuv participants, the words were formulated as an order – "Do not disembark" – whereas the ma'apilim accounts phrase it differently: "We will not disembark."[76] Moreover, the same decision to not disembark was reached on all three ships, whether or not an emissary from the Yishuv was present.

Although the *Exodus* affair was unusual and unique within Ha'apalah, it nonetheless teaches us about the enterprise in general.[77] When the ma'apilim of the *Exodus* first set out on their way to Palestine, they were no different from the ma'apilim who set sail from Italy and France before and after them. They were a representative cross-section of the population of the displaced persons camps in the American Occupation Zone of Germany, where more than 150,000 Jews resided. They represented the different generations of the DPs (in terms of their date of arrival to the camps), the variety of their countries of origin, and their wartime experiences. As a matter of fact, in comparison to the previous maritime voyages, the ma'apilim of the *Exodus* included more families with young children and more older people and lone immigrants ("ordinary Jews," to use the terminology of those days – that is, Jews who did not belong to any of the Zionist movements). We can therefore conclude that if this group passed the test, then this was all the more likely to be the case with the majority of their fellow ma'apilim.

The book *The Deportation Island* written by Nahum Bogner, who was among the ma'apilim imprisoned in Cyprus, was published ten years after the book *The Cyprus Deportation*, whose author David Shaari was an emissary to the camps there. Shaari's book uses the Hebrew term "*avak adam*" (human dust, or wrecked people)[78] and though it depicts the activities of the ma'apilim, it does not do so through their prism, and the sources he consulted were not written by ma'apilim. Bogner, on the other hand, provides more details regarding the activities of the ma'apilim and more information about them, and writes about "the community of ma'apilim." Both researchers agree that no leadership came from the ma'apilim[79] and that there were no charismatic leaders among them.[80]

In the 1980s, ma'apilim began to publish their own stories. A pioneering book in this context was *Yearnings and Upheaval* by *Exodus* ma'apil Yitzhak Ganuz, a literary text that combines memoirs and diary entries.[81] Other such texts were published later.

The studies of the second historiographical phase returned the ma'apilim to the story of the Ha'apalah and portrayed them as subjects and as a group with its own consciousness that was worthy of consideration in its own right.[82] As already noted, if the ma'apilim were related to at all in the previous phase of writing, they were cast primarily as objects whose treatment by Zionism, in addition to their contribution to the Zionist struggle and other instrumental and functional questions, needed to be examined. How can we interpret the difference between the first and the second phases in their account of the role of the ma'apilim? In addition to the fact that the perspective required for historical research now existed, the researchers of the second phase were typically younger and less personally and emotionally, ideologically and politically involved in the events of the time. Moreover, like all historians, the authors of the texts of the second phase were also a product of the society in which they lived. In the formative years of their lives, as part of Israeli society, they experienced the Eichmann trial, the "period of waiting" of May-June 1967 that preceded the Six-Day War, and the Yom Kippur War. These events increased their empathy toward the victims and survivors of the Holocaust. This must be understood in conjunction with the mounting tendency toward socially oriented historical research that takes interest in the individual, and toward the writing of history "from below." It is typical to suspect that the aim of historians is to debunk myths and prove their baselessness; however, the second phase of the historiography of Ha'apalah actually helped reinforce and solidify the real story of the quiet and touching heroism of the ma'apilim.

These changes in the spirit of the research also found expression in Israeli public discourse. In 1987, on the 40th anniversary of the *Exodus* affair, the events revolving around the occasion – a large ceremony at the Mann Auditorium in Tel Aviv and prime-time television programming on Rosh Hashana Eve – transpired in a calm atmosphere devoid of disagreement. By this point, the ma'apilim were already considered to be veteran residents of the country who were equal in status to their former escorts. A quarter of a century of events and new disagreements had given rise to a political partnership between the formerly competing parties, and an air of reconciliation and camaraderie between the ma'apilim and the Yishuv emissaries prevailed.

IV. The 1990s: Transforming the Ma'apilim from Subject to Object

Research on Ha'apalah in general and the role of the ma'apilim in particular continued into the 1990s and the first two decades of the twenty-first century through a number of channels, most of which will be discussed in the next section. The present section deals solely with the brief period of the 1990s, which witnessed the publication of several studies, the major innovation of which was accusations that the Zionist leadership engaged in cynical, instrumental, and even manipulative exploitation of the ma'apilim to meet the needs of the Zionist struggle. The texts of this phase of writing restored the ma'apilim to the role of objects – tools of the Zionist leadership and its emissaries.[83]

The leading scholar of this trend is Idith Zertal, who defined the ma'apilim as a "spearhead in the hands of the Zionist leadership in the struggle for the end of the British Mandate and the establishment of a Jewish state – putty in the hands of the leaders of this struggle and its not-to-be-condemned victim."[84] Although she qualifies her words by pointing out "that many of the ma'apilim/refugees, particularly those who were organized as members of the Zionist youth movements and political parties, did not see themselves as victims of the situation but rather as its willing emissaries and even its heroes," she continues as follows: "They included ordinary people, rank and file individuals, 'difficult human material' – as they were commonly referred to by the emissaries of the Yishuv – who accepted this fate due to lack of any other choice."[85] In *The Jews' Gold*, subtitled (in the Hebrew edition) *The Underground Jewish Immigration to Palestine, 1945-1948*, the Mossad Le'Aliyah Bet is the subject,[86] and the ma'apilim are the object. They are described as "some 80,000 human beings, Diaspora Jews who *were brought* to Palestine after World War II via 'illegal' paths by the Palestine Zionist organization under discussion."[87] The Mossad Le'Aliyah Bet transported the Jews of the Diaspora to the shores of Palestine,[88] and the Zionist leadership's treatment of the Diaspora was instrumentalist and political.[89] Not only is the population that was transported to Palestine not referred to as "ma'apilim," (in the original Hebrew version) as this term is part of the Zionist terminology, but Zertal displays no interest in the question of how this population defined itself[90] and does not rely on sources produced by the ma'apilim themselves.[91]

Yosef Grodzinsky, whose motivations for writing are already evident in his book's subtitle *Jews versus Zionists*, wrote in a similar manner. In his opening words, he clarifies that his book seeks to present an alternative story, a narrative that is different from the familiar history of the Jewish displaced persons in Europe following World War II. One of the questions he asks is: "What portion of them [the Jewish inhabitants of the displaced persons camp] did the Zionist emissaries succeed in bringing to the state of Israel?"[92] Grodzinsky reaches the conclusion that the Jewish remnants were not interested in immigrating to Palestine and that Ha'apalah was therefore against their will (or the result of having no other option). Tom Segev articulates a similar approach in his book *The Seventh Million*, in which the chapter dealing with Ha'apalah says almost nothing about the ma'apilim and focuses primarily on the emissaries, the Zionist leadership, and the political goals of the Zionists.[93]

An intriguing question is whether the political goals of Ha'apalah were consistent with the desires and interests of the ma'apilim or ran counter to them. Scholars of the third phase of writing did not bother to explore whether the ma'apilim identified with the goals of Ha'apalah. As we have seen, the authors of the second phase addressed this issue in the following spirit: the Zionist leadership exploited, or more precisely, harnessed the ma'apilim for the sake of the struggle it was leading, but the ma'apilim identified with it. According to Zeev Tzahor's formulation, the Holocaust survivors were not passive implements of action in the hands of Zionist politics; rather, the Zionist policy was the active tools of action of the Holocaust survivors."[94]

The texts that constituted the historiographical wave of the 1990s were written in the post-Zionist spirit and the style of the "new historians" that was prevalent in Israel at the time. They set the historiography of the Ha'apalah back in a number of ways, most notably in its treatment of the ma'apilim, who reverted to being objects, but this time, to use a post-modernist term from the school of deconstructionism, they were objectified. Actually, it was the authors of these texts who were responsible for this objectification, representing them as silent parcels that, ostensibly, could be moved based on the decision of the

Zionist leadership (and against their own will?) from camp to port, from port to ship, and so on. In their treatment of the ma'apilim, these authors appear to have done the opposite of what they intended: instead of rescuing the dignity of the ma'apilim from the hands of Zionism, which strived to make instrumentalist use of them, as they sought to do, they ended up restoring their status as an object: a population devoid of desires, which moved according to instructions "from above" and without any wants or leadership of its own. Their writing is tainted by the tendency to ignore the ma'apilim and by their distance and alienation from the individuals involved. It is also possible that the ma'apilim were silenced in Zertal's book to prevent their words from toppling her anti-Zionist thesis.[95]

An echo of the ma'apilim's treatment in this writing can be found in Yoram Kaniuk's book about *Exodus* commander Yossi Harel, in which Kaniuk writes, ostensibly as a mouthpiece for the ma'apilim: "They also met other people from the Yishuv who looked at them as if they were human worms…For some of the Yishuv inhabitants, they were no more than cargo being transported to the country."[96]

It seems that the most serious failing of these "new" writers lies in their total lack of understanding, or their ignoring, of the *zeitgeist*: the spirit of the time. When we evaluate the people involved between 1945 and 1948 and their motivations according to the scale of values of an affluent, satiated, occupying, and hedonist Western society like that of 1990s Israel, it is indeed difficult if not impossible to understand the behavior of the ma'apilim and their Zionism. And when we ignore the spirit of the time, we do not consider the possibility that Ha'apalah did not only take from the ma'apilim but may have also given them something, as proud people in search of personal and collective identity.

The post-Zionist writing about Ha'apalah (and about She'erit Hapleta, the surviving remnant of European Jewry) was part of an across-the-board attack on Zionism and the state of Israel aimed at proving that the state was born of sin. It was a multi-front attack, and in addition to the creation of the Palestinian refugee problem in the 1948 war and the treatment of the Jewish immigrants from the Muslim countries that followed, it trained its sights on the sin of the Yishuv's and Zionism's attitude toward European Jewry during the Holocaust and the survivors in its wake. This debate, which, as noted, teaches us more about the 1990s than about the period under study, raises questions regarding the work of the historian. Although the authors of the second phase of the historiography of Ha'apalah (and of the Yishuv and Palestine during the end of the British Mandate) were not as involved in the subject under study and its protagonists as their predecessors were, and although they made use of the critical tools that are customary in academia, we can nonetheless discern in some of them an element of Zionist identification. The writing of the authors of the third phase was characterized by heaping criticism, not only in the professional realm (a critical approach to sources and the like) but also in the ideological realm, and on multiple occasions their ideological approaches were clearly and explicitly revealed. It is generally agreed upon that in the humanities and the social sciences – certainly regarding topics as highly charged as the history of the Yishuv, the Holocaust, She'erit Hapleta, and Mandatory Palestine – researchers who enter the archive bring their baggage with them. The true test, therefore, is whether the researcher walks into the archive to confirm his or her thesis in a deductive manner and to use the archival material to draw circles around the arrow that is already stuck in the wall, or, alternatively, to discover "what really happened" – to develop a thesis and to reaffirm it while remaining aware of his or her ideological diversions, and to be open to the possibility of being "confused by the facts."

The writing about Ha'apalah that was published in the 1990s is not uniform. In addition to the texts mentioned above, texts were also published that were more characteristic of the second phase described in the previous section.[97] These texts were research-based and included in David Shaari's[98] and Dalia Ofer's[99] articles on the Cyprus detainees and the community of ma'apilim that formed there (this trend also continued in the decades that followed). They also included Shlomo Shealtiel's study of Ha'apalah from and through Bulgaria between 1939 and 1949, which approaches the subject from the perspective of the Jews of Bulgaria and reflects the ma'apilim's desire to immigrate to Palestine and the young state of Israel.

At the same time, texts were published that return to topics that had already been explored in the past but that consider them from a different, more personal angle. For example, Nissan Degani's *Exodus Calling*, which combines the perspective of Yishuv inhabitants and those of the ma'apilim, was written based on previous texts and does not presume to offer new facts.[100] The book contains recurring motifs in the spirit of the myth that began to take form during the period under study and that was nurtured during the first phase of writing: that the Ha'apalah enterprise in general, and the *Exodus* in particular, influenced the British decision to refer the matter of Palestine to the UN, as well as the UN's decision to partition Palestine and establish a Jewish state in part of it. Assertions along these lines can be found in other publications, including books written by ma'apilim. As these claims were written after the publication of a significant number of research-based texts that disprove them, historians may find themselves struck by a sense of "I cast out my sigh to the wind": that is to say, that as historians they made an effort in vain, spending their days in archives, linking document to certificate and proving, in signs and in wonders, where a cause and effect relationship existed and where things were different. The myth is stronger than the facts.

As a result of the cumulative effect of the writings in the spirit of the second historiographical phase, the third phase of writing, and processes that got underway in Israeli society – when the 50th anniversary of the *Exodus* affair arrived (1997), it was the subject of a television program along the lines of "*Popolitica*" (a former widely viewed Israeli television program in which aspects of the public agenda were debated in a round-table format), with the balanced participation of ma'apilim, Yishuv escorts, historians – "old" and "new" alike – and politicians. It seemed as if the historiography had reached an overall synthesis between the different orientations – between placing an emphasis on the role of the participants from the Yishuv and ignoring the ma'apilim, on the one hand, and shining a spotlight on the ma'apilim and leaving the others in the shadows, on the other hand. But during the first two decades of the twenty-first century additional changes occurred in the ma'apilim's status in Israeli historiography in its broad sense.

V. The Twenty-First Century: The Ma'apilim Return to the Story of Ha'apalah

Section III of the present article, titled "Returning the Ma'apilim to the story of Ha'apalah," dealt with studies by historians who reincorporated the ma'apilim into the narrative. The trajectory of the past decades, however, is best defined using active language and from the perspective of the ma'apilim: "the ma'apilim return" to the story, whether on their own or through the efforts of their descendants. As the academic research continues, we observe the accumulation of writings by ma'apilim; these texts are characterized by the fact that they do not limit themselves to recording memoirs but also draw political conclusions in the spirit of the myth of Ha'apalah's major contribution to the establishment of the Jewish state, without relying on primary sources or on the products of research that have already been published. This impressionistic trend regarding the Ha'apalah's role in the establishment of the state of Israel can be explained by the ma'apilim's desire to be active partners not only in the struggle but also in achieving its goals.

Here too, the historiographical changes also found public expression. When it came time to observe the 60th anniversary of the *Exodus* affair (2007), a large ceremony was held at the Cameri Theatre (known today as the Beit Lessin Theatre) in Tel Aviv, and the main speaker was ma'apilim leader Mordechai Roseman. Ten years later, the series of events marking the 70th anniversary of the *Exodus* got underway. If in the early years of statehood, as noted, the Ha'apalah was devoid of ma'apilim and the story was primarily one of operatives of the Mossad Le'Aliyah Bet and members of the Palmach, in 2017 the spotlight was on the ma'apilim. At the events marking the 70th anniversary, historians needed to remind the audience that there had been other participants in the *Exodus* affair aside from the ma'apilim – participants from the Yishuv and from the United States. The children of the Mossad Le'Aliyah Bet operatives and the Palmach members do not appear to regard their parents' involvement in the Ha'apalah enterprise as a central event in their life histories, whereas the further away we get from the period, the more significant the Ha'apala has been in the identity definition of the descendants of the ma'apilim. And in the spirit of today, they erect monuments and establish Facebook groups, hold events in Israel and abroad relating to Ha'apalah, and embark upon "roots" journeys with the last remaining ma'apilim and their descendants to the detention camps in Cyprus; the ports in France, Italy, and Germany; and other sites.

From unseen, mute objects overshadowed by members of the Yishuv, the ma'apilim have come to stand side by side with them, and, ultimately, to occupy front and center stage, while the members of the Yishuv have almost completely vanished from the stage. This might be explainable by the fact that the Yishuv's participants in the Ha'apalah enterprise subsequently took part in a difficult war that cast a shadow over their previous experiences (although some ma'apilim also took part in Israel's War of Independence); for the ma'apilim, on the other hand, Ha'apalah was, in real time and certainly in retrospect, a ray of light after a period of severe hardship, a transitional stage toward their integration into Israeli society.

Conclusions: The Ma'apilim and Ha'apalah – A Mutual Contribution

Like the presence of the Holocaust in Israeli society, which only intensifies with the passage of time, the same can be said of Ha'apalah's role in the lives of those who experienced it and their descendants. This trend suggests a notion that can be formulated as a paraphrasing of US President John F. Kennedy's challenge: "Ask not what your country can do for you – ask what you can do for your country." In our case, it is not enough to ask how the ma'apilim contributed to the Ha'apalah and to the struggle for the establishment of the state (around which there is already general consensus) – we also need to ask what participation in Ha'apalah did for the ma'apilim. How did it help their rehabilitation as proud individuals after years of war and suffering, as Jews creating a personal and collective identity for themselves? How were they influenced by the fact that people from the Yishuv in Palestine came to them and said: come with us, join us in a common struggle, in the spirit of David Ben-Gurion's words to displaced persons in 1945: "You are not only needy, but rather also a political force. When I look at you, I can see before me not only Jews who were slaughtered [but rather] also Jewish fighters."[101] A suggestion of the importance of the fact that, through Ha'apalah, Holocaust survivors were also required to give and not only to receive can be found in the difference between the critical approach of survivors in Germany and of the ma'apilim who were detained in Cyprus, toward the JDC on the one hand, and their supportive attitude toward the emissaries from the Yishuv on the other hand. The JDC carried out sacred work in the assistance it provided to displaced persons and ma'apilim, but it was a philanthropic organization with the aim of giving. It placed no demands on the recipients and made no requests, but it also did not give them a feeling of partnership.[102]

For the ma'apilim, and apparently also for their children, participation in the Ha'apalah was a formative and conscious searing experience that served as a ticket of entry to Israeli society.[103] In a book that recounts the events of the remote past by integrating them with the occurrences of the more recent past and with thoughts, memories, and interpretation of an adult, Arie Itamar, who was a child aboard the *Exodus*, explains that when the time came for him to be issued an identity card he decided to have it indicate that he was born in Haifa: "'I am from Haifa,' I said, without thinking twice, to anyone who was interested. This was not a complete lie, as in Haifa Bay, facing the Carmel, I was born again."[104]

In the spirit of the above mentioned assertion that history is the domain of the commemorators, we can say that after the first phase of writing, during which the commemorators were members of the Yishuv – in the twenty-first century it has been the turn of the ma'apilim and their descendants. They erect monuments, plaques, and other commemorative markings in ports (for example, at the Port of Hamburg in Germany, where the ma'apilim of the *Exodus* were taken off the deportation ships, and at the Port of La Spezia, Italy) and in other places. This process recently reached its peak when, at the initiative of Zvi Hatkevitz, who was born to *Exodus* ma'apilim in a deportation camp in Germany, it was decided to award an Israeli state (Ministry of Jerusalem and Heritage) "Ma'apil Medal" to all immigrants who arrived in Israel as ma'apilim between 1934 and 1948.

Endnotes

1 The Hebrew term *ha'apalah*, refers to organized illegal Jewish immigration to Mandate Palestine. The Hebrew term for illegal Jewish immigration is "illegal Aliyah", a fusion of the word "*aliyah*" (meaning Jewish immigration to Eretz Israel) and a phonetic Hebraization of the English adjective "illegal." This fusion is an attempt to resolve the dissonance between "*aliyah*" and "illegality," which, from a Zionist perspective, are inconsistent with one another. The non-Hebrew adjective suggests that this illegality existed solely in the eyes of the foreign regime, as the Zionist conception viewed Aliyah as a natural right of every Jew.

2 On these issues, which are not discussed in the present article, see Reuven Aharoni, *Leaning Masts: Ships of Jewish Illegal Immigration and Arms Purchase after World War II* (Efal, 1997) (Hebrew), and Nahum Bogner, *The Ships of Rebellion: Ha'apalah 1945-1948* (Tel Aviv, 1993) (Hebrew), especially pp. 70-84.

3 For details regarding the ships – including the names they were assigned during Ha'apalah, their original names, their ports and dates of departure, their places and dates of disembarkment, and the number and fate of the ma'apilim they carried – see Yehuda Slutsky (ed.), *History of the Haganah*, Vol. 3, Book 3 (Tel Aviv, 1972), pp. 1902-1903 (Hebrew).

4 See Shlomo Shealtiel, *From Birthland to Homeland: Immigration and Illegal Immigration to Palestine from Bulgaria and via Bulgaria, 1939-1949* (Tel Aviv, 2004) (Hebrew).

5 Some 800 ma'apilim from North Africa were aboard the *Yehuda Halevy* and the *Shivat Zion*, which sailed from Algiers, and another 1,700 sailed on ships that departed from Europe. Details regarding such information and the stories of the immigrants themselves can be found in Daniel Biton Bar-Eli, *Who are you, North African ma'apil? North Africans Who Immigrated to Palestine-EI between January 1947 and May 1948*, master's thesis, University of Haifa, 2012 (Hebrew).

6 Dalia Ofer, "She'erit Hapleta in the Israeli Historiography," *Iyunim: Multidisciplinary Studies in Israeli and Modern Jewish Society* 17 (2007), pp. 465-511 (Hebrew). On her decision to refrain from discussing Ha'apalah, see pp. 467-484. Later, Ofer published an article titled "Historiography and Memory: *Aliyah Bet* and She'erit Hapleta," *Moreshet: Journal for the Study of the Holocaust and Antisemitism* 12 (2015), pp. 96-138, in which she examines the interplay among memory, historical events, and reality in the present. Her discussion in this article deals primarily with memory, and only a small portion considers the impact of historical research. Much of the article addresses the period prior to and during World War II.

7 Y. Noded [Yitzhak Sadeh], "My Sister on the Beach," in Zerubavel Gilad (ed.), *The Palmach Book*, Vol. 1 (Tel Aviv, 1953), p. 725 (Hebrew) (emphasis in quote added).

8   See Aviva Halamish, "Illegal Immigration: Values, Myth, and Reality," *Studies in Zionism* 9 (1) (1988), pp. 47-62, especially p. 48; Idith Zertal, *From Catastrophe to Power: The Holocaust Survivors and the Emergence of Israel* (Berkeley, CA, 1998), pp. 7, 263-269.

9   Nathan Alterman, "Reply to an Italian Captain after Landing Night," *Davar*, January 15, 1946, reprinted in Nathan Alterman, *Writings in Four Volumes*, Vol. 2 (The Seventh Column I) (Tel Aviv, 1963), pp. 97-99 (Hebrew). See also Mordechai Naor, *The Eighth Column: An Historical Journey to the Current-Event Columns of Nathan Alterman* (Tel Aviv, 2006), pp. 132-136 (Hebrew).

10 See Halamish, "Illegal Immigration," p. 49.

11 See Aviva Halamish, The *Exodus Affair: Holocaust Survivors and the Struggle for Palestine* (Syracuse, 1998), p. 67.

12 Much has been written on the La Spezia affair. For a succinct summation, see Mordechai Naor, *At Sea, On Land, and in the Air: A New Look at Ha'apalah* (Israel, 2015), pp. 45-55 (Hebrew).

13 See, for example, Irit Keinan, "Between Hope and Fear," in Anita Shapira (ed.), *Ha'apala: Studies of the History of Illegal Immigration into Palestine, 1934-1948* (Tel Aviv, 1990), p. 215 (Hebrew).

14 See Dalia Ofer, "Holocaust Survivors as Immigrants: The Case of Israel and the Cyprus Detainees," *Modern Judaism* 16 (1996), pp. 6-8.

15 See Nahum Bogner, *The Deportation Island: Jewish Illegal Immigrants' Camps on Cyprus, 1946—1948* (Tel Aviv, 1991), pp. 222-234 (Hebrew), especially the notes on pp. 356-358, which contain examples of written and spoken remarks made during this period.

16 David Shaari, *The Cyprus Deportation, 1946-1949: Clandestine Immigration, the Camps, and the Immigrant Society* (Jerusalem, 1981), p. 85 (Hebrew), based on the Haganah Historical Archive (hereinafter, HHA), 14/452, the ship: *Mordei Hagetaot*.

17 *Haaretz*, May 26, 1947.

18 Shaari, *The Cyprus Deportation*, pp. 64-65, based on HHA 14/292, the ship: *Sh'ar Yishuv*.

19 Nathan Alterman, "Division of Duties," *Davar*, December 13, 1946. Reprinted in Alterman, *Writings*, Vol. 2, pp. 102-104 (Hebrew).

20 Halamish, "Illegal Immigration," p. 61.

21 Giora [Elhanan Vanchozker – subsequently Ishay] Recounts," Bracha Habas (ed.), *The Ship that Won: The History of Exodus 1947*, second edition (Tel Aviv, 1954), pp. 66-69 (Hebrew).

22 Hanan Reichman, August 26, 1947, Central Zionist Archive (hereinafter, CZA), S25/2630 (Hebrew).

23　Naor, *The Eighth Column*, pp. 140-141.

24　Nathan Alterman, "The War of Europe, 1947," *Davar*, August 25, 1947. Alterman did not include this column in the volumes of *The Seventh Column* that were published during his lifetime. It was printed in Nathan Alterman, *The Seventh Column*, Vol. 3 (Tel Aviv, 1978), pp. 156-157 (Hebrew).

25　Alterman, "The People and Its Envoy," *Davar*, September 5, 1947, reprinted in Alterman, *Writings*, Vol. 2, pp. 85-87 (Hebrew).

26　Alterman, "What is a National Holiday," *Davar*, September 12, 1947, reprinted in Alterman, *Writings*, Vol. 2, pp. 88-89 (Hebrew).

27　See Halamish, "Illegal Immigration"; Idith Zertal, "Vanishing Souls: The Ma'apilim and the Mossad Le'Aliyah Bet in the Struggle for Statehood and Afterward," *Hatziyonut* 14 (1989), pp. 107-126 (Hebrew).

28　The first edition was published in 1949, and the second edition was published in 1954. The references in the present article refer to the latter edition.

29　"In the Eyes of a 77 Year Old: A Grandfather's Account," in Habas, *The Ship That Won*, pp. 133-136; the quote: 136 (emphasis in original).

30　Haim Greenstein, "They Were With Us," in Habas, *The Ship That Won*, pp. 181-183. First printed in *Unzer Weg*, Munich, 1 Kislev 5708 (November 14, 1947).

31　August 4, 1947, in Habas, *The Ship That Won*, p. 185.

32　August 13, 1947, in Habas, *The Ship That Won*, p. 190.

33　In addition, I was unable to ascertain where the letters were archived. One of the ma'apilim whose letters appeared in the book (pp. 175-177) told me that his friends never received the letter (interview with Yosef Leichter, February 7, 1985). Lilia Bassevitch, a member of Kibbutz Ein Harod who was residing in Paris at the time, received many letters written by *Exodus* ma'apilim and published excerpts from them in *D'var Hapo'elet*, October 14, 1947. Particularly interesting is the evolution of the poem "Be Quiet, the Sea" by Hashomer Hatzair member Yehuda Pecker, who tried to pass it from his deportation ship to fellow movement members on the other ships. The poem never reached his friends and was instead published in Yiddish in Mapai's *Das Wort* and subsequently translated into Hebrew and published in *D'var Hapo'elet*. Interview with Yehuda Pecker, (February 7, 1985). The poem was included in Habas, *The Ship That Won*, p. 226, with no author indicated. See Halamish, *Exodus: The Real Story*, (Tel Aviv, 1990), p. 276, note 14 (Hebrew). This matter is not addressed in the English edition of the book (*The Exodus Affair*).

34　Habas, *The Ship That Won*, unnumbered page to the left of p. 12.

35　Arieh Boaz, *Unseen Yet Always Present: The Life Story of Shaul Avigur* (Tel Aviv, 2001), p. 309 (Hebrew).

36 "Waiting for a Message," in Gilad, *The Palmach Book*, Vol. 1, pp. 686-688.

37 Ibid., p. 583 (emphasis added).

38 Ibid., p. 589.

39 Yehuda Slutsky, *History of the Haganah*, Vol. 3, Book 2 (Tel Aviv, 1972) (Hebrew).

40 Ibid., p. 1092.

41 Ibid., pp. 1092-1093.

42 Ibid., p. 1092 (emphasis added).

43 Ibid., pp. 1123-1130.

44 Ibid., p. 1159.

45 Ibid., p. 1161.

46 Gilad, *The Palmach Book*, Vol. 1, p. IX (emphasis in original).

47 Shaul Avigur, Testimony. Recorded in writing by Bracha Habas, March 7, 1959, HHA 3403/278 (Hebrew).

48 Nathan Alterman, *City of the Dove* (Tel Aviv, 1957) (Hebrew). Citations here refer to the edition published by Hakibbutz Hameuchad in 1987. See also Dan Laor, *Alterman: A Biography* (Tel Aviv, 2014), pp. 504-566 (Hebrew).

49 "Poem of a Voyage," *City of the Dove*, pp. 13-14. See also Laor's interpretation in *Alterman: A Biography*, p. 513.

50 Alterman, "Sea Canopy," *City of the Dove*, pp. 15-17.

51 Alterman, "Poem of the Elderly," *City of the Dove*, pp. 22-23.

52 Alterman, "Poem of the Persecuted," *City of the Dove*, p. 21.

53 Alterman, "A Woman Born," *City of the* Dove, pp. 57-67.

54 Alterman, "Michael's Page," *City of the Dove*, pp. 25-27.

55 Laor, *Alterman: A Biography*, p. 509.

56 A Hebrew edition of Uris book *Exodus*, translated by Yosef Nedava, was published in 1959. On the film's reception in Israel see Rachel Weissbrod, "Exodus as a Zionist Melodrama," *Israel Studies* 4(1) (Spring 1999), pp. 129-152. See also Aviva Halamish, "Exodus, the Movie – Half a Century Later: The Interplay of History, Myth, Memory, and Historiography," in *Jewish Film & New Media: An International Journal* 5(2) (2017), pp. 123-142.

57 On the film's possible impact on Ada Sereni's treatment of the date on which the Exodus set sail in her book *Ship without a Flag* (Tel Aviv, 1975), p. 140, (Hebrew)

which differs from the telegram on the issue she wrote in July 1947, see Halamish, *The Exodus Affair*, p. 54.

58 See Halamish, *The Exodus Affair*, p. 89.

59 Ibid., p. 135.

60 Letter to the editor from Micha Perry, *Maariv*, November 25, 1964 (Hebrew). See Halamish, *The Exodus Affair*, pp. 273-274.

61 *Some Stories of Ha'apalah: An Anthology* (Hebrew), compiled by the Center for Information in Jerusalem, December 1964, unnumbered page following the title page.

62 Aryeh (Lova) Eliav, *The Ulua: Arthur's Story* (Tel Aviv, 1968), unnumbered page (Hebrew).

63 Ibid., p. 199.

64 Ibid., p. 193.

65 Zeev (Venia) Hadari and Zeev Tzahor, *Ships or a State: The Story of the Pan York and the Pan Crescent* (place and year of publication not indicated), pp. 58-74 (Hebrew).

66 Ibid., p. 62.

67 Ibid., p. 183.

68 For example, Ibid., p. 231.

69 Ahad Ha'am, "Moshe," first published in *Hashilo'ah* 13(2) (Shvat 5664 / January 1904) and subsequently reprinted in the various editions of *At The Crossroads* and *All the Writings of Ahad Ha'am* (Hebrew)

70 Upon the project's completion, the materials that were collected during its years of activity were deposited in the Haganah Historical Archives.

71 Zeev Venia Hadari, *Refugees Defeating an Empire: Chapters in the History of Aliyah Bet, 1945-1948* (Tel Aviv, 1985), p. 11 (Hebrew).

72 Ibid., p. 228.

73 Shapira, *Ha'apala*.

74 Of the nine monographs that were published as part of the project, only three dealt with Ha'apalah after World War II: Halamish's Hebrew version of *The Exodus Affair* (*Exodus: The Real Story*), Bogner's *The Deportation Island*, and Shealtiel's *From Birthland to Homeland*.

75 This is emphasized by the title of the book's English edition: *The Exodus Affair: Holocaust Survivors and the Struggle for Palestine* (Syracuse University Press, 1998).

76 This matter is discussed extensively by Halamish in *The Exodus Affair*, pp. 112-121, in the chapter titled "We Shall Not Land!"

77 See Aviva Halamish, "'Exodus': The Specific Case and the Overall Significance," *Ha-Ziyonut* 18 (1994), pp. 383-390 (Hebrew).

78 Shaari, *The Cyprus Deportation*, p. 189.

79 Ibid., p. 315.

80 Bogner, *The Deportation Island*, p. 271.

81 Yitzhak Ganuz, *Yearnings and Upheaval* (Tel Aviv, 1985) (Hebrew).

82 See, for example, Ofer, "She'erit Hapleta," p. 485.

83 Idith Zertal, "The Sacrificed and the Sanctified: Constituting a National Martyrology," *Zmanim* 48 (Spring 1994), pp. 26-45 (Hebrew). On p. 42, Zertal advances an argument that holds that the Zionists treated the ma'apilim like packages "which the porters pass to one another and unload indifferently onto one platform or another, in some station."

84 Zertal, "Vanishing Souls," pp. 107-108.

85 Ibid., p. 117.

86 Zertal, *From Catastrophe*, p. 2.

87 Ibid., p. 4 (emphasis added).

88 Ibid., p. 5.

89 Ibid., p. 9.

90 Ibid., p. 8.

91 Ibid., pp. 11. On this matter, see also Ofer, "She'erit Hapleta," p. 485.

92 Yosef Grodzinsky, *Good Human Material: Jews versus Zionists, 1945-1951* (Or Yehuda, 1998), pp. 178-179 (Hebrew) (emphasis added).

93 Tom Segev, *The Seventh Million: The Israelis and the Holocaust* (New York, 2000), pp. 123-139.

94 Zeev Tzahor, "The Holocaust Survivors and Zionist Politics: Who was the exploiter and who was exploited?" in Eli Tzur (ed.), *Old World, New Man: Jewish Communities in the Era of Modernization* (Jerusalem 1995), pp. 264-279: 279 (Hebrew). For an earlier version of this article, see Zeev Tzahor, "The Holocaust Survivors in Europe as a Political Factor," *Middle Eastern Studies* 24(4) (1988), pp. 432-444.

95　See Ofer, "She'erit Hapleta," p. 466: "For some researchers the primary goal is to undermine the overarching Zionist narrative on different levels, even at the price of distorting the historical data."

96 Yoram Kaniuk, *Exodus: The Odyssey of a Commander* (Tel Aviv, 1999), p. 155 (Hebrew).

97 Studies were also published on the ma'apilim's absorption and integration in Israel, though this is not the topic of the present article.

98 David Shaari, "Characteristics of the Ma'apilim Community in the Cyprus Deportation Camps," *Massuah* 25 (1997), pp. 48-62 (Hebrew).

99 Ofer, "Holocaust Survivors as Immigrants."

100 Nissan Degani, *Exodus Calling* (Tel Aviv, 1994) (Hebrew).

101 Shabtai Teveth, *Kin'at David, Vol. IV: A Man of Strife* (Jerusalem, 2004), p. 602 (Hebrew).

102 Bogner deals with this issue in his book *Deportation Island*, particularly on pp. 86-88.

103 See Ofer, "She'erit Hapleta," p. 497.

104 Arie Itamar, *Misty Mists: The Experiences of a Six-Year-Old on the Escape Route from Europe to the Voyage on the Exodus* (Israel, 2007) (Hebrew). Quote taken from the 2nd Edition (2019), p. 99.

Roni Stauber

Ben-Gurion and the Eichmann Trial: The Historiographical Debate

The goal of this article is to consider the historiographical debates surrounding the extent to which Israeli Prime Minister David Ben-Gurion intervened in the processes that resulted in the abduction of Adolf Eichmann in Buenos Aires and Eichmann's trial in Jerusalem. Did he authorize Eichmann's abduction and transfer to Israel ahead of time, with the intention of holding a historical trial that would generate a comprehensive account of the events of the Holocaust, even if the defendant was not involved in them all? Did he set educational and political goals for the trial? And what was the extent of his influence on the manner in which the prosecution was handled?

Eichmann in Jerusalem **and** *the Crooked Shall be Made Straight*

The assertion that Ben-Gurion had a decisive influence on the Eichmann Trial was first advanced, in an extremely profound manner, in Hannah Arendt's well-known book *Eichmann in Jerusalem*. Arendt covered the trial for the liberal American weekly *The New Yorker*, and her articles on the subject were published in five parts at the beginning of 1963.[1] According to Arendt, the book was written in the summer and autumn of 1962, shortly after the denial of Eichmann's appeal of his conviction and death sentence.[2]

Arendt maintains that Ben-Gurion devised the trial's trajectories and goals ahead of time, and that, based on the intention to use the trial to further educational, political, and ideological goals, he ordered that Adolf Eichmann be abducted from Argentina and brought to Israel. According to Arendt, Ben-Gurion was the "invisible stage manager of the proceedings," and Chief Prosecutor Gideon Hausner was his obedient emissary. The prosecution, argues Arendt, produced a show trial: that is, a trial planned for political purposes possessing the attributes of a play.[3] "Not once does he [Ben-Gurion] attend a session; in the courtroom he speaks in the voice of Gideon Hausner, the Attorney General, who, representing the government, does his best, his very best, to obey his master."[4] In this manner, Arendt maintains, the prosecution undercut the legal principle underlying the trial, which was meant to address Eichmann's crimes alone. The prosecution was conducted according to the instructions of the prime minster: "For this case was built on what the Jews had suffered, not on what Eichmann had done."[5] Only the judges tried to the best of their ability to stand firm by preventing the proceedings from degenerating into a show trial, and on a number of occasions they failed to do so. "The trial," writes Arendt, "is presided over by someone who serves justice as faithfully as Mr. Hausner serves the State of Israel."[6]

Eichmann in Jerusalem establishes a direct link between the words spoken by Ben-Gurion in his public addresses and interviews and the trajectory that guided the prosecution: emphasis on the hatred of the Jews throughout the generations, culminating in Nazi antisemitism and the Final Solution, and focus on Jewish suffering during the Holocaust. The prosecution operated according to the aims specified by Ben-Gurion. On the domestic level, the trial was meant to strengthen youth consciousness regarding the importance of the state of Israel and the change which the state's establishment had brought about in the Jewish People: now, unlike the Jews of Europe, the Jews of Israel can fight back. On the international level, the trial was meant to increase world awareness of the results of anti-Jewish hatred. Although Arendt does not say so explicitly, she appears to have believed that Ben-Gurion's intention was to increase the commitment of countries all over the world to the security of the state of Israel: "The audience at the trial was to be the world and the play the huge panorama of Jewish sufferings."[7] From Arendt's perspective, this approach of depicting the role of Eichmann and his associates in implementing the Final Solution solely from the perspective of anti-Jewish hatred was consistent with the perception of Jews around the world and the Jews of Israel in particular. However, it overlooked the Final Solution's deep universal meaning "as a crime against humanity that was perpetrated against the body of the Jewish People." This was the view of prominent figures such as philosopher Karl Jaspers, who called for an international trial. The attempt at complete annihilation that was organized by the German state apparatus using technological means – or "administrative massacre," to use Arendt's words – must serve as a warning sign for humanity as a whole. This warning should have been issued from Jerusalem, but the narrow perception that was adopted at Ben-Gurion's direction during the trial – that of the "the most horrible pogrom in Jewish history" – precluded discussion of the universal meaning of the "unprecedented crime," although it was clear that "this type of killing can be directed against any given group, that is, that the principle of selection is dependent only upon circumstantial factors."[8]

Immediately following the publication of Arendt's series of articles and her book, a deep-seated controversy erupted among intellectuals in different parts of the world, and especially Jewish intellectuals in the United States. The controversy and fundamental criticism focused on two theses advanced by Arendt:

1. The character of the perpetrator – Eichmann - was described as an average, "normal" bureaucrat whose actions were motivated not by the hatred of Jews or ideological conviction but rather by diligence and the aspiration for promotion. According to this account, Eichmann was an official who committed serious crimes under circumstances that precluded him from knowing or sensing the intensity of the injustice he was perpetrating.

2. The cooperation of the Jewish leadership as an important element of the success of the Final Solution – According to Arendt, "Jewish officials…became instruments of murder."[9]

Although the controversy revolved around these two primary claims, Arendt's negative depiction of the prosecutor as Ben-Gurion's emissary and Ben-Gurion's characterization as the trial's "stage manager" also sparked reproach. This criticism was articulated primarily in the book *And the Crooked Shall be Made Straight* by international law expert and Holocaust scholar Jacob Robinson.[10] Between the two world wars, Robinson served as the head of the Jewish faction of the Lithuanian parliament and Lithuania's envoy to the League of Nations, where he earned a reputation as an expert in international law in general and minority rights in particular. Following the Soviet invasion of Lithuania in June 1940, Robinson was issued an entry visa to the United States, and in 1941 he established the Institute of Jewish Affairs (IJA) in New York under the auspices of the World Jewish Congress. Following the war, he served as a special advisor to Robert Jackson, the chief US prosecutor at the Nuremberg Trials, on the subject of the murder of European Jewry, in an ultimately unsuccessful attempt to engage the Holocaust as a unique Jewish event that was distinct from other crimes discussed during the trials. After the establishment of Israel, Robinson served as legal advisor to the Israeli delegation to the United Nations. During the 1950s and the early 1960s, he served as a special advisor to Yad Vashem. Hausner asked Robinson to join the prosecution team in the Eichmann Trial, and the latter had immense influence on the manner in which the prosecution was handled.[11]

According to Robinson, *And the Crooked Shall be Made Straight* was intended to present a reliable and well-based historical and legal picture as an alternative to the distorted picture that Arendt had presented. Its goal was to refute that which Robinson characterized as "vast falsehoods, lies, and fabrications…Hannah Arendt's malicious words that lay blame on the martyrs." Therefore, in an effort to expand the trial's scope to include an exploration of the historical and legal issues pertaining to the trial, the book deals with Eichmann's character and actions, the Jews' steadfastness in light of the Holocaust, the legal aspects of the Nuremberg Trials, and the conduct of the Eichmann Trial. In the chapter dealing with the conduct of the trial, Robinson – who, as noted, played a substantial role in formulating the strategy of the prosecution – addresses Arendt's claims regarding the show trial envisioned by Ben-Gurion and the chief prosecutor who did his bidding. Robinson altogether repudiates Arendt's claims regarding Ben-Gurion's involvement in demarcating the guiding approach of the prosecution, as well as her conviction that he demanded that the trial be subordinated to ideological and educational goals, thus imbuing it with the character of a show trial.[12]

According to Robinson, the trial's testimony-based broad engagement with the suffering of the Jews by no means deviated from criminal law's principle of addressing the charges alone. Robinson maintained that the prosecution was obligated to prove the outcome of the crime – as "where there is no injury, there is no crime" – and the many testimonies made a great contribution. Robinson did not deny the assumption that the trial had moral and educational aims;

rather, he maintained that these aims were not the purpose of the trial as far as the prosecution was concerned and did not run counter to the trial's true aim: proving Eichmann's guilt. They also did not cause the trial to stray from the principles of criminal law, as "the aim of bringing criminals to justice is metajuridical…The metajuridical purpose does not, however, contradict the immediate purpose of doing justice…It is inevitable that certain trials, especially trials such as those conducted at Nuremberg and Jerusalem, generate side effects not directly related to their judgments."[13]

The Decisions regarding Eichmann's Abduction and the Trial in Jerusalem

A generation elapsed between the publication of *Eichmann in Jerusalem* and *And the Crooked Shall be Made Straight*, on the one hand, and the first studies that dealt, among other things, with Ben- Gurion's role in Eichmann's abduction and trial, on the other. The latter studies, which were published primarily in Israel during the 1990s and the first years of the twenty-first century, marked the beginning of a trend that gained momentum in the years that followed: the study of Holocaust consciousness in Israel. Published at the beginning of the 1990s, Tom Segev's book *The Seventh Million* was one of the most noticeable portents of this field. Despite its criticism by the community of historians in Israel immediately following its publication, it was undoubtedly a groundbreaking and influential study on the formation of Holocaust consciousness in Israeli society.[14]

In the chapters dealing with the Eichmann trial, Segev presents a somewhat toned down version of Arendt's account of Ben-Gurion's involvement. Like Arendt, he relates to Ben-Gurion as the one who paved the way for the trial. According to Segev, from the very outset, on the eve of the abduction, Ben-Gurion had clear goals for the trial, which was intended to influence Holocaust consciousness on both the national and international levels. Had this not been the case, Segev reasons, "he [Eichmann] could have been assassinated on Garibaldi Street."[15] In the international realm, the aim of the trial was to "remind the countries of the world that the Holocaust obligated them to support the only Jewish state on earth." In this context, Segev relies largely on an interview that Ben-Gurion granted to *The New York Times* in late December 1960, in which he explained that "the world must learn from the trial where hatred of the Jews…led – and then it must be made ashamed of itself." At the same time, maintains Segev, the trial was meant "to impress the lessons of the Holocaust on the people of Israel, especially the younger generation and immigrants from the Arab countries." From this interview Segev cites Ben-Gurion's call for the youth to learn from the trial about the revolution that had occurred within the Jewish People as a result of the establishment of the state of Israel: "that Israelis are not like lambs to be taken to slaughter, but rather a nation that is able to fight back."[16]

Segev maintains that the trial was also linked to ethnic tension in Israel. From his perspective, the decision to conduct the trial stemmed, among other things, from the desire "to unite Israeli society" through "some collective experience, one that would be gripping, purifying, patriotic, a national catharsis," against the background of the Wadi Salib riots and the sense of threat to the hegemony of the Mapai-led Ashkenazi establishment. The chapter, however, cites no pre-trial evidence to support this explanation, but only a brief statement that Ben-Gurion made more than two years after it had been decided to hold the trial. At that time, the prime minister was relating to the national need, which existed prior to the Eichmann trial, to expose Israelis who had "lived in Asia or Africa" to the events of the Holocaust.[17] On the other hand, at the first meeting of the Israeli Government that discussed the abduction and in interviews he gave before the trial got underway, including an interview in *The New York Times*, Ben-Gurion referred to the generation that had grown up in Israel, and not to the Jews who had immigrated to Israel from Arab countries. "It is essential for us. There is a new generation that has heard things but did not live through it. We cannot blame Sabras [native born Jewish Israelis] who do not feel it."[18]

Also absent is documentary evidence of Segev's other explanations for Ben-Gurion's decision to hold the trial, some of which, as we will see, were adopted by Idith Zertal – such as "to restore Mapai's control of the legacy of the Holocaust," "to erase the historical charges that had stuck to Mapai since the Kastner Trial," and "to prove that despite its relations with Germany, Ben-Gurion's government was not indifferent to the memory of the Holocaust" (see below).[19]

At the end of the first of the two chapters dealing with the Eichmann Trial (the chapter dealing with the preparations for the trial), Segev quotes and appears to accept Arendt's assessment of the event as a show trial without critically engaging it. Elsewhere, he characterizes the trial as "historical" but does not distinguish between the two terms (see below) and describes it as "a production far more elaborate than what was necessary to convict Adolf Eichmann in court."[20]

Approximately a decade after the publication of Segev's book, two books published at approximately the same time discussed the Eichmann Trial's impact on Holocaust consciousness and its major role in Israeli society: Hanna Yablonka's *The State of Israel vs. Adolf Eichmann*, published in 2001, and Idith Zertal's *Death and the Nation* published in 2002. These books represent different views on the question of whether Ben-Gurion ordered Eichmann's abduction and trial based on the assessment that it could be shaped as an educational and ideological tool to influence Israeli society.

Zertal's book is a collection of articles, a few of which had already been published in other formats. It dedicates one chapter to the trial, with an emphasis on Ben-Gurion's role in it. In this chapter, titled "From the People's Hall to the Wailing Wall," Zertal examines the relationship between the political narrative of the Holocaust, which she maintains was shaped during the Eichmann Trial, and the fear of extermination that gripped Israeli society during the "period of waiting" that immediately preceded the Six-Day War. During these weeks, according to Zertal, a "Holocaust discourse" was implemented for the first time, which meant the construction of a false representation of a threat – emanating from Israel's Arab enemies – of individual physical extermination of the Jews living in Israel.[21]

The arguments advanced by Zertal in this chapter constitute one layer of the book's overall thesis, which casts Holocaust memory and commemoration in Israel as a means of achieving national goals. The most important of these goals was to create a "consciousness of strength" as an ideal, through an emphasis on the Jewish helplessness that characterized the period of the Holocaust. According to Zertal, the state leadership's overall interest in Holocaust commemoration stemmed solely from the desire to intensify the feeling of being threatened by the Arab world around them – a fear of destruction that the state of Israel never truly faced.

Without reservation, Zertal adopts Arendt's claim that Ben-Gurion envisioned the direction and goals of the trial ahead of time, with the intention of taking advantage of it for educational, political, and ideological purposes. She notes Arendt's "prophetic words" in this context even before Arendt left Jerusalem, and she argues that they reflect a mere fraction of what occurred during the trial. Zertal notes that it was Arendt who first defined the Eichmann Trial as a show trial and agrees that this classification was indeed reflective of the proceedings. It was designed as such ahead of time, she holds, and was meant to achieve "goals that were extra-legal, ideological, political, propaganda-related, educational, and cultural."[22]

"Why now?" Zertal asks rhetorically. Why did Ben-Gurion barely address the Holocaust in the 1950s only to begin aggressively promoting national engagement with the extermination of European Jewry in the early 1960s? Zertal offers a number of answers to this question. Like Segev, and, we can assume, following his lead, she resolutely states that the trial was intended, among other things, as Ben-Gurion's "belated answer," against the background of the Kasztner-Gruenwald trial and Israel's Reparations Agreement with Germany, to the charge that he had "'forgotten' the Holocaust, 'sold' the memory of the victims for German money."[23] Again, these assertions have no documentary basis whatsoever and are difficult to accept even in conjecture. Both in terms of the Reparations Agreement and Israel's developing economic and security ties with Germany, Ben-Gurion was not deterred by controversy with those who disagreed with his views. He once again proclaimed that strengthening the state of Israel, even by means of German support, was the fulfillment of the last testament of the victims. He spoke these words just a few months before authorizing Eichmann's abduction.[24] There is also no evidence to establish the claim that Ben-Gurion felt a need to prove that he had not "forgotten" the Holocaust, nor that he sought to defend himself against the charges made during the Kasztner Trial regarding the conduct of the Yishuv leadership during World War II. Moreover, it is unclear how the trial was supposed to serve Ben-Gurion's interest in this matter, and it is difficult to accept Zertal's claim that the trial was meant "to reestablish Ben-Gurion's already waning narrative as 'the father of the nation'."[25] One month before the order was issued to capture

Eichmann, Mapai, under Ben-Gurion's leadership, achieved its most impressive electoral victory ever, winning 47 of the Knesset's 120 seats. At the heart of Mapai's election campaign had been the slogan "*imru ken lazaken*" – "say yes to the old man." It was Ben-Gurion's victory and an expression of confidence in him and his leadership. With justification, Segev writes: "Ben-Gurion was then at the height of his power as prime minister. He did not need the Eichmann Trial to reinforce his power."[26]

These arguments advanced by Zertal regarding the factors that motivated Ben-Gurion to order the capture and trial of Eichmann are secondary to her main thesis, which can be summed up by pairing the words "Holocaust" and "power." The thrust of this thesis is that the Israeli establishment's manipulative use of the memory of the Holocaust and of Jewish suffering to achieve educational goals was destructive. The progenitor of the sin was Ben-Gurion, with the "national pedagogy" that, to a great extent, he dictated to the state of Israel by means of the Eichmann Trial. This approach was rooted in the tension between the ostensive threat looming over Israel of extermination by the Arabs, and Israel's ability to fight back, in contrast to European Jewry's helplessness during the Holocaust. The testimonies during the trial were meant to highlight the tragedy that lies in weakness. At the same time, Ben-Gurion's speeches, which repeatedly compared Hitler and the Nazis to Nasser and the Arabs, and the attempt during the trial to overstate the involvement of the Mufti of Jerusalem, al-Haj Amin al-Husayni, in the Final Solution, were intended to emphasize that only power against the enemy plotting the Jews' destruction and a willingness for total sacrifice on the part of young Israelis could prevent another Holocaust. The sin, to use Zertal's terminology, lies "not only [in] the creation of the false illusion of an immediate threat of extermination" and demonization of the Arabs and their leaders, but also in the injury to the memory of the murdered, the devaluation of "the suffering and death of the victims and the grief of the survivors."[27]

The sources clearly indicate that Ben-Gurion sought to use the trial to highlight the dramatic change that the Jewish People had undergone thanks to the establishment of the state of Israel, and its resulting ability to fight back against and punish its enemies. It is also clear that an effort was made during the trial to exaggerate the Mufti's involvement in the Holocaust. Nonetheless, the assertion that "Holocaust and power are the subtext of the entire trial" is inconsistent with the evidence. Zertal completely disregards the possibility that it was the intention of the prosecutor to use the testimonies to create empathy for and recognition of the suffering of the Jews during the Holocaust and their struggle for existence. For her, it appears implausible that Ben-Gurion sought, to use the words of Alterman, "exposure of the essence of the crime and its denunciation," although the Prime Minister had spoken explicitly in this spirit at the first meeting of the Government following his announcement of Eichmann's capture before the Knesset (see below).

It should also be noted that Ben-Gurion's depiction of the revolution that had occurred within the Jewish People in its realization of the importance of military power, as a lesson of the Holocaust, contained nothing vis-à-vis things he had said in the 1950s. Change was also not evident in his view of the plot to annihilate the state of Israel that was being pursued by Arab leaders in general and Nasser in particular as students, according to Ben-Gurion, of the Nazis. Unlike the impression created by Zertal's words, the sources offer no indication that at the end of the 1950s, Ben-Gurion sought a "spectacle," to use the words of Zertal, to convey these messages. According to Zertal, "Eichmann, like other Nazi leaders who survived, were in Israel's 'sights' even earlier, but the authorization to capture him was only granted at the end of the 1950s." That is to say, the information existed, and Ben-Gurion decided on the timing. In agreement, she quotes historian Hugh Trevor-Roper, who wrote: "For the whole Eichmann policy is, in a particular way, personal to Mr. Ben-Gurion; he and he alone authorized and ordered the entire process."[28]

The picture that emerges from the historical sources is a completely different one. Eichmann was not in the Mossad's cross-hairs, and Ben-Gurion did not initiate the search for Eichmann. In fact, at no time did the prime minister convey to the head of the Mossad that he viewed the capture of a Nazi criminal as a means of "national pedagogy." No one in the Israeli political or security systems initiated the abduction, even though unconfirmed reports regarding Eichmann's residence in Argentina had apparently reached the Mossad as early as 1954.[29] Eichmann's capture was initiated by Hessen District Attorney Fritz Bauer, who, in 1957, conveyed to the Mossad reliable information regarding his place of residence in Buenos Aires. The Mossad, however, "dragged its feet," did not deal thoroughly with the affair, and failed in its analysis of the material with which it had been provided, although the focus of this article precludes us from discussing its conduct here. The change occurred in the autumn of 1959. Bauer succeeded in corroborating the information he had communicated some two years earlier from an Argentinian Jew named Luther Hermann who had arrived as a German refugee in 1939. He had done so with the assistance of another party, whose name he resolutely refused to pass on to the Israelis. He informed Israel that Eichmann had arrived in Argentina in 1950 and was living under the false identity of Ricardo Clement. At the end of December 1959, Ben-Gurion was informed that Eichmann had been identified in Buenos Aires, and he authorized his abduction.[30]

Yablonka presents a different thesis than that of Segev and Zertal, which distinguishes between two periods in Ben-Gurion's attitude toward the trial. During the first period, until just before the trial got under way, Ben-Gurion viewed it only in the international context, and particularly in the context of world Jewry – that is, the glorification of Israel's international standing, and Israel's favored status in the eyes of the Jewish People. Yablonka maintains that at this point in time, Ben-Gurion did not understand the trial's significance from an Israeli domestic perspective.[31] His interest in the trial increased just before it began, when he realized its powerful impact on the Israeli public. Only then did the prime minister and the political establishment as a whole also come to understand the international community's great interest in the trial, and only then did their involvement in its management increase. Despite the political involvement and the attempts to set aims for the trial that would be consistent with the ideological approach of the Israeli establishment and Israeli state interests, Yablonka rejects its classification as a show trial. Unlike Arendt, Segev, and Zertal, she makes a clear distinction between a "show trial," the outcome of which is determined in advance, and a "historical" trial, which, despite its expanded scope of discussion, preserves the principles of law and justice.[32]

Surprisingly, the argument that Ben-Gurion did not understand the importance of the impending trial until just before it began is based on only one source: a brief exchange which, in my opinion, can also be interpreted differently. Moreover, as we will see below, other sources completely refute this assertion. This single source is a question that *Maariv* editor Aryeh Dissentshik addressed to Ben-Gurion during a meeting with the Editors' Committee in September 1960, on Rosh Hashana Eve: What did he regard as the most important event that had taken place in Israel over the past year? After providing an answer that did not mention Eichmann and being questioned briefly on this point by eminent Journalist Shalom Rosenfeld, he said that the event had been important from a journalistic perspective. Yablonka takes this as evidence that, at the time, Ben-Gurion did not appreciate the trial's importance to Israeli society. According to Yablonka, his insight into the importance of the trial emerged only seven months later at its onset, when he realized the public interest it stimulated.[33]

Yablonka's reliance on these few sentences that were exchanged by Ben-Gurion and two senior journalists raise a number of questions that introduce cracks to her thesis. First, we must ask: If Ben-Gurion initially ascribed importance to the trial's international aspect, why did he not say so in his response to the queries of the newspaper editors? Second, in December 1960, some three months after the meeting of the Editors Committee in question and approximately four months prior to the beginning of the trial, Ben-Gurion granted an interview to *The New York Times*, which appears to have been his most explicit reference to the imminent trial. In the interview, Ben-Gurion emphasized the importance he assigned to the trial's anticipated influence on the Israeli domestic realm, and especially on Israeli youth.[34] The December interview, in conjunction with Ben-Gurion's remarks at the first meeting of the Israeli Government that was held following his announcement to the Knesset of Eichmann's capture (see below), completely refute the argument that he initially did not understand the trial's domestic significance. Moreover, we can also propose an alternative interpretation to that of Yablonka regarding the manner in which Ben-Gurion related to Eichmann in his meeting with the Editors' Committee. The Prime Minister was asked about the most important event of the *past* year – the Jewish year 5720, or 1959/60, and we can assume that when Eichmann was mentioned in the meeting it was in relation to his abduction, which from Ben-Gurion's perspective was not an event of national and educational significance. He therefore responded in the past tense: "It was an event from a journalistic perspective." That is to say, he was referring to the event that had already occurred and not the impending trial. Support for this interpretation can be found in Ben-Gurion's response shortly afterward, when, asked by *The New York Times* about the goal of the trial, he provided, as noted, a clear and focused answer about its expected impact on Israeli society.

In addition to the problem of relying on only a single source to establish her argument, Yablonka offers no satisfactory answer for Segev's fundamental question: Why was Eichmann abducted to Israel as opposed to being assassinated on Garibaldi Street? This question assumes greater importance in light of the special relationship that Ben-Gurion had forged with West German Chancellor Konrad Adenauer, and the assurance he had received of West German security and economic support of Israel. Yablonka rightfully notes Ben-Gurion's sensitivity "regarding Germany, Adenauer, the German public, and concern regarding the possibility of the trial doing damage to the delicate fabric of the understandings between the two countries." She notes the distinction between West Germany and Nazi Germany, which the prime minister repeatedly emphasized, and his concerns regarding the prospects of the name of Adenauer's loyal aide Hans Globke coming up in the trial.[35]

Yablonka does not go into detail on the matter, however, in their conversations with their Israeli counterparts, West German diplomats repeatedly emphasized their concern that the trial had the potential to rekindle hatred for Germany in all the countries that had experienced the horrors of Nazi occupation. At a press conference held approximately one month before the trial, Adenauer acknowledged that "the trial against Eichmann of course causes me some concerns. Not the trial as such. I repeat: Eichmann's fate will be as he deserves. I have full confidence in Israeli law, but I am concerned about the impact the matters raised there will have on the general opinion of us Germans." At the time, concern was expressed not only regarding the possibility that Globke's name might come up, but also the possibility that the defense would highlight the integration of many former loyal servants of the Nazi regime within the bureaucracy of the Federal Republic, especially within the legal and law enforcement system and the West German Foreign Service.[36]

Due to the sensitive nature of Israel's relations with West Germany, as Yablonka notes, and due to the diplomatic difficulties the abduction was expected to create vis-à-vis Argentina, it is unreasonable to assume that Israel would have carried out the entire complex operation simply in order to highlight the Israeli state's status in the eyes of the Jewish People. Yablonka does not make this claim, but rather advances a simple argument: Not only did Ben-Gurion not spearhead the measures leading up to the trial, as Segev claims, but rather he was "dragged into it." According to Yablonka, "at least with regard to the capture of Adolf Eichmann and his trial in Israel, it was not the same Ben-Gurion, planning ahead, contemplating, and deciding, but rather a Ben-Gurion who to some degree followed and was even dragged into the events.[37]

Yablonka's approach to the subject has been adopted by a number of scholars. A prominent example is Anita Shapira, whose article "The Eichmann Trial: Things Seen from Here Are Not Seen from There" was first published in 2002. The article addresses Hannah Arendt's and Haim Gouri's different perspectives on and insights into the Eichmann Trial. Shapira also takes the opportunity to express her views regarding the trial's impact on Israeli society's Holocaust consciousness and notion of negation of the Diaspora. Although Ben-Gurion's attitude toward the trial is addressed only marginally in her article, Shapira begins the article with Ben-Gurion's meeting with the Editors' Committee that is mentioned in Yablonka's book, and determines, with no further consideration, that "Ben-Gurion did not initiate Eichmann's capture, and when Eichmann was captured, he did not recognize the importance of the event."[38]

Deborah Lipstadt also embraces Yablonka's argument, despite the fact that it is based on a single source that can be interpreted differently. In her book on the Eichmann Trial, Lipstadt argues that the assertion that Ben-Gurion regarded youth education as a goal when he decided on Eichmann's abduction is not well based. Her evidence is that "Hanna Yablonka, who has researched the Israeli response to Eichmann's abduction and trial, has shown that he [Ben-Gurion] identified the educational realm as a goal only after Eichmann was captured."[39]

Published eight years later, an approach that runs completely counter to that of Yablonka is articulated by Yechiam Weitz in his article "The Founding Father and the War Criminal's Trial: Ben-Gurion and the Eichmann Trial."

In contrast to Yablonka's suggestion that Ben-Gurion's being dragged along reflected cracks that were beginning to emerge in his leadership, Weitz points out that "the Eichmann Trial symbolizes his apex and the Lavon Affair his decline." According to Weitz: "Ben-Gurion's role in the decision to capture Eichmann and transport him to Israel was decisive. The fact that he himself announced Eichmann's abduction before the Knesset and the public was neither coincidental nor formal. It was indicative of his important role in the decision making process pertaining to Eichmann."[40]

With regard to Eichmann's abduction, Weitz is undoubtedly correct in his use of the word "decision" as opposed to the word "initiative," which appears at the beginning of Shapira's argument. As already noted, Ben-Gurion was informed that Eichmann had been located and identified at the end of December 1959, after Mossad Chief Isser Harel was convinced that the man in question was in fact Eichmann. Harel and Attorney General Haim Cohen informed Ben-Gurion that the information regarding Eichmann's place of residence had been conveyed by Bauer. If Israel failed to act, they explained, Bauer intended to approach the German government and request Eichmann's extradition from Argentina. "I suggested he be asked to not tell a soul and to not demand his extradition," Ben-Gurion wrote in his diary. "If we establish that he is there, we will capture him and bring him here." These few words reflect Ben-Gurion's historic decision to hold the historical trial in Jerusalem.[41]

The most important source regarding the debate over the significance that Ben-Gurion ascribed to the trial as a historic event in general, and its possible impact on the youth in Israel in particular, appears to be his remarks at the first meeting of the Israeli Government following his announcement of Eichmann's abduction and impending trial.[42] During the two decades in which the studies discussed in this article were written, this source had still not been released for examination by scholars. As a result, Weitz relates only to the summary of the meeting, which was open to scholars when he wrote his article,[43] and he therefore makes only one comment regarding Ben-Gurion's words: that the main thing was not the punishment but rather the importance he ascribed to the trial.

Weitz links this to the following remark made by Ben-Gurion half a year later: "The matter of the Jews has not been comprehensively recounted, even at Nuremberg." Unlike the other scholars referred to in this article, Weitz maintains that in Ben-Gurion's eyes, the trial's significance was manifested first and foremost in "the presentation of the story of the murder of the Jewish People in Europe."[44]

The full protocol of the Government meeting of May 29, 1960 has since been opened for viewing, and its reading reveals unequivocal remarks made by Ben-Gurion regarding the goals and the historical importance of the trial. These words refute Yablonka's assertion that "it was not the same Ben-Gurion, planning ahead, contemplating, and deciding," as well as Shapira's closing assertion that "when Eichmann was captured, he [Ben-Gurion] did not recognize the importance of the event." The full protocol also supports Weitz's assertion that Ben-Gurion's primary aim was to facilitate an overall account of the Jewish tragedy, as opposed to the other scholars whose studies are discussed in this article, who ascribe to Ben-Gurion a purely instrumental approach with regard to the trial. For example, Yablonka writes as follows: "The decisive points pertaining to Ben-Gurion show that at the basis of things, the trial that was going to take place in Israel was, for Ben-Gurion, a means. This applies especially to the context outside of Israel [particularly in terms of highlighting the state's preferred status in the eyes of the Jewish People]."[45]

Prime Minister Ben-Gurion spoke after his ministers heard Harel's general report on the execution of the abduction operation. In his remarks, Ben-Gurion resolutely stated that his goal in bringing Eichmann to Israel was to conduct a historical trial, articulating before the ministers a historical-moral position as the primary motivating factor for holding the trial:

> We will not limit ourselves to the misdeeds of Eichmann alone.
> Rather, it will be necessary to recount the entire affair. This will require
> thorough preparation, so the trial can give the Jewish People and the
> world a picture of all that European Jewry experienced during that
> period – not only what was perpetrated by Eichmann, but by all the
> Nazis....this is **historical justice** [my emphasis]: that the criminal,
> one of the most major criminals, be judged by the same people, a
> sovereign people, against whom the transgression was committed.[46]

The term "historical justice" here refers to the revolution that the Jews experienced as a result of the establishment of the state of Israel: the Jewish People's extrication from the state of political helplessness that was so fundamentally demonstrated during the Holocaust, and the revival that enabled the Jewish collective to take action against those actively seeking its destruction. In the name of the murdered, the state of Israel would recount the atrocities committed against the Jewish People when it was unprotected. Alongside the historical moral aspect, he also noted the political implications that could emerge from the trial. He viewed it as a historic opportunity to explain in detail the tragedy of the Jewish People, especially as the Nuremberg Trials did not focus on the murder of the Jews: "The matter of Nuremberg was against Germany, against the Nazi leaders. It was a political issue, and so they did not pass judgment on the Jewish matter, which was a side issue…that the world wants to forget. People are also getting tired of it. At the moment, there is a summit [of the four superpowers in Paris]. Everything must be revitalized."[47]

Moreover, in total contrast to Lipstadt's conclusion and unlike Yablonka's thesis, Ben-Gurion recognized the trial's importance in the domestic Israeli context from the outset, with an emphasis on the realm of education.[48] Ben-Gurion was of course unable to assess the intensity of the impact the trial would have on the Israeli public ahead of time. This was something that no one could do. Nonetheless, his words make it clear that he sought for the trial to be an important historical and educational collective experience for Israeli society in general and the youth of Israel in particular.

The Question of Ben-Gurion's Involvement in the Trial and Hausner's Independence

The research has yielded differing versions regarding Ben-Gurion's involvement in the conduct of the trial and the independence of the prosecutor. Zertal, following Arendt, maintains that Ben-Gurion was the architect, director, and supervisor of the preparations for the trial and subsequently of the trial itself. Although he intentionally refrained from making appearances in the courtroom and expressed himself in a measured and calculated manner in public, she continues, he navigated the trial from behind the scenes according to the goals he had set.[49] On the other hand, Zertal makes no reference to Hausner as a party with influence on shaping the trial.

Unlike Zertal, Segev underlines Hausner's substantial influence on the direction of the trial. It is true that the chief prosecutor identified with the goals that had been set by Ben-Gurion. Nonetheless, he played a decisive role in determining the nature of the trial in accordance with his own legal, historical, and educational conceptions. Based on a historical, national, and educational perspective, "Hausner sought to design a national saga that would echo through the generations," writes Segev, highlighting Hausner's historic decision to have the trial revolve around the testimony of survivors. In this context, it is important to note Robinson's significant influence, which stemmed in part from his criticism of the manner in which the trials were conducted at Nuremberg.[50]

Like Segev, Yablonka also emphasizes Hausner's impact on the historic decision to make testimonies the focus of the trial. She notes the disagreements that emerged in this context between Hausner and members of the Israeli police force's Bureau 06, which compiled the case for the prosecution. "Overall," she writes, "we can say that the members of Bureau 06 stitched together the criminal case, on which Hausner assembled the historical case, which consisted mainly of 110 live witnesses."[51] Nonetheless, she stresses the political pressures that were exerted on Hausner, which he himself denies in his book *Justice in Jerusalem*. According to Yablonka, the pressures were exerted primarily by Justice Minister Pinchas Rosen and Foreign Minister Golda Meir. Unlike Zertal, Yablonka notes that the pressure regarding the Mufti came from the foreign minister and officials within her ministry, and not from Ben-Gurion.[52] Still, Yablonka holds, Ben-Gurion played a role in the trial. During the preparatory stages, Ben-Gurion intervened by throwing all his weight behind an attempt to expand the scope of the trial. According to Yablonka, this was in response to a memorandum authored by Ultra-Orthodox journalist and writer Moshe Prager, but she provides no documentation for this assertion.[53] Although the government had announced that the Eichmann Trial would be a historical trial, she maintains, "it was unclear whether this term was used to mean that, for the first time, the Jewish People was putting on trial those who had acted against it, or that the intention was to present a historical chapter in its entirety." In actuality, in the meeting of the Government that took place approximately one week after Eichmann was brought to Israel, Ben-Gurion resolutely proclaimed: "We will not limit ourselves to the misdeeds of Eichmann alone. Rather, it will be necessary to recount the entire affair."[54] Even if the scope of the trial was not determined ahead of time, the direction was undoubtedly clear to Hausner and the investigators of Bureau 06.

Another topic addressed by Yablonka is the "Hungarian affair" in general and the testimony of Joel Brand in particular. Yablonka relates with extreme brevity to the concerns of officials from the Prime Minister's Office regarding the testimony of Brand, which could again spark the fundamental questions that were raised during the Kasztner-Gruenwald trial and the public controversy that ensued. They mostly feared a renewed discussion of the question of who was responsible for Brand's failure to rescue thousands of Hungarian Jews. Immediately following the testimony's conclusion, documents relating to the Jewish Agency's responses to Brand's mission were published for the first time. The documents were meant to clarify the efforts of the Yishuv's leadership to help Brand, the manner in which the British thwarted the mission, and other actions taken by the leadership of the Yishuv and the Zionist movement. Yablonka discloses a letter from the Foreign Ministry's legal advisor indicating that the publication of the documents had been initiated by the political echelon. The documentation on this matter, it should be noted, contains no proof of direct involvement by Ben-Gurion as argued by Yablonka, although it is possible that the matter was brought to his attention.[55]

Unlike in the "Hungarian affair," Ben-Gurion's involvement in the affairs pertaining to West Germany was clear and documented. It occurred against a background, explained above in brief, of German concern regarding the possible tarnishing of the image of West Germany, and especially the exposure of involvement of senior officials in the West German state institutions in various aspects of anti-Jewish persecution during the period of Nazi rule. Ben-Gurion demonstrated great sensitivity with regard to this concern in accordance with the understandings that had been reached with Adenauer vis-à-vis West German economic and security aid to Israel a few months before the beginning of the trial.

The studies by Segev, Yablonka, and Weitz all address two episodes: the changes that Ben-Gurion sought to introduce to Hausner's opening arguments, and the former's attempt to prevent the presentation of a document that exposed the involvement of Globke – alongside a representative of Eichmann – in efforts meant to expropriate the property of German Jews who had "emigrated" or been deported. Weitz maintains that when it came to legal matters, Ben-Gurion tried to avoid intervening out of adherence to the principle of separation of powers between the executive and judicial branches. On the other hand, Weitz explains, "the issues in which he was involved reached him not at his own initiative."[56] This assessment by Weitz appears to not be reflective of the relations between the prime minister and the prosecutor, or of Ben-Gurion's intervention on the subject of West Germany. Hausner's appeal plainly stemmed from his clear knowledge regarding the subject's extreme political sensitivity, and the fact that, at least on this matter, Ben-Gurion demanded that he be consulted and that his approval be secured. Still, it is important to note that Hausner refused to make his decisions subject to the wishes of the prime minister, if doing so ran counter to professional considerations.

Hausner submitted his opening statement for the trial, in which he invested a great deal of work, to Ben-Gurion toward the end of March 1961. Ben-Gurion responded within a few days. He read the initial sections, until the section dealing with the extermination in Poland, but said he could read no further due to his other responsibilities. He thought, however, that there was no need to continue reading the remaining sections, as "they are of no special political significance." In this way, he clarified his involvement in the trial: he did not intervene in the principles that guided the prosecution in its management of the trial, but rather only in issues with potential foreign political impact – that is, that could damage Israeli foreign relations. This was in reference primarily to West Germany. Ben-Gurion pointed out three elements in Hausner's opening statement that were in need of change. The first had to do with Hitler's decisive role. The beginning of the remarks, Ben-Gurion argued, should pertain to Adolf Hitler and not to Adolf Eichmann; Eichmann may have been the defendant, but Hitler was the "major key party." His second point was that "every time we say what it is that Germany did to us, we need to say 'Nazi Germany'" – that is, a Germany that was different from the Germany that existed prior to the rise of the Nazis, particularly in light of the political sensitivity, as the latter was regarded as completely distinct from West Germany, which Ben-Gurion characterized as an "other Germany." It should be noted that although the phrase "Nazi Germany" is commonplace in Hausner's opening remarks, the word "Germany" alone also appears frequently, contrary to Ben-Gurion's request. Neither Segev nor Weitz mentions this fact, and Yablonka also refrains from emphasizing it.[57] The third point was opposition to the deterministic approach to history in general and to the course of Germany in particular. "I doubt whether it is desirable or correct to speak of the inevitability of Nazism and its atrocities, as you attempt to prove in the introduction."[58]

What these three points have in common is the status of Nazism and Hitlerism – which Ben-Gurion regarded as one and the same – as the force from which all actions emerged. The rise of Nazism was not inevitable – that is to say, it was not a necessary outcome to which the history of Germany had led, and the conduct of the democratic countries had a decisive influence on the path that ultimately led to the war. Segev justifiably writes that these points were "all aimed at protecting West Germany's image and diminishing the guilt of the German People."[59]

As noted, Ben-Gurion's involvement in all aspects related to Germany did not end with his comments on Hausner's opening arguments. According to Hausner, he and Ben-Gurion disagreed regarding the former's decision to introduce to the court a document from the Nuremberg Trials that had been conveyed to the prosecution in Jerusalem,[60] which indicated that, according to the conclusion of the prosecutor, there had been "close contacts between Globke and Eichmann."[61] The document did not link Globke to the Final Solution (this issue was the focus of the investigation of the prosecutor in Bonn and the charges of slander that were submitted by the Chancellor and his aide). However, from a public and political perspective, it was extremely problematic; it revealed Globke's participation, as a representative of the Ministry of the Interior alongside senior ministry official Hermann Hering, in discussions pertaining to the deportation of German Jewry and the theft of Jewish property.

Yablonka makes only brief mention of this issue, and as a result details providing important insight into the Prime Minister's involvement, and the limitations of this involvement, are not clarified for the reader. In this context, she quotes from Ben-Gurion's diary, which reveals that he asked Felix Shinnar, head of the Israeli Purchasing Mission in Cologne and the senior Israeli representative in West Germany, to speak with Hausner and Justice Minister Rosen about the document in which Globke is mentioned. Yablonka asserts that Ben-Gurion's explicit instructions were to prevent the document's submission, which she concludes based on a short excerpt from his diary, and perhaps also based on Hausner's testimony in his book on the Eichmann Trial. Unlike Segev and Weitz, Yablonka does not mention the fact that Hausner objected to Ben-Gurion's request and maintained that the document had important bearing on the charges against Eichmann and that he was obligated to submit it. She also does not indicate that the document was in fact submitted to the court.[62] On the other hand, in Segev's and Weitz's presentations of the document, it is not at all clear that Ben-Gurion asked Shinnar to intervene after Hausner refused his request, and that Hausner stood fast in his noncompliance even after Shinnar's intervention.[63]

Segev holds that before Ben-Gurion approved Hausner's use of the document, he sent Shinnar to Bonn to explain to the West German Chancellor that the document's submission to the court was unavoidable. Contrary to this assertion, however, the document's submission was not at all dependent on Ben-Gurion's approval or Adenauer's advance knowledge. Hausner explained to Shinnar, apparently with Rosen's knowledge, that the prosecution could not avoid submitting such a fundamental document, and it was therefore decided to provide Adenauer, and, through him, undoubtedly also Globke, with knowledge of the document in order to prevent surprises during the trial. In this manner, an attempt was made to minimize the possible damage to the relations between the two countries.

Weitz holds that neither the prosecutor nor the defense attorney mentioned Globke's name during the trial and that the document was merely submitted to the court, although this is only partially true. When it was presented by the prosecution, Justice Benjamin Halevy employed a simple and intentional rhetorical measure aimed at highlighting Globke's participation. By presenting a brief question to the prosecutor, he emphasized Globke's name on the long list of meeting attendees. Moreover, as the prosecution had introduced the document, the defense also addressed it during Eichmann's examination by his attorney Robert Servatius. Servatius offered excerpts from the protocol that proved, he argued, that the expropriation of German Jewish property was initiated by Interior Ministry officials, including Hering and Globke, who are listed among the attendees.[64]

Conclusion

Most of the studies discussed in this article were published during the 1990s and the first decade of the new millennium. Since their publication, new documents have been opened for the use of researchers in Israel and elsewhere. On the one hand, these documents allow us to reach a clearer verdict regarding the question at hand; on the other hand, they deepen and expand the discussion to encompass aspects that are insufficiently clear or were hitherto unknown.

For example, the protocol of the meeting of the Israeli Government that took place approximately one week after the announcement of Eichmann's capture clearly reflects that, from the outset, Prime Minister Ben-Gurion recognized the profound historical significance of Eichmann's standing trial in Jerusalem. It establishes that Ben-Gurion authorized Eichmann's abduction and his transfer to Israel with the intention of holding a historical trial. His authorization was based on profound consideration and forward thinking; Ben-Gurion was not "dragged" into it. The protocol, which was hitherto not open to researchers in its entirety, also establishes that from the outset, the trial's importance in Ben-Gurion's eyes lay primarily in the domestic Israeli realm. The protocol also proves that Ben-Gurion's primary goal, more than any other consideration, was to enable an all-encompassing account of the tragedy of European Jewry.

On the other hand, the substantial documentation that has been released in recent years by both the Israel State Archive and archives in Germany and the United States, and particularly the CIA files dealing with Adolf Eichmann and Hans Globke, indicates that the prime minister's intervention – which was aimed at preventing injury to the image of West Germany, against the background of the complicated relationship between the Israeli security establishment and West Germany – was deeper than previously depicted by the research. These documents further emphasize the diplomatic importance of the Eichmann Trial and the cooperation of the American, Israeli, and West German intelligence services in an effort to prevent the trial from being exploited by the Eastern Bloc as part of its propaganda war against West Germany.[65]

Endnotes

1   Deborah E. Lipstadt, *The Eichmann Trial* (New York, 2011), p. 178.

2   Arendt covered the Eichmann trial for *The New Yorker*, and in contrast to the impression given by her articles and book, and her impressions of the witnesses, her account was largely based on the protocol of the trial and only partially on her impressions of the few sessions she attended. According to Arendt, the articles that were published in February and March 1963 were a slightly abbreviated version of her book *Eichmann in Jerusalem: A Report on The Banality of Evil*, which she completed in November 1962. The book's first English-language edition was published in May 1963. In a new edition containing minor revisions, published approximately half a year later, Arendt relates to the fundamental controversy sparked by the book. See Hannah Arendt, *Eichmann in Jerusalem: A Report on the Banality of Evil* (New York, 2006), "Introduction"; Deborah E. Lipstadt, *The Eichmann Trial* (New York, 2011), p. 178.

3   Hanna Yablonka, *The State of Israel vs. Adolf Eichmann* (Tel Aviv, 2001), p. 266 (Hebrew). See note 32. below regarding Yablonka's definition of the trial as a "historical trial."

4   Arendt, *Eichmann in Jerusalem*, pp. 4.

5   Ibid., p. 6.

6   Ibid., p. 5.

7   Ibid., p. 8.

8   Ibid., pp. 288.

9   Ibid., p. 116. For an extensive discussion of the controversy surrounding Arendt's thesis and its fundamental criticism, especially in the United States, see Lipstadt, *The Eichmann Trial*, pp. 148-187.

10   Jacob Robinson, *And the Crooked Shall be Made Straight* (Jerusalem, 1965) (Hebrew).

11   Boaz Cohen, "Holocaust And Justice, Dr. Jacob Robinson, the Institute of Jewish Affairs and the Elusive Jewish Voice in Nuremberg," in David Bankier and Dan Michman (eds.), *Holocaust And Justice* (Jerusalem, 2010), pp. 81-100; Roni Stauber, *A Lesson for this Generation: Holocaust and Heroism in Israeli Public Discourse in the 1950s* (Jerusalem, 2000), p. 172 (Hebrew); Yablonka, *The State of Israel vs. Adolf Eichmann*, p. 115. Yablonka maintains that Robinson was the "guiding hand" of the trial.

12   Robinson, *And the Crooked Shall be Made Straight*, p. 101.

13 Ibid., pp.123-124.

14 Tom Segev, *The Seventh Million* (Tel Aviv, 1991) (Hebrew).

15 Ibid., p. 337.

16 Ibid., p. 311.

17 Ibid., p. 312.

18 Minutes of the Government of Israel, May 29, 1960, ISA 12968/10.

19 Segev, *The Seventh Million*, pp. 311-312.

20 Ibid., p. 325. See note 32 below on Yablonka's distinction between a "show trial" and a "historical trial" and the Eichmann Trial's classification as the latter.

21 Edith Zertal, *Death and the Nation: History, Memory and Politics* (Tel Aviv, 2002), p. 138 (Hebrew). In one of the book's other chapters, titled "Between Love of the World and Love of Israel," Zertal discusses theses that Arendt advances in *Eichmann in Jerusalem* and in correspondences with Gershom Scholem.

22 Ibid., p. 144, 155.

23 Ibid., p. 152.

24 Knesset protocol, July 1, 1959, *Divrei Knesset* Website, https://fs.knesset.gov.il/3/Plenum/3_ptm_251590.pdf (accessed on January 29, 2020).

25 Ibid. On this topic, see also Ora Herman's criticism of Zertal in Ora Herman, *The Furnace and the Reactor* (Tel Aviv, 2017), pp. 113-115 (Hebrew).

26 Segev, *The Seventh Million*, p. 311.

27 Zertal, *Death And the Nation*, pp. 137-161.

28 Zertal, *Death And the Nation*, p. 153.

29 This information was conveyed by Simon Wiesenthal to both the Israeli consul in Vienna and World Jewish Congress Chairman Nahum Goldmann. See Tom Segev, *Wiesnethal: A Biography* (Jerusalem, 2010), p. 14 (Hebrew). In his book about Eichmann's capture, Isser Harel explains that the Mossad had received (albeit unconfirmed) reports that Eichmann was residing in Buenos Aires, including reports from 1956 "that referred explicitly to Argentina." See, Simon Wiesenthal, *The House on Garibaldi Street* (Tel Aviv, 1990), p. 37 (Hebrew).

30 See, for example, Yablonka, *The State of Israel vs. Adolf Eichmann*, pp. 19-20; Lipstadt, *The Eichmann Trial*, pp. 10-14.

31 Yablonka, *The State of Israel vs. Adolf Eichmann*, pp. 63-64.

32 Ibid., pp. 264-271. Yablonka highlights primarily the manner in which the trial was conducted by its judges, who prevented it from being a show trial; unlike the prosecutor, they were completely detached from and independent of the political echelon. In addition, according to the principles of criminal law, their ruling "did not aspire, in a demonstrative manner, to tell the story of the Holocaust but rather to establish or refute Eichmann's direct guilt." And although the testimonies of Holocaust survivors were the focus of the trial, the ruling convicted Eichmann based on documents alone and did not uphold all the arguments of the prosecution.

33 Ibid., p. 64.

34 *New York Times*, December 18, 1960.

35 Yablonka, *The State of Israel vs. Adolf Eichmann*, pp. 16, 66. Among other things, Globke was responsible for one of the authoritative interpretations of the Nuremberg Laws, as well as of other laws and regulations enacted against the Jews of Germany. To Ben-Gurion's chagrin, Globke's name was ultimately mentioned during the trial, which will be discussed later in this article.

36 For a lengthy discussion on this topic, see Roni Stauber, "The Impact of the Eichmann Trial on Relations between Israel and the Federal Republic of Germany," in Rebecca Wittmann (ed.), *The Eichmann Trial Reconsidered* (Toronto, 2020) (forthcoming).

37 Yablonka, *The State of Israel vs. Adolf Eichmann*, pp. 67, 266.

38 Anita Shapira, *Jews, Zionists, and in Between* (Tel Aviv, 2007), p. 111 (Hebrew).

39 Lipstadt, *The Eichmann Trial*, p. 13. Another example is the comprehensive study by David Cesarani, which also devoted a chapter to the trial. It should be noted that Cesarani's presentation of Yablonka's position is imprecise. He writes that Ben-Gurion understood the potential of the trial after Eichmann was already in Israel and his abduction had sparked international controversy. Elsewhere, he writes with hyperbole that Ben-Gurion had, for a period of months, contended with the debate surrounding Eichmann's abduction and Israel's right to try Eichmann, and not with the importance of the trial. Cesarani, *Becoming Eichmann: Rethinking the Life, Crimes, and Trial of a "Desk Murderer"* (New York, 2007), pp. 15, 256.

40 Yechiam Weitz, "The Founding Father and the War Criminal's Trial: Ben-Gurion and the Eichmann Trial," *Yad Vashem Studies* 36 (2008), p. 36 (Hebrew).

41 Eichmann's abduction is described extensively in the memoirs and the scholarship. See, for example, Yablonka, *The State of Israel vs. Adolf Eichmann*, pp. 19-20; Lipstadt, *The Eichmann Trial*, pp. 10-14; Cesarani, *Becoming Eichmann*, pp. 221-228.

42 The meeting was held six days after Ben-Gurion announced Eichmann's capture to the Knesset. The previous meeting of the Government had taken place on the day

that Eichmann was brought to Israel: May 23, 1960. During this meeting, Ben-Gurion briefly informed the ministers that Eichmann was in Israel and that he intended on making an announcement to that effect before the Knesset. See the protocols of the meetings of the Israeli Government of May 23 and 29, 1960 on the Israeli State Archive website.

43 See Weitz, "The Founding Father," note 138, in which he states that the protocols of the Government meetings held after 1959 were not open for viewing, and that only their summaries and decisions were accessible.

44 Weitz, "The Founding Father," p. 34.

45 Yablonka, *The State of Israel vs. Adolf Eichmann*, p. 67.

46 Protocol of the Government of Israel, May 29, 1960, ISA 12968/10. Similar words regarding the desire for "historical justice" as a primary motivation appear in Ben-Gurion's letter to Yitzhak Y. Cohen, April 10, 1960.

47 Protocol of the Government of Israel, May 29, 1960, ISA 12968/10.

48 Protocol of the Government of Israel, May 29, 1960, ISA 12968/10. According to Bar-Zohar, Ben-Gurion said the following during a meeting with Isser Harel and Haim Cohen: "Bring him alive or dead! Then he thought for a moment and added: I would prefer it if you brought him alive. It will be very important for the youth from a moral perspective." Bar-Zohar, *Ben-Gurion: A Biography* (Tel Aviv, 1975), p. 1375. Bar-Zohar presents no source for this quote.

49 Zertal, , *Death And the Nation* p. 97.

50 Segev, *The Seventh Million*, pp. 319-320. Yablonka, *The State of Israel vs. Adolf Eichmann*, pp. 115.

51 Yablonka, *The State of Israel vs. Adolf Eichmann*, p. 103.

52 Ibid., pp. 99-102.

53 Ibid., pp. 81-82.

54 Minutes of the Government of Israel, May 29, 1960, ISA 12968/10 (Hebrew)

55 Ibid., pp. 138-139.

56 Weitz, "The Founding Father," p. 36.

57 Attorney General to Prime Minister, March 24, 1961; Ben-Gurion to Attorney General, March 28, 1961, Ben-Gurion Archive (hereinafter, BGA), Correspondences/1961; Segev, *The Seventh Million*, p. 327; Yablonka, *The State of Israel vs. Adolf Eichmann*, p. 101; Weitz, "The Founding Father," p. 21.

58 Attorney General to Prime Minister, March 24, 1961 (Hebrew).

59 Segev, *The Seventh Million*, p. 327.

60 The document in question was the protocol of a conference of departmental representatives discussing the legal status of the Jews, January 15, 1941, NMT3, NG 300.

61 Gideon Hausner, *The Eichmann Trial in Jerusalem* (Bnei Brak, 2011), p. 301 (Hebrew).

62 Yablonka, *The State of Israel vs. Adolf Eichmann*, p. 66. Hausner consulted with Ben-Gurion on the matter of Globke once again in February 1962, leading up to the proceedings pertaining to the conviction and sentencing. Eichmann's attorney Robert Servatius decided to use, or at least considered using, the collection of documents that had been published about Globke in Germany, and the comments on the documents conveyed by Eichmann (a few dozen pages), in the proceedings before the justices of the Supreme Court. In response to Hausner's question regarding whether there were political reasons for preventing its use in the trial, Ben-Gurion said that indeed there were: i.e., to avoid doing injury to Globke. This time, however, unlike in the case of the document that he submitted to the first instance against Ben-Gurion's wishes, Hausner had no problem accepting the political justification, as the documents pertaining to Globke had already been published, were not part of the prosecution's evidence, and had no bearing on establishing Eichmann's guilt. On the contrary, they were meant to support the arguments of the defense.

63 Segev, *The Seventh Million*, p. 322; Weitz, "The Founding Father," p. 24. Weitz, it should be noted, erroneously refers to multiple episodes, although they were actually all the same matter.

64 Session 38, May 12, 1961, *Eichmann Trial Records*, I (Jerusalem, 1963), p. 573.

65 I explore this topic at length in a forthcoming manuscript to be published by Yad Vashem in Jerusalem titled *Diplomacy in the Shadow of Memory: Past and Present in Israeli-West German Relations, 1963-1965* (Hebrew).

Graciela Ben Dror

Pius XII and the Jews during the Holocaust: New Historiographical Aspects in the Twenty-First Century

The public debate and the debates among historians regarding Pope Pius XII's silence during the Holocaust began in earnest during the first half of the 1960s, following the publication of Rolf Hochhuth's play *The Deputy*, in which the Pope is accused of indifference toward the fate of the Jewish People. These debates assumed greater importance during the final decade of the twentieth century in light of Pope John Paul II's intention to award Pius XII sainthood. Although this was a Catholic theological title pertaining to Pius's status in the world to come, it had implications for this world in the eyes of devout Catholics and people in general. The process of beatification, a step towards the status of sainthood, began during the time of Pope Benedict XVI. Jewish institutions asked the Papacy not to bestow the title of sainthood upon him until the Vatican opened its archive about his rule from 1939 onwards and historians might learn more about his policy and conduct.

According to Catholic doctrine, the Church is "One, Catholic, Apostolic, and Roman" (meaning, a single organizational institution with a hierarchal and universal missionary structure based in Rome, with the Pope occupying the top position in the pyramid). This structure gives the Pope a unique status in this world. Moreover, in the second half of the nineteenth century he was endowed with the status of "infallibility". However, despite the fact that the Church views itself as a single unit, it has many different faces and numerous voices.

This article explores what different historians have written about the actions, the silence, and the motivations of Pius XII regarding the Jews during the Holocaust. It focuses not at the beginning of the debate in the 1960s, but on research that has been carried out over the past twenty years – that is to say, during the twenty-first century. One question it considers is: What was Pius XII's policy and what factors led him to adopt one position as opposed to another? Another is whether the Vatican archives' 2003 opening of documents pertaining to the tenure of Pius XII's predecessor, Pius XI, who headed the Church until his death in 1939, contain material that sheds additional light on Eugenio Pacelli, who served as Cardinal Secretary of State until Pius XI's death and was subsequently appointed his successor.

At the outset of the historians' debate in the 1960s, emphasis was placed on political, ideological, and moral aspects. The intense debate began after the publishing of the play *The Deputy* by Rolph Hochuut, when Saul Friedländer presented the first historical research about *Pius XII and the Third Reich. Documents*, in 1964.[1]

Under the impact of the discussion accusing Pius XII for being silent while millions of Jews were being murdered, and others making his apology, four Jesuit historians were asked to work in the Vatican archive, resulting in eleven volumes published by the Vatican between 1965 and 1981, under the name *Actes et Documents du Saint Siège relatifs à la Seconde Guerre mondiale.*[2]

Later in the debate, in the 1970s and 1980s, the discussion highlighted the theological aspect of the issue, while several Catholic historians were very active and placed their emphasis on the impact of the anti-Jewish tradition and teaching of the Catholic Church over the centuries and its impact during the Holocaust.[3] Moreover, in the 1980s Friedländer came to the conclusion that Pius XII was aware in real time about the mass murder of the Jews, but he maintained public silence. Not a word was said or written against the Nazis as perpetrators and not a word about the Jews as victims. He brought several examples of internal and external bodies asking him to speak out – such as the request of the Archbishop of Lvov, and the request of the Jewish Agency report, sent through Myron Taylor, the personal ambassador from Roosevelt to the Vatican, in the second half of 1942, and there are several other testimonies that he knew about the special mass murder of the Jews. According to Friedländer's interpretation, the Pope's stand was due to several primary reasons. First, because of his will to keep the Church unified during the War and his fear of any division inside the Church. Second, because he saw Communism as an ideology as the most dangerous threat against the Christian world. He therefore did not wish to make any declarations in favor of the Jews as victims, which might weaken Nazi Germany during the war. And third, perhaps because of his warm relationship with Germany, since the time he was the nuncio of the Holy See in that country, and was friendly with the German people and its culture.[4]

New points in the debate were articulated in the 1990s, and the question of whether Pius XII was antisemitic became one factor among many in the historiographical debate as a result of the 1999 publication of *Hitler's Pope* by John Cornwell.[5] Although Cornwell was invited to the Vatican archives to locate documents testifying to the Pope's assistance to the Jews, the book's title is indicative of its content. He also assigned the section of the book dealing with Italy the subtitle "Antisemitism" and explained why the Pope and his environment were saturated with antisemitism, which was customary at the time, and which served as one motivation among many for his actions during the Holocaust.

A number of other studies have been published since Cornwell's book. Some have been extremely critical and others quite defensive. Some have sought to strike a balance between those denouncing Pius XII and those defending him, to examine what can be agreed upon by the contemporary research on the subject, and to note the disagreements that remain unresolved. Some of those who have denounced Pius XII have reiterated the assertion that his primary motivation was antisemitism, which, in the 1950s, Jules Isaac referred to as the Catholic Church's "teaching of contempt." Isaac was among the leading intellectuals in France calling for a change in the approach to Jews in Catholic doctrine during the Second Vatican Council, which culminated in the issuing of the *Nostra Aetate* of 1965, the positions of which marked a genuine change by retracting the collective charge of deicide against all Jews throughout the generations.

The Historians' Debate at the Beginning of the Twenty-First Century

On the eve of the twenty-first century, new studies on the subject continued to be published. The historians who offered new explanations for understanding the behavior of Pius XII included Italian historian Giovanni Miccoli, who emphasized the anachronism of the conservative behavior that precluded the Pope from finding an appropriate means of response that suited the gravity of the hour.[6]

On the other side of the divide, the researchers who came to the defense of Pius XII, by highlighting his inability to act differently in the historical circumstances that had emerged, included Ronald Rychlak, who had served as an advisor to the Holy See's Permanent Observer Mission to the United Nations and was therefore part of the Church establishment. Rychlak's research has been critical of Cornwell's abovementioned position. Unlike Cornwell, who holds that Pius XII was tainted by antisemitism, Rychlak draws attention to the Aktion that was perpetrated in Italy on October 16, 1943 and states that the Pope's intervention resulted in its cessation and in the release of two hundred Jews. Rychlak also asserts that the Pope played a notable role in rescuing the Jews of Denmark and instructed the bishops of Europe to take action against racism. He also argues that the Pope sent a letter to the bishops instructing them to open all monasteries, convents, and religious orders to provide sanctuary for Jewish refugees.[7] Rychlak's conclusions, however, are not substantiated by the necessary documents.

In the work of some researchers, theological, moral, and educational aspects play a major role. For example, in 2000, Garry Wills, a former Jesuit seminary student and one of the Catholic scholars who views theological factors as a basis of antisemitism, published the book *Papal Sin: Structures of Deceit*. In it, he focuses on the weighty responsibility borne by the Catholic Church in its entirety – as opposed to Pius XII alone – for the dissemination of antisemitism throughout Europe over the course of history.[8]

It is difficult to assess the impact of theology as a motivating force for taking or abstaining from action. However, we can assume that it was a constant and fundamental factor that was relied upon by the Catholic Church hierarchy and that was therefore one of a host of ideological and political motivations that were relevant during the war.

In his 2002 book *A Moral Reckoning*, Daniel Goldhagen also emphasizes the theological moral aspect of the message that was conveyed by the Church for centuries, including during the Holocaust, and accuses the Church of disseminating antisemitism throughout the generations. He views it as responsible for the Church's actions and inaction during the Holocaust, and he judges it for as of the date of publication, not having apologized for its actions. Goldhagen's book returns to the argument that the primary motivating factor for what subsequently occurred during the Nazi era was antisemitism, as the continuity of anti-moral policy – which is a weighty accusation.[9]

James Carroll, who was educated in Catholic institutions and formerly served as a Catholic priest, also thoroughly examined his experiences as a Catholic and noted, based also on personal testimony, that the teachings of the Catholic Church was a major factor that contributed to antisemitism. His study attracted great interest as well as the criticism of the Catholic Church, which regarded it as not objective.[10]

However, not all studies focused on the realm of theology, the "teaching of contempt," and the dimension of modern antisemitism, which the Church incorporated into the education of its devout members and into the public discourse. In 2000, Michael Phayer published a comprehensive study of Pius XII during the Holocaust from the perspective of the dioceses in Germany. At the beginning of the twenty-first century, in the absence of new documents with the exception of those that were published by the Vatican between 1965 and 1981 in *Actes et Documents* already mentioned, Phayer focused on the topic of the Holocaust with an emphasis on Germany.[11] His book provides an extensive account of the Catholic positions on the Jews prior to the Holocaust, the genocide which the Germans carried out against the Poles when they entered Poland in 1939, and the 1941 genocide in Croatia, which was a satellite state of Nazi Germany. In the context of the Jews, he focuses on the views of a few of the German and European bishops who, during the Holocaust, tried to protect them. He also depicted the Catholic attempts to rescue Jews during the Holocaust as part of the Catholic Church's effort in a broader sense.

The importance of Phayer's study lies in its provision of an in-depth explanation of each case and its explanation of how Pius XII sometimes came to the aid of the Jews and at other times did not. Still, the major gap highlighted by those researching the Pope during World War II and the Holocaust is the absence of relevant documents from this era. For example, *Actes et Documents* does not contain Bishop Preysing's letters to the Pope, even though Preysing is known to have consistently demanded that the Pope make his voice heard. Were these letters lost, asks Phayer, and if not, why were they not published?[12]

Phayer adds that Catholic dogma since the First Vatican Council in 1870 has endowed the Pope with a status of infallibility, and the Catholics of the modern era have been educated accordingly. The Pope instructs Catholics what to believe and what not to believe and what is right to do in every situation. That being the case, one can conclude that during the Holocaust, in the absence of instruction and leadership, individuals acted on their own – sometimes with courage and heroism. Some bishops and Catholic institutions took part in the rescue efforts, as did some diplomats, especially in the East. These include Angelo Roncalli, who was the Pope's delegate in Turkey and was later appointed Pope John XXIII. We can therefore presume that Pius XII acted on behalf of the Jews through the diplomatic echelon, although this is only a conjecture.[13]

He assigns significant importance to Pius XII's anti-Communist views. He maintains that, in both the moral and the financial realm, the Pope did not support the rescue of Jews and that the explanation for this has to do first and foremost with his role as a diplomat. However, he also maintains that Cornwell's claim that Pius XII was antisemitic is mistaken, as at times he did act on behalf of the Jews. Moreover, he argues that the Pope did not work alone, despite his position as head of the Church, and that responsibility should therefore be shared among the church leaders on all levels.

Phayer views the entire church as responsible, due to its past and its anti-Jewish tendencies over the years, and assigns responsibility to the Church establishment as a whole and therefore to its members, as the Holocaust occurred in Europe, a Christian continent with a Christian majority. Notwithstanding, he also ascribes importance to the role of particular personality in history as opposed to deterministic forces alone. Like most historians who engage in the Holocaust, Phayer believes that even if another leader had been elected to serve as pope, he would certainly not have been able to prevent the murder of the Jewish People. He may, however, have been able to instruct Catholics as to the best possible response. According to him, the history of the Church during the Holocaust would have been different had Pius XI remained in the Holy See or had Roncalli been elected as Pope John Paul XIII in 1939 as opposed to 1959 (although we of course have no way of knowing what could have been). According to him, Pius XII was preoccupied by his fear of Communism, and it was this fear, in addition to his concern for the unity of the Catholic Church, that constituted his top priority. In this way, Phayer brings us back to the beginning of the research on the subject as established by Saul Friedländer in the 1960s, who was the historian who paved the way for the historiographical debate.[14]

Phayer adds further arguments. Pius XII's silence, even in the face of Germany's deportation of the Jews of Rome in October 1943 after the conquest of Italy, apparently stemmed from three primary considerations: (a) concern that in response to his speaking out, the Nazis would deport even more Jews from Rome; (b) concern that he himself would be harmed; (c) concern for the destruction of the city of Rome. Phayer concludes that Pius XII's views on the Jews were characterized by an inability to decide and an inability to adhere to decisions. His hesitation influenced the reactions to the Holocaust of high-level and everyday Catholics alike. He also concludes that had a clear voice called for helping the Jews, this would have helped to some degree. Pius XII's adherence, for the most part, to the diplomatic approach, and the absence of clear instructions and statements, influenced the Catholics of Europe.[15]

In 2008, Phayer published another book titled *Pius XII, the Holocaust, and the Cold War*. This book is divided into two parts – one on the period of the Holocaust and another on the subsequent period – and expands the research on the Pope's views during the Cold War. In his conclusion of the second study he articulates greater understanding for the Pope's policy, this time based on documents pertaining to the tenure of Pius XI that were released by the Vatican in 2003 and that provide a better understanding of Pacelli's motivations as Cardinal Secretary of State, before his appointment to the papacy in 1939. Based on these documents, Phayer concludes that Pacelli was not an antisemite but rather that his top priority was the unity of the Church, as opposed to considerations of morality and compassion. According to Phayer, Pius acted primarily out of his opposition to Communism and his anticipation of a new post-war world order devoid of Communism. For this reason he took action to rescue refugees and figures of different backgrounds. This included the rescue of Nazi war criminals after the war, in the interest of helping those in need on all sides according to his overall approach and for the sake of his image as Pope. The murder of the Jews during the war, in contrast, was not his top priority. These views led him to adopt a position that was neither moral nor universal and that suited neither the status nor the power of his position as head of the Church, considering the fact that the main issue at the time was Nazi Germany's extermination of the Jews.[16]

On the other hand, he reminds us that rescuing Jews during the Holocaust was no trivial matter, and that the rescuers were forced to operate under extremely difficult conditions. According to Phayer, during the events of October 16, 1943, when the SS rounded up more than 1,000 of Rome's Jews and sent them to their deaths, the Pope did little to change the situation. Nonetheless, Phayer's study considers other factors that prevented the Pope from responding. Overall, Phayer joins the ranks of those who blame the Pope – even if he moderated his positions somewhat – particularly regarding insights into what Pius XII said or did not say in his December 24, 1942 speech, in which he referred to the ongoing murder of innocent people because of their religion, and their race (*stirpe*), but not explicitly to the Jews.[17]

Prominent among the works that are critical of the Pope, based on research that has been conducted on the Catholic Church in Italy and on Pope Pius XII during the Holocaust from the 1980s until the present, are the studies of Susan Zuccotti.[18] In *Under His Very Windows* – one of the most professional and in-depth studies of the race laws that were enacted by Mussolini's Fascist government and of the antisemitic policies of Mussolini's Italy during the tenure of Pope Pius XI and Pope Pius XII – Zuccotti focuses on the Pope's response to the Jewish Holocaust in Italy. She also researched Pius XII's policy on Jewish immigration and Jewish refugees, and on the Italian Jews who were sent to forced-labor camps, and clarified what the Pope knew about the Holocaust. Against the background of the political situation in Italy, Zuccotti places special emphasis on discoveries regarding the rounding up of more than 1,000 of Rome's Jews, the Aktion of October 16, 1943, and the Pope's and the Vatican's responses to these events. The book's importance stems also from its examination of the absence of an unequivocal instruction by the Pope to hide Jews in monasteries and convents.

A large portion of Zuccotti's book deals with the hiding of Jews throughout Italy between October and December 1943. Through monasteries, convents, Catholic schools and hospitals, and houses that belonged to the Vatican, Zuccotti researched the situation in different places throughout Italy. Her conclusion was that monasteries and convents throughout Italy opened their doors to Jewish refugees who had been hiding since Germany's invasion of the country. However, she also concludes that these acts of hiding and rescue were not the outcome of an order or instruction issued by the Pope but rather the result of local initiatives of each individual monastery and convent and a network of nuns and monks, priests in regional churches, and a few bishops willing to take the risk of providing assistance to these initiatives out of a sense of humanity, compassion, and mercy. According to Zuccotti, prominently absent is an instruction "from above" to hide Jews in monasteries and convents.[19] She also maintains that the documents at our disposal do not provide a documentary foundation for the various arguments that have been used to paint a positive picture of the Pope's policy regarding rescuing Jews in Italy.[20]

In 2003, a conference on Christian teachings pertaining to Jews, attended by Protestant, Catholic, and Jewish historians engaged in the subject from different countries, facilitated a comparison of the ways in which different Catholic and Protestant churches around the world reacted to the Holocaust. The papers presented at the conference, which was held at the Tacoma Theological University in Washington State, were published in a volume of *Kirchliche Zeitgeschichte: International Journal for Theology and History*, edited by historian Gerhard Besier. The hosts' intention, as reflected in the words of historian Robert Ericksen, was twofold: First, to constitute an initial effort to expand discussion on the subject from the perspective of theology and the Christian teachings of various churches; and second, to compare the teachings and views regarding Jews during the Holocaust espoused by different Catholic and Protestant churches that were exposed to the events of the Holocaust. According to Ericksen, although the Germans decided on a policy of murdering the Jews, this also impacted the Christians throughout Europe because they were part of the reality of murder in different ways: as perpetrators, as bystanders, and as rescuers and Righteous among the Nations. The fate of the Jews in the different countries of Europe varied according to the conditions in each. The goal of the conference was to focus on the educational approach to Jews of churches in different countries and to assess whether differences existed. On the other hand, it was important to examine the contents of the teachings that were disseminated to devout Christians in religion classes and in the Church press, in the "catechism", in the religious education in the text books, and in sermons in order to understand and consider the reasons for differences among the churches in each country and the primary contents pertaining to the Jews during the Holocaust.[21]

Most of the papers dealt with Christian education and antisemitism in different Christian denominations and in different countries. A few addressed education in the Catholic Church, and most examined the realm of education in the Protestant denominations in various countries.

An emphasis on Catholicism's "teaching of contempt" as another motivation for the Pope's policy during the Holocaust reemerged in full force during the initial decades of the twenty-first century, as said before. In his 2001 book *The Popes against the Jews: The Vatican's Role in the Rise of Modern Antisemitism*, historian David Kertzer also shows how Catholic teachings over the years were replete with anti-Jewish images of religious origin. This content continued to be published in the modern era and emanated prominently from the top of the hierarchal pyramid, as reflected in the documents of the popes of the nineteenth and the early twentieth centuries. Kertzer offers an historical account of the "teaching of contempt" and the Catholic Church's contribution to modern antisemitism, which, beginning in the second half of the nineteenth century, found expression in Papal documents, including those of Pius IX, Leo XIII, and Pius X, as well as in respected Catholic newspapers such as the Jesuit bimonthly *Civiltà Cattolica*.[22]

Kertzer highlights the antisemitic view that was expressed in *Civiltà Cattolica*. Until the 1930s, this paper's editors articulated extreme anti-Jewish hostility both in their theological explanations and their explanations of modern antisemitism, which had not been subject to papal censure. This view underwent some change when the public learned about the murder of the Jews during the Holocaust.[23]

In his essay at the Tacoma Conference, Kertzer highlights the role of antisemitism, based on generations of Catholic tradition, as a major factor motivating the behavior of Pius XII. Kertzer is critical of the Vatican's 1998 document "We Remember: A Reflection on the Shoah," which deals with the memory of the Holocaust, due to the content and the topics it does *not* address, such as the ongoing antisemitism in the Church hierarchy and its manifestation in Catholic public opinion in the nineteenth and the twentieth centuries. In his view, not only did the popes of the period in question not prevent antisemitism – they encouraged it. The 1998 document makes no mention of the fact that, at the end of the nineteenth century and the beginning of the twentieth century, the popes supported Catholic parties whose platforms were antisemitic in content. In other words, it fails to mention Catholic antisemitism and the popes' support of regimes and heads of government who did not grant equal rights to Jews. The Vatican, Kertzer adds, employed modern antisemitism, as well as racist antisemitism, and even supported blood libels in the twentieth century.[24]

Kertzer's book was severely criticized by Vatican spokespeople. In 2002, in the name of the Vatican and in defense of the Holy See, Father Giovanni Sale wrote of the need to distinguish between anti-Judaism on religious grounds and modern antisemitism, which was unrelated to Catholicism.[25] According to Kertzer, the Church had maintained a clear and distinct antisemitic approach, and not only in the nineteenth century. As an example to prove this claim, he refers to Enrico Rosa's article on "The Jewish Threat" that appeared in *Civiltà Cattolica* in 1928 and contained known antisemitic stereotypes. Most serious, he maintains, was the fact that the article was published by a highly respected journal of the Jesuits, a religious group centered in Rome.[26]

The Vatican Archive's Opening in 2003: The Tenure of Pope Pius XI

The opening of the archives pertaining to the tenure of Pius XI up to 1939 has facilitated an examination of the views and policies of Cardinal Secretary of State Eugenio Pacelli during the 1930s and allows us to draw conclusions regarding his views on various issues.

Prominent during the first decade of the twenty-first century were studies of the two orientations discussed above – those who are critical of the Pope and those who come to his defense – based on the new documentation. Among the historians who have researched the tenure of Pius XI in the archives that have been opened, we can learn from Thomas Brechenmacher, who has researched the position of the Holy See vis-à-vis Germany between 1933 and 1939 from a political perspective. His conclusion is that the major pursuit of the Vatican during the years in question was to ensure the future existence of all the institutions of the Catholic establishment in Germany during the period of Nazi rule. The "Reichskonkordat" of 1933 between Nazi Germany and the Vatican was meant to serve this policy of tending first and foremost to the needs of the Catholic Church. This treaty, however, was quickly trampled by the Nazi regime.

Immediately following the establishment of the Nazi Party, Pacelli was aware of its negative attitude toward Judaism and toward the Jews. In 1924, he also took note of the Nazi Party's negative attitude toward the Holy See, based on its comparison of the Vatican to the Jews and its denunciation of both. This comparison in the Nazi propaganda influenced the views of Pacelli, who rejected the comparison on the grounds that, in accordance with the Christian doctrine that prevailed during this period, Christianity was the successor of Judaism. According to Brechenmacher, Pius XI and Pacelli, "without being openly antisemitic, were so rooted in traditional doctrine, by no means free of antisemitism." Moreover, based on the published documents, Brechenmacher shows that Pacelli sent a letter to Nuncio Orsenigo in Germany to consult with him regarding how a possible condemnation of the "antisemitic excesses" would be received in Germany. Pacelli explained the reason for his consultation as follows: "It is traditional for the Holy See to carry its universal mission of peace and love to all people, regardless of class or religion…"[27] This correspondence is of great importance because it establishes that Pacelli initially considered Christian morality, which calls for compassion and mercy, but that in real time, this approach was subsequently replaced with internal considerations of political expedience for the Catholic Church.

In March 1937, Pope Pius XI issued two encyclicals: *Mit brennender Sorge*, on the state of the Church in Germany, which addressed race theory as running counter to Christianity, but says nothing about the German Nazi Regime, and *Divini Redemptoris*, which dealt in its entirety with total opposition to Communism, both as an ideology and as a threat in specific regimes, such as the Soviet Union, Mexico and Republican Spain. These two encyclicals, in conjunction with the April 1938 letter to the Vatican's Congregation of Seminaries and Universities that called on all Catholic institutions of higher learning to fight the fraudulent racial doctrine, was the crowning glory of the Church's condemnation of Communism and Racism. Later, when it was realized that this condemnation of racism had not been assigned its due significance because it was not issued as an encyclical, a discussion was initiated that was meant to result in the formulation of an explicit encyclical against racism and antisemitism, which Pius XI requested from Jesuit Catholic priest John La Farge. La Farge remitted the draft of the encyclical, which he composed in collaboration with French Jesuit Gustave Desbuquois and German Jesuit Gustave Gundlach, to the Superior General of the Society of Jesus in Rome when Pius XI was already very ill.[28]

Based on these documents, Brechenmacher deduces Pacelli's positions vis-à-vis Nazi Germany and his views on the Catholic Church, Communism, Racism, and racial antisemitism. These documents were known because they were published in real time. However, the opening of the archive of Pius XI offered a glimpse into the internal debate that each of these documents sparked at the highest echelons of the Church hierarchy, that is, at the level of the Pope, his close aides, and the Cardinal Secretary of State.

Brechenmacher's conclusion regarding the ideologies that were denounced in 1937 is that while Pacelli was quite aware of the heretical nature of the racial ideology that underlay the National Socialist regime and regarded it as a genuine threat to Christianity, it can be assumed that Communism was viewed as the foremost threat. As it turns out, therefore, the initial decision to issue an encyclical against racism and antisemitism on moral grounds was halted based on diplomatic and political considerations, which trumped morality.

The draft encyclical also had theological problems. If Pacelli read the draft when it was written, he would have been aware of the theological difficulties it created with regard to the Jews. Even if he believed in the anti-Jewish theology articulated in the draft encyclical, which was the prevailing theology at the time, he also believed that from a political perspective it would be counter-intuitive to publicize these views in 1939, when antisemitism was at its height.[29]

With regard to antisemitism, the public position of Pius XI was constant between 1928 and 1938. In 1928, he stated that antisemitism was inconsistent with Christian teachings, as "we are all Semitic in a spiritual sense," and in 1938 he reiterated this statement before Belgian pilgrims who visited the Vatican in that year: "Antisemitism is not acceptable. In the spiritual sense we are all Semites." These statements are indicative of the continuity of thought that characterized Pius XI between 1928 and his death one decade later. Even if Communism was the chief enemy of Christianity, Pius XI had no interest in turning National Socialism into a bulwark against the Communist threat. He regarded both totalitarian forms as equally dangerous, as both actively opposed the Catholic Church. In 1937, Pope Pius XI was ready to upset the order of things and to make a public statement against Nazi Germany, but the concern raised by the German bishops – that protest may not be the right course of action, as it could break the unity of the Catholic Church in Germany – prompted the Vatican to return to its previous policy of refraining from issuing an encyclical dealing entirely with opposition to racism and antisemitism. In 1938, the senior church leadership at the Vatican pondered the major question of whether issuing an encyclical would add fuel to the fire – a question that remained unanswered.[30]

The decision to refrain from issuing the encyclical stemmed primarily from political considerations. Hitler's standing rose in the international arena following the signing of the Munich Agreement in 1938, and the confrontation with Fascist Italy intensified following the enactment of the race laws of the same year. In Hitler's view, the Vatican was economically dependent on Italy, and it was important for the Pope to confirm the continuation of the Lateran Pacts of 1929, which enabled the Vatican to exist in exchange for its political neutrality. In addition, among the other considerations, the Vatican did not regard the need to issue an encyclical dealing solely with racism as particularly pressing, as the documents of 1937 and 1938 had already effectively clarified the Church's position on this matter. Therefore, when Pacelli was appointed Pope Pius XII, he buried the *Humani Generis Unitas* encyclical deep in a drawer. According to Brechenmacher, the Vatican archives contain no other documents that further illuminate this issue.

As noted, one issue that has occupied historians has been the role of Christian theology in motivating the Pope and the institutions of the Catholic Church during the Holocaust. In a 2007 article, the historian Sister Grazia Loparco paints a comprehensive picture of the assistance provided by the Catholic institutions in general, and by convents and monasteries in particular, to the rescue of Jews throughout Italy (which will be discussed more extensively below). Based on her research, Loparco reaches conclusions regarding the role of Christian theology in practice that are completely different from those that had been advanced up to that point. According to Loparco, between the autumn of 1943 and June 1944, during the Nazi occupation and the period that was most dangerous for Jews, Catholic institutions saved thousands of Jews, and as a result, there are convents and monasteries that are deserving of the title "Righteous among the Nations." Of Rome's 10,000-12,000 Jews, 4,500 were rescued with the assistance of convents, monasteries, and other Catholic institutions. Loparco's interpretation and conclusions regarding this rescue illuminates a different aspect of Christian faith. In her view, the main reasons for this extensive rescue effort were "Christian compassion and a natural sense of pragmatism." As a result of the pressing nature of the undertaking, doors were opened and Jews were taken in throughout Italy. During the German occupation of Italy, she concludes, the monasteries, and especially the convents, were extremely active. Unlike the existing theory, which holds that Christian theology and teachings resulted in antisemitism, Loparco concludes that monks and nuns were actually motivated to rescue Jews by the theology they carried with them. The decision was made easier by their theological consciousness, which stressed compassion and mercy.[31] This interpretation, facilitated by a deep gaze into the theology and constituting a new trajectory for the familiar historiography, stands to help researchers analyze and understand Catholic institutions that displayed compassion and mercy when they learned of the Germans' murder of the Jews in Europe and elsewhere.

Using Vatican documents that were opened in 2003, historian Paul O'Shea highlights a number of explanations for Pacelli's conduct as Cardinal Secretary of State and subsequently Pope Pius XII. Among other things, his research also emphasizes the Christian theological explanation of "supercessionism," which teaches that Judaism is no longer valid and was succeeded by Christianity, which has assumed its role. O'Shea's conclusions are completely different than those reached by Loparco,[32] and this theological basis, he maintains, is important for understanding the Pope's conduct at the time.

O'Shea also holds that, with regard to the Jews, Pius XII believed that he was doing the most that he could. He left the choice of how to proceed in the hands of the local bishops throughout Europe, whom he hoped would adopt positions in accordance with the conditions of the Church in each country. His personal policy was one of full adherence to impartiality during the war. He believed that it was his job to refrain from making a clear statement regarding the murder of the Jews, and he did so by choice. The Pope understood the war as an ideological battle between Christian civilization and the evil of National Socialist racial ideology and Communist Satanism. Moreover, according to Pius XII, the danger posed by Bolshevik atheism in 1942-43 was greater than all others. In this manner, O'Shea relates to the explanations that had been offered by Friedländer since the 1960s. The Pope hoped that the two totalitarian regimes would cease to exist – that they would spill each other's blood in battle and emerge from the war in a weak state, unable to cause further damage. As the war continued, he had to decide how to preserve a united Church in Italy and in Europe. As Friedländer already noted, it was a choice between different political and moral options.

According to O'Shea, the Pope was under immense pressure to speak out against the murder of the Jews and against Hitler. He did not submit to the pressure of the major powers. Rather, he acted based on his conscience and his convictions and left the solutions in the hands of God, whom he believed would bring an end to the war. Although this explanation may seem unreasonable to many historians, O'Shea maintains that it cannot be avoided. As Pius XII was a devout man, he believed that the history and fate of the nations were not in Hitler's or Churchill's control, but in the hands of God. Therefore, his passivity and his failure to make a clear statement stemmed also from his theological conception.

O'Shea also points to the personality of Pius XII as a reason for his silence. The Pope, he explains, was a man devoid of evil and hatred. He believed in the use of diplomacy and explanation to solve problems, and he believed that what was best for humanity would ultimately win out. During this period he was confronted with the question of whether to risk all he believed in. He was limited in his ability to see the reality that was taking shape before his eyes with regard to the murder of the Jews, and he lacked an army and the financial means to provide wide-scale assistance. He neither spoke nor issued warnings or condemnations, for, as the Pope himself explained to those who demanded his intervention, he could not abandon and endanger those whom he had already rescued in Rome and elsewhere. But why did he not speak out in 1942, when he learned of the murders, and especially in light of the Jews' removal from Rome in 1943? According to O'Shea, among the various explanations, the Church's long history of hatred of the Jews was decisive and caused him to remain silent. In the Pope's eyes, the Jews' fate was in God's hands. The Jews could always manage and always suffered as victims less than others. This is O'Shea's hard conclusion: that all of the defensive explanations that were offered for the Pope's silence are acceptable, but that after October 16, 1943, when the Jews of Rome were removed from their homes and sent to into the unknown, justification could no longer be found. At that point, a change was called for but did not occur.[33]

After the Vatican archive's opening of documents up to the year 1939, including the tenure of Pope Pius XI, during which Pacelli served as Cardinal Secretary of State from 1930 onward, numerous other studies were written on the period in addition to those mentioned here. However, as this article focuses on Pius XII during the Holocaust and is less concerned with Pacelli as Cardinal Secretary of State, we suffice with a general summary pending the Vatican's opening of the archives pertaining to the tenure of Pope Pius XII in 2020.[34]

The 2009 Workshop at Yad Vashem as an Interim Summation

In 2009, Yad Vashem and the Saint Peter and Saint Paul Silesian Theological Institute in Jerusalem invited senior scholars on the subject of Pius XII and the Jews during World War II to a first-of-its-kind workshop on the current state of research on the subject. Following the event, new studies written during the first decade of the twenty-first century were assembled, alongside the workshop lectures and the responses to them, in a book that was published in English in 2012 by Yad Vashem on behalf of both institutions. The book edited by David Bankier, Dan Michman, Yael Nidam-Orvieto – titled *Pius XII and the Holocaust: Current State of Research* – also featured new documents that were presented by the speakers.[35]

The main goal of the workshop was to understand the current state of the research according to the Vatican's archival material until 1939, and the contribution of the recent studies conducted since the opening of the archive. The scholars and experts on the subject espoused a variety of opinions of Pius XII; some were fundamentally critical of the Pope, whereas others came to his defense and explained his motivations based on their own interpretations. The subjects discussed encompassed the dilemmas, the silence, the passivity, and the rescue efforts of members of the Catholic Church. In light of the sensitivity of the issue, the willingness of these historians to meet and to engage in these controversial subjects was an achievement in itself.

The book *Pius XII and the Holocaust: Current State of Research* contains the workshop discussions divided according to the session topics and based on the expertise of the different historians. After a presentation of the points of division regarding each topic, the participants engaged in focused discussion on each. The topics were as follows:

1. Pacelli's Personality and the Jew – Presented by Andrea Tornielli and Michael Phayer.
2. Pacelli before his Pontificate – Presented by Jean-Dominique Durand and Paul O'Shea.
3. Pius XII, Orsenigo and the German Bishops – Presented by Thomas Brechenmacher and Sergio Minerbi.
4. Pius XII's Messages to European Bishops, Leaders and Governments – Presented by Matteo Napolitano, Paul O'Shea, and Michael Phayer.
5. Pius XII and Hiding in Italy – Presented by Grazia Loparco and Susan Zuccotti.
6. Pius XII and German Diplomats – Presented by Susan Zuccotti, Sergio Minerbi, Andrea Tornielli, and Thomas Brechenmacher.
7. Two topics from the post-war period were also explored: Pius XII and assistance to fleeing Nazi criminals, and the Vatican's post-war policies on Jewish children who had been hidden in convents and monasteries. These topics were presented by Michael Phayer and Matteo Napolitano.

The book reflects the proceedings of the presentations and the discussions themselves, revised as required by the participants for the purpose of the book's publication.

Due to its limited scope and the large number of relevant topics, this article deals with the issues pertaining primarily to Pacelli's conduct and policy as Cardinal Secretary of State and as Pope Pius XII, and not to issues pertaining to the bishops of occupied Europe. Indeed, the opening of the Vatican archival documents pertaining to the period up to 1939 sheds light on Pacelli's policy as the Cardinal Secretary of State of Pius XI, his papal predecessor, and provides some insight into his motivations during the period preceding his appointment as Pope Pius XII. Historians Tornielli, Brechenmacher and Durand noted that the new documentation provides a better understanding of Pacelli's attitude toward Nazism and the Jews, and the historians who took part in the workshop were in agreement that the atmosphere and setting in which Pacelli served were replete with traditional Christian anti-Jewish conceptions. However, they also showed how the new documents reflect Pacelli's disgust for National Socialist ideology, which he viewed as one of the greatest heresies of his time. This conclusion sheds new light on previous studies that sought to establish the opposite view. In any event, the anti-Jewish traditions of Catholicism that influenced Pacelli and his generation did not prevent him from privately expressing his disgust for Nazi antisemitism and German policies prior to the war.[36]

During the workshop, Phayer re-emphasized that European culture was steeped in anti-Jewish elements of religious origin and modern antisemitism. He also presented Pius XII's desire to avoid rupturing the unity of the Catholic Church in Germany as one of the most important reasons for his silence on the murder of the Jews. However, he also proposed a reassessment of the documents that were at the heart of the debate, such as the Pope's speech of December 24, 1942. In his view, a re-examination of this controversial address precludes us from continuing to speak about silence. According to him, the Pope's statement regarding the victims was universally understood as a condemnation of the Jewish genocide that the Germans were perpetrating, even if he did not say so explicitly. Based on his formulation, it was abundantly clear that he was referring to the Jews. It is also necessary to consider the Pope's attitude toward the Jews in the more general context of his treatment of other subjects during the war, which was always guided by the internal interests of the Catholic Church. In terms of his ability to sway the bishops of Germany, Pope Pius XII refrained from intervening; he did not seek ways of influencing them, and he did not try to encourage them to adopt a more positive attitude toward the Jews. Church Unity was above all other considerations. According to Phayer, the Pope's silence stemmed from his belief that any statement he made could cause a rupture in Church unity.[37]

Also at the Yad Vashem workshop – and in contrast to Phayer – O'Shea, whose above-mentioned research resulted in his invitation by Yad Vashem, assigned responsibility for not speaking out clearly against the treatment of the Jews to the Catholic Church as a whole, as opposed to the Pope alone (as he had argued in his book). The Church is more than just the Pope, he held; it consists of all devout Catholics and is a Church of all of its believers.[38] The new documents, he explained, enhances our understanding of the subject by revealing the tensions and the complexity in the relations between the Pope, the Cardinal Secretary of State, and the consensus in different countries. In this way, they reflect the complex circumstances that influenced the responses.

One of the major issues examined to assess the Pope's approach is the events that occurred in Italy itself. This subject was presented at the workshop by Loparco and Zuccotti, whose books are mentioned above. At the Yad Vashem workshop, the new research on Italians' rescue of Jews during the Nazi occupation of Italy aroused an old but fundamental debate: Were the rescue efforts a product of the intervention of Pius XII and an order "from above," or were they local initiatives by individual convents, monasteries, and Catholic institutions?

Loparco's comparative study of the rescue of Jews in Italy adds a new dimension to the discussion. Unlike Zuccotti, Loparco concludes that Pope Pius XII's involvement in the rescue of the Jews of Italy in general and in Rome in particular was greater than typically thought. According to Loparco, we cannot separate the Church's hiding of Jews from the assistance it provided to other persecuted groups in occupied Italy in the name of Christian compassion – such as certain political elements and their families; individuals who deserted from the army; young Italians in danger of being detained; refugees; orphans; and

Italian, British, German, and partisan soldiers.[39] Assistance to the Jews was provided in the same context.

In her response to Loparco's study at the Yad Vashem workshop, Zuccotti highlighted the fact that even after the study, the absence of a document by Pius XII instructing the nuns and monks of Catholic convents and monasteries to extend assistance to the Jews was still conspicuous. On this subject, there is almost no difference between the facts presented by the critics and the defenders of Pius XII. The difference lies in their interpretation of the absence of such a document.

Zuccotti's book – *Under His Very Windows: The Vatican and the Holocaust in Italy* – as said above- deals extensively with Pius XII. It focuses on opportunities to rescue Jews of which he did not take advantage, and it sparked renewed debate on the issue. At the workshop at Yad Vashem, she continued defending her argument that those who rescued Jews were acting solely on their own accord. Had the Pope personally intervened, she argued, we can assume that more Jews would have been saved. However, the bulk of the charge against him is that the Jews of Rome were taken away for extermination "under his very windows," and that he did not stop the transports. Pius XII was motivated by various considerations, Zuccotti argued, but Christian compassion was not one of them.[40]

Another significant topic discussed at the Yad Vashem workshop was whether the Pope recognized that the Jews posed a unique problem – that is, whether he regarded the murder of the Jews as something unique and exceptional in Nazi policy. According to Tornielli, he did not. It has already been proven that a number of bishops and priests on the ground recognized the exceptional nature of the murder of the Jews and petitioned the Vatican on the matter. Dina Porat noted that during her own research in the archive, she observed that Roncalli, the Pope's representative in Turkey (who was later appointed Pope John XXIII), expressed both his concern and his disappointment with the Pope's actions regarding the Jews.[41] The Pope was aware of the pressures from within the Church. Tornielli holds that the bishops who were situated at the sites of the killing were attentive and understood what was transpiring before their eyes better than those situated elsewhere. The Pope did not directly observe a problem of special crimes directed against the Jews, but rather regarded the case of the Jews as another issue in the context of the war and the other war crimes that were being perpetrated. Therefore, when assistance was provided to the Jews, it stemmed from Christian compassion for others. There was no comprehension that the mass killings of Jews, were special crimes against them as a collective. According to Tornielli, there is no doubt that, in the discussion of what should have been said and done, it has been proven that the Catholic Church and its members reacted inappropriately to what befell the Jews during the Holocaust, considering the scope of the tragedy. But we must also consider the general context, which was the fact that the entire world had reacted inappropriately to this exceptionally tragic event. In a discussion on the matter conducted within the Church, it was decided to exercise caution in public statements in certain cases, but this was a mistake. Some thought that the Church should have acted differently by instructing the general public to help the Jews. In contrast, in Tornelli`s view, the Pope and Cardinal Secretary of State thought that exercising caution in public statements would allow the rescue effort to spread, which was also noted by the Red Cross.[42]

In contrast, Matteo Napolitano argued that because the Holocaust was an event that transcended the limits of human imagination, diplomatic activity, certainly in its classical sense, would not have helped. What was required was an alternative diplomacy, a "diplomacy of catacombs," based on a closer, grassroots connection with the field. Its base was the lower clergy and the monasteries and convents, which, using their network of connections around the world, succeeded in rescuing some of the victims of Nazism.[43]

According to Napolitano, the Pope was limited in a number of ways. First, unlike World War I, World War II was a conflict with ideological dimensions – a war between world powers that was simultaneously a war between two opposing ideologies – and until 1942, it was unclear whether the liberal democracies would be capable of defeating the Nazis. Second, the Holocaust was an unprecedented event, creating a problem of priorities.[44]

According to Napolitano, then, as shown at the workshop at Yad Vashem, the Pope should have abandoned classical diplomacy. The Holy See could have succeeded only if its voice was heeded by the authorities and policy makers – only if they followed its instructions. However, the Pope lacked the political power necessary to influence other countries. For this reason a new diplomacy was needed, one that would protect the entire network of the papal diplomatic representatives – the nunciature – and the bishops as a living and breathing body: a "diplomacy of catacombs." Here, Napolitano was referring to an underground diplomacy aimed at mitigating the suffering of all the victims, Jews included, by means of the Vatican's representatives and the bishopries that still existed. In Napolitano's eyes, what happened after the war was an example of the success of this diplomacy. According to reports, immediately following the Holocaust the Jewish institutions, and some survivors, articulated immense gratitude for the Pope's actions and viewed him as a great friend.[45]

Pius XII's actions, Napolitano explained, were guided by a number of factors that did not include anti-Communism. The Pope's anti-Communism was along the lines of American anti-Communism. Napolitano's interpretation, as presented at the workshop, in part ran contrary to everything that had been written until then, particularly with regard to Communism. He is one of the only historians who does not accept that the Pope's action was guided by the anti-Communist ideology.

As for the prevailing attitude toward Hitler, it should be remembered that for some time Hitler was considered to be an accepted statesman, as reflected in the fact that nobody severed relations with Nazi Germany after Hitler enacted the anti-Jewish laws.

With regard to Zionism, Napolitano maintained that Pius XII expressed doubts regarding the establishment of a Jewish state in Mandatory Palestine. This position, however, did not prevent him from working to send Jews to Palestine via the rescue network, which proceeded via papal representative Roncalli in Istanbul.

One of the issues raised at the workshop was whether there was any documentary evidence of the Pope's assistance to the Jews, or whether conclusion of his assistance was based on interpretation alone. Napolitano argued that such evidence does exist. Information collected in the Baltic States proves that the Vatican ran a network that undoubtedly worked to the benefit of the Jews. This network did not differentiate between Jews who had converted to Christianity and Jews who had not been baptized, perhaps due to the fact that time was of the essence. Pius XII received the cooperation of the American Jews, which started in

1940. Three documents, in which the Cardinal Secretary of State offered financial assistance to inmates of a concentration camp in southern Italy, were not contained by the collections published by the Vatican between 1965 and 1981 (*ADSS*). One of these letters was signed by Giovanni Montini, one of Pius XII's advisors from 1944 onward, who was subsequently appointed Pope Paul VI.[46]

On the subject of the Pope's silence, Napolitano asked whether it was a silence reflecting guilt, or reflecting the caution required by the situation. In his view, *Summi Pontificatus* of October 12, 1939, Pius XII's first encyclical, was welcomed by Britain, as reflected in the War Cabinet's meeting of October 30. Should the explanation for the Pope's silence, then, be searched for in the Vatican archives or, alternatively, in the words of Pius XII and how those who read them understood his intentions? This question can be considered in the context of the October 1939 encyclical – which did not explicitly specify who was the victim and who was the occupier – after the German invasion of Poland, as well as to the Pope's well-known Christmas radio broadcast in 1942, in which he used the term *stirpe* (meaning "race" or "descent"), instead of the explicit word "Jews," when referring to the victims. The *New York Times* reported extensively on the speech and asserted that the Pope had finally made a clear public statement regarding what was happening. Only a study comparing the existing documents thus far and the Vatican documents pertaining to the tenure of Pius XII can provide the information necessary to fill out this picture.[47]

The workshop at Yad Vashem expanded the scope of many topics, and David Bankier, one of the initiators of the workshop, sought to focus on the reaction of Pope Pius XII, as opposed to that of the Church and all its institutions. The major question that Bankier continued considering was whether we can identify a turning point in the Pope's approach – a point at which he said: "enough is enough." According to Bankier, although this question has yet to be clarified, it appears that Pius XII never reached such a turning point in his policy and never said "enough is enough." However, others did, and Bankier bases this conclusion on the fact that points of change can be identified in other places and other institutions outside the Church. One example was the German generals who, at a certain point in 1944, decided to mutiny. They knew they would be unable to assassinate Hitler, but they reached a point at which enough was enough. Another was among "regular" Germans, and even in the Nazi leadership, the army, the Jews imprisoned in the ghettos, and the bystanders. A related question is whether they had examined other options for rescuing more. It is also important to remember that during World War II, a few Germans dared to take action against the murder being perpetrated by the Nazis. On this basis, Bankier asked at what point, if any, did the Pope and all Church leaders wonder whether they needed to change their response in light of the reality with which they were faced.[48] This question remains unanswered, as food for thought.

An important question of Bankier that was discussed at the workshop was whether Pius XII was responsible for the rescue activity conducted by the regular clergy, or whether they were the product of their own initiative. This question was asked twice: both in relation to the rescue of Jews during the war, and, in the words of Bankier, in relation to whether there was a point in time at which the Vatican diplomats acknowledged to themselves that the previous approach was not working: that by working "behind the scenes" they could save 2,000 people per day, but that by making a statement to the media they could save 4,000. Bankier also wondered whether the situation in the summer of 1944, when the Nazis were killing some 12,000 people per day in the gas chambers, caused Pius XII to realize that there were no longer two options but rather only one: that of issuing a public statement, despite the risks involved, because it was no longer possible to remain silent. Enough was enough.[49]

These and other important issues were also addressed by Michman in his conclusion to the workshop. Although agreement was not reached during the meeting, Michman held, an important process had gotten underway: the effort to present different views and different interpretations of the published documents, with an emphasis on both the broad historical processes and the minute details of the documents themselves. Many issues have not yet been researched, but the overall agreement was that many questions regarding Pius XII's policy during the war could only be answered after the opening of the Vatican archives pertaining to the period from 1939 up to 1945, as well as other archives. Until then, many issues will continue to be interpreted differently based on the same sources. According to Michman, one of the main problems concerns the linkage between politics and theology and between politics and morality. The Church is an all-embracing institution in its religious and moral dimensions, and the Vatican is also a state with political dimensions. In many cases, the balance between these aspects is overlooked when dealing with the Vatican and the Pope. Finally, Michman highlighted the period between the end of November 1942 and the early months of 1943, which witnessed a host of highly significant events: the Battle of El Alamein, the December 17, 1942 Allied statement regarding the murder of the Jews, the Pope's Christmas address of December 24, 1942, and the German defeat at Stalingrad at the beginning of 1943. These events certainly cultivated an awareness of the wartime events and the turn on the battlefield, and as a result, the United States and the Soviet Union began thinking seriously about the end of the war, each in its own way. It is important here to clarify what, at this point in time, the Church and the Pope were planning for the future. In his conclusion to the workshop at Yad Vashem, Michman noted that thus far little was known about the churches in the free world as a whole – Latin America and North America included.[50]

The Pope's Silence from the Perspective of Latin America

The research on the Catholic churches located outside the theatres of war, such as in Latin America, has emphasized the absence of a clear statement by the Pope regarding the Jews, whether by document or public address, and that this had distinct consequences. In the absence of explicit instructions to assist the Jewish victims and in light of the traditional anti-Jewish Christian theology and its manifestation in the "teaching of contempt," each Catholic church in each country had to decide independently how to proceed. It is evident that the approaches to the Jews were diverse, but each country had its central message. Ultimately, the Catholics were influenced by the political climate in each country more than by the position of the Pope, who did not openly make his voice heard and left his position unknown.[51]

At the beginning of 1939, the rescue of the Jews of Europe was on the agenda of two different cardinals in Latin America who had the ability to help: Cardinal Sebastião Leme, the Archbishop of Rio de Janeiro; and Cardinal Santiago Luis Copello, the Archbishop of Buenos Aires. In March 1939, both men were in Rome for the election of the new Pope, Pope Pius XII. In response to a request made by Cardinal Faulhaber, on his own behalf and on behalf of other German bishops, these cardinals sought to intervene with their governments to allow the immigration of "non-Aryan Catholics" (Jews who had converted) to their countries. As a result of the benevolent willingness of these senior clergymen to intervene in this manner, Cardinal Faulhaber and Archbishop Adolf Bertram met with Pius XII and asked him to conduct negotiations with the governments of Brazil and Argentina to acquire entry visas for "non-Aryan Catholics." To the Pope, Faulhaber emphasized that he knew that the policy in Germany was pushing for quick emigration, and that if this did not occur they would be deported to the concentration camps.[52]

In the case of Brazil, progress was made on the issue despite all the difficulties noted in the research on the subject. Ultimately, Brazil absorbed 1,000 Jewish refugees of the 3,000 to which its government had committed itself.[53] In the case of Argentina, no progress was made on the issue, and had it not been noted in the Vatican documents contained in *Actes et Documents* (it is mentioned nowhere in the publications of the Catholic Church in Argentina of the time) we would have no idea that such a request was also made to the Archbishop of Argentina. Also unknown is whether a petition was made by the Vatican and whether such a request was conveyed to the government.[54]

Discussion on the policy, the conduct, and the silence of Pius XII is still underway. In 2014, an American Catholic couple, a lawyer and his wife, who researched the policy of Pius XII during the Holocaust and continue to do so, published a book. Based on a photo published in *Der Stürmer* in 1934, they embarked upon research of Argentina's convening of the 34th International Eucharistic Congress (an international gathering of the Catholic Church in which all church heads from around the world – archbishops, bishops, and papal representatives – take part), in October 1934 in the presence of Cardinal Secretary of State Eugenio Pacelli, its guest of honor. On this occasion, Archbishop Copello of Buenos Aires blessed the swastika-bearing German flag that had been raised in the San Isidro Church.[55] A different picture of Archbishop Copello's blessing of the flags of the countries who participated in the International Eucharistic Congress, including the flag bearing the swastika, appears on the cover of the 2003 Spanish-language edition of my book on the Catholic Church in Argentina, *Católicos, Nazis y Judíos*. This photo was also taken from the German newspaper

Der Sturmer in real time and was reprinted in 1935, the following year, in an official publication issued by the Catholic Church of Argentina to mark the one year anniversary of the Congress.[56]

These examples highlight Pacelli's explicit conduct as Cardinal Secretary of State in 1934 and the absence of a public position against Nazi Germany in the early days of the regime. On the other hand, they also leave many unanswered questions regarding Pacelli's future policy and path as Pope Pius XII and his failure to approach the rulers of the Catholic countries of Latin America, which is indicative of the lack of a focused and efficient effort.

Conclusion

Since the early 1960s, a fundamental historiographical debate has been underway regarding Pope Pius XII's silence and policy vis-à-vis the Jews, and regarding the factors that resulted in this policy. Engaged in by Jewish and Christian historians, the discussion initially proceeded based on documents that were uncovered after the war, but without a foundation of documents from the Vatican itself. Because of this ongoing discussion, between 1965 and 1981, the Vatican published 11 volumes of material selected from the archive, and the debate continued with greater intensity.

Historians were able to hone their research and dig deeper with the 2003 opening of the Vatican archives pertaining to the tenure of Pope Pius XI, which ended in 1939. Until that year, as we known, Eugenio Pacelli served as Cardinal Secretary of State, and the released documents offered insight into his positions prior to the outbreak of World War II.

Despite the different approaches and the debate between the critics and the defenders of Pope Pius XII, the new research enhances the initial research and is indicative of partial interpretations, some based on the same facts and documents, and others based on new documents, new questions, and other interpretations. In conclusion, we can say that the historians agree that only after the opening of the archives dealing with the years 1939-1945 will it be possible to ground the different interpretations in a foundation of the facts regarding Pius XII's policy and motivations vis-à-vis the Jews and the Holocaust.

It is widely agreed that the Pope knew what the Nazi regime was doing to the Jews in real time, although he did not speak out publicly. The disagreements pertain to whether or not he understood that the Jewish problem was unique and about the ways he dealt with it. Many argue that he regarded the Jewish problem as comparable to the problems posed by the other victims of the war, as opposed to a special problem involving the planning and execution of total genocide.

Some maintain that the Pope bears responsibility on both a political level, as head of the Vatican state, and on a religious and moral level, as head of the Catholic Church. At the junctures at which Pope Pius XII needed to make decisions, he tended first to the members of his flock, and the moral issues became of secondary importance. The Pope acted first and foremost to maintain the unity of the Church and therefore did not express a public position out of concern that Church unity could be compromised as a result of such remarks. This policy intensified as the strength of Hitler and Nazi Germany grew during the war. In the eyes of Pius XII, it was a war between two anti-Christian ideologies: Communism and Nazism.

Most historians believe that, in his ideological and political view, the Pope objected to Communism more than to Nazism. Some historians view his failure to make an explicit statement opposing the German oppressor and the Jewish victim as an expression of the political view that a victorious Nazi Germany could serve as a bulwark against the advancement of Communism. In this sense, Nazism was the lesser of two evils, and after the war, the Pope hoped, it could be moderated. Many historians have concluded that the political concerns eclipsed the moral concerns. Others hold that as a religious man, the Pope believed that, in any event, God had the last word and that for this reason too, he refrained from intervening on behalf of the Jews.

Many historians understand the Pope's silence regarding the murder of the Jews as a manifestation of a psychological block and a deep emotional connection to the German nation and German culture, stemming from his many years of service as Apostolic Nuncio in Germany (1917-1930).

Most historians, including the Catholics among them, stress that the traditional anti-Jewish theological message and the many years of "teaching of contempt" for the Jews deeply penetrated all levels of the Church, including the popes themselves. John Cornwell has presented an extreme view of this aspect, writing that Pope Pius XII was an antisemite. Others believe that the opposite is true: that the compassion and mercy that are ingrained in the Christian theology, were the main reason for the rescue efforts in Italy. The case of Italy strengthens the position of those who argue that a broad network to assist in the rescue of Jews was established by convents and monasteries, and that this network succeeded in rescuing thousands of Jews after the German invasion of Italy, based on a sense of Christian compassion and mercy.

Disagreement remains regarding the Pope's role in this rescue effort. Some hold that the rescue efforts by the regular clergy in Italy would not have occurred without the instruction of the Pope, or at least an understanding that this was his desire, although we have no documents to support this approach. Zuccotti, for example, writes that the Jews of Rome were sent to Auschwitz "under his very windows" without his public intervention, even though he was obligated to protect them in his capacity as the Bishop of Rome. Numerous researchers have proven that the local efforts and the rescue network among the local clergy, undertaken for humane and religious reasons alike, were the product of local decisions. No such document has been found thus far.

One of the major questions that have been asked during the twenty-first century and that featured prominently in the 2009 workshop at Yad Vashem was whether we can identify a turning point in the Pope's conduct and silence during the war –whether there was a moment at which Pope Pius XII said "enough is enough!" and changed his position on the murder of the Jews by Nazi Germany. The case of Italy was a test case, but there were other cases as well. This question is extremely important for the interpretation of the facts that have been revealed thus far. Most likely, there was no turning point in the diplomatic policy of "catacombs" – diplomatic activity behind the scenes on behalf of the Jewish victims. No change occurred in the course of the war, even though the crimes were revealed on an increasingly frequent basis. His concern for his own flock outweighed all moral considerations. Another question that has been asked is whether a clear statement could have changed the reaction of everyday Catholics – whether it would have motivated Catholics to rescue many more Jews across occupied Europe, even if, as is widely agreed, they could not have prevented the Holocaust. The interpretation of this policy remains a source of disagreement.

At the close of this publication, we have come to learn that, as promised, in March 2, 2020, the Vatican archive relating to Pope Pius XII term was opened, as Pope Francis announced in 2019. But, the archive had to close its doors shortly after because of the coronavirus crisis. Prof. Hubert Wolf from the University of Munich and his team were working at the archive during the first week and already made some important discoveries. He talked to the Catholic weekly *Kirche + Leben*, saying that his team had found documents that were not included in the eleven volumes of *Actes et Documents* published by the Vatican between 1965-1981. Their report was published on April 22, in the newspaper *Die Zeit*. [57]

The conclusions from the documents they revised in the short time they were able to work in the archive are that Pope Pius XII knew about the mass killing of Jews in real time. In September 1942 the United States diplomat gave the Pope a report prepared by the Jewish Agency in Switzerland that documented the mass murder of some 100,000 Jews from the Warsaw ghetto. It also said that 50,000 Jews were killed in Lvov in German occupied territories. The US ambassador asked the Vatican if they could confirm the report from their own sources and they responded that they could not. But now, Prof. Wolf and his team have discovered a note confirming that Pius XII had read the American report, as well as two documents showing that the Vatican had corroborated the reports of the mass killings. One is a report from the Ukrainian Greek Catholic Archbishop of Lvov, Andrey Sheptytsky, sent in August 1942, a month before the American report talked about 200,000 Jews massacred in Ukraine under the "outright diabolical" German occupation. The second was a report from an Italian businessman who told Monsignor Giovanni Battista Montini, the future Pope Paul VI, of the "incredible butchery" of Jews he had seen during a visit to Warsaw. Montini reported it to Maglione, the report stated. These two reports were detailed in a memo by another staffer at the Secretariat of State, Angelo Dell`Acqua . He wrote in his memo that the Vatican should be careful, because the Jews "easily exaggerate and the "orientals", meaning the Archbishop of Lvov, "are really not an example of honesty". According to Wolf and his staff this is a key document, and a new discovery that helps understand the antisemitic atmosphere around the Pope. The Pope also received many documents and photos from concentration camps, letters and pictures, asking for help.[58]

The full picture of Pius XII's attitude and policy will be further explored in the coming years, the more the research continues and answers given to the relevant questions that are still missing, like when he first knew about Jews being mass murdered, and why he subsequently did not change the way he acted, and other key questions that may give an answer as to why he did not mention the Jews in any document or declaration, why he did not condemn Nazi Germany, and so on. The responses to the main questions, as well as the omissions, are in the documents in the Vatican archive.

Endnotes

1   Saul Friedländer, *Pie XII et le IIIe Reich. Documents* (Paris, 1964). On the historiography of Pius XII since the beginning of the historiographical debate, see the bibliography chapter in Graciela Ben Dror, *Christianity without Mercy: The Vatican, the Catholic Church, and the Jews of Argentina, Brazil, and Uruguay in Light of the Holocaust – Comparative Aspects, 1933-1945* (Moreshet–Givat Haviva, 2018) (Hebrew), pp. 272-278.

2   P. Blet, R. A. Graham, A. Martini and B. Schneider (eds.), *Actes et documents du Saint Siège relatifs à la Seconde Guerre mondiale* (Vatican City, 1965 – 1981).

3   For example: John F. Morley, *Vatican Diplomacy and the Jews during the Holocaust, 1939-1943* (New York, 1980); John Conway, "Catholicism and the Jews during the Nazi Period," in Otto Dov Kulka and Paul R. Mendes-Flohr (eds.), *Judaism and Christianity under the Impact of National Socialism* (Jerusalem, 1987), pp. 435-451, 435-436, John P. Palikowski, O.S.M., *The Challenge of the Holocaust for Christian Theology* (New York, 1978. Second ed. 1982).

4   See Friedländer in his publication of 1980: Saul Friedländer, "Vatican Policy toward Jews during the Holocaust in the light of the new Research". *The Shlomo and Shoshana Strochlitz Chair in Holocaust Studies*, Publication no.3, University of Haifa, pp. 5-18.

5   John Cornwell, *Hitler's Pope: The Secret History of Pius XII* (London, 1999), p. 295.

6   Giovanni Miccoli, *I dilemmi e i silenzi di Pio XII: Vaticano, Seconda Guerra mondiale e Shoah* (Milan, 2000).

7   Ronald J. Rychlak, *Hitler, the War and the Pope* (Columbus, MS, 2000), pp. 137, 142; Ronald J. Rychlak, "Goldhagen v. Pius XII," *First Things* (June/July 2002), pp. 37- 54.

8   Garry Wills, *Papal Sin: Structures of Deceit* (New York, 2000).

9   Danaiel Goldhagen, *A Moral Reckoning: The Role of the Catholic Church in the Holocaust and its Unfulfilled Duty of Repair* (New York, 2002).

10   James Carroll, *Constantine's Sword: The Church and the Jews* (Boston, 2000).

11   Michael Phayer, T*he Catholic Church and the Holocaust, 1930-1965* (Indiana University Press, 2000).

12   Ibid., pp. xii-xv.

13   Ibid., pp. xi-xvii. On Roncalli, see also Dina Porat, *Trapped Leadership* (Tel Aviv, 1986), third printing (2004), pp. 300, 336-343 (Hebrew).

14   Saul Friedländer, *Pie XII et le IIIe Reich. Documents* (Paris, 1964).

15   Phayer, T*he Catholic Church and the Holocaust*, p. 222.

16   Michael Phayer, *Pius XII, the Holocaust, and the Cold War* (Indiana University Press, 2008).

For a critique of this book, see Ruth Brauda, "The Holocaust as a Marginal Matter, Pius XII and the Jews: Michael Phayer, Pius XII, The Holocaust, and the Cold War," *Yad Vashem Studies* 36(2), pp. 203-219.

17 Michael Phayer, "Helping Jews is not an easy thing to do," *Holocaust and Genocide Studies* 21(3) (2007), pp. 421-453.

18 Susan Zuccotti, *The Italians and the Holocaust: Persecution, Rescue, and Survival* (University of Nebraska Press, 1987); Susan Zuccotti, *Holocaust Odysseys: The Jews of Saint Martin Vesubie and their Flight through France and Italy, 1939-1945* (Yale University Press 2007).

19 Susan Zuccotti, *Under His Very Windows: The Vatican and the Holocaust in Italy* (Yale University Press, 2000); Susan Zuccotti, *Pope Pius XI and the Rescue of Jews in Italy* (Washington, 2004).

20 Susan Zuccotti, *Two Popes and the Holocaust: An Examination of the Controversy*, Occasional Paper no. 9, The Center for Holocaust Studies at the University of Vermont, 2005, pp. 18-19.

21 Robert P. Ericksen, *Kirchliche Zeitgeschichte* 16(1) (2003).

22 David Kertzer, *The Popes against the Jews: The Vatican's Role in the Rise of Modern Antisemitism* (New York, 2001).

23 Ibid., pp. 76-91.

24 David Kertzer, "Antisemitism and the Vatican: On Anti-Judaism, Antisemitism, and the Holocaust," in *Kirchliche Zeitgeschichte* 16(1), pp. 69-91. In the same publication, on the anti-Jewish elements in Catholic education, see Graciela Ben Dror, "Catholic Teaching about Jews in Spain compared with Argentina during the Holocaust Era, 1933-1945," in *Kirchliche Zeitgeschichte* 16(1) (2003), pp. 92-111; Ana Lysiak, "The Rev. Kruszynski and Polish Catholic Teachings about Jews and Judaism in Interwar Poland," *Ibid.*, pp. 52-75.

25 Giovanni Sale, "Antigiudaismo o antisemitismo? Le accuse contro la Chiesa e la *Civiltà Cattolica*," *Civiltà Cattolica* II (2002), (No. 3647).

26 Enrico Rosa, "Il pericolo giudaico e gli Amici d' Israel," *Civiltà Cattolica* II (1928), p. 340.

27 Thomas Brechenmacher, "Pope Pius XI, Eugenio Pacelli and the Persecution of the Jews in Nazi Germany, 1933–1939, New Sources from the Vatican Archives," *Bulletin of the German Historical Institute in London* 27(2) (2005), pp. 24-25; Thomas Brechenmacher, *Der Vatikan und die Juden* (Munich, 2005); Thomas Brechenmacher, *Das Reichskonkordat 1933* (Munich, 2007).

28 Brechenmacher, "Pope Pius XI," pp. 24-25; See also Georges Passelecq and Bernard Suchecky, *The Hidden Encyclical of Pius XI* (New York, 1997).

29 Brechenmacher, "Pope Pius XI," p. 25.

30 Ibid., pp. 26-27.

31 Gracia Loparco, "La Assistenza prestata dalle Religiose di Roma agli Ebrei durante la Seconda Guerra Mondiale," in Luigi Mezzadri and Maurizio Tagliaferri (eds.), *Le Donne nella Chiesa e in Italia* (Rome, 2007).

32 Paul O'Shea, *A Cross too Heavy: Eugenio Pacelli, Politics, and the Jews of Europe, 1917–1943* (Australia, 2008), pp. 328-344.

33 Ibid.

34 Articles on this subject have been written in English, French, Polish, German, and of course Italian and have shed light on different aspects of Pacelli's tenure as Cardinal Secretary of State. See, for example, Gary DeGregorio, *Pope Pius XII and His Silent War* (Independently Published, 2019); Hubert Wolf, *Pope and Devil: The Vatican's Archives and the Third Reich* (Cambridge, MA, 2016); Jacques Kornberg, *The Pope's Dilemma: Pius XII Faces Atrocities and Genocide in the Second World War* (University of Toronto Press, 2015); Margherite Marchione, *Did Pope Pius XII help the Jews?* (Mahwah, NJ, 2007); Pancratius Pfeiffer, *Der Verlangerte Arm Von Pius XII* (Rome, 2013); Robert S. Wistrich, *Pius XII and the Shoah* (Jersualem, 2006); Klaus *Kühlwein, Pius XII und di Judenrazzia in Rom* (Berlin, 2013); Frank J. Coppa, *The Policies and Politics of Pope Pius XII: Between Diplomacy and Morality* (New York, 2011); Frank J. Coppa, *The Life and Pontificate of Pope Pius XII: Between History and Controversy* (Washington, D.C., 2013); Marcel Rustemeyer, *Die Paepste zur zeit des Nationalsozialismus* (Nordestedt, 2018).

35 David Bankier, Dan Michman, and Iael Nidam-Orvieto (eds.), *Pius XII and the Holocaust: Current State of Research* (Jerusalem, 2012).

36 Andrea Tornielli, "Pacelli's Personality and the Jews," in Ibid., pp. 28-36; Jean-Dominique Durand, "Pacelli before his Pontificate," in Ibid., pp. 46-59; Thomas Brechenmacher, "Pius XII, Orsenigo and the German Bishops," in Ibid., pp. 68-74.

37 Michael Phayer, "Pius XII's Messages to European Bishops, Leaders and Governments," in Bankier, Michman, and Nidam-Orvieto, *Pius XII,* pp. 90–98, 103. Phayer emphasizes the pressure exerted by Bishop Preysing to clarify what happened to those who were sent to the camps.

38 Paul O'Shea, "Pius XII's Messages to European Bishops, Leaders and Governments," in Ibid., pp. 90-98.

39 Grazia Loparco, "Pius XII and the Hiding in Italy," in Ibid, pp. 115–125.

40 Susan Zuccotti, Pius XII and the Hiding in Italy," in Ibid, pp. 126-135. Zuccottii has also written a number of studies on rescue by different figures and groups within the Catholic Church, the most recent of which (published in 2013) deals with the rescue stemming from the dedication of Father Marie-Benoît.

41 Dina Porat, in Bankier, Michman, and Nidam-Orvieto, *Pius XII,* pp. 38-39.

42 Andrea Tornielli, in Ibid, pp. 17, 112.

43 Matteo Naplolitano, in Ibid, p. 17.

44 Andrea Napolitano, in Ibid, pp. 84-95, quoting Richard Breitman, *Official Secrets: What the Nazis Planned, What the British and Americans Knew* (New York, 1998).

45 *Actes et Documents (ADSS)* 10(10); Napolitano, in Bankier, Michman, and Nidam-Orvieto, *Pius XII*, pp. 85-86.

46 Napolitano, in Ibid, pp. 87-88.

47 Ibid., pp. 89-90.

48 David Bankier, Ibid., pp. 112-114.

49 Ibid., p. 114.

50 Dan Michman, "Conclusion," in Bankier, Michman, and Nidam-Orvieto, *Pius XII*, pp. 198-201.

51 Graciela Ben Dror, *La Iglesia Católica ante el Holocausto. España y América Latina 1933-1945* (Madrid, 2003); Ben-Dror, *Christianity without Mercy*.

52 ADSS 6(8), pp. 63-65.

53 Avraham Milgram, *Os Judeus do Vaticano* (Rio de Janeiro, 1994).

54 Graciela Ben Dror, *The Catholic Church and the Jews: Argentina, 1933-1945* (Nebraska, 2008).

55 Stephen and Diane Galebach, *Why did the Vatican Honor the Swastika?* (Massachusetts, 2014). http://investigation2.galebachlaw.com/itimeline.html (accessed January 30, 2020).

56 For a photo of the swastika-bearing flag at the International Eucharistic Congress in Buenos Aires in 1934, see the cover of Graciela Ben Dror, *Católicos, Nazis y Judíos. La Iglesia Argentina en los tiempos del Tercer Reich* (Buenos Aires, 2003).

57 *Die Zeit*, 22.4.2020, quoted in *The Time of Israel*, (Online) 2.5.2020

58 Ibid.

Judy Tydor Baumel-Schwartz

Women, Gender, and the Holocaust: A Historiographical Survey

Introduction

A few days ago, I noticed a news item regarding the publication of a new book dealing with women in the Holocaust. After reading the report, I was pleased for my friend who had written the book, I sent her my congratulations, and I continued reading. A few minutes later, however, I returned to the item announcing the book's publication to take another look. I was struck by what a long way we have come since I began researching this subject more than three decades ago. In those days, publication of a research book on women in the Holocaust was considered to be a rare, exceptional, and in some cases even problematic event. Every such book could expect to receive critical and at times insulting reviews by those who found the very subject unworthy of research. Such reviews also had practical implications, as criticism leveled at the authoring scholar and her research on more than one occasion left her position of employment uncertain. Today, the situation is different. In most places, the subject has long since become mainstream Holocaust research, and studies on the subject are considered to be appealing to those interested in the Holocaust and are an almost routine undertaking.

Routine undertakings, however, must begin somewhere and evolve over time until they become routine. This raises the question of how routine research on Jewish women in the Holocaust came into being. When were the first efforts made to research the subject, and what aspects did the initial studies explore? Why was it decided to emphasize some aspects of women's experiences in the Holocaust while completely ignoring others? And finally, how can we understand the disregard that was demonstrated for this subject for so many years, despite the fact that the figure who had become the symbol of the Holocaust for millions of people around the world was actually a woman, or, to be precise, a Jewish adolescent girl who, while living in hiding from the Nazis, wrote a diary that would emerge as the most widely sold Holocaust-related book in the world: *Anne Frank: The Diary of a Young Girl*?[1] In the following discussion, we will explore these and other related questions.

This article will consider the five waves of writing on Jewish women in the Holocaust, according to the fullest definition of the event (from the Nazis' rise to power through the end of World War II), that have constituted the literature on the subject between the end of the war and the present day. Each wave is associated with a number of factors that helped bring it about, such as public and political events, developments in the research, and changes in the personal lives of survivors, as well as with the content of the publications it encompassed.

The First Wave of Writing on Women in the Holocaust

Although the first books about women during the era of Nazi rule were published in Germany immediately following World War II, these works dealt primarily with German women who lived in the Third Reich as opposed to Jewish women living under Nazi rule.[2] A significant number of studies have considered the activity of women in the anti-Nazi underground movements, but most of these books do not fall within the category of "women's studies" due to their focus on the acts of resistance as opposed to the women themselves.[3]

When did historians begin to take an interest in the lives and behavioral patterns of Jewish women in the Holocaust? Use of terms such as "women's studies" and "gender studies" in the context of the Holocaust is a relatively new practice, although the phenomena they explore are not. Almost 80 years ago, Jewish historian Emanuel Ringelblum researched the life and behavioral patterns of Jewish women in the Warsaw Ghetto. During the war, among other things, he charged Cecilia Slepak – a journalist and translator who was active in the secret "*Oyneg Shabes*" archive he had established in the ghetto – with interviewing women in the ghetto about their lives as women, motherhood, and wifehood prior to the war, during the war, and during their time in the ghetto.[4] Their responses were intended to lay the foundation for a comprehensive study on the life of women in the ghetto. Slepak managed to interview 16 women, but before the major project was completed the ghetto was liquidated and its women were sent to Treblinka extermination camp.

During the initial years following the war, few studies were published on the Holocaust in general and women in the Holocaust in particular. One of the latter was Denise Dufurnier's 1948 book on the women's camp at Ravensbrück.[5] The Holocaust literature produced during this early period was similar to memoirs in its conveyance of stories of survivors who spent the war in hiding, in ghettos, in camps, or in the underground movements. Among the authors of these texts, women outnumbered men. We have no way of knowing for certain whether this was the result of a more developed historical consciousness among women, a stronger need among women to document their experiences, or the fact that more women than men survived the Holocaust. One explanation attributes the phenomenon to the fact that female survivors were ostensibly typically afforded a longer rehabilitation period than male survivors before they were required to rejoin productive society. However, as many women survivors became mothers only a year or two after liberation and therefore were not afforded slow rehabilitation, this explanation fails to convince. Another explanation has to do with the prevalence of a culture of gender that encouraged women to engage in activities that were considered to be "feminine," such as writing memoirs. Therefore, after an initial period of physical rehabilitation, they could be psychologically cleansed and document what they experienced during the war.

The memoirs that were published during this period include books by Ruzka Korczak and Zivia Lubetkin, members of the Jewish underground movement in Eastern Europe; books by Olga Lengyl and Gisella Perl, Jewish doctors who survived Auschwitz;[6] the memoirs of Kitty Hart, also a survivor of Auschwitz;[7] the diaries of Mary Berg and Gusta Dawidson;[8] and, of course, the diary of Anne Frank.

Unlike the diaries that were preserved by chance, most of the memoirs that were published during this period were written by major figures in the underground movement in Eastern Europe or by women who played central roles in the concentration camps. These women had better chances of surviving, and their stories were considered to be of greater public interest than the stories of 'regular' survivors. This was particularly true of memoirs written in Israel by former activists of the underground movements. For more than two decades after the end of the war, the Israeli public exhibited an "orientation of armed resistance" and harbored reservations about what it regarded as the passive and diaspora-like behavior of most victims of the Holocaust. On more than one occasion during the period in question, survivors were accused of going "like sheep to the slaughter," a phrase coined by Abba Kovner in the Vilna Ghetto.[9] At the time, Israel's national day of mourning in memory of the victims of the Holocaust was known as "Holocaust and Uprising Remembrance Day" (*Yom Hashoah ve'Hamered*),[10] before its name was changed to "Holocaust and Heroism Remembrance Day" (*Yom Hashoah ve'Hagevura*).[11] During this period, the political movements in Israel called on their members to document their activities during the war.[12] Here too, women initially answered the call at a higher rate than men.

How can we characterize the first memoirs written by Holocaust survivors? First, we consider their level of reliability. Memoirs that were written immediately following the war typically depict their author's experiences much more accurately than those that were written after their memories faded. Second, we consider the level of preaching they contain. Although the memoirs written during this period reflect the ideological background of their authors, they also contain a primarily factual, albeit sometimes emotional, description of their experiences during the war. They reflect no effort to preach or to lead readers to far-reaching conclusions, which are two attributes that are characteristic of many of the memoirs that were written later. Third, many of the memoirs written by Holocaust survivors during this period pertained to experiences from "women's society". This was unusual, as it was a time in which people did not conceptualize issues that were contingent on the sex of the individual. Fourth, most of the women who wrote their memoirs during this period began their accounts in September 1939 and devoted only a few lines to the years preceding the outbreak of the war. Most men, on the other hand, devoted more space to their accounts of the interwar period. Finally, almost all the women emphasized the centrality of mutual assistance among women as an essential aspect of their survival. These accounts would later serve as a key resource for researchers studying the unique dynamics of the survival of women during the war.

The Publications of the 1950s and 1960s

The second wave of publications dealing with women in the Holocaust began in the 1950s and lasted for almost two decades. These years are sometimes considered to constitute a period of inactivity with regard to Holocaust awareness due to the fact that they were situated between two periods of greater awareness regarding the issue: the period immediately following the war and the period that began in the mid-1970s. During this period, almost no methodical studies were conducted on women in the Holocaust.

In the 1950s and 1960s, women continued to publish memoirs about their lives during the Holocaust, the number of which increased toward the end of the 1960s.[13] Here too we note the high representation of former female members of the underground movements and women who held senior positions in the camps. This period also witnessed the publication of collections of children's memoirs, including memoirs of girls who were in their mid-to-late teens during the war. One was the collective autobiography, edited by Karen Gershon, of the Jewish refugee children who arrived in Britain in 1938 and 1939.[14]

Why was the writing on the Holocaust so meagre during this period? At the time, many survivors were forced to defer their urge to bear testimony for future generations due to their focus on rebuilding their lives in the present.[15] Moreover, a significant number of survivors who sought to document their experiences during the war discovered that they had almost no audience for their stories. In those days, the social and cultural frameworks of survivors, especially the younger ones, were not encouraging of deviation. Until the onset of the cultural pluralism that emerged at the beginning of the 1970s, many survivors, especially those living outside of Israel, sought to play down their past in order to ease their integration into society in their new homelands. Some wrote accounts that were meant for their own desk drawer, but few were ready to actually publish their memoirs and, in so doing, to highlight their foreign origin. An economic factor was also at play here: cultural consciousness of the Holocaust only increased in the mid-1970s, which meant that, until then, publishers did not regard Holocaust literature as a profitable investment. As a result, little effort was made during this period to acquire manuscripts of the memoirs of Holocaust survivors, as publishers would do later.

The absence of synthetic research on the Holocaust during the 1950s and 1960s, particularly with regard to women, was also a product of the prevailing cultural and social climate at the time. The small number of memoirs, the lack of historical consciousness regarding the importance of issues pertaining to women and gender, and political considerations all precluded methodical research on subjects related to women and gender in the Holocaust.[16]

The Publications of the 1970s and 1980s

The third wave of publications dealing with women and gender in the Holocaust began in the 1970s. These publications were directly related to two international phenomena: mounting interest in the Holocaust, and the academic development of Women's Studies and Gender Studies. At the time, Holocaust literature dealing with women and gender could be divided into three major categories: memoirs of women survivors, compilations of testimonies, and academic studies.[17]

During the quarter-century that had elapsed since the end of World War II, most Holocaust literature consisted of memoirs. The increased awareness of the Holocaust that began in the mid-1970s – as a result of publicity in the media, generational changes, and other factors – served to increase the pace of publication of memoir literature. Many survivors who had previously been hesitant about putting their life stories down in writing now decided to take on the challenge, as the world was already interested in their accounts and ready to hear them. As a result, at the encouragement of friends, family members, staff members of Holocaust centers, and representatives of publishers, many survivors who had never before considered writing their stories now began to do so.

What characterized the memoirs of women Holocaust survivors that were published from the mid-1970s onwards? First, like the initial wave of memoirs, these later texts also highlighted the unique female experience of Jewish women during the Holocaust. And here too, many of the authors emphasized women's mutual assistance for one another as a major reason for their survival.

Second, whereas the first wave of memoirs began with an account of the outbreak of the war, most of the memoirs written during this period also dealt with the authors' lives prior to the Holocaust. We can assume that, in most cases, this expanded chronological scope stemmed from the increased historical awareness of the authors, which developed over time and with age. Readers were therefore provided with important background information and a window into the social and cultural world of Jewish women during the interwar period.

Third, this group of memoirs was characterized by significant modesty regarding intimate experiences. Although most female authors revealed their emotion they refrained from discussing issues of female sexuality. In this way, these memoirs differed from those that were written in the 1950s and 1960s, which, surprisingly, usually dealt with such issues almost explicitly. One conjecture regarding the cause of this turn in the approach to such issues pertains to the fact that during the initial period, "Stalag fiction," with its pornographic tendencies, was at its height.[18] This writing influenced the overall Holocaust literature that was published during the years in question. A different explanation holds that the openness regarding intimate matters was a function of the authenticity of the first wave of memoirs, in which female authors were not expected to embellish the past. The memoirs of the 1970s, written by men and women alike, also lacked the ideological foundation that dominated the memoirs of the earlier waves. In many cases, however, these later memoirs contained religious or moral aspects. This may have stemmed from the fact that most memoirs during the wave in question were written by "regular survivors," as opposed to party activists or former members of the underground groups that emerged from the socialist Zionist youth movements.

Who were the women who published their memoirs during the 1970s and 1980s? They were survivors of concentration camps, ghettos, transit camps, and family camps. They included women who had lived in hiding, women who had lived on the Aryan side, and women who had fought with the partisans. They included some who had experience in writing, some who had never written before, and some who had written for their families. In summation, all types of Holocaust survivors engaged in the writing of memoirs during this period. Individuals who had never considered putting down their experiences in writing now began to publish their memoirs from the Holocaust and the period that preceded it. Most notable were those women who had been very young during the Holocaust and who, in their current stage of life, had already began devoting more time to coping with the past. Part of the cathartic process was facilitated by writing memoirs more than three decades after the end of the war. In this manner, female (and male) authors became links in an international chain reaction that emerged from the need to "bear testimony" about what they had experienced during those horrible times.

Compilations of women's Holocaust testimonies were also published during this period, including Lore Shelley's *Secretaries of Death*, which assembled testimonies of Jewish women who worked in the Gestapo offices in Auschwitz; a book by Czech underground member Vera Laska, who was not Jewish but who wrote about women in the underground and the Holocaust; and a collection of testimonies of former prisoners of the Canada Commando at Auschwitz, which I edited.[19] Some of these collections were illustrated and others were only narrative. All contained documentary material that holds unique value for historians seeking to research the experiences of women in the Holocaust.

These collections of testimonies differed from the memoirs of women that had been published earlier in a number of ways. First, almost all were edited by Holocaust historians and scholars and were not composed by the survivors alone. They were thus an indication of academic research's growing interest in subjects pertaining to women and gender in the Holocaust. Second, most of the collections were the product of cooperation among groups of survivors who were willing to publically reveal their intimate experiences. This phenomenon could have only occurred during a period of growing awareness of the historical importance of the Holocaust. The collective testimonies were typically thematic, and, as such, they paved the way for the academic research of women and gender in the Holocaust.

In addition to the collective and individual memoirs published from the mid-1970s onward, women in the Holocaust were also the subject of analytical studies, such as Marion Kaplan's socio-historical studies of Jewish women in pre-war Germany or the volume edited by Marion Kaplan, Atina Grossmann, and Renate Bridenthal, which also explored the issue of Jewish women in Germany.[20] Another group of studies dealt with women refugees.[21] Other studies, such as Marlene Heinemann's *Gender and Destiny: Women Writers and the Holocaust*, dealt with literary aspects of the subject.[22] And still others, such as those by Joan Ringelheim, focused on philosophical and social-ideological aspects of women's lives under Nazi rule.[23] Another prominent scholar of this period was Sybil Milton, who wrote about the everyday life of women under Nazi rule and particularly about the lives of women who were imprisoned in Nazi camps.[24]

Why were so many studies conducted on the changing roles of Jewish women in Germany? During this period, the United States witnessed the organization of a group of scholars that wrote about women studies and Germany studies, held gatherings, and encouraged research on the subject. It was only natural that a few of the scholars, themselves daughters of female immigrants and refugees from German speaking countries, would choose to research Jewish women in Germany under Nazi rule. Other studies dealt with Jewish women in Eastern Europe and other occupied countries. During this period, one could perceive the beginnings of a generational transition as most of the women writing were relatively young, were not Holocaust survivors, and wrote primarily from a historical perspective. These studies were composed not only as a result of increased awareness of the Holocaust during the years in question, but also due to the ongoing development of Women's Studies and Gender Studies in the West, which began to take form in academia as a result of the feminist revolution of the late 1960s and early 1970s.[25] This factor also resulted in the first conference on women in the Holocaust ("Women Surviving the Holocaust"), which was organized in New York in 1983 by Joan Ringelheim[26] and Esther Katz[27] and which placed the topic of Jewish women in the Holocaust on the public and the academic agenda.[28]

The Publications of the 1990s and the Early 21ˢᵗ Century

The early 1990s witnessed the onset of a new wave of publications pertaining to women and gender during the Holocaust. During this wave too, the subject found expression in a variety of literary and academic forms, such as diaries, memoirs, collective autobiographies, poetry, and studies in communications, history, sociology, and other disciplines. Like the previous wave, this one was characterized by a large number of publications in English, Hebrew, and German – the spoken and written languages of the countries in which the Holocaust was deeply ingrained in public consciousness.[29]

During these years, research, commemoration, and literary writing concerning the Holocaust were already familiar and accepted phenomena both in academia and in public life. Thousands of books and articles had already been published on the subject, and many more were on the way. Institutes for Holocaust research and monuments erected in commemoration of the Holocaust had become a familiar facet of the public and academic landscape in Israel, Europe, and elsewhere, as well as locations that are geographically and culturally more remote from the West, such as the Japanese city of Fukuyama.[30]

At the same time, political usage of the Holocaust continued. Germany witnessed the outbreak of a "debate of historians" regarding the extent of Germany's guilt for the events of World War II. This debate stemmed from an attempt to re-understand the period as a whole and to determine Germany's position on the ladder of responsibility.[31] A growing number of publications dealing with Holocaust denial had been published in Europe, Canada, and the United States, resulting in increasing legislation against their dissemination.[32] The collapse of the Communist regime in Poland sparked the beginning of a discussion on Poland's conduct during the Holocaust. One expression of this discussion was a series of articles published in the Roman Catholic weekly *Tygodnik Powszechny* at the end of the 1980s, the point of departure of which was Polish poet Czesław Miłosz's (1911-2004) poem "A Poor Christian Looks at the Ghetto."[33] Even some in Israel regarded the increasing use of the Holocaust to legitimize political and military activity as an understandable and welcome phenomenon, whereas others viewed it as an almost demonic manipulation of the history of the Jewish People.[34] Due to all of the above, the Holocaust remained at the center of public discussion and continued to serve as a subject of academic and literary publications.

In the 1980s, in both the academic and the literary arenas, emphasis was already shifting from the heroic dimension of the Holocaust to interest in the everyday life of the Jews living during the period. Consequently, publishers began to take an interest in the memoirs of male and female survivors who had previously been considered "a-heroic" figures.[35] Through the publication of these memoirs, the publishers strengthened the academic orientation that already existed and that called for researching the lives of groups that had previously been considered marginal in Holocaust research, such as children, refugees, Jews who had survived by hiding or impersonating non-Jews, girls and women, "mixed-race" girls, and Aryan women who were married to Jews.

The memoirs and research literature dealing with women and gender in the Holocaust that were published during this period had four major attributes. In the autobiographical literature of the 1970s and 1980s, it is difficult to identify a common denominator among the authors, with the exception of the fact that they had all survived the Holocaust. In addition, a generational shift was observable among the survivors who were writing their stories. Indeed, as time passed, the authors of most of the memoirs and autobiographies by women had not experienced the war as adults; it was now the turn of younger women survivors who had lived through the war as children and adolescents. Two or three decades earlier, when the first major wave of Holocaust memoirs were being published, these survivors were in their 30s and 40s and were occupied with day to day affairs, professional development, and building families. By the mid-1990s, however, they were approaching retirement age, which provided them with the time and perspective to reassess their wartime experiences and consider the importance of leaving testimony for future generations. As the years passed, the number of living survivors who had experienced the war as adults began to dwindle, and the relative importance of those who had lived through the war as children and young adults increased. As a result, publishers began to focus on this group and to search its ranks for potential authors of memoirs and autobiographies. An example is Jana Renée Friesová's book about her adolescence in Terezin.[36]

A second common denominator of autobiographical literature written by women survivors beginning in the mid-1990s pertained to the authors' biographies. During the preceding decades, many authors had been survivors of ghettos and camps. Unlike this group, many of the women whose works were published during the new wave had spent most of the war years in hiding or living under false identities or outside occupied Europe. For years, these women had considered their wartime experiences to be less important than those of the survivors of concentration camps and labor camps, ghetto fighters, and the like. The reassessment of Holocaust experiences, which was expanded to include Jews who had not spent the Holocaust in ghettos and camps, as well as those who had managed to flee Europe during the Nazi era, enabled these women survivors to redefine their identity and their relationship with the Holocaust. Consequently, many women survivors in these groups felt that the time had come to publish autobiographies dealing with their experiences during the war. Memoirs and studies published during this period included an autobiographical collection edited by Philip K. Jason and Iris Posner, which contained the stories of child refugees from Europe who found safe haven in the United States during the Holocaust, as well as stories about the women, primarily social workers, who helped these children reach the United States from Germany and to integrate into their new homeland.[37]

A third feature of this wave was an increasing tendency to expand the limits of the Holocaust and to examine it through a universal prism. In the past, non-Aryan Christians and Christian women who were married to Jews had gone virtually unmentioned in the Holocaust literature, whereas during this period they became the focus of memoirs, autobiographies, and historical studies. Secondary groups included the memoirs of non-Jews, especially non-Jewish women who, in their younger years, were imprisoned in camps on political or religious grounds. Although the term "Holocaust" was applied solely to Jews from the outset, these groups were also part of the new wave of Holocaust literature. One example of this phenomenon is Nanda Herbermann's memoirs, which relate her experiences as a Catholic woman in the women's camp at Ravensbrück where she was imprisoned due to her underground activity.[38]

These three characteristics pertain to the age of the authors, their biographical background, and their religious-racial classification. However, they do not explain why a high percentage of the authors at the time were women. One possible explanation lies in the fourth attribute – that is, the authors' sociological and psychological self-awareness regarding gender and identity. These female survivors were part of a generation that was affected to some degree by the struggle for gender equality and self-expression that began to find expression in the 1960s. The feminist movement influenced not only these women, who reached adulthood during the decade in question, but also women who had gone through adolescence half a generation earlier. Sometimes, this occurred through autobiographical writing. The result, an increasing number of memoirs and autobiographies written by women who were children and adolescents during the Holocaust, was augmented by this generation's early retirement in comparison to their male colleagues, which left them with ample time to think about closing the circle of their past.

In addition to autobiographical writing, at the same time, a new wave of historical studies appeared, focusing on special groups of women in the Holocaust and World War II, particularly those who took part in military activity. One example was Nigel Fountain's study of women in wartime, which concentrated largely on World War II[39] and was accompanied by an exhibition at the Imperial War Museum in London.

The 1990s and the early twenty-first century was also a productive time for academic research on women and gender in the Holocaust. The first anthology on the subject, Carol Rittner and John Roth's *Different Voices: Women and the Holocaust*,[40] was published in 1993. Though somewhat eclectic, this anthology paved the way for those who followed and raised fundamental questions regarding the absence of discussion on women and the Holocaust. This awakening also encouraged academic gatherings on the subject. Two years after the anthology was published, Dalia Ofer of the Hebrew University of Jerusalem and Lenore J. Weitzman of George Mason University organized a research workshop in Jerusalem on "Women in the Holocaust," and in 1998 the two scholars edited and published a collection of articles based on the meeting.[41]

Academic writing on women in the Holocaust continued to flourish. In 1996, *Contemporary Jewry* devoted a special issue to the study of women in the Holocaust. The issue contained nine articles written by historians, sociologists, and scholars of literature and philosophy but lacked contributions by scholars from Israel, perhaps due to the fact that the subject had thus far not been substantially explored there. Although Israel was then home to a significant number of female Holocaust scholars, the few who had begun researching women in the Holocaust had done so only recently. One of the main trajectories of most of the articles was confrontation with the silence which until then had characterized research pertaining to the linkage between gender and the Holocaust, especially in non-historical realms; explanation of the causes of this silence; and the proposal of means of rectifying it.[42]

Writing and research on the subject continued to flourish throughout the 1990s. In addition to Ofer and Weitzman's book, 1997 and 1998 witnessed the publication of another six books dealing with gender and the Holocaust: my book about the "double jeopardy" of women and the Holocaust;[43] Marion Kaplan's book on Jewish women in Nazi Germany;[44] a collection of testimonies of female survivors edited by Brana Gurewitsch;[45] Lilian Kremer's literary study of women's literature in the Holocaust;[46] Roger Ritvo and Diane Plotkin's study of women doctors and nurses in the camps;[47] and *Women in the Holocaust*, a collection of studies edited by Esther Fuchs.[48]

By the beginning of the twenty-first century, a pattern had emerged that would characterize the issue in the years to come: academic gatherings dealing with women and the Holocaust followed by the publication of studies that had been presented there; the examination of "major" Holocaust subjects, but this time from the perspective of gender; and the flourishing of research on women in the Holocaust in various fields within the humanities and the social sciences, but not in history. In 2003, Elizabeth Baer and Myrna Goldenberg published a collection of articles inspired by an academic gathering on the Holocaust and the churches that had been held a few years earlier, in which two panels considered the fate of women.[49] In 2003, a special issue of *Women in German Yearbook* was devoted to women in the Holocaust following a conference that was held at the University of Minnesota on the feminist perspective on the Holocaust.[50] 2004 witnessed the publication of Rochelle G. Saidel's book, which considered the fate of women at Ravensbrück Concentration Camp.[51] The fields of literature and theology also experienced a flourishing of research on women and the Holocaust, with Ruth Linden's book on feminist reflection on the Holocaust,[52] Lilian Kremer's book on women's writings on the Holocaust,[53] and Melissa Raphael's book on the "female face of God" at Auschwitz.[54] During this period, studies were also published by women who began to analyze the Holocaust testimony of women not as documentary material for studies on the subject but rather as a body of documentation in itself that required examination and clarification. Such were Zoe Waxman's articles, which focused on a reassessment and deconstruction of women's testimony from the Holocaust.[55]

This wave of publication also included academic studies on women in the Holocaust conducted by women who themselves were survivors and who integrated a personal dimension into their research. Such were Felicia Karai's research and autobiographical works dealing with young women at the Hasag-Leipzig labor camp and Nechama Tec's book on men and women in the Holocaust.[56] Like those published beginning in the 1970s, these texts integrated tools from the social sciences and the humanities and presented readers with studies that were distinctively interdisciplinary in nature.

In terms of both the academic and commercial presses, the symbiosis between academia and publication impacted not only the research of women in the Holocaust but also the development of teaching of the subject. The first course was taught by Konnilyn Feig in the United States in the mid-1980s. However, it was a workshop that did not require the reading of substantial research literature, which was still unavailable.[57] This lack of research was also reflected at the first gathering on women and the Holocaust, which was held in 1983 and which included only one academic lecture, although the program was based primarily on the testimonies and memoirs of female survivors.

By the end of the twentieth century, Holocaust researchers had already produced an expanding corpus of academic research on women and gender in the Holocaust that could serve as a bibliography for courses on the subject. A number of these women scholars also taught in academia, and to them the thought of teaching such a course was a natural extension of their research. There was also a demand among college and university students for courses and study tracks on the Holocaust in general and women and gender in particular, particularly in the fields of history, sociology, and literature. Initially, such courses were only taught outside of Israel, but in 1994, for the first time, I taught a course dealing with "Women in the Holocaust and among the DPs" at Touro College and at the University of Haifa, two places where I taught during the 1990s. The course was extremely successful, and by the end of the decade Dalia Ofer was teaching a similar course at the Hebrew University of Jerusalem. When I moved to Bar-Ilan University I taught the same course there, and the subject began to gain momentum among Holocaust lecturers (especially women) in Israel and elsewhere. By the first decade of the twenty-first century, it was no longer unusual to encounter courses on gender or women in the Holocaust in Israeli institutions of higher learning.

Publications of the Twenty-First Century

By the mid-2000s a new wave of publications on women and gender in the Holocaust began. This wave, which continues up to the present (2019), has three main attributes. The first pertains to the identity of the female authors of memoirs and autobiographies. During the years in question, almost no memoirs were published by women who reached adulthood prior to the Holocaust because most had already passed away. Continuing the trend that began during the previous wave, almost all survivor autobiographies of this period have been written by women who were born at the end of the 1920s or the beginning of the 1930s and were children or adolescents during World War II. Examples include *Love in a World of Sorrow* by writer and philanthropist Fanya Gottesfeld Heller, who founded Bar Ilan University's Center for the Study of Women in Judaism, where she placed an emphasis on the fate of women in the Holocaust;[58] Marika Roth's *All the Pretty Shoes*, which describes her experiences as a 12 year old in Budapest around the time of liberation;[59] and *If Only It Were Fiction* by Elsa Thon, who wrote about her wartime experiences as a youth in Warsaw and in the Płaszów concentration camp.[60] When these women wrote their memoirs they were already in their seventies and eighties and regarded it as their last opportunity to tell the world their story and to put it down in writing for posterity. Like the initial waves of publications, the writing during this period has been notable for its openness regarding intimate experiences. This may have been a reflection of the substantial time that had passed since the events took place, as well as the authors' desire to document as many details as possible, intimate details included, for future generations.

These books were joined by a sub-genre that emerged during the third wave, in the 1980s and the 1990s that was subsequently forgotten: group autobiographies written by survivors or researchers. These works focused on the story of groups of Jewish women in the Holocaust who were connected by bonds of friendship, family relations, or time spent in the same camp. In some, the authors wove the individual memoirs into a joint narrative. Others presented the story of each woman as an individual in her own right. Examples include Isabelle Choko's book on five women who survived the Holocaust,[61] Rina Gellisen and Heather Macadam's book about two sisters in Auschwitz,[62] and Wendy Holden's book about three young mothers who together survived an extermination camp.[63]

The two other primary features of this wave have to do with the nature of the research literature and the identity of the authors. Many of the publications were follow-up studies based on the topics of the previous wave, including Dalia Ofer's articles on women in the ghettos of Eastern Europe, Atina Grossmann's book on women in Germany after the Holocaust, and my study on the identity and selfhood of the women of She'erit Hapleta.[64] The trend of anthologies dealing with women in the Holocaust also continued, as reflected in Esther Hertzog's edited volume on women and family in the Holocaust, Myrna Goldenberg and Amy Shapiro's volume on gender and the Holocaust, and a special issue of the Hebrew-language journal *Nashim* ("women") that was devoted to the subject.[65]

There have also been innovations. The current wave has also witnessed the first serious discussion of a subject that until recently has received only sporadic mention: sexual violence against Jewish women in the Holocaust. This may have stemmed from the changing nature of memoir literature, which already contained more than mere suggestions of the phenomenon. Although the women survivors interviewed during this period have also displayed a greater willingness to answer questions on the subject, numerous researchers have noted that most spoke about the rape of other women but almost never acknowledged having been raped themselves. The first authors to write about this phenomenon included Doris Bergen, Kirsty Chatwood, Na'ama Shik, Helene Sinnreich, Sonia Hedgepeth, and Rochelle Saidel. Hedgepeth and Saidel also published an edited volume of studies dealing with sexual violence against women in the Holocaust.[66]

The final feature of this wave has been a generational shift among scholars. Toward the end of the previous wave, we witnessed the publication of studies by young women authors, such as Pascal Bos and Zoe Waxman, who had started to take an interest in the fate of young Jewish women in the Holocaust.[67] With the onset of the fifth and current wave of publications, Ofer explains, these authors were joined by young women "belonging to the third and fourth generation of Holocaust researchers."[68] These scholars include Lisa Pine, who has explored gender and victimization in the Holocaust; Natalia Aleksiun, who has written about gender and the daily lives of Jews hiding in Galicia; Sharon Geva, who has focused on female Holocaust heroes in Israeli society; and Frederica (Clementi) Schoemann, whose book deals with mothers and daughters in the Holocaust.[69] Pascal Bos and Zoe Waxman have also continued their research – Bos with work on sexual violence against Jewish women in the Holocaust and Waxman with feminist historical writing on the Holocaust.[70] This has marked the coming of age of a new generation of women researchers, some of whom were still in elementary school when the serious academic research on women and gender in the Holocaust began.

Discussion and Conclusions

In this article, I have analyzed the five waves of autobiographical and research literature pertaining to women and gender in the Holocaust. I noted that the initial publications dealing with women and gender were largely memoirs or studies written by survivors. Although memoirs and diaries continue to be published up to the present, they were joined, over time, by the analytical studies that appeared during the second wave of writing. Ultimately, a new group of scholars emerged, most of whom were born after World War II (and some of whom were born during the final decades of the twentieth century). This group engaged in – and continues to engage in – research on women and gender in the Holocaust. Their studies provided the subject with the conceptualization it had been lacking up to that point.

Nonetheless, some questions remain unanswered. What led to the emergence of each new wave? Were they related to events that occurred in the world, to new historical interpretations, or perhaps to developments in the academic world? Are there any common denominators among the subjects selected for research – subjects related to women and gender in the Holocaust? What were the factors that shaped the exploration of these subjects?

It appears that the waves of interest in women, gender, and gender in the Holocaust were almost completely uninfluenced by international events relating to the Holocaust, to World War II, to identity, and to the survival of Jews. In the juridical realm, neither the Kastner trial, nor the Eichmann trial, nor the Demjanjuk trial resulted in special studies on women and gender in the Holocaust. There was no connection between the establishment of diplomatic relations between Israel and Germany, the debate in Israel surrounding the Reparations (*Shilumim*) Agreement, the Six-Day War, the Yom Kippur War, the First Lebanon War, and the Second Lebanon War, on the one hand, and the waves of publications dealing with women and gender in the Holocaust, on the other hand. During the initial decades of research, the only factors that increased interest in these subjects were the development of Holocaust awareness in the 1970s and the academic interest in "women's culture" and gender studies that began to take form during this period.[71] It is possible, however, that the studies of the final wave, especially those dealing with sexual violence against Jewish women in the Holocaust, were in fact related to international events to an extent – particularly, to the violence against women that characterized the civil war in Bosnia in the mid-1990s.

Since the mid-1970s, interest in research pertaining to the histories and behavioral patterns of women and gender in the Holocaust has been on the rise. The forms and essence of the resulting studies have been shaped first and foremost by the available types of documentation, but they have also been influenced by the personal orientations of the researchers and the popularity of the subject under discussion. Overall, it appears that most of the studies in these areas began not as independent historical analyses but rather as appendices to more general Holocaust research. For example, studies on the problem of the refugees from the Nazi occupied countries that were published during the 1970s resulted in studies, produced in the 1980s, on refugees and children and on the women who worked on behalf of these children in their countries of origin and in the countries in which they settled. Studies conducted in the mid-1980s on religious life during the Holocaust resulted in studies written the following decade on mutual assistance among groups of religious women in the ghettos and the camps. It also appears that the general trend of researching everyday life in the Nazi camps, which emerged in the mid-1980s, resulted in studies on dynamics in the women's camps that were published in the late 1990s. Many of the studies on women and gender in the Holocaust have therefore been responses to existing forms of research and to areas of academic study that were already examined as part of broader studies.

Nonetheless, most of the studies conducted on issues of gender during the initial decades of Holocaust research remained components of the social and cultural history of the Holocaust and said little about the more weighty issues of Holocaust research, such as the Final Solution and Jewish leadership. Only during the final wave of publications have we seen articles and books dealing with the gender aspects of these subjects, integrating the study of women in the Holocaust into the core issues of this field.

What, might we ask, delayed the publication of studies dealing with women and gender in the Holocaust? Two factors played a central role in determining these studies' date of publication: 1) the accessibility of documentary material and 2) awareness of the importance of the issues under discussion. Although these factors of course influenced Holocaust research as a whole, Holocaust research only began to flourish in the 1970s due to the accessibility of the increasing Jewish documentation and the world's mounting interest in the Holocaust; indeed, research on Jewish woman and gender in the Holocaust took another half generation to emerge. Only then was the corpus of autobiographical documentation required for research created, and only then did Gender Studies and Women's Studies begin to develop in universities. Therefore, only in the twenty-first century did historians begin to incorporate studies on women's culture into general women's studies.

In the Israeli context, many women have researched and continue to research the Holocaust, but only a handful have focused their attention on Jewish women in the Holocaust since this issue first became a subject of academic investigation in Israel in the 1990s. Dalia Ofer and I were among the first Israeli women to publish books on the subject, and over the years we have been joined by a small number of others, including Esther Hertzog, Sharon Geva, Yehudit Kol Inbar, Na'ama Shik, Ilana Rosen, and the late Felicia Karai, who herself was a survivor. With the passage of time, books have also been written on major women figures who were leaders in the underground movements or Jewish paratroopers from the Jewish Yishuv, such as Hannah Szenes and Haviva Reik. In most cases, however, such studies have not been written from the perspective of Women's Studies or Gender Studies but rather as Zionist stories. Women in the She'erit Hapleta have also been examined, for example, in my studies and those of Michal Shaul. But despite the impressive response of female students who have opted to write master's theses and doctoral dissertations on the subject, Israeli research on women in the Holocaust has remained the domain of a relatively small group of scholars.

The future direction of research on women and gender in the Holocaust is still unclear. It is too early to tell whether it will be naturally integrated into general Holocaust research as a gender aspect of all topics, or whether it will remain an independent subject and an element of gender studies. What is clear, however, is that as time passes, the young women researchers in the field are encountering fewer of the obstacles that challenged the women scholars of my generation when we began researching Jewish women in the Holocaust – most notably, the request that we "find a more serious subject" in which to specialize. In a previous article, I address former *Commentary* editor Gabriel Schoenfeld's arguments, of more than three decades ago, against the legitimacy of combining gender research and Holocaust research. Although there has been no fundamental change in Schoenfeld's view on this matter, it is hard to imagine such a debate occurring today, in the gender and cultural climate that currently prevails in academia and the press. Library shelves and research databases are filled with studies on the diverse aspects of the life and death of Jewish women in the Holocaust and the rehabilitation of women survivors among She'erit Hapleta. Courses on this subject are widespread in the academic fields of history, literature, and sociology in Israel and around the world, each with its own suitable methodology and rich and diverse bibliography.

As I noted in a historiographic article a decade and a half ago, it is still not possible to anticipate how Holocaust research in general, and research regarding Jewish women and gender in the Holocaust in particular, will develop in the future, especially after the last survivors leave us. But today, at the beginning of the third decade of the twenty-first century, it is hard to imagine the field losing its legitimacy. Studies on gender and the Holocaust no longer begin with a preliminary note justifying the choice of topic, as Rochelle Saidel noted in a review published in 2000.[72] Today, not only is the topic of women in the Holocaust considered to be a legitimate field of research, but ego-documents (memoirs) are increasingly being written by women who have researched the subject since its beginnings, and by women researching it today, documenting their personal and professional experiences stemming from their choice of this topic of research. A senior historian recently noted that researching researchers of a specific field is typically a sign that that field has become established. I hope that this is true of the study of Jewish women in the Holocaust.

Endnotes

1   Millions of copies of the diary of Anne Franke have been published in Holland, West
    Germany, France, Britain, the United States, East Germany, Italy, Denmark, Sweden,
    Norway, Finland, Iceland, Hungary, Poland, Romania, the Soviet Union, Czechoslovakia,
    Yugoslavia, Japan, Israel, India, South Korea, Thailand, the People's Republic of China,
    South Africa, Indonesia, and Bulgaria. On the history of the journal and its various
    editions see its full version, published in Dutch in 1986 under the title *De Dagboeken van
    Anne Frank* (The Hague, 1986; Amsterdam, 1986).

2   Many years before the increased general awareness regarding issues related to
    women's culture, German scholars began researching women-related topics in
    the political, social, economic, and military contexts of the Third Reich. See, for
    example, Gabriele Bremme, *Die politische Rolle der Frau in Deutschland* (Goettingen,
    1956); Marja Kubasec, *Sterne uber adem Abgrund: Aus den Leben der Antifascisten
    Dr. Maria Grollmuss* (Bautzen, 1961); Ursula von Gersdorff, *Frauen im Kriegsdeinst,
    1914-1945* (Stuttgart, 1969). Later studies include Gertrud Meyer, *Frauen gegen
    Hitler: Berichte aus dem Widerstand* (Frankfurt, 1974); Angelika Reuter and Barbara
    Poneleit, *Seit 1848: Frauen im Widerstand und im Faschismus* (Munich, 1977); Dörte
    Winkler, *Frauenarbeit im "Dritten Reich"* (Hamburg, 1977); Hanna Elling, *Frauen
    in Deutschen Widerstand: 1933-1945* (Frankfurt, 1981); Frauengruppe Faschismus
    Forschung (ed.), *Mutterkreuz und Arbeitsbuch* (Frankfurt, 1981); K. Klinkseit, *Die
    Frau im NS-Staat* (Stuttgart, 1982); Annette Kuhn and Valentine Rothe, *Frauen im
    deutschen Faschismus* (Duesseldorf, 1981); Maruta Schmidt and Gabi Deitz (eds.),
    Frauen under Hakenkreuz (Berlin, 1983); Georg Tidl, *Die Frau im Nationalsozialismus*
    (Vienna, 1984); Marianne Lehker, *Frauen im Nationalsozialismus* (Frankfurt, 1984).
    Studies on these subjects have also been published outside of Germany, and some
    were follow-ups to studies conducted during and prior to the war. For example, see
    Clifford Kirkpatrick, *Nazi Germany: Its Women and Its Family Life* (New York and
    Indianapolis, 1938); Katherine Thomas, *Women in Nazi Germany* (London, 1967);
    Jacques R. Pauwels, *Women, Nazis and Universities: Female Students in the Third Reich*
    (Westport, 1984); Rita Thalmann (ed.), *Femmes et Fascismes* (Paris, 1986).

3   Many of these studies were born out of a desire to provide justification for wartime
    collaboration. See Helen Astrup and Bernard Louis Jacot, *Oslo Intrigue: A Woman's
    Memoirs of the Norwegian Resistance* (New York, 1954); Nicole Chatel (ed.), *Des
    Femmes Dans la Resistance* (Paris, 1987); Benedicta Maria Kempner, *Nonnen unter
    dem Hackenkreuz* (Wuerzburg,1979); Kevin Sim, *Women at War: Five Heroines Who
    Defied the Nazis and Survived* (New York, 1982); Antonia Hunt, *Little Resistance*
    (London, 1982); Margaret L. Rossiter, *Women in the Resistance* (New York, 1986);
    Lore Cowan, *Children of the Resistance* (New York, 1971).

4   Dalia Ofer, "Her View through My Lens: Cecilia Slepak Studies Women in Warsaw,"
    Yalkut Moreshet 75 (April 2003), pp. 111-130 (Hebrew).

5   Denise Dufurnier, *Ravensbrueck, the Women's Camp of Death* (London, 1948).

6   Ruzka Korczak, *Flames in the Ashes* (Merhavia, 1946) (Hebrew); Zivia Lubetkin, *The Last Ones on the Wall* (Ein Harod, 1947) (Hebrew); Olga Lengyl, *Five Chimneys* (Chicago, 1947); Gisella Perl, *I was a Doctor in Auschwitz* (New York, 1948).

7   Kitty Hart, *I am Alive* (London, 1946).

8   Mary Berg, *The Diary of Mary Berg* (New York, 1945); Gusta Draenger, *Pamietnik Justyny* (Cracow, 1946).

9   This phrase appeared at the top of Abba Kovner's September 1, 1943 proclamation calling for an uprising in the Vilna Ghetto. Yitzhak Arad, Israel Gutman, and Abraham Margaliot, *Documents on the Holocaust* (Jerusalem, 1978), pp. 344-346 (Hebrew).

10 On the treatment of Holocaust survivors in Israel during the early years of statehood, see Hannah Yablonka, *Foreign Brothers: Holocaust Survivors in the State of Israel, 1948-1952* (Jerusalem, 1994) (Hebrew).

11 On the history of this day of commemoration and its historical significance, see my book *A Voice of Lament: The Holocaust and Prayer* (Bar Ilan University Press, 1992), pp. 65-69 (Hebrew).

12 Dina Porat, "With Mercy and Forgiveness: Ruzka Korcak's Encounter with the Yishuv and its Leadership," *Yalkut Moreshet* 52, April 1992, pp. 9-33 (Hebrew).

13 This wave of women's and children's memoirs also included: Rachel Auerbach, *In the Streets of Warsaw* (Tel Aviv, 1954) (Hebrew); Batya Berman-Temkin, *Underground Diary* (Tel Aviv, 1956) (Hebrew); Chayka Grossman, *People of the Underground* (Merhavia, 1965) (Hebrew); Helena Szerszewska, *The Last Chapter: Memories from the Warsaw Ghetto* (Tel Aviv, 1960) (Hebrew); Helena Szerszewska, *The Cross and the Mezuzah* (Merhavia, 1969) (Hebrew); Fredka Mazia, *Comrades in the Storm* (Jerusalem, 1964) (Hebrew); Grete Salus, *Eine Frau Erzaehlt* (Bonn, 1958); Marga Minco, *Bitter Herbs: A Chronicle* (New York, 1960); Gemma La Guardia Gluck, *My Story* (New York, 1961); Reska Weiss, *Journey Through Hell* (London, 1961); Halina Birnbaum, *Nadzieja umira ostatnia* (Warwaw, 1967); Elisabeth Singer, *Children of the Apocalypse* (London, 1967); Judith Strick Dribben, *A Girl Called Judith Strick* (New York, 1970); Donia Rosen, *The Forest, My Friend* (New York, 1971); Vladka Meed, *On Both Sides of the Wall: Memoirs from the Warsaw Ghetto* (New York, 1972).

14 Karen Gershon, *We Came as Children: A Collective Autobiography* (London, 1956). See also Inge Deutschkron, *...denn ihrer war die Hölle: Kinder in Ghettos und Lagern* (Cologne, 1965); Giorgina Bellak (ed.), *Donne e bambini nei lageri nazisti* (Milan, 1960).

15 On the psychological rehabilitation of survivors in the United States see William B. Helmreich, *Against All Odds* (New York, 1992).

16 The lack of Holocaust research focusing on women can be contrasted to the state of research on German women and their families in the Third Reich. The Nazis' engagement with mothers and feminism encouraged studies on these subjects, which were conducted immediately following the war. A different explanation casts these studies as part of a general trend in the research of the post-war period – studies on life in the days of fascism – and maintains that they cannot be regarded as a vanguard of gender studies or social history as we know them today. A third explanation focuses on the condition of the sources, maintaining that the large number of testimonies of women and youth in Germany constituted another factor encouraging studies on these issues. The cultural aspect is also important, as during the Weimar Republic German scholars were interested in issues related to women and families, and it was natural to continue these studies when the Nazi period came to an end. On the academic interest in women and families during the Weimar era, see Alex De Jonge, *The Weimar Chronical: Prelude to Hitler* (New York, 1978).

17 The memoirs of women and children in the Holocaust that were published during this period appeared in the following books: Eva Heyman, *The Diary of Eva Heyman* (Jerusalem, 1974); Corrie Ten Boom, *The Hiding Place* (New York, 1975); Bryna Bar Oni, *The Vapor* (Chicago, 1976); Fania Fenelon, *Playing for Time* (New York, 1977); Ilse Koehn, *Mischling, Second Degree: My Childhood in Nazi Germany* (New York, 1977); Isabella Leitner, *Fragments of Isabella* (New York, 1978); Charlotte Delbo, *None of Us Will Return: Auschwitz and After* (Boston, 1978); Leesha Rose, *The Tulips Are Red* (New York, 1979); Johanna Reiss, *The Upstairs Room* (New York, 1979); Liliana Ziker-Bujanowsky, *Liliana's Journal* (New York, 1980); Bertha Ferderber-Satz, *And the Sun Kept Shining* (New York, 1980); Jack Kuper, *Child of the Holocaust* (New York, 1980); Livia E. Bitton-Jackson, *Elli: Coming of Age in the Holocaust* (New York, 1980); Georgia M. Gabor, *My Destiny: Survivor of the Holocaust* (Arcadia, CA, 1981); Frida Michelson, *I Survived Rumbuli* (New York, 1981); Aranka Siegel, *Upon the Head of a Goat: A Childhood in Hungary* (New York, 1981); Sara Zyskind, *Stolen Years* (New York, 1981); Gerda Schild Haas, *These I do Remember: Fragments from the Holocaust* (Salt Lake City, 1982); Kitty Hart-Moxon, *Return to Auschwitz* (New York, 1982); Agnes Sassoon, *Agnes: How my Spirit Survived* (Edgeware, Middlesex, UK, 1963); Judith Kerr, *When Hitler Stole Pink Rabbit* (London, 1983); Nechama Tec, *Dry Tears: The Story of a Lost Childhood* (New York, 1984); Aranka Siegal, *Grace in the Wilderness* (New York, 1985); Clara Asscher-Pinkhof, *Star Children* (Detroit, 1986); Frida Scheps Weinstein, *A Hidden Childhood* (New York, 1986); Thomas Geve, *Guns and Barbed Wire: A Child Survives the Holocaust* (Chicago, 1987); Alicia Appleman-Jurman, *My Story* (New York, 1990); Tzila (Tzesia) Rosenberg-Amit, *Maintain Humanity* (Tel Aviv, 1990) (Hebrew); Bela Ya'ari-Hazan, *My Name is Bornislava* (Tel; Aviv, 1991) (Hebrew); Lily Tau, *I Remained Myself: The Story of a Girl from Lvov* (Tel Aviv, 1991) (Hebrew).

18 "Stalag fiction" was a genre of erotic paperbacks published in Israel during the 1960s that dealt primarily with soldiers imprisoned in Nazi prison camps and their sexual abuse by female Nazi guards.

19 L. Shelley (ed. and trans.), *Secretaries of Death: Accounts by Former Prisoners who worked in the Gestapo of Auschwitz* (New York, 1986). An exceptional book published at a relatively early stage was *Women's Warfare* (Tel Aviv, 1979) (Hebrew). Other books in this category include Judy Tydor-Baumel (ed.), *Voices from the Canada Commando* (Jerusalem, 1989) (Hebrew); Vera Laska (ed.), *Women in the Resistance and in the Holocaust: The Voices of Eyewitness* (Westport and London, 1983); Ruth Schwertfeger, *Women of Theresienstadt: Voices from a Concentration Camp* (Oxford and New York, 1989); Karin Berger, Elisabeth Holzinger, Lotte Podgornik, and Lisbeth N. Trallor, *Ich geb Dir einen Mantel, dass Du ihn noch in Freiheit tragen kannst: Widerstehen im KZ Oesterrichische Frauen erzaehlen* (Fulda, 1987).

20 Marion Kaplan, *The Making of the Jewish Middle Class* (Oxford University Press, 1991); Marion Kaplan, *The Jewish Feminist Movement in Germany: The Campaigns of the Judischer Frauenbund, 1904-1938* (Westport, CN, 1979); Renate Bridenthal, Atina Grossmann and Marion Kaplan (eds.), *When Biology Became Destiny: Women in Weimar and Nazi Germany* (New York, 1984); Claudia Koonz, *Mothers in the Fatherland: Women, the Family and Nazi Politics* (New York, 1987). Additional studies include Rita Thalmann, "Juedische Frauen nach dem Pogrom 1938," in Arnold Paucker, Sylvia Gilchrist, and Barbara Suchin (eds.), *The Jews in Nazi Germany, 1933-1945* (Tuebingen, 1986), pp. 283-293; Claudia Koonz, "Courage and Choice Among German Jewish Women and Men," in Paucker, Gilchrist, and Suchin, *The Jews in Nazi Germany, 1933-1945*, pp. 295-302.

21 Andreas Lixi Purcell, *Women of Exile: German Jewish Autobiographies since 1933* (New York and Westport, CN, 1988); Gabriele Kreis, *Frauen Im Exil: Dichtung und Wirklichkeit* (Dusseldorf, 1984).

22 Marlene E. Heinemann, *Gender and Destiny: Women Writers and the Holocaust* (Westport, CN, 1986).

23 Joan Ringelheim, "Women and the Holocaust: A Reconsideration of Research," *Signs* 10 (1985), pp. 741-761; Joan Ringelheim, "The Unethical and the Unspeakable: Women and the Holocaust," *Simon Wiesenthal Center Annual* 1 (1984), pp. 69-87.

24 Marion Kaplan, *The Jewish Feminist Movement in Germany: The Campaigns of the Judischer Frauenbund, 1904-1938*; Lixi Purcell, *Women of Exile*; Kreis, *Frauen Im Exil: Dichtung und Wirklichkeit*; Ringelheim, "Women and the Holocaust"; Ringelheim, "The Unethical and the Unspeakable: Women and the Holocaust," Rita Thalmann, "Juedische Frauen nach dem Pogrom 1938," in Paucker, Gilchrist, and Suchin, *The Jews in Nazi Germany, 1933-1945*, pp. 283-293; Claudia Koonz, "Courage and Choice Among German Jewish Women and Men," in Paucker, Gilchrist, and Suchin, *The Jews in Nazi Germany, 1933-1945*, pp. 295-302.

25 Barrie Throne with Marylin Yalom, *Rethinking the Family: Some Feminist Questions* (New York, 1982); Hunter College Women's Studies Collective, *Women's Realities, Women's Choices: An Introduction to Women's Studies* (New York, 1983); Ellen Carol DuBois, Gail Paradise Kelly, Elizabeth Lapovsky Kennedy, Carolyn W. Korsmeyer, and Lilian S. Robinson, *Feminist Scholarship: Kindling in the Groves of Academe* (University of Illinois Press, 1984).

26 At the time, Dr. Joan Ringelheim, a scholar of gender and philosophy, was a research fellow at Wesleyan University's Center for the Humanities. She later served as the Director of Education and then Director of Oral History at the United States Holocaust Memorial Museum. Author's correspondence with Joan Ringelheim, August 13, 2018.

27 At the time, Dr. Esther Katz was a historian at New York University, where she served as deputy director of the Center for Historical Research. She currently directs NYU's Margaret Sanger Papers Project. Author's correspondence with Esther Katz, August 6, 2018.

28 Ava F. Kahn, Review of Esther Katz and Joan Miriam Ringelheim, *Women Surviving the Holocaust* (New York, 1983), in *The Public Historian* 7(3) (Summer 1985), pp. 104-106; "Focus on Issues: Women Surviving the Holocaust," JTA, March 29, 1983, https://www.jta.org/1983/03/29/archive/focus-on-issues-women-surviving-the-holocaust (accessed on August 5, 2018).

29 Dan Michman, "One Theme, Multiple Voices: The Role of Linguistic Cultures in Holocaust Research," in Shmuel Almog, David Bankier, Daniel Blatman, and Dalia Ofer (eds.), *The Holocaust: The Unique and the Universal. Essays Presented in Honor of Yehuda Bauer* (Jerusalem, 2001), pp. 8-37.

30 The Holocaust Education Center in Japan (in memory of the 1.5 million Jewish children) was established by Makoto Otsuka in June 1995. When Otsuka met with Otto Frank, the father of Anne Frank, in 1971, he already expressed a desire to establish a center to teach and commemorate the Holocaust.

31 On this subject, see articles by Martin Broszat, Ernst Nolte, Jürgen Habermas, Christian Meier, Eberhard Jäckel, and Israel Gutman in *Yad Vashem Studies* 19 (1988).

32 Rivkah Knoller, "The Phenomenon of Holocaust Denial," *Mahanaim* 9 (December 1994), pp. 238-247 (Hebrew).

33 Jan Blonski, "The Poor Poles Look at the Ghetto," *Yad Vashem Studies* 19 (1988), pp. 271-281.

34 Yehuda Elkana, "The Need to Forget," *Haaretz*, March 2, 1988, p. 13 (Hebrew); Boaz Evron, "The Holocaust: A Danger to the People," *Iton 77-Literary Magazine* 21 (June 1980), pp. 12-17 (Hebrew); Dan Michman, "The Image of the Holocaust

in Israeli Public Debate: Remains and Manipulation," *Gesher* 135 (Summer 1997), pp. 52-60 (Hebrew).

35 For example, see: Judith Isaacson, *Seed of Sarah: Memoirs of a Survivor* (Chicago, 1990); Liana Millu, *Smoke over Birkenau* (Philadelphia, 1991); Giuliana Tedeschi, *There is a Place on Earth: A Woman in Birkenau* (New York, 1992); Charlotte Delbo, *Auschwitz and After* (Yale University Press, 1995); Lucie Adelsberger, *Auschwitz: A Doctor's Story* (London, 1996); Joy Miller, *Love Carried Me Home: Women Surviving Auschwitz* (Deerfield Beach, FL, 2000).

36 Jana Renée Friesová, *Fortress of My Youth: Memoir of a Terezin Survivor* (University of Wisconsin Press, 2002). See also Suzanne Mehler Whiteley, *Appel is Forever: A Child's Memoir* (Detroit, 1999); Anita Brostoff, *Flares of Memory: Stories of a Childhood during the Holocaust* (Oxford University Press, 2001).

37 Philip K. Jason and Iris Posner, *Don't Wave Goodbye: The Children's Flight from Nazi Persecution to American Freedom* (Westport, CT, 2004). Other examples are: Vivette Samuel, *Rescuing the Children: A Holocaust Memoir* (University of Wisconsin Press, 2002); Lena Jedwab Rozenberg, *Girl With Two Landscapes: The Wartime Diary of Lena Jedwab 1941-1945* (New York and London, 2002); Ava Kadishon Schieber, *Soundless Roar: Stories, Poems and Drawings* (Northwestern University Press, 2002); Faye Walker and Leo Rosen, *Hidden: A Sister and Brother in Nazi Poland* (University of Wisconsin Press, 2002).

38 Nanda Herbermann, *The Blessed Abyss: Inmate #6582 in Ravensbrueck Concentration Camp for Women* (Wayne State University Press, 2000); Cynthia Crane, *Divided Lives: The Untold Stories of Jewish-Christian Women in Nazi Germany* (New York, 2000).

39 Nigel Fountain (consulting ed.), *Voices from the Twentieth Century: Women at War* (London, 2002).

40 Carol Rittner and John Roth, *Different Voices: Women and the Holocaust* (New York, 1993).

41 Dalia Ofer and Lenore Weitzman, *Women and the Holocaust* (Yale University Press, 1998).

42 *Contemporary Jewry* 17(1) (1996).

43 Judy Tydor Baumel, *Double Jeopardy: Gender and the Holocaust* (London, 1998).

44 Marion Kaplan, *Between Dignity and Despair: Jewish Life in Nazi Germany* (Oxford University Press, 1998).

45 Brana Gurewitsch (ed.), *Mothers, Sisters, Resisters: Oral Histories of Women Who Survived the Holocaust* (University of Alabama Press, 1998).

46 S. Lilian Kremer, *Women's Holocaust Writing: Memory and Imagination* (University of Nebraska Press, 1999).

47 Roger Ritvo and Diane Plotkin, *Sisters in Sorrow: Voices of Care in the Holocaust* (Texas A&M University Press, 1998).

48 Esther Fuchs, *Women and the Holocaust* (University Press of America, 1999).

49 Elizabeth Baer and Myrna Goldenberg (eds.), *Experience and Expression: Women, the Nazis, and the Holocaust* (Wayne State University Press, 2003).

50 See, for example, Lisa Disch and Leslie Morris, "Departures: New Feminist Perspectives on the Holocaust," *Women in German Yearbook* 19 (2003), pp. 9-19.

51 Rochelle G. Saidel, *The Jewish Women of Ravensbrueck Concentration Camp* (University of Wisconsin Press, 2004).

52 Ruth Linden, *Making Stories, Making Selves: Feminist Reflections on the Holocaust* (Ohio State University, 1993).

53 Kremer, *Women's Holocaust Writing*.

54 Melissa Raphael, *The Female Face of God in Auschwitz: A Jewish Feminist Theology of the Holocaust* (London, 2003).

55 Zoe Waxman, "Unheard Stories: Reading Women's Holocaust Testimonies," *The Jewish Quarterly* 47(177) (2000), pp. 53-58; Zoe Waxman, "Unheard Testimonies, Untold Stories: The Representation of Women's Holocaust Experiences," *Women's History Review* 12(4) (2003), pp. 661-677.

56 Felicia Karai, *Mortars and Rhymes: The Hasag-Lepizig Women's Camp* (Tel Aviv, 1996/97) (Hebrew); Nechama Tec, *Resilience and Courage: Women, Men and the Holocaust* (Yale University Press, 2003).

57 The first course on this subject appears to have been taught by Prof. Konnilyn Feig at Foothills College in Los Altos Hills, California. R. Ruth Linden, "Troubling Categories I Can't Think Without: Reflections on Women and the Holocaust," *Contemporary Jewry* 17 (1996), pp. 18-33.

58 Fanya Gottesfeld Heller, *Love in a World of Sorrow: A Teenage Girl's Holocaust Memories* (New York, 2005).

59 Marika Roth, *All the Pretty Shoes* (Deadwood, OR, 2011).

60 Elsa Thon, *If Only It Were Fiction* (Toronto, 2013).

61 Isabelle Choko, *Stolen Youth: Five Women's Survival in the Holocaust* (New York, 2005).

62 Rena Gellisen and Heather Macadam, *Rena's Promise: A Story of Sisters in Auschwitz* (Boston, 2015).

63 Wendy Holden, *Born Survivors: Three Young Mothers and their Extraordinary Story of Courage, Defiance, and Hope* (New York, 2015).

64 Dalia Ofer, "The Contribution of Gender to the Study of the Holocaust," in Marion Kaplan and Deborah Dash Moore (eds.), *Gender and Jewish History* (Indiana University Press, 2011), pp. 120-135; Judy Tydor Baumel-Schwartz, "The Identity of Women in the She'erit Hapleta: Personal and Gendered Identity as Determinants in their Rehabilitation, Immigration and Resettlement," in Dalia Ofer, Francoise Ouzan, and Judith Baumel-Schwartz (eds.), *Holocaust Survivors: Resettlement, Memories, Identities* (New York and Oxford, 2012), pp. 16-45; Atina Grossmann, *Jews, Germans and Allies: Close Encounters in Occupied Germany* (Princeton University Press, 2007).

65 Esther Hertzog, *Women and Families in the Holocaust* (Tel Aviv, 2006) (Hebrew); *Nashim: A Journal of Jewish Women's Studies and Gender Issues* 27 (2014), Special Issue: "Gender and the Holocaust: New Research"; Myrna Goldenberg and Amy Shapiro (eds.), *Different Horrors, Same Hell: Gender and the Holocaust* (University of Washington Press, 2013).

66 Doris Bergen, "Sexual Violence in the Holocaust: Unique and Typical," in Dagmar Herzog (ed.), *Lessons and Legacies VII: The Holocaust In International Perspective* (Northwestern University Press, 2006), pp. 179-200; Kirsty Chatwood, "(Re)-Interpreting Stories of Sexual Violence: The Multiple Testimonies of Lucille Eichengreen," in Esther Hertzog (ed.), *Life, Death, and Sacrifice: Women and Family in the Holocaust* (Jerusalem and New York, 2008), pp. 161-179; Na'ama Shik, "Sexual Abuse of Jewish Women in Auschwitz-Birkenau," in Dagmar Herzog, *Brutality and Desire: War and Sexuality in Europe's Twentieth Century* (London, 2009), pp. 221-246; Helene Sinnreich, "'And it was something we didn't talk about': Rape of Jewish Women during the Holocaust," *Holocaust Studies: A Journal of Culture and History* 14(2) (2008), pp. 14-22; Sonia M. Hedgepeth and Rochelle G. Saidel (eds.), *Sexual Violence against Jewish Women during the Holocaust* (Brandeis University Press, 2010).

67 Pascal Rachel Bos, "Women and the Holocaust: Analyzing Gender Differences," in Baer and Goldenberg (eds.), *Experience and Expression*, pp. 35-48; Zoe Waxman, "Unheard Testimony, Untold Stories: The Representation of Women's Holocaust Experiences," *Women's History Review* 12(4) (2003), pp. 661-677.

68 Dalia Ofer, "Introduction," *Nashim: A Journal of Jewish Women's Studies and Gender Issues* 27 (2014), pp. 11.

69 Lisa Pine, "Gender and Holocaust Victims: A Reappraisal," *Journal of Jewish Identities* 1(2) (2008), pp. 121-141; Natalia Aleksiun, "Gender and the Daily Lives of Jews Hiding in Eastern Galicia," *Nashim: A Journal of Jewish Women's Studies and Gender Issues* 27 (2014), pp. 38-61; Sharon Geva, *To the Unknown Sister: Holocaust Heroines in Israeli Society* (Tel Aviv, 2010) (Hebrew); Federika Clementi, *Holocaust Mothers and Daughters: Family, History, and Trauma* (Brandeis University Press, 2013).

70 Pascal Bos, *Her Flesh is Branded 'For Officers Only': Scandalizing Sexual Violence in Holocaust Literature and Film, 1942-1961* (forthcoming); Zoe Waxman, *Women and the Holocaust: A Feminist History* (Oxford University Press, 2017).

71 A discussion of the factors responsible for Holocaust research on different topic and in different countries can be found in Israel Gutman and Gideon Greif (eds.), *The Holocaust in Historiography* (Jerusalem, 1988) (Hebrew).

72 Rochelle Saidel, "New Books in Print," *Yad Vashem Studies* 28 (2000), pp. 363-378.

Dan Michman

Comparative Research on the Holocaust in Western Europe: Its Achievements, its Limits and a Plea for a More Integrative Approach

Introduction: On Eastern Europe and Western Europe in the Conceptualization of the Holocaust

In 1989 the sociologist Zygmunt Bauman published the study *Modernity and the Holocaust* which for a while left a considerable impact on students of the Holocaust and was awarded an important prize. In it he claimed that the Holocaust was the example *par excellence* of "modern genocide", modern genocide being characterized as a type of genocide "with a purpose", "a means to an end": "modern genocide is an element of social engineering, meant to bring about a social order conforming to the design of the perfect society".[1] Yet his conceptualization of "the Holocaust" was in fact limited to the systematic murder of Jews in the annihilation camps, of which Auschwitz served as the ultimate example; the extensive murder campaign carried out by the *Einsatzgruppen* and the *Wehrmacht* in Eastern Europe was, amazingly as it sounds even for that stage of research (the 1980s), not included at all in his study. In excluding the persecution and murder of the Jews in the areas occupied by Germany during *Fall Barbarossa* and in Serbia, Bauman's study was probably the most extreme example of a tendency apparent in the decades preceding the downfall of the communist bloc in Eastern Europe: viewing the essence of the Holocaust through the prism of "industrial murder". One may say that this view stemmed from a non-Eastern European perspective in which the annihilation camps and the network of deportations to them stood central, a view resulting from the very restricted inaccessibility up to that moment of sources stored in the Soviet Union.[2]

The collapse of the communist bloc around 1990 and the ensuing opening of Eastern Europe in general and the former Soviet Union in particular and of the archives there to research, gradually changed the perception and emphasized the enormity of the vast and brutal mass murders by shooting in the territories of the Soviet Union occupied by Nazi Germany.[3] Yet, the pendulum has recently swung to the other extreme, culminating in a series of comprehensive studies which almost entirely disregard the Holocaust in Western (and southern!) Europe; "the Holocaust" is now interpreted in some studies as the genocide of the Jews as well as that – or as part - of a broader genocidal wave including other ethnic groups in *Eastern* Europe.[4] If the main reason for this recent development is indeed to be found in the impressive volume of research on Eastern Europe in the past three decades, there is nevertheless another reason which played a role in my opinion: the fact that research on the Holocaust in western Europe, though also considerable, was often written in the local languages only, and that scholars from these countries (and in the first place from The Netherlands, Belgium and France) barely tried to participate in and integrate Western Europe sufficiently into the major discussions on the evolution and decision-making on overall anti-Jewish policies in the Third Reich which have been raging since the end of the 1980s.[5]

In this context one important facet of Holocaust research in general has to be emphasized: the fact that the bulk of it deals with the national chapters of the Holocaust.[6] The general background being usually invoked only in introductions to studies on the "local Holocaust", these studies do not go in their analyses beyond national borders and consequently limit the scope and horizon of their findings.[7] And that section of Holocaust research which has tried to trace and delineate the overall development of anti-Jewish policies, and especially of the decision-making process leading to the Final Solution, although having applied a broader view looking beyond political borders, has predominantly used German source material in combination with the perspective of the "decision-making" bureaucratic bodies, either in Berlin or in the periphery linked to Berlin.[8] It is within this section of research that the focus has so swung to focus on Eastern Europe. But even within this type of research, only some details are being picked up from the national scenes: those details that are relevant for the decision-making process which culminated in the murder campaign. Attempts to produce a comprehensive integration of all facets of anti-Jewish policies are rare.[9]

However, it should be emphasized that "The Holocaust" consisted not only of the horrendous chapter of the Final Solution: the scope of persecutions before – since 1933 – and also during the implementation of the Final Solution went far beyond the murder campaign itself. The volcanic outburst of antisemitic energy aimed at exorcising the polluting "Jewish spirit" and its carriers (i.e. the living Jews) was a broad undertaking which encompassed a variety of actions which have to be integrated in their entirety into the narrative.[10] One of the possible methodologies which can be applied in order to achieve this is comparative research. However, until today such research has been very limited and – amazingly enough - carried out only regarding Western Europe. What can we learn from these attempts?

To the best of my knowledge, there have been close to twenty attempts to combine the western European countries into one cluster, which, according to the authors, differed from the "Eastern European model" of the Holocaust.[11] The "crowns" of this approach are the project on division-of-labor of the Final Solution in Western Europe conducted by a team of researchers headed by Wolfgang Seibel,[12] and more so the impressive study by the Dutch scholars Pim Griffioen and Ron Zeller published in September 2011.[13] In the following I shall try to analyze and evaluate the attempts of comparison; in the last part of this article I will suggest an additional path of research - that of a broader conceived framework of *integrative* history, which will help not only to better understand the separate national chapters of the Holocaust, but also to balance the extremity of the above-mentioned Eastern-European-centred current tendency. Thus, the rationale behind my proposal and the deep need for it is here juxtaposed with the comparative approach.

Concepts and Definitions: "Comparisons" and "Western Europe"

There are two major questions regarding the possibility of carrying out comparative research in history: a) what kind of insights do we expect to gain from our comparisons? b) are the compared cases really comparable, i.e. can they really serve us in attaining the desired goal?

Regarding the first question the major issue which has bothered scholars of the Holocaust in Western Europe is: why do the percentages of murdered Jews differ so much from country to country? Comparison(s) might enable us to learn more about the differences and peculiarities of the situations and processes in each country – be it regarding perpetrators, bystanders or victims.[14] Similarities in actual persecution might also help us in finding larger patterns of action applied by the German authorities, patterns which sometimes cannot be well extracted from the regular documentation; the comparison may thus point to some oral planning or to modes of behavior and functioning stemming from a shared background – a common former training, for instance. By applying a comparative approach, we can thus overcome the obstacle of detaching local cases from broader patterns and sometimes the lack of sufficient documentation.

Regarding the second question – are the compared cases really comparable? – one may say that it is widely assumed that there are some basic common denominators to the three Western European countries France, Belgium and the Netherlands. Indeed, some scholars have tried to slightly broaden the scope: in the beginning of the 1970s Leni Yahil tried to compare the Netherlands and Romania; and in the 1980s Hans Blom made a comparison which included the Scandinavian countries Denmark and Norway in Western Europe. In recent years, the impressive project *Die Verfolgung und Ermordung der europäischen Juden durch das nationalsozialistischen Deutschland* (2008-2020) also included these countries and Luxemburg in one package (volumes 5 and 12 out of 16 volumes).[15] Yet the three above-mentioned countries – the Netherlands, Belgium and France (with Luxemburg sometimes included at the sidelines) - have usually been presented in many studies as one "block", which is the "center" (or essential nucleus) of "Western Europe."

However: what are the reasons behind the creation of this very common conceptual construct? It seems that there are three such reasons:

1. The democratic tradition of those countries, as well as their having a most well-organized modern state bureaucracy, a tradition which can be traced back to the end of the 18th century (to the French revolution and its impact); this criterion can be defined as relating to the *bystanders* aspect;

2. The occupation of those countries *en bloc*, at the same moment, with the invasion which started on May 10, 1940; this criterion relates to the geographical and the general chronological *context of the occupation*;

3. The inclusion of the three countries by the Eichmann Department IVB4 in one planning scheme for the deportations in the spring of 1942 and the interactive implementation of these deportations as from July of that year (regarding the instrument of deportations - by trains; regarding the pace of the deportations; regarding the similar system of directing the deportees through a main *Judendurchgangslager*, etc.); this criterion relates to the *perpetrator* aspect of the Final Solution.

Lacunae

If indeed these are the major reasons underpinning the common tendency to put those three countries in one bag – and these *are* valuable reasons in my eyes – than we can proceed to an analysis of the weak points of this conceptualization.

(a) It emphasizes the democratic and organizational tradition of those countries (point 1 above), but does not take into account at all the aspect of Jewish history, i.e. the composition of the Jewish communities and the processes they went through before the occupation; the <u>victim</u> aspect, as it is often called – even though I do not like this definition – is neglected. Jews remain an *object* of persecution only.

(b) It pays much attention to the structural frameworks of occupation and planning for the Final Solution (points 2 and 3), assuming a large extent of coherence. It does not give much weight, however, to the overall development and shaping of anti-Jewish policies in Nazi Germany *before* 1942 and to their origins – policies which were characterized by varying driving forces and goals of persecution![16]

(c) It focuses on large stuctures and groups, while disregarding the role and impact of individuals and the differences which different decisions by certain people could make (an insightful example for this aspect is the weight of the role played by Hans Biebow, the German official in charge of the Lodz ghetto, on the prolonged existence of this ghetto);[17]

(d) It looks upon those countries in a relatively static way - as one of the patterns of a more general "Holocaust phenomenon" which is applied in varying modes "everywhere", thus disregarding the option to view them as being links in a chain of development, i.e. that these countries present differences resulting from larger, separately developing issues (or lines), and that developments in themselves impacted afterwards on other, even remote countries. This static view is very much the outcome of the enormous impact Raul Hilberg had, with the political scientific model which he created, on Holocaust research.[18]

In the following I would like to show that in order to cope with these lacunae – not in order to oppose the insights gained from comparative analyses - we need to look for links with more countries and areas throughout Europe, and we have to do so through the application of an evolutional integrative approach too, not only a comparative "static" approach.

Links Between the different Western European Jewries and their counterparts in other European (and non-European) countries

(1) *Jewish history in modern times*. A very common characteristic of the writing about the Holocaust is the generalizing way in which Jewish society and its behavior is depicted. This is a result of several causes: first, the historical fact that Nazi ideology and policies related to the Jews in a generalized, mythologized way; second, the professional situation that many scholars of the Holocaust are ignorant about Jewish history; third, the historiographical state of affairs that much of Jewish historiography of the Holocaust, as well

as Jewish commemoration and religious martyrological depictions, have related to "the Jews" as a quite homogeneous collectivity.[19] However, European Jewry on the eve of the Holocaust was immensely diverse, as a result of - and vis-à-vis - the modern developments of emancipation, secularization, politicization, nationalism, liberalism, socialism, and especially migration. Thus, even though still having a very powerful shared tradition and many common characteristics (which so impacted on the gentile societies to perceive them as different), Jews had been disputing and quarelling among themselves and disagreeing about almost everything, mostly about Jewish identity and about what goals to pursue; and they had been splitting into many groups and sub-groups. The history of their relationship with their host countries was also very different from place to place.[20]

Consequently, the character of the *Jewries* in each of the three western European countries was very different. Most – about 85% - of the 140,000 Jews living in The Netherlands in 1940 were long-rooted in the country.[21] Nevertheless, in the peculiar segmentation of Dutch society (*"verzuiling"*), Dutch Jewry showed a relatively low percentage of intermarriages on the eve of the Holocaust (about 15%).[22] From cultural and legal perspectives, Dutch Jews had been very much integrated in the Netherlands, yet socially they had kept together and apart, remaining a clearly recognizable segment in Dutch society. One pre-1940 historian, Sigmund Seeligmann, even suggested to view Dutch Jews as a special "species" - "Species Hollandia Judaica". His interpretation was definitely an over-simplification;[23] nevertheless, it is a fact that Dutch Jewry was only slightly interwoven into the many trans-national Jewish networks which had developed since the second half of the nineteenth century. Thus, for instance, secularization had made deep inroads and Dutch Jews had abandoned (Western European) Yiddish as their colloquial tongue, but traditional orthodox Judaism remained the official representative of "Jewishness" and Reform Judaism of any kind existed in the Netherlands only on the margins; and as for orthodox Judaism itself – it had a strong Western European flavor while the very powerful Eastern European orthodox currents – "Lithuanian" orthodoxy and Chassidism – were non-existent in the Netherlands.[24] Also, the many Jewish political factions which existed in Eastern Europe, especially the socialist Bund which had become the largest Jewish party in Poland on the eve of WWII, were not present in the Netherlands whatsoever, except for general Zionism (and its sub-streams *Mizrachi* and *Poalei-Tzion*), and Agudath Israel. Good faith in the correctness and fairness of the Dutch state structures was deeply ingrained, and the dispersion of Jews over the country was such that about 60% of them lived in Amsterdam (more then 80,000 souls).[25]

Belgian Jewry, on the other hand, consisted of about 70,000 souls on the eve of the occupation, almost 94% of them foreigners, who in many ways represented characteristics of interwar Polish Jewry (with additional aspects introduced by Jews from other Eastern European countries such as Russia and Hungary, and German Jewish refugees who had arrived after the Nazi ascendance to power in Germany). Even among the Jews with Belgian nationality many were of Eastern European origin, and had been naturalized after World War I. The Belgian Jewish community, mainly concentrated in Brussels and Antwerp, was deeply affected by secularization and segmented into many quarrelling parties and factions, including a variety of strong socialist, communist and other ultra-left groupings, but also containing typical ultra-orthodox groupings. As dominantly foreign, with (Eastern European) Yiddish being the leading language among them, the Jews were very different from other Belgian ethnic communities: Flemish or Walloon (no Jews settled in the German speaking east of Belgium). Yet, there were strong organizational contacts between leftist Jews of varying groupings with Belgian leftist organizations, first and foremost the communist organizations for immigrants.[26]

French Jewry, the largest western European community at the moment of occupation (about 300,000 souls), was different from both the Netherlands and Belgium. It was generally divided into two major segments: the veteran French Jews *("israélites")* who had lived in France for many generations – the *"Juifs d'État"*, as Pierre Birnbaum has called them [27] - whose number was about 90,000; and the Eastern European Jews, who were only partially naturalized. The first category – even the Jews of rural Alsace – were much more integrated into French society than Dutch Jews and extremely identified themselves with the state. The segment of Eastern European Jews however, should be seen as an extension of Eastern European Jewry, with its Yiddish culture (although many embraced French culture too), intensive politicization and strong representation of radical socialist trends; this segment of French Jewry much resembled that of Belgian Jewry in its internal structure and characteristics. Yet there were in France also Jews from North African countries, and from Turkey and Greece.[28]

Thus, when we look upon the composition, backgrounds and interpretation of identities of the Jewries of these countries, we observe immense differences.[29] During the Nazi occupation, this diverse composition and nature of the three Jewish communities impacted on the ways in which Jews reacted to persecutions, including the trans-border contacts they could establish, and the links which they could create with Gentile resistance organizations, especially the communist and socialist ones. Thus, in Belgium we observe the emergence in 1942 of an underground *Comité de Défense des Juifs* (CDJ) through the cooperation of Jewish political activists of differing and even rivaling colors (but many of them speaking Yiddish and French) among themselves and with the communist underground *Front de l'Indépendance*. The CDJ became for many the counter-pole to the German-imposed *Judenvereingung in Belgien/Association des Juifs en Belgique* (AJB). In the Netherlands such a phenomenon never happened. There, the Jewish roof-organization which was established vis-à-vis the occupation, the *Joodsche Coördinatie Commissie* (Jewish Coordination Committee), was typically established in December 1940, i.e. in the early, pre-Final Solution period, when open or semi-open activities were still tolerated; it faded away precisely when anti-Jewish policies radicalized, as a result of the strengthening of the position of the *Joodsche Raad* (the Jewish Council/Judenrat), and none of its members continued its activities in some underground manner. Although Jews carried out underground activities, this was mostly done as part of general underground groups, very different from Belgian Jewry.[30]

Consequently, from the point of view of *Jewish* history, the three countries cannot just be put together in one bag: each Jewry had a separate story, and Belgian Jewry and about two-thirds of French Jewry can in certain respects be better linked to Poland and some other East-European countries (but also to North African Jewries) than to Dutch Jewry. The paths of emancipation and integration of Dutch Jewry and of the other third of French Jewry also differed, as a result of the different compositions and political cultures of the societies of which they were part.[31] Moreover, the ways in which different types of Jews and

Jewish groups within those countries behaved and reacted during the period of occupation can be understood only in the larger context of the processes of modern Jewish history.[32]

(2) *The overall development and shaping of anti-Jewish policies in Nazi Germany before 1942 and their origins.* As stated above, the view of the three countries as a unit has its justifications from the point of view of the beginning of the planning of the systematic Final Solution in the spring of 1942. But most historians of the national scenes of these countries have hitherto also perceived the persecutions of the two preceding years of occupation as a corridor *leading* in an almost linear way to the Final Solution; they consequently tended to make comparisons in that context. For instance, the establishment of the *Joodsche Raad voor Amsterdam* in February 1941, and the AJB in Belgium and the *Union Générale des Israélites de France* (UGIF) in France at the end of November 1941, have always been viewed as being part of the organisation of local Jewries for the purpose of the implementation of the Final Solution. Hilberg's model of the evolution of anti-Jewish policies – definition-expropriation-concentration-annihilation – has consciously and unconsciously served as the basis for this conceptualization.[33] However, from the point of view of the general development of anti-Jewish policies as we comprehend it now, this is not correct. Before the decision(s) about the Final Solution, which by itself was a complex process which took several months, several German authorities competed over and proposed differing directions for the right path to a "solution of the Jewish question"; and one of the novelties of the Final Solution stage was that its goal - and the bureaucratic structures serving it - principally (but not entirely) overrode the pre-existing host of instances which were active in the field of searching for the "right" solution. This does not mean that the general impulses for persecution as analyzed by Hilberg did not exist; they were, however, carried out in very different ways, not as consecutive but often as parallel steps, and in many cases without being fully coordinated.[34]

For instance, expropriation policies in the Netherlands, especially regarding bank accounts, were developed against the background of the experience gathered in Austria after the *Anschluss*. This notion is, of course, not new: the input of the Austrian Nazis, in this context especially Dr. Hans Fischböck, has long been recognized by historians of the occupation and the Holocaust in the Netherlands.[35] Yet this knowledge has usually been limited to a brief and general mentioning of their former activities in Austria, not accompanied by a very deep-seated analysis comparing the specifics of the Dutch and Austrian cases. The reports of the official Austrian enquiry committee, established and working about two decades ago, now allow for comparisons in that direction.[36]

A similar remark has to be made regarding the organization of the Jews by the representatives of Eichmann in Western Europe. The model developed by Eichmann in Vienna in 1938 (a reorganization of the Jewish community in the form of a *Zwangsvereinigung* subordinated to a special SS authority, which in Vienna was the *Zentralstelle für jüdische Auswanderung*), was later, in June 1939, repeated and further developed in Prague.[37] Two years later in France, on March 18, 1941 Theodor Dannecker, the Paris-based representative of the Eichmann office for Jewish affairs in Berlin, "announced to the leaders [of the Charities Coordination Committee] that two Viennese Jews will be sent to them [Israel Israelowicz and Wilhem Biberstein] who have experience with the organisation that exists in Germany, an organisation which is the model to be followed."[38]

So once again the organization of the Viennese Jewish community (this is what actually was meant by the expression "the organisation that exists in Germany") served as a model for organizing the French Jews.[39] In the Netherlands, in mid-March, at about the same time and parallel to what happened in Paris, Eichmann sent three of his accomplices in Prague, among them the SS officer Erich Rajakowitsch, and two leaders of the reorganized Jewish community there, Jacob Edelstein and Richard Friedmann, to Amsterdam, where they stayed for about a month, giving advice to the local Jewish Council; meanwhile a supervising *Zentralstelle für jüdische Auswanderung* was also established in Amsterdam – similar to the ones in Vienna and Prague.[40] These actions have thus to be seen in a context including (in this case) Vienna, Prague, Paris and Amsterdam – which excludes, in this central issue, Belgium. On the other hand, when the Belgian AJB was established at the end of November 1941, this was done "nach dem Muster der Reichs-Vereinigung" ("according to the Reichsvereinigung model")[41] in Germany.

On other occasions, the Polish case was of decisive importance. This can be proved by the material fact of two apparently very different documents being kept together in one file. One is a report on "Die Juden in Holland" ("The Jews in Holland"), composed by experts of SD II 112, the Jewish Department of the SS *Sicherheitsdienst* (SD) headed by Herbert Hagen; the document is dated March 28, 1939 – i.e. 14 months *before* the occupation of The Netherlands by Nazi Germany.[42] Most interestingly, this document is immediately followed in that same file by a memo (*Vermerk*) of May 9, 1939, titled "Verbindungen nach Polen" (contacts with Poland), which dealt with preparations to register the Jews of Poland in case it would be needed for the activities of "a possible *Einsatzkommando*" in Poland, i.e. for the invasion, an invasion which happened three and a half months later.[43] What one can learn from this is that those preparations for anti-Jewish policies in the Netherlands and Poland which were taken care of by the Jewish Department of the SD, were made in a common unit and context– *before* the invasion of those countries. This had resulted from an "Arbeitsanweisung" (working instruction) dated December 22, 1938, i.e. in the wake of *Kristallnacht*, to SD II 112 to intensify the monitoring of "Jewry" in all countries neighboring with Germany.[44] There are, therefore, non-western European contexts and earlier stages to developments that occurred in Western Europe; and sometimes these are relevant for only some of the western European countries, not for all of them *en bloc*.

Moreover, should we view the Western European countries only as "final stations" of certain lines of developments? Should not the establishment of the *Jevrejska Zajednica* (Jewish Council) in Belgrado on April 19, 1941[45] be seen in context with the establishment of the Joodsche Raad in Amsterdam two months earlier? If documentation proving such an assumption in this case is lacking, we do have proof for such a link in the evolution as far as Romania is concerned. Gustav Richter, Eichmann's emmissary there, was the driving force behind the establishment of a central Jewish organisation, the *Centrala Evreilor din Romania* in December 1941. Richter explained to Prime Minister Ion Antonescu "dass auch neuerlings Frankreich in der Lösung seiner Judenfrage einen wesentlichen Schritt getan hätte, durch die Aufhebung aller jüdischen Organisationen in Frankreich und die Errichtung einer Judenzentrale in Frankreich an deren

Stelle" ("that recently France too took a major step forward in its Solution of its Jewish Question by repealing all Jewish organizations in France and establishing a Jewish Center for France instead");[46] the establishment of the UGIF in France thus served as a model for Romania.

(3) *Influential individuals.* The Nazi empire was a huge chess board on which SS officers, military commanders and bureaucrats were moved from one place to another. The experience which Wilhelm Harster gained as *Befehlshaber der Sicherheitspolizei* (BdS) in western Galicia in the months following the invasion of Poland (the end of 1939 and the beginning of 1940), was undoubtedly used by him when he was transferred to the Netherlands and appointed there as BdS. Similarly, *Judenberater* (advisor on Jews) Kurt Asche, Eichmann's representative in Brussels, formerly served for several months in the Jewish Department under the infamous *SS und Polizeiführer* of the Lublin district, Odilo Globočnik. And Theo Dannecker continued from his position as *Judenberater* in France to similar positions in Bulgaria and Hungary. However, Dutch researchers did not check the impact of Harster's Polish period on his deeds in Holland, Belgian researchers did not do the same thing for Asche; only for Dannecker has this European-wide scope of activity been partially checked.[47]. The same is true for other personalities. So we see again, that there are much broader contexts for the developments in western Europe than merely western Europe – and they have not been properly checked by scholars till today.

Conclusion

Comparisons depend on *our* decision what to include, and what not. Comparative analyses of the Holocaust in Western Europe have undoubtedly contributed new insights to our understanding. Yet the comparisons have their limits: they are basically synchronic, linked to models in order to be meaningful; they put (national) units next to each other, and do not trace back developments beyond the defined scope. Comparisons also limit themselves to those cases which allow for many aspects to be compared; thus, they exclude per definition cases which may have only a low number of comparable elements. Moreover, in seeking for models, in-depth studies of the role of individuals and their personal geographical itinerary and career development over time is usually overlooked or downplayed.[48] These aspects have caused, according to my understanding, the exclusion of "Western Europe" from being integrated in the larger picture of both the research on the overall escalation of anti-Jewish policies, and of the understanding of cross-European elements of the comprehensive picture of "the Shoah", be it from the perspective of Jewish history[49] or that of the history of perpetration and so-called bystanding.

For a fuller historical understanding of the picture we shall have to overcome our mental subordination to national, political and linguistic borders, and to keep in mind the entire extent of Nazi domination over Europe and North-Africa,[50] the overall ideologically driven intention to deal with "Das Weltjudentum" ("World Jewry"), wherever it was found, and the all-European dimensions of "Jewish geography" and history. Therefore, only through the examination of issues in their entire scope and through tracing twisted, border-crossing developments – i.e. through *integrative* history – shall we be able to get closer to an understanding of many still unsolved facets of the Holocaust – in Western Europe and elsewhere. Such an endeavour is a "must" in this state of Holocaust research - in order to balance the tendency in research which puts almost all the weight of the Holocaust on the Eastern Europe theatre.

Endnotes

1 Zygmunt Bauman, *Modernity and the Holocaust*, (Ithaca, NY 1993), S. 91. For an analysis of this book see: Dan Michman: *Holocaust Historiography: A Jewish Perspective. Conceptualizations, Terminology, Approaches and Fundamental Issues*, (London 2003), pp. 43-45.

2 The Israeli scholar Shalom Cholawski, who specialized on Vohlynia and Byelorussia, once compared (in a discussion at Yad Vashem at the end of the 1970s in which I participated) the challenges he faced in his research with those of archeologists of Antiquity.

3 Of course, the murder in the territories of Fall Barbarossa was not "unknown", and it was included in the comprehensive histories of the Holocaust in one way or another from the earliest stages of Holocaust research (see for instance Raul Hilberg, *The Destruction of the European Jews*, (Chicago 1961), and later editions and translations). Some very important partial studies focusing on Eastern Europe were also carried out, most notably Helmut Krausnick and Hans H. Wilhelm, *Die Truppe des Weltanschauungskrieges. Die Einsatzgruppen der Sicherheitspolizei und des SD 1938-1942*, (Stuttgart 1981). Yet, altogether, and seen in the light of the information available to researchers today, knowledge about these areas and the space allotted to the Eastern European scene were very limited.

4 See Mark Mazower, *Hitler's Empire: How the Nazis Ruled Europe*, (London 2008); Timothy Snyder, *Bloodlands*, (New York 2010).

5 No Dutch, Belgian or Danish historians have participated in the debate at all. French historians having contributed original research to the debate are less than a handful: Joseph Billig, "The Launching of the 'Final Solution'", in: Serge Klarsfeld (ed.), *The Holocaust and the Neo-Nazi Mythomania*, (New York 1978) (who belongs to the first generation of Holocaust historians); Philippe Burrin, *Hitler et les Juifs. Genèse d'un genocide*, (Paris 1989); and Florent Brayard, *La solution finale de la question juive: La technique, le temps et les catégories de la decision*, (Paris 2004). For a recent contribution which does not deal with decision-making but with the mindset that emerged in Nazi Germany and the attitude to the Jews in it see Johann Chapoutot, *La loi du dang. Penser et agir en nazi*, (Paris 2014) (English edition: *The Law of Blood. Thinking and Acting as a Nazi* (Cambridge, MA and London, England 2018).

6 This state of affairs has to be attributed to a large extent to the fact that much of this research on the Holocaust has emerged in European countries – since the 1970s in Western Europe and since the 1990s in Eastern Europe – within the context of coping with the traumatic national pasts on the eve of and during World War II.

7 Interestingly – and surprisingly – first comprehensive studies by German scholars on the Holocaust in these countries followed these national approaches; the authors explicit reasoning for that was that, next to bringing fresh insights, they wanted to

provide surveys of these countries to the German public whose knowledge about what happened in these countries was almost nil; see Insa Meinen, *Die Shoah in Belgien*, (Darmstadt 2009); Katja Happe, *Viele falsche Hoffnungen. Judenverfolgung in den Niederlanden 1940-1945*, (Paderborn 2017).

8   In the earlier comprehensive surveys and analyses of the Holocaust, by Gerald Reitlinger, *The Final Solution*, (London 1953); Raul Hilberg, op. cit., and Nora Levin, *The Holocaust*, (New York 1968), and in the more recent study by Peter Longerich, *Politik der Vernichtung*, (München 1998), countries are dealt with separately. The ultimate example is Lucy Dawidowicz, T*he War Against the Jews 1933-1945*, (New York 1975): in the original English edition all countries (except for Germany and Poland) are dealt with in the appendix, not in the narrative! (in the German edition this was not called "appendix" but "Part III", yet the basic conceptualization was not changed).

9   See for instance the minimal place allotted to the enormous scope of economic spoliation throughout Europe in Christopher R. Browning, *The Origins of the Final Solution. The Evolution of Nazi Jewish Policy, September 1939-March 1942*, (Lincoln and Jerusalem 2004).

10 For this understanding of "the Holocaust" as a historical event see Dan Michman, "The Jewish Dimension of the Holocaust in Dire Straits? Current Challenges of Interpretation and Scope", in Norman Goda (ed.), *Jewish Histories of the Holocaust. New Transnational Approaches*, (New York 2014), pp. 17-38.

11 Leni Yahil, "Holland ve-Romania bi-Tekufat ha-Shoa (Hebeytim shel Mechkar Mashveh)" ("The Netherlands and Romania During the Holocaust Period (Aspects of Comparative Research)], *Divrey ha-Kongres ha-Olami ha-Chamishi le-Mada'ey ha-Yahadut* [Proceedings of the Fifth World Congress for Jewish Studies], (Jerusalem 1972), pp. 195-200; Leni Yahil, "Methods of Persecution: A Comparison of the Final Solution in Holland and Denmark", *Scripta Hierosolymitana XXIII*, (Jerusalem, 1972), pp. 279-300; Alan Mitchell: "Polish, Dutch and French Elites under German Occupation", in: Henry Friedländer and Sybil Milton (eds.): *The Holocaust: Ideology, Bureaucracy and Genocide*, (Millwood, NY 1980), pp. 231-241 [reprint from the Wiener Library Bulletin]; Michael R. Marrus and Robert O. Paxton, "The Nazis and the Jews in Occupied Western Europe 1940-1944", in: François Furet (ed.), *Unanswered Questions. Nazi Germany and the Genocide of the Jews*, (New York 1989), pp. 172-198 [reprint from: *Journal of Modern History* 54 (1982), pp. 687-714]; Johannes C.H. Blom, "The Persecution of the Jews in The Netherlands in a Comparative International Perspective", in: Jozeph Michman (ed.), *Dutch Jewish History II, Assen*, (Maastricht and Jerusalem 1989), pp. 273-289 [also published in English and Dutch, with slight alterations, in other periodicals]; Dan Michman, "The Uniqueness of the Joodse Raad in the Western European Context", in: Jozeph Michman (ed.), *Dutch Jewish History III*, (Jerusalem 1993), pp. 371-380 [abridged English version of: "De oprichting van de 'Joodsche Raad voor

Amsterdam' vanuit een vergelijkend perspectief', in: David J. Barnouw, Dick van Galen Last, Marion de Keizer, René Kok, Peter Romijn, Erik .M. Somers and C. Touwen-Bouwsma (eds.): *Oorlogsdocumentatie '40-'45*, 3, (Zutphen 1992), pp. 75-100]; Bob Moore, "Conclusion", in: Bob Moore, *Victims and Survivors. The Nazi Persecution of the Jews in the Netherlands 1940-1945*, (London, New York, Sydney, and Auckland 1997), pp. 253-258 [also published in Dutch]; Dan Michman, "Jewish 'Headships' under Nazi Rule: The Evolution and Implementation of an Administrative Concept," in Dan Michman: *Holocaust Historiography: A Jewish Perspective. Conceptualizations, Terminology, Approaches and Fundamental Issues*, (London 2003), pp. 159-175; Maxime Steinberg, "The Judenpolitik in Belgium Within the West European Context: Comparative Observations", in: Dan Michman (ed.), *Belgium and the Holocaust: Jews, Belgians, Germans*, (Jerusalem 1998), pp. 199-222; Chris J. Lammers, "Persecution in the Netherlands During World War Two: An Introduction", *Netherlands Journal of Social Sciences* 34/2 (1998), pp. 111-125; Jan Willem Griffioen and Ron Zeller, "A Comparative Analysis of the Persecution of the Jews in the Netherlands and Belgium During the Second World War", *The Netherlands Journal of Social Sciences* 34/2 (1998), pp. 126-164 [varying versions of this article were published in German, Dutch, French and Hebrew]; Dan Michman, "The Place of the Holocaust of Dutch Jewry in a Wider Historical Fabric: Approaches of Non-Dutch Historians", in: Chaya Brasz and Yosef Kaplan (eds.), *Dutch Jews as Perceived by Themselves and by Others*, (Leiden: Brill, 2001), pp. 373-391. Most of these comparisons have in my eyes the deficiency that the comparison is usually being done from the viewpoint of one country, which than stands in the center; the comparisons are thus not of equal chapters – on the same level and comprehensive - but trying to illuminate some aspects relating to that specific country or that specific issue. Bob Moore, *Survivors. Jewish Self-Help and Rescue in Nazi Occupied Western Europe*, (Oxford 2009), is different in treating the different countries equally; however, there are no real comparisons in the book and the stories are told separately for each country (except for several cases where rescue crossed the borders).

12 Wolfgang Seibel, "The Strength of Perpetrators – The Holocaust in Western Europe, 1940-1944", in: *Governance – An International Journal of Policy, Administration, and Institutions* 15 (2002), pp. 211-240; Wolfgang Seibel, "Staatsstruktur und Massenmord. Wass kann eine historisch-vergleichende Analyse zur Erforschung des Holocaust beitragen?", in: H. Berding (ed.), *Genozid und Charisma*, (Göttingen 1998) pp. 539-569 [Sonderheft aus: Geschichte und Gesellschaft 24/4 (1998), pp. 539-569].

13 Pim Griffioen and Ron Zeller, *Jodenvervolging in Nederland, Frankrijk en België 1940-1945. Overeenkomsten, verschillen, oorzaken*, (Amsterdam 2011). This is the only study comprehensively comparing The Netherlands, France and Belgium in an equal and systematic mode. Although being extremely important in its high resolution examination of these countries, the focus of this study is, however, on the "how" of the occupation, i.e. the way policies developed and were implemented; it does not deal with ideological drives and intentions, cultural aspects, etc., and only slightly with broader contexts.

14 This is done in a most extensive way by Griffioen and Zeller, *Jodenvervolging*.

15 *Die Verfolgung und Ermordung der europäischen Juden durch das nationalsozialistischen Deutschland 1933-1945* [vol. 5]: *West– und Nordeuropa 1940 – Juni 1942*, compiled and edited by Michael Mayer, Katja Happe, Maja Peers, (Munich 2012); [vol. 12]: *West- und Nordeuropa Juni 1942 – 1945*, compiled and edited by Katja Happe, Barbara Lambauer und Clemens Maier-Wolthausen, (Munich 2015). An English edition of this series – *The Persecution and Murder of the European Jews by National-Socialist Germany 1933-1945*, Institute for Contemporary History Munich, Freiburg University, German Federal Archives and Yad Vashem, Munich and Jerusalem, is currently in the process of publication and volumes 5 and 12 are planned to be published in 2021.

16 Indeed, Griffioen and Zeller, *Jodenvervolging* is different: they pay much attention to the period 1940-1942 in order to explain the differences in victimization later. Nevertheless, the German occupation authorities are presented en bloc and the internal ideological currents and interactions within the German bureaucracy are not dealt with sufficiently as driving forces.

17 See: Michal Unger, *Lodz: Ahron haGettaot bePolin* [*Lodz: The Last Ghetto in Poland*], (Jerusalem 2005) (Hebrew).

18 Raul Hilberg, *The Destruction of the European Jews*, (Chicago 1961) (and later editions and translations). For an analysis of this aspect see: Michman, *Holocaust Historiography: A Jewish Perspective*, pp. 16-20.

19 See for instance: Dawidowicz, *The War Against the Jews*.

20 For an analysis of these issues see Michman, *Holocaust Historiography: A Jewish Perspective*, pp. 59-88. For a panoramic in-depth picture of European Jewry in the 1930s see Bernard Wasserstein, *On the Eve. The Jews of Europe Before the Second World War*, (London 2012).

21 Jozeph Michman, Hartog Beem and Dan Michman, Pinkas. *Geschiedenis van de joodse gemeenschap in Nederland*, (Amsterdam 1999).

22 See Emanuel Boekman, *Demografie van de Joden in Nederland*, (Amsterdam 1936).

23 See my own argumentation against exaggerating the "uniqueness" and "separateness" of Dutch Jewry: Dan Michman, "Migration versus 'Species Hollandia Judaica'. The Role of Migration in the Nineteenth and Twentieth Centuries in Preserving Ties between Dutch and World Jewry", *Studia Rosenthaliana*, special issue, September 1989, pp. 54-76.

24 Dan Michman, *Het Liberale Jodendom in Nederland 1929-1943*, (Amsterdam 1988).

25 See J.C.H. Blom and Joël J. Cahen, "Joodse Nederlanders, Nederlandse Joden en joden in Nederland (1870-1940)", in: J.C.H. Blom, Rena G. Fuks-Mansfeld and Ivo Schöffer (ed.), *Geschiedenis van de Joden in Nederland*, (Amsterdam 1995), pp. 247- 310.

26 See: Dan Michman, "Belgium", in: *Encyclopedia of the Holocaust*, (New York 1990), pp. 160-169; Daniel Dratwa, "The Zionist Kaleidoscope in Belgium", in: Michman, *Belgium and the Holocaust*, pp. 43-62; Rudi Van Doorslaer, "Jewish Immigration and Communism in Belgium, 1925-1939", in: Michman, *Belgium and the Holocaust*, pp. 63-82; Jean-Philippe Schreiber, "Belgian Jewry Reacts to the Nazi Regime Prior to the Occupation: The Case of the Economic Boycott, 1933-1939", in: Michman, *Belgium and the Holocaust*, pp. 83-114;

27 Pierre Birnbaum, *Les fous de la République: Histoire des Juifs d'Etat de Gambetta à Vichy*, (Paris 1992); Yerachmiel (Richard) Cohen, "Dat uMoledet – leDarka shel haKonsistoriya haMerkazit beTsarefat biTkufat Milhemet ha'Olam haSheniyah", in: Shmuel Almog e.a. (eds.), *Beyn Yisrael la'Umot. Kovetz Ma'amarim Shay liShmuel Ettinger* [Israel Among the Nations. A Volume Presented in honor of Shmuel Ettinger], (Jerusalem 1988), pp. 307-334.

28 David Weinberg, *Les Juifs à Paris de 1933 à 1939*, (Paris 1974); Asher Cohen, *Persécutions et sauvetages. Juifs et Français sous l'Occupation et sous Vichy*, (Paris 1993), pp.25-30; Renée Poznanski, *Être juif en France pendant la seconde Guerre mondiale*, (Paris 1994), pp. 23-47 (English edition: *Jews in France during World War Two*, (Hanover and London 2001).

29 A striking example is the fact, that on the eve of the German occupation, i.e. in the 1930s, almost no organizational ties existed between Dutch and Belgian Jewries, in spite of their living in neighboring countries. And thus, Hashomer Hatza'ir in Antwerp, for instance, organized joint hachshara (preparation for pioneering in Palestine) summer camps for its members together with their fellow members from France and as far as from Tunisia (!), but not with young Dutch Zionist socialists. See Dan Michman, "The Belgian Zionist Youth Movements During the Occupation", in: Michman, *Belgium and the Holocaust*, pp. 373-395, esp. 386-387.

30 Some of these issues are mentioned by Griffioen and Zeller, *Jodenvervolging*, in ch. 15 (pp. 583-633), though very briefly (due to the focus of their work). On Jewish resistance in the Netherlands see Ben Braber, *'Zelfs als wij zullen verliezen'. Joden in verzet en illegaliteit in Nederland 1940-1945*, (Amsterdam 1990).

31 Dutch Jewry never encountered bold antisemitic outbursts since the emancipation in 1796; yet only a handful of Jews made it to top positions in Dutch society, the most shining example being the president of the Supreme Court in the 1930s until his removal by the German occupier, Lodewijk E. Visscher; but Jewish government ministers there had been only two between 1796 and 1940, both Ministers of Justice, one at the end of the 18th century (!), the other during the second half of the 1850s (!) and no one later! In France antisemitism was outspoken and much fiercer; yet a considerable number of Jews climbed the social and economic ladder and made it to the highest positions, among them Prime Minister Léon Blum.

32 See Michman, *Holocaust Historiography: A Jewish Perspective*, pp. 59-88.

33 See in this context my review of Bob Moore's 1997 book *Victims and Survivors* in: *Journal of Modern History* 71/4 (December 1999), pp. 977-980.

34 For an analysis and critique of Hilberg's model see Dan Michman, "Getting it Right, Getting it Wrong: Recent Holocaust Scholarship in Light of the Work of Raul Hilberg", *The 2017 Annual Raul Hilberg Memorial Lecture*, University of Vermont (Vermont: Carolyn & Leonard Miller Center for Holocaust Studies, 2017).

35 See: Lou de Jong, *Het Koninkrijk der Nederlanden in de Tweede Wereldoorlog*, vol. 4a, 's (Gravenhage 1972), pp. 101-103; and index.

36 See: Theodor Venus und Alexandra-Eileen Wenck, *Die Entziehung jüdischen Vermögens im Rahmen der "Aktion Gildemeester". Eine empirische Studie über Organisation, Form und Wandel von "Arisierung" und jüdischer Auswanderung in Österreich 1938-1941*, Österreichische Hstorikerkommission, (Wien, 2002); and Gabriele Anderl and Dirk Rupnow with editorial assistance by Alexandra-Eileen Wenck, *Die Zentralstelle für jüdische Auswanderung als Beraubungsinstitution*, Österreichische Hstorikerkommission, (Vienna 2002).

37 See Michman, *Holocaust Historiography: A Jewish Perspective*, p. 165.

38 In the original French: "a annoncé aux dirigeants [du Comité de coordination des œuvres de bienfaisance] qu'il allait leur envoyer deux Juifs viennois [= Israel Israelowicz et Wilhelm Biberstein] qui avaient l'expérience de l'organisation existant en Allemagne, organisation qui etait le modèle auquel il fallait aboutir."

39 Léo Hamon, "Étude sue la situation des juifs en zone occupée", in: Léo Hamon and Renée Poznanski, *Avant les premières grandes rafles. Les Juifs sous l'Occupation (juin 1940-avril 1941), Les Cahiers de l'IHTP, Cahier No. 22* (Décembre 1992), p. 100; see also Cynthia J. Haft, *The Bargain and the Bridle. The General Union of the Israelites of France, 1941-1944*, (Chicago 1983), pp. 3-5.

40 Ruth Bondy, Edelstein *Neged haZeman* [Edelstein *Against the Current*], (Tel Aviv 1981), pp. 249-251.

41 "Sonderbericht. Das Judentum in Belgien", [31.1.1942], Archive Marburg (now in CEGES/SOMA, Brussels), *Film XIV*, p.124, note 56; quoted also in Serge Klarsfeld and Maxime Steinberg, *Die Endlösung der Judenfrage in Belgien. Dokumente*, (New York 1981), p. 12. For an overview of the developments towards Jewish forced organizations in France, Belgium and The Netherlands see: Michman, "De oprichting van de 'Joodsche Raad voor Amsterdam' vanuit een vergelijkend perspectief", pp. 75-100.

42 Dan Michman, "Preparing for Occupation? A Nazi Sicherheitsdienst Document of Spring 1939 on the Jews of Holland", *Studia Rosenthaliana* 32/2 (1998), pp. 173-189.

43 See: Dan Michman, "Why Did Heydrich Write the Schnellbrief? A Remark on the Reason and on its Significance", *Yad Vashem Studies* 32 (2004), pp. 438-440.

44 See document relating to this order in Michman, "Preparing for Occupation?", p. 179.

45 Menachem Shelach, "Serbia", in: Idem (ed.-in-chief), *Toledot Hashoa: Yugoslavia* [*A History of the Holocaust: Yugoslavia*], (Jerusalem, 1990), p. 76 (Hebrew).

46 Richter to von Killinger, "Aktennotiz, Betr. Unterredung mit dem Stv. Ministerpräsident Mihai Antonescu am 12.12.1941", December 15, 1941, *Yad Vashem Archives*, TR-3/573.

47 Claudia Steur, *Theodor Dannecker Jodenvervolging: Funktionär der Endlösung*, (Stuttgart 1977).

48 An exception is Ulrich Herbert's fine biography of Werner Best, a leading personality both in France and Denmark, although Herbert's main focus is not on explaining the Holocaust in Western Europe; see Ulrich Herbert, *Best: Biographischen Studien über Radikalismus, Weltanschauung und Vernunft, 1903-1989*, (Munich 2016) (new edition).

49 In this context Saul Friedländer's 2-volume comprehensive history has to be mentioned: he definitely integrates a Jewish perspective into his narrative, yet his emphasis is on the individual Jews, and only in a limited way on Jewish society; see: Saul Friedländer, *Nazi Germany and the Jews: The Years of Persecution, 1933-1939*, (New York 1997); *The Years of Extermination: Nazi Germany and the Jews, 1939-1945*, (New York, 2007).

50 An important attempt to present a broad view of this kind is the above-mentioned 16-volume project of annotated documents *Verfolgung und Ermordung der europäischen Juden durch das nationalsozialistischen Deutschland 1933-1945*, though this project has excluded developments in North Africa under Vichy, Italy and Germany.

Dina Porat

The Jachin and Boaz of Holocaust Research: Israel Gutman and Yehuda Bauer on the Uniqueness of the Holocaust

I would like to start out by quoting Eliezer Schweid of the Hebrew University of Jerusalem regarding the subject in general:

> We begin by citing a fact obvious to all readers of the wide-ranging literature on the Shoah: Philosophers have no monopoly on the question of whether the Shoah was a completely aberrant, unprecedented event that cannot be compared with any other historical or contemporary occurrence, or whether it can be discussed together with other attempts at genocide, especially with contemporary outbreaks of mass killing. Almost everyone who studies the Shoah addresses this question seriously…[1]

Indeed, a stormy debate has been underway over the past two decades in the research world, with reverberations in society at large, over the question of whether the Holocaust was a unique historical event – meaning, an event possessing unique attributes that are characteristic of it alone – or a genocide that, although extreme, should nonetheless be located on the continuum of genocides that occurred before and after it.[2] Put differently: Should the Holocaust be examined exclusively as an event that was planned and carried out against the Jewish People and regarded as a national catastrophe and a Jewish tragedy alone? Or should it be studied as an event whose implications transcend the unique context of a specific national group of victims and that holds international significance from which we can also derive lessons on a human and universal level?

In this article, I will try to examine the views of Israel Gutman (who passed away in 2013) and Yehuda Bauer (may he have a long life) – the Jachin and Boaz of Holocaust research, who were active in Israel in the decades following the Holocaust – on these questions in general, and the question of the uniqueness of the Holocaust in particular, even before the onset of the abovementioned debate. I will also explore the possible implications of their conclusions for the current research. To conclude, I will attempt to propose a third possibility: that there is no fundamental contradiction between these two approaches – the view of the Holocaust as wholly unique and the view of the Holocaust as an extreme and unprecedented event on the continuum – and that an effort should at least be made to bring them closer together. This third possibility is proposed here with the utmost caution, and with due consideration of whether it is reasonable to propose a synthesis in the case in question. We have learned from Georg W.F. Hegel that the wave that follows thesis and antithesis is synthesis, and that the pendulum stimulating the research swings from one side to the other and back again, at least until midpoint. However, based on an examination of the writings of Gutman and Bauer, who sometimes relate to the possibility of synthesis, can we say that these two approaches are actually two sides of the same coin and that they complete one another? After all, uniqueness does not preclude us from relating to and closely examining other events, and we are also capable of proposing formulations such as "an unprecedented event with unique characteristics."

As we are dealing with the years immediately following the Holocaust – both Gutman and Bauer began writing and publishing in the 1950s – we can perhaps ask whether there is any significance to the fact that Gutman was a survivor who experienced a number of the circles of hell during the Holocaust – in the Warsaw Ghetto, in Auschwitz, and in Majdanek – whereas Bauer's family immigrated with him to Palestine from Prague in 1939, on the eve of the war. Could it be that Holocaust survivors hold a certain view on the subject under discussion that differs from that of those who lived in a safe place during the Holocaust? This is a sensitive question due to the broader question that underlies it, pertaining to the impact of the life circumstances of the historian or scholar on his or her conclusions. "Leaving the event as an unexplained and unresearched event fulfills Holocaust survivors' deep mental need to give expression to their feeling that what happened to them was unique in intensity and scope," writes one Yad Vashem employee who has been in consistent contact with survivors for many years.[3] Of course, historians, and survivors in general, devote themselves to researching and explaining the Holocaust and to not leaving it as an event that is unexplained and unresearched. Still, the question remains: Did the experiences of the two scholars that are the focus of this article lead them with greater vigor to the conclusion that the Holocaust was unique, or to the opposite conclusion? Another question that emerges from the period under discussion here is whether devotion to the Zionist idea, and to the aspiration within Israel of building research and teaching that is consistent with this idea, had an impact on the conclusions.

The possible influences on the research also include interpersonal relations, as work relations and friendship/rivalry have always existed in academia and among scholars in general, although such relations do not necessarily correspond with the differences in perspective. Gutman and Bauer would meet up with Abba Kovner and talk. All three were members of kibbutzim of Hashomer Hatzair, and questions pertaining to Jewish history and the fate of the Jewish People were pressing for all three. Bauer and Gutman were close friends for a number of decades, and together they established a number of infrastructure enterprises in the field of Holocaust research. Kovner was an inspiration for both men. Their personal relationship, however, did not require fundamental agreement between them, and they disagreed on a number of key issues, including a particularly extended difference of opinion regarding the uniqueness of the Holocaust. In other words, their views have neither been consistent with nor determined by interpersonal relations; toward the end of the article I return to the question of whether their views interface with their histories as individuals.

Gutman's Approach: Uniqueness

Gutman categorically opposed defining the Holocaust as an ongoing general phenomenon or framework and locating it on a continuum of genocides that occurred before and after it. It cannot be included on a continuum of other murders that were perpetrated for territorial, religious, or ethnic reasons, Gutman maintained. "The more I have explored the subject over the decades, the more I have come to recognize the uniqueness of the Holocaust, which cannot be turned into another episode in history."[4] Nazi antisemitism also cannot be seen merely as the most extreme link in the phenomenon of antisemitism, he noted. The Nazis undoubtedly exploited the negative image that had been instilled by the church for many centuries prior to the emergence of the Nazi party, and the Jew's transformation into a Satan that opposes humanity, which, unlike all other cases in history, continued for thousands of years and served as a backdrop for murder. However, in addition to the consistent elements of antisemitism, Nazism also mobilized new and different components; first and foremost was the Jews' placement "beyond the realm of humanity" and "their physical, spiritual, and cultural eradication…as a necessity in clearing a path for the redemption of humanity." This total and apocalyptic removal was one of a kind.

> The Holocaust's uniqueness stems from the role of antisemitism in general, and of racial antisemitism in particular, in the worldview of Hitler and National Socialism, and from the stages of the implementation of this worldview in the Nazi Third Reich and in the course of the war. The Holocaust is an event that stands alone in the history of humanity, which is why it has been so difficult for Jews and non-Jews alike to understand and internalize it.[5]

Gutman expounded his outlook in two lectures that subsequently became key articles: "The Holocaust and its Impact on Jewish History"[6] and "Notes and Reflections for a Discussion on the Uniqueness and Universal Nature of the Holocaust,"[7] a title that says simply that the uniqueness and the universal nature of the Holocaust go hand in hand with and complete one another, as "the dimensions of the crime alone endow it general human significance that transcends the history of one nation."[8] After examining the attributes of the totalitarian regimes in his articles, Gutman quotes Saul Friedländer, who wrote:

> The absolute character of the anti-Jewish drive makes it impossible to integrate the extermination of the Jews not only within the general framework of Nazi persecution, but also within the wider

aspects of contemporary ideological-political behavior, such as fascism, totalitarianisms, economic exploitations, and so forth.[9]

Gutman's argument also finds support in Nathan Rotenstreich's words on the uniqueness of the persecution of the Jews: "Even if the Holocaust can be viewed as the height of persecutions implemented against the Jews by the nations of the world," we cannot "ignore the fact that the Holocaust is a special type of persecution, and that the difference between the persecutions is a genuinely qualitative one."[10] In addition, with regard to the fundamentally anti-Jewish foundation of Nazism, Rotenstreich asks whether the Holocaust is a unique phenomenon constituting a type in itself, and answers his question as follows: "It seems to me that despite the proximity between traditional antisemitism and National Socialist antisemitism, it is the latter that is a unique phenomenon."[11]

The same is true of the work of Ben-Zion Dinur. Indeed, in accordance with his well-known study "Diasporas and Their Destruction," in which he analyzes the cyclicality of the destruction of Jewish centers and the construction of others, during the Holocaust Dinur believed that the cyclicality of the destruction was part of the affliction of exile, and therefore that the Holocaust was not a new episode in our history: "It is new in its form and its scope, and its calculated organization and its menacing dimensions, but not at all in its essence."[12] However, after the Holocaust, when the intensity of the loss and the tragedy became clear, he wrote:

> And nonetheless, what happened to us was unique and completely different. It is something that has never before occurred. Never before has the blood of an entire nation been abandoned with this being proclaimed publically. Before the eyes of the entire world, we were removed from the human race. Before the eyes of the entire world, we were executed and destroyed using all means and all methods. We should see things as they are and not conceal them.[13]

Jacob Talmon explored European history as the backdrop for the Holocaust and reached the same conclusion:

…the world has never seen such a campaign of annihilation. Not
an outburst of forces of wild religious extremism, not a wave of
pogroms initiated from above, not the act of an incited mob…
but rather the act of a "legal" government that handed over
an entire people to murderers…That is how this campaign of
extermination differed completely from all other massacres, mass
murders, and acts of spilling blood and forsaking life in history…
The Nazis' extermination of the Jews of Europe is different and
deviates from all of these mass killings [previously referred to by
Talmon] in the conscious, detailed, and precise planning that
preceded it and in its systematic implementation; in the absence of
a factor of emotional outburst; in the meticulously implemented
decision to destroy everything, without leaving a trace; and in the
prevention of any possibility of someone escaping when his turn
came to be killed.[14]

After drawing on the writings of colleagues, Gutman sums up by stating that
the Holocaust differed from similar crimes and constituted an unprecedented
event in Jewish history and the history of the world in that it was an attempt at
the total murder of a people, grounded in ancient antisemitism and carried out
with meticulous planning, as the world bore witness to the murder.

Obfuscating the uniqueness of the Holocaust, or integrating it into
a long list of crimes, even when done with good intentions, helps
distort the historical picture…Understanding and remembering
this uniqueness are the vaccine against the crime.

And he continues with greater force: "The Holocaust is an act that is included
in the complex of crimes that have been defined as genocide, but genocide does
not say all there is to say about the ideological basis of 'the Final Solution for
the Jewish People'," even as defined in the UN Convention on the Prevention of
Genocide.[15] When they speak of genocide, he emphasizes, they are talking about
something that has happened and that will happen again – wars and murders

have occurred in human society since its inception; in this way, they negate the murder of the Jews, which by nature was a singular event.[16] According to Gutman, the Jews had no way of escaping the repercussions of racial theory, because no change of name, profession, or place –or even assimilation or conversion to Christianity – were of any help. On the contrary, religious conversion was viewed as an attempt to infiltrate and corrupt the Aryan race.

The evil spirit that gripped Germany at the time precludes us from speaking about ordinary people, Gutman maintains, with regard to the title of Christopher Browning's book *Ordinary Men*,[17] which became a turn of phrase and a term that Gutman totally opposed. He thought that the opposite was true: that the continuously intensifying dynamics of political and military power, the course of which was dictated by ideology, resulted in the murder of the Jewish People being assigned supreme importance in the Nazis' priorities; in practice, it became one of the main war aims that an entire nation was trained to implement with cruelty so chilling that those involved cannot be characterized as ordinary people.[18] Gutman was the editor in chief of the Encyclopedia of the Holocaust, in which he wrote the entry for "Genocide":

> According to all the experts, genocide was one component of the Holocaust. However, the crime that the Nazis committed against the Jewish people in Europe involved planning; the administration of a system; the construction of extermination facilitates; the forced transfer of the entire Jewish population in underhanded ways; and, above all else, assigning them [the Jews] blame and the stigma of conspirators and pests, whose physical extermination was required for the rehabilitation of society and the future of humanity. In this way, it alone constitutes a distinct type of crime that is broader and more all-encompassing than genocide.[19]

The approach of Gutman and his supporters can perhaps therefore be summed up in the following sentence: It was the uniqueness of Nazi ideology's approach to the Jews and its horrific implementation in reality that made the Holocaust unique.

Yehuda Bauer's Approach: The Holocaust as an Unprecedented Event

Yehuda Bauer's approach to the subject developed over time. His initial remarks reflect complexity and uncertainty, which found expression in a number of his writings. This has been pointed out, for example, by Yair Auron, a scholar of the Armenian genocide, who notes that Bauer regards the Armenian genocide as the closest parallel to the Holocaust, but distinguishes between "genocide" on the one hand, and "Holocaust," or total extermination, on the other hand, meaning that total extermination did not occur: "Not to see the difference between the concepts, not to realize that the Jewish situation was unique, is to blur history," writes Bauer,

> On the other hand, to declare that there are no parallels, and that the whole phenomenon is inexplicable, *is equally a mystification* [emphasis added – the original Hebrew text reads: "is also a mistake, one of mystification"]…To view the Holocaust as just another case of man's inhumanity to man, to equate it with every and any injustice committed on this earth…to say that the Holocaust is the total of all the crimes committed by Nazism in Europe, to do any or all of this is an inexcusable abomination *based on the mystification of the event* [the original Hebrew text reads: " abomination that blurs the event"]. On the other hand, to view it as totally unique is to take it out of history and out of the context of our everyday lives, and that means opening wide the gates for a possible repetition. We should properly use the term "Holocaust" to describe the policy of total physical annihilation of a nation or a people. To date, this has happened once, to the Jews under Nazism.

Therefore, at the time, at the beginning of the 1980s, Bauer preferred to make use of the term "epoch making," and also introduced a similar term: "alpine event." These original terms were not integrated into the discourse on the definition of the Holocaust, but they constitute a stage in Bauer's thinking about the event; and a few pages later, Bauer also makes perhaps the first use of the term an "unprecedented event."[20]

Other scholars have also addressed the development of Bauer's later thinking in the 1990s. Eliezer Schweid, who analyzed the situation using the chisel of the philosopher, wrote:

> The cautious and precise among the scholars who maintain that the Holocaust was an exceptional and unprecedented event (here we refer especially to the worldview of Yehuda Bauer, according to its most recent version) acknowledge that although we can also find similar foundations…in other attempts at genocide, only in the Nazi attempt to murder the Jewish people, based on Nazi ideology, do we find these features playing a central, exclusive, and unadulterated role. Therefore, even if the Holocaust can be placed on a continuum of the execution of such plans, it is located at the end of the continuum, as the complete embodiment of the meaning of the concept of genocide – in terms of ideology, planning and execution – and must therefore also be characterized as exceptional and unique within it.[21]

We will return to the matter of similar foundations later in this article. In the meantime, we take note of Schweid's recognition of the caution and precision that characterized the development of Bauer's thinking in his aspiration to find the exact formulation. We also emphasize that according to Schweid's formulation, "exceptional" and "unprecedented" are adjectives that are mutually complementary, as opposed to contradictory, which was also the view of philosopher Emil Fackenheim.[22]

A second scholar who addressed the development of Bauer's later thinking is A. Dirk Moses of the University of Sydney, who pays significant attention to the writings of Yehuda Bauer and Steven T. Katz during the 1990s and reaches the conclusion that they locate the Holocaust at the heart of Jewish life and Jewish identity. Therefore, they must necessarily resolutely insist on the uniqueness of the Holocaust, as not doing so would undermine their individual identities and their concept of collective Jewish existence. The significance that Katz and Bauer ascribe to the Holocaust has no basis, he writes, if the Holocaust is "just" another instance of mass murder that highlights human history. In his view, they also ascribe theological significance to the Holocaust, endowing its victims, and its victims alone, with the status of sanctity.[23] This is Moses's major argument, which he does not always develop out of respect for Katz and Bauer and their perspectives, particularly when disregarding the possibility that the linkage between Jewish identity and Holocaust memory, which all recognize, does not require us to reach the conclusion that the Holocaust was unique. Katz vehemently objects to this erroneous presentation of his views, which is not based on excerpts from his writing, and in decisive remarks that were recently published[24] again stresses his unequivocal position that the Holocaust was unique – not for theological reasons or due to a mystification of the event and its victims, nor due to his support for Jewish identity after the Holocaust, but rather based on his research as a historian and a phenomenologist. Katz disagrees with Bauer but emphasizes that the latter is a secular man who led a movement for secular Judaism, and that he also decisively rejects all mystification and theological meaning like that assigned by Elie Wiesel. Katz notes that additional scholars have adopted Moses' approach without evaluating it and shows, ironically, that even they cannot avoid expressions such as "exceptionality" and "extremity" in their discussion; they too are unable to escape the uniqueness of the Holocaust.[25]

In remarks made at a conference held by the Israel Academy of Sciences and Humanities in 2012, Bauer presented a refined summary of the view to which he arrived after years of thought, out of the anxiety that has accompanied his studies and his activity in international organizations and that guides his analysis – the Holocaust, despite its extreme nature, has not prevented subsequent murders; the twentieth century was a bloody century during which many tens of millions of civilians were murdered (it is difficult to estimate exactly how many); and who knows how many will be murdered in the century that follows.[26] First, he spoke about a subject that is close to his heart and that he repeatedly emphasizes: the issue of suffering. It is clear that all survivors of genocide each focus on their own suffering and that a competition of victimhood prevails among them, which he believes constitutes a cover for political interests and attempts to profit from the status of the victim and runs counter to all moral and historical perception. Second, he addressed the question of comparison: suffering, torture, and sadism cannot be ranked, he argued, because no genocide is any better or easier than another. In the event that scholars are trying to identify parallels between genocides, they must also identify the differences between them, which can only be done through comparison. Comparison is particularly essential for Holocaust Studies, as it alone can clarify the extent to which the Holocaust has unique foundations.

The question of the unique foundations of the Holocaust led Bauer to examine the factors resulting in genocide and to ask whether there are certain factors or elements that led to or were present in the Holocaust and that have not been found together in other genocides. He enumerates these factors as follows:

1. Totality – The aim of identifying and killing all Jews, down to the last one.

2. Universality – That is on a universal scale, everywhere in the world – first in Europe and then around the globe. Indeed, many peoples, or segments of many peoples, were party to the execution of the Holocaust.

3. The absence of rational motivating factors – There were no practical, economic, military, or political motivations for the murder of the Jews as there were in other cases of genocide. After all, Jewish property was already in German hands prior to the murder, and neither in Germany nor in any other country did the Jews constitute a threat. The main motivating factor was irrational ideology that was detached from reality and from German interests. Even when economic, military, and other considerations ran counter to the ideology, the latter had the upper hand. Here, we can perhaps add to Bauer's assertions that this ideology created – particularly among a fanatical group – a surreal and unfounded picture of the world promoted by a leader for whom the fear of the Jews became an obsession, and who swept up almost all of society, as if he were a messiah striving for redemption by eradicating the Jews.

4. Racial theory – The surreal race theory that brought about the Holocaust required the physical and intellectual eradication of the Jews because they constituted a biological antithesis as well as an antithesis in principle: it was a case of intentional destruction of an entire culture, or of a principle – the principle of equality – and of those who brought to the world democracy, liberalism, and men's equality before God, all of which run counter to race theory based on inequality. And again we might add: when we speak of genocide we are limiting the actions of the Germans and their collaborators to murder, whereas the Holocaust involved the systematic destruction of an entire culture, as well as intentional harassment, isolation and dispossession, discrimination, and abuse that eased the subsequent murder.

5. Industrialized murder in the heart of Europe – The Holocaust involved planned murder not perpetrated in an outburst of fury but rather in a level-headed manner with special attention to detail, in offices and through bureaucracy, and systematically, using a system that had never been tried on such a scale.

6. A point that Bauer has referred to on other occasions – The nature of the victim, and the civilization the Jews created throughout the generations, are what caused the uniquely obsessive approach toward them and their perception as the polar opposite of everything the Nazis stood for. This, it should be added, is perhaps the greatest compliment the Jewish People could ask for.

In Bauer's view, each of the six components he presents together in order to oppose the notion of uniqueness also appear separately in the murder of other peoples, such that none are unique to the Holocaust. As a result, the Holocaust is not unique in terms of its components but rather "unprecedented," as he has characterized it in recent decades, in that it involved all the components together. The Holocaust, therefore is the most extreme genocide – "the complete embodiment of the meaning of the concept of genocide," to use the words of Schweid. Bauer explains with candor that he examines these components from the Jewish perspective. "Viewing the Holocaust from the perspective of the Jewish victim is the main thing, and…doing so does not undermine in-depth exploration of the perpetrators of the crimes," he maintains. "Indeed, I am in favor of a Judeocentric view of the Holocaust," which is the title of one of his articles. At the same time, however, he again argues that this view does not necessitate the Holocaust's classification as unique, but rather as unprecedented.[27]

In a discussion that developed following Bauer's lecture, the respondents debated questions regarding the Holocaust's uniqueness and unprecedented nature. Dan Michman highlighted the path that led from the term unique to the term unprecedented and the fact that the Holocaust was much broader than simply murder; it was the destruction of an entire culture through severe all-encompassing measures, not murder alone, and therefore cannot be defined merely as genocide. Moreover, due to its scope and its depth, it cannot serve as a paradigm for other genocides, because it does not enable us to understand their variation. Next, Juergen Zimmerer asked how one exceptional case can be a scale for other cases; after all, long-standing multifaceted antisemitism is the core of the Holocaust, and no other genocides have been characterized by a comparable component. It is therefore necessary to take into account the uniqueness and singularity of antisemitism, and to understand that we can learn from the Holocaust without detracting from its specificity.[28]

The limited framework of this article precludes us from expanding our discussion into one on the general debate between the two views, as the writing on the subject, which continues today, is broad and rich, and scholars and philosophers have articulated views in both directions. For example, Raul Hilberg, Léon Poliakov, Elie Wiesel, Emil Fackenheim, Eberhard Jäckel, and Richard Rubenstein, each from his own perspective, all articulated the view that the Holocaust is unique,[29] and a younger generation has continued their arguments. For example, in their article on "the uniqueness of the Holocaust," Avishai Margalit and Gabriel Motzkin present the event's uniqueness as a human experience of a unique quality, based on the unique manner in which the Nazis linked humiliation and murder.[30]

On the other hand, there has been no lack of scholars who objected to the notion of uniqueness and debated its advocates; Irving L. Horowitz, for example, attacked the eight arguments listed by Fackenheim for the uniqueness of the Holocaust,[31] on the grounds that they are the product of theological thinking; and Wiesel's words on the world of the concentration camps that is located outside, if not beyond, history,[32] on the grounds that it reflects the mystical trend against which Bauer also spoke. Richard Evans defended himself against Helen Fine's charge that he played down the scope of genocides in general and focused only on the Holocaust: the Jewish genocide.[33] In the course of the historians' debate that took place in Germany in the mid-1980s, German historians also addressed the question of uniqueness, and a few, most notably Ernst Nolte, offered a long list of comparisons of genocides to the Holocaust, thereby expressing opposition to its uniqueness. As noted, these are only a few examples of the extensive literature on the subject.

Questions and Suggestions

We now return to the questions with which this article began, and we begin with the possibility that historians and philosophers who were survivors, and who worked in Israel during the era in which the Zionist enterprise was the motivating force behind the work overall, knew that the assertion of the Holocaust's uniqueness served to reinforce the feeling that a unique Jewish society was being built in Israel in its aftermath, and that the world needed to recognize the terrible injustice that had been caused to its brothers and sisters. It is true that historians, like all people, are molds of the landscape of their homelands; however, the fact that a long list of historians and philosophers who were working outside of Israel and were not obligated to the sentiments or the frameworks that emerged there have reached the conclusion that the Holocaust was unique, and have debated those who thought otherwise, indicates that this conclusion has stemmed from the research and the thinking of each scholar, and not necessarily from the needs of their surroundings.

Second, even if relating to the Holocaust as a unique phenomenon was characteristic of many of the philosophers and the historians working in Israel in the initial decades following the Holocaust and the establishment of the state, the tendency to view it as a link in the chain of genocides intensified over time, especially from the 1980s onward, following the genocide that occurred in Cambodia, and in the 1990s with the mass murders in Rwanda and Cambodia. A look at the debate that occurred in the research community of the 2000s reveals an increase in this tendency, especially in western universities, which are gradually abandoning the notion of the uniqueness of the Holocaust and have come to regard it as an anachronistic idea that confines understanding to a narrow horizon.[34] Debate among historians does not always stem from the heart of the academic research, as many scholars of the phenomenon of genocide are not familiar with the history of the Holocaust and are first introduced to the subject via engagement with varied disciplines and eras; debate has become an outcome of political interests and fashions.

Third, on the question of synthesis – the Holocaust's classification as unique in no way serves to disrespect or detract from the severity of other murders and atrocities or to exclude them from the discussion. On the contrary, deeper exploration of the histories of other genocides and their outcomes, and their comparison to the Holocaust, can result in empathy for the suffering of the other and a move away from the ranking of suffering. Bauer also believes that there is no contradiction between Jewish specificity and universality, as these are two sides of the same coin.[35] We can therefore say that there is no necessary contradiction between the research of the Holocaust as a unique phenomenon and the research of other murders, but rather completion and cross-fertilization, or synthesis, as suggested by the title of Gutman's article on "the uniqueness and universal nature of the Holocaust." Another title in this spirit was formulated by Michael Berenbaum, former director of the United States Holocaust Memorial Museum in Washington, for his article "The Uniqueness and Universality of the Holocaust," and Dan Stone has stressed that, even if he does not agree with them, a new generation of scholars is no longer taking part in the debate but rather pointing out the possibility of synthesis.[36]

Depicting the Holocaust as a unique event does not necessarily encompass a view of the event on a religious, ethical, metaphysical or mystical level, as Moses maintains, but rather is the outcome of its examination as a historical event which, like all historical events, has its own characteristics. It also does not necessarily stem from a Jewish and Israeli feeling that the Jewish People and its history are unique, but rather from the feeling, from the emotional realm, and the recognition, from the realm of logical analysis, that the Holocaust was such an exceptional event that it can be viewed as unique, regardless of the general Jewish self-perception. Jews during the Holocaust felt that the events occurring around them had never occurred before – that they were living on borrowed time in a world that had been turned upside down in a manner that could not be understood. It was a period of "sadistic tortures that even a tyrant of the Middle Ages would have been ashamed to publish…" wrote Chaim Kaplan of the Warsaw Ghetto. "This period, so full of darkness and catastrophe…is unparalleled since we became a people." It was darkness for humanity as a whole, not just for the Jewish People.[37] The same was true of Jews following the Holocaust:

> Members of this generation [following the Holocaust] do not allow themselves the perspective of distance, as they tend to regard the continued involvement from within as an absolute moral obligation resting on their shoulders…It was a consensus that was perceived as virtually self-evident by Jewish scholars of the Holocaust. It reflected the feeling, of members of the generation of Holocaust survivors, that what occurred went beyond all evil that could be expected from man, even against the backdrop of the Jewish People's history of trouble and calamity.[38]

Indeed, recognition of the uniqueness of the fate and the treatment of the Jewish People, whether living in the Land of Israel or not, is accompanied by a heavy feeling and is not self-evident. It also involves a sense of shared fate and the burden of responsibility for this fate. Is the assumption that the Holocaust is not part of this uniqueness, but rather an extreme genocide located on the continuum of genocides that occurred before and after it, not an attempt to escape this heavy feeling and to be part of a broader universal framework that is shared by many nations?

Bauer clearly defines his position on this subject and agrees that the attempt to say that the Jews are like all nations encompasses a dimension of escapism:

> All these universalizing attempts [regarding the Holocaust] seem to
> me to be, on the Jewish side, efforts by their authors to escape their
> Jewishness. They are expressions of a deep-seated insecurity; these
> people feel more secure when they can say 'we are just like all the
> others'. The Holocaust should have proven to them that the Jews
> were, unfortunately, not like the others. Obviously it did not.[39]

Dan Michman, who belongs to the intermediate generation of Holocaust scholars,
between that of Gutman and Bauer on the one hand and the third generation that
is active today on the other hand, related to this assumption as follows:

> Is the Holocaust one case of genocide and nothing more? I reject
> this assertion…The Holocaust is not the "genocide of the Jews."
> Defining it as such ignores and fails to understand the largely
> anti-Jewish activities that occurred in the era of the Third Reich,
> including what they referred to as de-Judaization…But also
> during the period of the murder itself – the genocide – there are
> features that are absent from all other cases of genocide…because
> there was uniqueness in the Holocaust… Characterization of the
> Holocaust as "unique" has come under attack in recent years by
> various researchers, but I am not afraid of it.[40]

To accentuate his words, he drew attention to a basic aspect that was neglected
in the heat of the debate: the dictionary's definition of the adjective "unique," as
it appears for example in the Oxford dictionary, as "the only one of its kind" and
"very special or unusual." According to this definition, unique is not an absolute
term. Therefore, Michman continues, it does not necessarily mean that it is
detached or not comparable, but rather that it "possesses extremely exceptional
characteristics, and not because it belongs to me and not the other."[41]

Michman also noted the immense interest in the Holocaust that continues
to grow: Bauer repeatedly emphasizes that if the Holocaust were unique, there
is no reason to research or address it, as uniqueness means singular – that it will
not repeat itself, and it can be left behind our wall. However, uniqueness is the

reason for the great interest in the Holocaust, which today is tenfold what it was decades ago when scholars laid the foundations for this research in Israel and elsewhere. At the time, we – members of the intermediate generation – were still students of the first. The Holocaust is fascinating and intriguing to explore precisely because it is an exceptional event pertaining to the Jewish People, but also one that holds universal human meaning and has implications for all realms of individual and public life: leadership, the sweeping-up of society, ideology and power, people at moments of spiritual elevation and decline, loss and destruction, sophisticated killing mechanisms, and war lasting years and claiming victims on an incomprehensible scale – all of which still lie at the heart of individual and public life today, 75 years after the tragedy known as World War II came to an end. As recently formulated by Nigel Pleasants, who advocates the uniqueness of the Holocaust: "We are haunted by the Holocaust precisely because there is reason to say it is unique."[42]

Befitting an intermediate generation, Michman seeks the path of synthesis, showing that Yad Vashem's selection of Christopher Browning to write its volume on the evolution and implementation of the Final Solution is indicative of the need for synthesis, which can occur only when the debate is bona fide and not conducted out of political rivalry and not out of an agenda that fuels opposition, against anyone who advocates uniqueness, that at times seems genuinely personal for the scholars from the field of genocide. According to Michman, Browning's book constitutes a bridge between the approach advocating uniqueness and the approach tending toward universality, and proves that synthesis is possible.[43]

In conclusion, Bauer has said that Abba Kovner wrote his "Epilogue to the Historians" with him in mind, as a result of their close relationship.[44] Kovner, whose testimony in the Eichmann Trial stressed that he could tell the truth and nothing but the truth, but not the whole truth, sought to engage in in-depth and unbiased research that was as objective as possible and that was based on documentation and study. However, "it seems to me," he wrote,

> that behind all the documents is a hard core, things that are
> difficult to decipher because it means taking a risk that we will do

more harm than good, and that it is best to leave them unclear, as they are, troubling and burning with questions, forever…It is doubtful whether those who think that they are capable of coming to know the whole truth about the Holocaust – of comprehending the meaning of existence in the avalanche and annihilation, and of proposing a solution to the riddle of the human motivations for their destruction and their survival, based on information they have accumulated or on their own judgment – actually understand that the Holocaust was a Holocaust.[45]

But despite this warning, Bauer, and Gutman, each in his own way, continued searching for the answers to the burning questions, proposing solutions and explanations for one of the most enigmatic and highly debated events in human history and attempting to understand that the Holocaust was a Holocaust.

Endnotes

1   Eliezer Schweid, "Is the Shoah a Unique Event?" in Steven T. Katz, Shlomo Biderman, and Gershon Greenberg (eds.), *Wrestling with God: Jewish Theological Responses during and after the Holocaust* (Oxford University Press, 2007), p. 221.

2   One example of this debate is the controversy that erupted around an international conference on genocide that was held at the Hebrew University of Jerusalem on June 29, 2016.

3   Ehud Amir "The Uniqueness of the Holocaust,"*Alachson* 16 (July 2017) (Hebrew).

4   Quoted in Dina Porat, "The Jerusalem School," *Haaretz, Books*, February 4, 2009 (Hebrew).

5   Israel Gutman, "The Impact of the Holocaust on Jewish History," *Newsletter: The World Union of Jewish Studies* 23 (1984), pp. 14, 27-32 (Hebrew).

6   Ibid.

7   Gutman, "Notes and Reflections for a Discussion on the Uniqueness and Universal Nature of the Holocaust," *Yalkut Moreshet* 28 (1979), pp. 77-94 (Hebrew).

8   Ibid., p. 77.

9   Saul Friedlander, *Some Aspects of the Historical Significance of the Holocaust* (Jerusalem, 1977), p. 7.

10 See Nathan Rotenstreich, *On Jewish Existence in This Era* (Merhavia and Tel Aviv, 1972), pp. 111-112 (Hebrew).

11 Nathan Rotenstreich, *Holocaust and Revival: A Symposium* (Jerusalem, 1975), pp. 124-134 (Hebrew).

12 Ben-Zion Dinur, "Diasporas and Their Destruction," in *Generations and Records* (Jerusalem, 1978), p. 175 (Hebrew).

13 Ben-Zion Dinur, "Our Fate and Our War in These Times," in *Remember: The Holocaust and Its Lesson* (Jerusalem, 1958), p. 36 (Hebrew).

14 Jacob Talmon, "European History as Background for the Holocaust," in *In the Era of Violence* (Tel Aviv, 1975), pp. 265-266 (Hebrew). Gutman does not quote Talmon.

15 Gutman, "Notes and Reflections," pp. 79 and 92, see points of conclusion.

16 In conversation with Gutman while preparing the critique in Porat, "The Jerusalem School."

17 Christopher Browning, *Ordinary Men: Reserve Battalion 101 and the Final Solution in Poland* (New York, 1993).

18 Gutman, "Notes and Reflections," p. 23.

19 Israel Gutman (ed.), *Encyclopedia of the Holocaust*, Vol. 2 (Tel Aviv, 1990), pp. 391-392 (Hebrew). The entry was written by Gutman and Marion Mushkat.

20 Yehuda Bauer, "Against Mystification: The Holocaust as a Historical Phenomenon," in *The Holocaust; Historical Aspects* (Tel Aviv, 1982), pp. 75-76 (Hebrew). Unprecedented: p. 81.

21 Eliezer Schweid, *Battle until Dawn* (Tel Aviv, 1991), p. 146 (Hebrew).

22 See Emil Fackenheim, "The 'Shoa' as a Novum for History, Philosophy, and Theology," *Daat: A Journal of Jewish Philosophy & Kabbalah* 15 (1985), pp. 121-129 (Hebrew).

23 A. Dirk Moses, "Conceptual Blockages and Definitional Dilemmas in the 'Racial Century': Genocides and Indigenous People and the Holocaust," *Patterns of Prejudice* 36(4) (2002), p.13.

24 Steven T. Katz, *The Holocaust and New World Slavery: A Comparative History* (Cambridge University Press, 2019).

25 See Katz's response to Moses in ibid., pp. 13-17. Katz addresses the arguments of Donald Bloxham and Dan Stone which appear repeatedly in their writings.

26 Bauer, "Holocaust and Genocide," remarks delivered at the opening of the symposium on the Holocaust and genocide (Jerusalem, September 2-4, 2012), published in *Igeret* (publication of the Israel Academy of Science and Humanities) 34 (December 2012), pp. 34-39 (Hebrew). In his lectures, Bauer repeatedly quotes Rudolph J. Rummel, who examined the numbers of those who were killed during the twentieth century. See Rudolph J. Rummel, *Statistics of Democide: Genocide and Mass Murder since 1900* (Charlottesville, VA, 1997).

27 See my and Dalia Ofer's interview with Bauer in this issue, as well as Bauer's response to Daniel Blatman in *Haaretz*, August 16, 2019 (Hebrew).

28 Michman's and Zimmerer's remarks were not published but can be found in the video footage of the academic conference that was uploaded to YouTube.

29 See, for example, Richard Rubenstein, *The Cunning of History* (New York, 1975).

30 Avishai Margalit and Gabriel Motzkin, "The Uniqueness of the Holocaust," *Philosophy and Public Affairs* 25(1) (Winter 1996), pp.65-83.

31 See Moses, "Conceptual Blockages and Definitional Dilemmas in the 'Racial Century'."

32 Elie Wiesel, "Now We Know," in Richard Arens (ed.), *Genocide in Paraguay* (Temple University Press, 1976), p. 165; Irving Louis Horowitz, "Taking Lives, Genocide and the Reconstruction of Social Theory," *Armenian Review* 37(1) (Spring 1984), p. 2.

33 Richard J. Evans, *In Hitler's Shadow: West German Historians and their Attempt to Escape from the Nazi Past* (Tel Aviv, 1991), p. 38 (in Hebrew).

34 See Moses, "Conceptual Blockages and Definitional dilemmas in the 'Racial Century'."

35 Conversation with Bauer when preparing the critique in Porat, "The Jerusalem School."

36 Michael Berenbaum (ed.), *A Mosaic of Victims: Non-Jews Persecuted and Murdered by the Nazis* (New York University Press, 1990); Dan Stone, "The History of Genocide: Beyond 'Uniqueness' and Ethnic Competition," *The Journal of Theory and Practice* 8(1) (2004), pp.127-142. See "the new generation" in the executive summary.

37 Chaim Kaplan, *Scroll of Agony: The Warsaw Diary of Chaim A. Kaplan* (Indiana University Press, 1999), November 5 and December 17, 1939, pp. 64 and 88.

38 Schweid, *Battle until Dawn*, pp. 143, 267.

39 Yehuda Bauer, "A Past that will not go away," in: Michael Berenbaum and Abraham J. Peck (eds), *The Holocaust and History* (Indiana University Press, 1998), p. 20.

40 Dan Michman, "Researching and Teaching Holocaust and Genocide in the Context of Conflict and Trauma," lecture delivered at the fifth biennial conference of the International Network of Genocide Scholars, June 29, 2016.

41 Ibid.

42 Nigel Pleasants, "The Question of the Holocaust's Uniqueness: Was it Something More Than or Different from Genocide?" *Journal of Applied Philosophy* 33(3) (August 2016), p. 297.

43 See Michman's article in this issue of *Moreshet Journal*.

44 See my and Dalia Ofer's interview of Bauer in this issue.

45 Abba Kovner, *On a Narrow Bridge: Essays*, edited by Shalom Luria (Tel Aviv, 1980), p. 224 (Hebrew).

Esther Webman

Is there an Arab historiography of the Holocaust?

The Arab discourse on the Holocaust deals little if at all with the events of the Holocaust itself. Arab intellectuals, academics and journalists have not demonstrated a significant interest in the processes that led to the Nazis' decision to exterminate the Jews and have rarely referred to the acts of murder themselves. They have not taken an interest in the experiences of the victims in the ghettos or in the concentration and death camps, in the ways of survival of the Jews, or the inhumane and dead-end dilemmas they faced. There has been no systematic engagement in studies or reports, but rather an eclectic reference to events and a focus on their repercussions. It might be said that an authentic discourse has developed without a coherent narrative in parallel to the Western and the Soviet discourses.

The public Arab discussion has not addressed the historiographic debates about the Holocaust and its meaning, and it has not accepted the limits of its representation in the Western discourse. Rather, it has focused on the Holocaust's political implications for the Arab-Israeli conflict and for the status of Israel and Zionism. Referring to the Holocaust as part of the ongoing debate with Israel and Zionism, Arab writers from all ideological streams have adopted a set of terms, ideas, concepts, and arguments that have fueled and reinforced one another for more than seventy years, creating a well-defined intellectual and ideological climate and discourse on the Holocaust. These elements have also been reflected in the Arab academic field. Unlike Holocaust research in the West, which became a fully-fledged field in the study of history, the Holocaust was never subject to comprehensive Arab research as was Zionism, Judaism, and Israel, which have been extensively researched, often with a clear ideological bias and frequent obfuscation of the difference between academic and polemic writing. Scholar Hassan Barari, who has explored scholarship on Israel in the Arab world, argues that Arab scholarship has not contributed any real insight to

Israel studies and that it is burdened by bias, ideological distortion, predisposition, and the need to expose rather than to understand or explain the 'other'. The Arab writing on Israel has to a great extent been fueled by the ongoing Arab-Israeli conflict and is "more of a tool of resistance against Israel than a mechanism for understanding."[1] Although Barari does not address the Arabs' approach to the Holocaust, his assessment is applicable to this issue as well.

The main argument of the current article is that there is no Arab historiography of the Holocaust itself. Still, the many references to the Holocaust in Arab public discourse create narratives that permeate and settle in the collective consciousness, and in some senses these narratives in themselves constitute a historiography of sorts. Thus, we can distinguish between two periods: until the 1990s, and from the 1990s onward. The first period was characterized by alienation from and lack of interest in the Holocaust; not only was there no Arab scholarship on the subject and no translations of western – not to mention Israeli – academic literature, but books by Holocaust deniers were translated and published in Arabic soon after their publication, providing reinforcement to studies challenging the Zionist and the western narrative on the subject. In the 1990s, as a result of a shift in the public discourse on the representation of the Holocaust and its impact on general political perceptions, Arab scholars began engaging in new research topics, which did not focus on the Holocaust but nonetheless related to it as an undisputed historical fact. These studies have dealt with two major issues: Arab attitudes toward the Holocaust, and the link between the Palestinian Nakba and the Holocaust.

The current article is based largely on a study that reviewed a wide range of academic and non-academic works, as well as newspapers and periodicals published since the end of World War II that made mention of the Holocaust.[2] The article is divided into four parts: the first part briefly reviews the major themes in the representation of the Holocaust in the Arab public discourse; the second part deals with the indirect discussion of the Holocaust in the historiographical literature on Zionism, the Jews, and the Palestinian Nakba; the third part examines the changes in the writing on the Holocaust since the early 1990s; and the fourth part tackles the question of why there is no Arab historiography of the Holocaust.

Themes in Holocaust Representation in the Arab World

In Arab public consciousness, the immediate context of the Holocaust is the establishment of the state of Israel and its attempts to achieve legitimacy and consolidation. The Holocaust is perceived as a European matter that does not concern them and which they were not involved in perpetrating, but for which they continue to pay with the Palestinians' dispossession of their land. According to this view, the Jews were the true victors of World War II, whereas the Palestinians were the victims' victims. Zionism is perceived as cynically exploiting the Holocaust, or even as inventing it in order to achieve its goals. Concomitantly, it has imbued and nurtured the West with a sense of guilt, and extorts it financially and psychologically. The symbols of the Nazi era, its terminology, its caricatures, and its ideology are projected onto Zionism and Israel, transforming the Jews from victims into persecutors. From this point of departure, different approaches to the Holocaust have developed, ranging from recognition to denial. On this scale, we can identify the following themes:

1. Recognition
2. Justification of the Holocaust
3. Charges that Zionism collaborated with the Nazis in the extermination of European Jews
4. Equation between the ideology of Zionism and the ideology of Nazism, and between Israeli policy toward the Palestinians and the Nazi German policies toward the Jews
5. Reversal of the role of victim and criminal and the Palestinians' casting as the true victims of the Holocaust
6. Minimization of the dimensions of the Holocaust by denying the number of victims, the existence of the gas chambers, and the reason for the death of the Jews during the war
7. Relativization of the Holocaust, whether by comparing it to the number of other victims during the war or by placing it on the same level as other historical cases of genocide, such as the massacre of the Native Americans in America
8. Outright denial of the Holocaust and its representation as a Zionist invention.

Despite the Arabs' point of departure that the Holocaust ostensibly did not concern them, they could not avoid relating to it at the end of the war, when – as part of the international efforts to find a solution for the problem of the displaced persons and the "Jewish problem" – the idea of establishing a state for Jews in Mandate Palestine became more concrete than ever before. Already in 1964, Egyptian journalist and leftist intellectual Ahmad Baha' al-Din effectively defined the dilemma facing Arabs when relating to Jews and to the Jewish problem. "We Arabs found ourselves, against our will, party to all that is linked to Jews, including the story of antisemitism," he explained, adding:

> Because the Jews who have suffered for many years from persecutions…, which culminated in the gas chambers that Hitler built to annihilate the Jewish race, found that the only solution to their problem is…the establishment of a homeland and a state on the ruins of a million Arabs. In this way, without wanting to, we found ourselves forced to be attentive to everything said about the Jews and the Jewish problem.[3]

Baha' al-Din's words sum up the basic Arab approach to the Holocaust: it had nothing to do with them, but its repercussions ended up on their doorstep and they had no choice but to relate to it and to everything pertaining to the Jews.

The Holocaust, therefore, was perceived in Arab society as the primary factor in Zionism's success in achieving its goals, creating a direct linkage between it and the establishment of the state of Israel. Arabs' opposition to the establishment of the state impeded their ability and desire to recognize and sympathize with the tragedy of the Jews, and this distorted their historical view of the Holocaust and made it difficult to separate its moral aspects from what are perceived to be its political repercussions. The Arab discourse on the Holocaust has developed as part of the Arab-Israeli conflict and serves as an additional means for the construction of the negative image of the enemy: the 'other'. Moreover, the discourse on the Holocaust has become part of the intellectual discussion of issues on the public and political agenda in the Arab world, such as the future of the states in the region after the war; the nature of their regimes;

their attitude toward the West; their place in the new world order; and their cultural and social character.

From the outset this discourse contained clear contradictions. One example is the inherent contradiction between rejection of the Holocaust as irrelevant on the one hand, and its frequent mention in political discourse, even using a precise term – *al-Mahraqa*, on the other hand. Minimizing its scope to the point of denial has also stood in contradiction to its adoption as a benchmark for suffering and evil and to charges that Zionism played an active role in its execution, disclosing an admission of its occurrence. The Holocaust and Nazism has penetrated the public Arab consciousness as a metaphor and a paradigm of the embodiment of evil, as it has throughout the world, but not out of recognition of the uniqueness of the Jewish experience at Auschwitz.[4]

With the collapse of the Soviet Union, the beginning of the peace process, the signing of the Oslo Accords and the peace treaty between Israel and Jordan, and the emergence of ideas regarding a new world order, the mid-1990s witnessed the beginning of a wave of critical intellectual discourse regarding the state of the Arab world, which, unlike the previous waves of self-criticism, also related to the Holocaust and called for a reassessment of the Arab approach to it. This facilitated an open discussion of a new kind in Palestinian, Lebanese, and North African intellectual circles, which were later joined by Egyptian liberals supporting reforms and democratization, including globalization and a change in the conception of the conflict with Israel. They noted the contradictions in the traditional Arab approach to the Holocaust and the damage it has caused the Arab, and in particular the Palestinian cause, and called for separating the human and political aspects in the discussion of the Holocaust and for recognizing the suffering of the Jews as a crime against humanity. One of the prominent spokespeople of this approach has been liberal Lebanese journalist Hazim Saghiya, who holds that the traditional Arab approach – that the Holocaust "is none of our affair" – is the product of an erroneous understanding of European history, laziness, lack of curiosity, and a substantial degree of opportunism. The Arabs certainly cannot be viewed as responsible for the Holocaust, he noted, but if they want to be accepted into the international community, they need to recognize humanity's joint responsibility for the tragedy. In order to understand the world's sympathy for Israel, he argues, the Arabs must understand the Holocaust and demonstrate greater sensitivity toward it. Only in this manner can they also win sympathy for the Palestinian tragedy. Other articles in this spirit, including Edward Said's article on the "Bases of Coexistence," were published in 1997 and 1998, sparking a vigorous public discussion.

This new approach was influenced by the terminology and approaches to the Holocaust in the West, just as Holocaust denial and other motifs in Holocaust representation were influenced by western and Soviet literature. Many of its spokespeople live in the West, where they are exposed to the Holocaust's role in western culture, and, despite their limited number, they have succeeded in expanding the boundaries of the mainstream discourse, confining denial primarily to Islamist circles.

Thus, the taboo on discussion of the Holocaust in the Arab world was lifted at the end of the twentieth century, perhaps due to the time that had elapsed since the events themselves and to the fact that, in the era of satellite communication and the internet, it was more difficult to control and limit the flow of information. Calls for original Arab studies and for the dissemination of information on the Holocaust, as well as Arab visits to the extermination camps and to the United States Holocaust Museum in Washington, have become open and more frequent, and represent a marked change from the past. However, the open discussion of the Holocaust, not surprisingly, has also elicited a counter-reaction advocating active denial. Both streams recognize the Holocaust's importance to Jewish and Israeli identity and to western culture; however, whereas one identifies with those who view it as an event with universal moral implications and for actualizing national aspirations, the other continues to adhere to the view that the Holocaust is a tool employed by Zionism and Israel and that recognizing it hinders the realization of Palestinian national aspirations. This duality – recognition of the Holocaust as a criminal act against the Jewish People on the one hand, and the need to deny the Holocaust and to equate Zionism with racism on the other hand – is a major feature of the Arab discourse on the Holocaust. It is dictated by the political dynamics and the reality of the Arab-Israeli conflict, and it has found expression in the public discussion in the Arab media that has emerged in response to various affairs since the mid-1990s.[5]

Lack of Interest but Intensive Indirect Preoccupation with the Holocaust

The Arab public discourse on the Holocaust and its repercussions which appeared in the Arab press has also been reflected in the broad literature, written against the background of the Arab-Israeli conflict, on Zionism, its ostensive links to Nazism,[6] the Jews,[7] and World War II.[8] This literature has denied the Holocaust, blamed the Jews for its occurrence, justified Hitler's actions, and equated Zionism and Nazism on ideological and practical levels.

Holocaust denial began in the Arab World, independent of its development in the West, first and foremost in order to refute the Zionists' claims. Prior to 1948, most expressions of Holocaust denial were veiled and indirect. However, beginning in the 1950s, as the Arab-Israeli conflict intensified, they became more explicit. The Eichmann trial, which in 1961 put an end to the relative indifference to the Holocaust in Europe and the United States, was also an important milestone in Arab responses. The third stage in the development of this discourse, from the 1970s onward, was the adoption of arguments articulated by "professional" Holocaust deniers from the West. Toward the end of the twentieth century we can discern a fourth stage, with the publication of books by Arab writers that deal solely with Holocaust denial or with Hitler's personal exoneration, representing an antithesis of the new approach to the Holocaust. The intensification of Holocaust denial in the Arab discourse was to a large degree a mirror image of the Holocaust's mounting importance in Israeli collective identity and in western cultural and political discourse.[9]

Like in the West, Holocaust denial has also been manifested in Arab discourse in a number of ways, the most important of which are: total denial of its occurrence, as if nothing happened to the Jews during World War II, and its description as a Jewish-Zionist hoax aimed at extorting funds and political assistance from the West in general and from Germany in particular; recognition of the death of no more than a few thousand Jews during the war and the assertion that these were part of the general loss of civilian life during the war due to starvation, disease, and random acts of terrorism carried out by the Nazis; rejection of the existence of a Nazi policy that targeted the Jews with the intention of exterminating them; minimization of the number of Jewish victims in order to negate the Holocaust's significance as a genocide; and the assertion that the Nazis "persecuted" Jews, and particularly German Jews, as they had the French and the Dutch, but that they did not exterminate them.

The major change in Holocaust denial since the 1980s has been the growing reliance on western Holocaust deniers and the translation of their work into Arabic. These publications lent denial pseudo-scientific support, as if they were verifiable historical studies based on documents and statistical data. The fact that these deniers came from the West, which was ostensibly being held captive by the Zionist myth "inside the same house in which the massacre supposedly occurred," to use the words of Palestinian journalist Khayri Mansur, increased the importance and respectability of their claims.[10] This reliance also reflected an implicit or subconscious admiration of the West and of western sources, despite the resentment toward them. For example, the articles of French Holocaust denier Robert Faurisson were translated into Arabic and compiled in a book titled *The Historical Lie: Did six million really die?* which articulated his arguments and the debate they sparked.[11] Years later, Roger Garaudy's *The Founding Myths of Israeli Politics* (*Les mythes fondateurs de la politique Israelienne*),[12] Fred Leuchter's *The Leuchter Report: The End of a Myth*, and Norman Finkelstein's *The Holocaust Industry: Reflections on the Exploitation of Jewish Suffering* were also translated into Arabic.[13] These books received positive reviews in the Arabic media. For example, *The Leuchter Report*, which denied that the Jews were killed by gas in Auschwitz and Majdanek based on dubious technical claims, was reviewed in a long, two-part article in *al-Ahram al-'Arabi* even before it was translated into Arabic. The review praised Leuchter, Ernst Zündel (a Holocaust denier living in Canada), and Faurisson for their work. Since the end of World War II, it argued, the victors had imposed their hegemony on history and invented the "lie of the Holocaust," in order to extort the entire world. Every time these researchers voiced the truth, the article continued, western democracies dealt with them in the same manner that the Catholic Church had related to Galileo Galilei. Zündel, it added, had joined Galilei "as one of the victims of the truth facing the forces of ignorance, lies, and deceit."[14] The report was on sale at the 2001 Cairo International Book Fair.[15]

Books by Arab authors based on the works of Holocaust deniers that presumed to reflect an academic approach were also published, in addition to texts by Holocaust deniers and translations of such texts. The most prominent example of such reliance on western Holocaust deniers has been Mahmud 'Abbas's (Abu Mazen) book *The Other Side: The Secret Relationship between Nazism and Zionism*, which was based on his doctoral dissertation, submitted to the Oriental Studies Institute in Moscow in 1982. The book was meant to 'prove' the Zionist-Nazi collaboration in exterminating the Jews, but in its introduction 'Abbas addresses the number of Jewish victims and cites Faurisson to refute the "myth" of the gas chambers. He also cites Canadian Holocaust denier Roger DeLorme to support his assertion that the number of victims was considerably less than six million.[16] DeLorme also served Rafiq Natshe, a member of the Fatah Central Committee in the 1980s and subsequently a minister in the Palestinian National Authority, as a major source for his book *Colonialism and Palestine: Israel, A Colonialist Project*, to refute the "imagined" (*al- maz'uma*) acts of murder. Natshe explained that it was not his intention to belittle the severity or the scope of the Nazis' crimes but rather only to show how "the Zionists exploited, in the most despicable way…a whole series of myths and fables to attain financial and political remunerations."[17] He concedes that Hitler did kill some Jews, but "only the old and those opposed to Zionism." The young were sent to Palestine, "their pockets filled with money," while the killing and the emigration from Germany proceeded under Zionist supervision.[18]

The 1990s marked the beginning of a new stage in Arab Holocaust denial, with the publication of a number of books devoted entirely to denial and Hitler's personal exoneration.[19] This change apparently came in response to the mounting efforts in Europe to establish the Holocaust as a central event in the universal collective memory, as reflected in the establishment of Holocaust museums and international memorial ceremonies. This process sometimes led to a separation between the Holocaust as a universal symbol and the Jewish tragedy; yet, concern that Israel would derive benefit from this trend, and deep resentment toward the West, especially among Islamists, triggered an intensified effort of denial. It was also a response to the discourse that rejected denial, which had started to emerge in the Arab world. Ibrahim Alloush, an Islamist living in Jordan, reflected this approach in his conclusion that the Arabs were in need of "a coherent, principled, cognizant response to the campaign to Zionize

the Arab mind. Therein lies the promise of historical revisionism for us Arabs."
According to Alloush:

> Painstaking research findings are not enough: revisionist findings
> should be popularized in pamphlets and articles aimed at the
> average person, who has neither the time nor the background
> to delve into thick volumes. The research findings of historical
> revisionism can only become politically effective if they reach
> the people. Therefore, revisionist work should proceed along
> two parallel trajectories: the serious academic work of debunking
> the 'Holocaust' myths, and the even more important work of
> popularizing revisionism.[20]

Muhammad Nimr al-Madani's book *Were the Jews Burned in the Gas Chambers?*
sums up all the themes in the Arab discourse on the Holocaust: from the
charges of Zionist collaboration with the Nazis, to the charge of Jewish
responsibility for the Holocaust, to the portrayal of the Allies as the real war
criminals, to complete denial. Al-Madani's discussion focuses on the writings
of various Holocaust deniers, particularly Faurisson, Henri Rock, Leuchter, and
Roger Garaudy, and praises them for well-documented "meticulous scientific
research" in which they refute the major historical lies and the claims that the
Jews were exterminated.[21] The book's introduction, titled "The End of Israel
Begins Here," notes the direct connection between Holocaust denial and the
delegitimization of Israel. Madani asserts that the "Final Solution" to the Jewish
problem was indeed one of the Nazis' main plans and was completely consistent
with the Zionists' desire to concentrate all Jews in Palestine. It was put into
action based on a mutual agreement regarding mass Jewish emigration from
Germany and Europe to Palestine. Hitler, he states, did a great service for the
Jews, and in return the Jews supported him when he started the war. During
the war, however, the Jews betrayed Hitler and began to disseminate the lie that
he was exterminating their people. Al-Madani acknowledges that the Jews were
detained in German camps, like other national groups, but argues that there
is abundant documentary evidence showing that Germany did not murder

these Jews but rather used them to manufacture weapons like the rest of the prisoners. As proof, he points to the cynical, fraudulent motto that appeared on the gates of Auschwitz and other camps: *Arbeit macht frei* ("work sets you free"). According to al-Madani, not only was there no extermination as the Zionists claimed, but the years after the war were a period of success and prosperity for the Jews, culminating in the establishment of the state of Israel.[22]

The Arab political and intellectual discourse that denies the Holocaust is aimed first and foremost at undermining the historical-moral basis of Zionism. The most blatant use of denial in this manner, according to the needs of the user, has been its assertion from time to time alongside claims justifying Hitler for murdering the Jews and charges that the Zionists collaborated with the Nazis in the mass murder of the Jews. The prevalent view in the Arab World has been – and to a large extent remains – that because Zionism has no moral or historical justification, it is based on unfounded historical myths and total falsifications. Thus, the Arab deniers regard the Holocaust as one of the central myths that the Zionists invented for the purpose of creating a guilt complex in the West, and therefore as playing a major role in cultivating sympathetic public opinion in support of the establishment of the state of Israel.[23] At the foundation of Holocaust denial, therefore, lies the assumption that disproving the "lie" would completely undermine the international standing and legitimacy of Israel.

The themes of Holocaust justification and blaming the Jews for what befell them, of equating Zionism and Nazism and highlighting the collaboration between the two movements, were meant to undermine the Jews' legitimacy and to expose their ostensive treachery, maliciousness, and hostility to the whole of humanity.[24] "Those who are surprised by Hitler's hatred of the Jews will be less surprised when they learn the reasons for this deep, total hatred," declared Husayn Mu'nis, one of the most important Egyptian historians in the Nasserist era in the 1960s. The real reason, according to Mu'nis, was that international Zionism had forged an alliance with France in order to control Germany and ensure its eternal humiliation.[25] Hitler waged an intifada against the Jews in Germany, argued Algerian author Muhammad Jarbu'a, implicitly equating Israeli control over the Palestinians with the Jewish 'control' over the Germans prior to 1933. Germany was subject to Jewish terror, and Hitler's actions amounted to a just

sentence against traitors. He did what many had wanted to do but did not dare –
he rescued his country from the Jews.[26] Following these serious accusations against
the Jews, some writers who had spoken favorably about Hitler were infuriated by
the reactions of the Jews and the world to Hitler's justified aspiration to exterminate
the Jews.[27] According to 'Ali Imam 'Atiyya, Hitler "made a significant contribution
to the world by exterminating the Jews."[28]

In the years following the signing of the Egyptian-Israeli peace treaty, Holocaust
justifiers included some senior members of the religious establishment in Egypt
whose writings dealt with the Jews and their relations with the Muslims, and also
related to the modern era. Most prominent among them was Shaykh Muhammad
Sayyid al-Tantawi, who was then serving as rector of Cairo's prestigious al-Azhar
University and the senior-most figure in Egypt's religious establishment. His book
The Children of Israel in the Qur'an and the Sunna, which was published in 1997
during his tenure as rector, is a 700 page work based on his 1967 doctoral dissertation.
Al-Tantawi did not limit himself to a description of the Jews' atrocious acts against
the prophet Muhammad but also surveyed their history in Europe, with extensive
quotations from *The Protocols of the Elders of Zion* as a major historical source. In
addition to initiating the two world wars of the twentieth century for profiteering,
"the most prominent example" of the Jews' conduct was "their treacherous acts"
against Germany during World War I, which led to its defeat. They were rewarded
for their treachery with the Balfour Declaration, which recognized Zionism's claims
to Palestine. The Jews, al-Tantawi argues, had been exploiting the German people in
the basest manner ever since the eighth century when they settled in its land. They
achieved almost total control of German finances through high-interest money
lending and a host of other unacceptable means in order to accumulate money. It
is therefore no wonder that the German people rose up against them on a number
of occasions, using all possible means of killing, expulsion, and robbery. Hitler
was one of those "who put together all of the treacherous deeds" and took action
against them. Al-Tantawi concludes with a quote attributed to Hitler: "If the Jews
are victorious, it will mean the end of the Human race…and when I am defending
myself against the Jew, I am struggling to defend God's creation."[29]

Although Holocaust justification has always been less common then the motif
of denial, it was more widespread among the political and intellectual streams in

the 1950s and 1960s, when the conflict was perceived as an existential problem. Manifestations of justification decreased during the 1980s when the conflict changed in nature, albeit only partially, into a conflict between two countries. The increasing sophistication and the circulation of such manifestations, as well as the intensification of the negative approach to Nazi Germany in the political and cultural discourse in the Arab world, also contributed to this orientation. The motif of Holocaust justification remained typically, though not exclusively, the domain of writers from the Islamist camp: establishment religious figures and members of radical organizations. These groups adhered to a strict ideological conception of the conflict, adopted extreme and intolerant views of their adversaries, and had fewer inhibitions about articulating explicit justification of the Nazis' actions against the Jews. A few of them even called for the annihilation of the Jews. Holocaust justification was more common among Egyptians than others, despite the signing of the Israeli-Egyptian peace treaty of March 1979. The opposition to the peace treaty may have encouraged the publication of anti-Jewish texts in Egypt, as many of the writers and intellectuals who opposed the treaty and viewed it as their country's failure in realizing its national aspirations expressed their frustrations with numerous verbal attacks on the Jews, particularly in the literature dealing with Jews and Judaism. Another possible reason was the existence of a silent agreement between the government and intellectuals in Egypt, which allowed them to direct their anger and their pens against the Jews and the United States in exchange for refraining from criticism of the government's domestic failings.[30]

The equation between Zionism and Nazism in public Arab discourse began around the end of World War II and served all the ideological streams, as well as Arab spokespersons in various international forums. It was not the result of Soviet ideological and political influence as was thought in the past, although later, in the 1970s and 1980s, it drew motifs from the Soviet literature that represented Israel in this manner.[31] Like Holocaust denial, the depiction of Zionism and Israel as Nazis became a major rhetorical means to delegitimize them. It can be assumed that Arab writers were aware of the Israeli sensitivity to such comparisons in light of the Jews' suffering at the hands of the Nazis. They sought to strip the Jews of their human dignity by comparing them to their most notorious oppressors.

MORESHET · VOL. 17 · 2020

Moreover, such charges not only turn Jews from victims into perpetrators but also threaten them with the fate met by the Nazis.

This theme, like the others, has been characterized by a high degree of continuity along with a growing sophistication in the argumentation, including pseudo-scientific substantiation and academic studies published by universities.[32] Still, despite the broad agreement among the different ideological streams in the Arab world regarding the similarities between Zionism and Nazism, there are disagreements over how to explain them. Those who make use of this motif recognize that the Nazis committed atrocities against the Jews, but they usually play down the number of Jewish victims and deny the existence of a Nazi policy of total extermination of the Jews. The equation is typically based on a major exaggeration of Israel's ostensive crimes, as well as on the distortion of Judaism in general and Zionist ideology in particular through the use of partial and patently inaccurate quotes or taking them out of context.

These comparisons reflect the common view that Nazism and Hitler represent the pinnacle of evil. However, in their portrayal of Nazism as simply one of many racist movements, they clearly indicate, wittingly or unwittingly, a misunderstanding of the essence of Nazism, the most prominent attribute of which was murderous racism. The comparisons are frequently intended to reduce the atrocities committed by the Nazis to oppression, persecution, or military aggression. Egyptian leftist Ahmad Baha' al-Din, maintained, for example, that the clash between Nazism and Zionism was natural and inevitable in light of their similar nature as racist movements. The fact that the Nazis killed Jews, and not vice-versa, does not prove that the Jews were right or innocent but rather that the Nazis were stronger. Had the Jews been stronger, they would have massacred the Germans in a similar manner. Such a statement is not meant to exonerate or justify the Nazis but rather to clarify that although Nazism was a dark page in human history, so is Zionism. Both ideologies are based on the same ideas and the same racist philosophies, "which should be wiped off the face of the earth."[33]

The most complex and comprehensive comparison between Zionism and Nazism since the 1970s is undoubtedly that of 'Abd al-Wahhab al-Masiri, an Egyptian scholar who was considered an expert on Judaism and Zionism. Unlike others, al-Masiri sought to extricate the Arab discussion on the Holocaust from the confines of the Arab-Israeli context and examine it in a broader context with a historical critique of western culture. In this respect, he joins a long list of Muslim authors who have compared the "rationalist-materialist" West to "spiritual" and "moral" Islam. At the same time, he sought to establish his analysis on a philosophical-historical basis. Unlike other authors, he made extensive use of western academic literature on the Holocaust and on Nazism, in addition to the writings of various Holocaust deniers. He was also influenced by philosophers such as Martin Heidegger and Zygmunt Bauman, who were critical of the foundations of western rationalism and enlightenment.[34]

Al-Masiri authored numerous books on Judaism and Zionism, and in 1999 he published an eight-volume encyclopedia on these subjects. He did not deviate from the earlier theses that sought to condemn Zionism, its ideological conceptions, and its patterns of action. During his three decades of writing, his arguments underwent marked development, shifting from crude Holocaust denial in the 1970s to acceptance of the destruction that befell the Jews as historical fact, using his own unique interpretation. Unlike his early writings that rejected the "fraudulent number six million" and minimized the scope of the Holocaust, al-Masiri's later texts opposed paying excessive attention to numbers, which miss the main historical point with regard to Nazism.[35] He called for detaching the discussion of the human aspects of the Holocaust from the political discussion of its repercussions, but he continued to reject western academic findings on the Holocaust, to express doubts about its scope and its uniqueness, and to stress Zionist-Nazi collaboration.

Like the studies of Faris and Abu Mazen, al-Masiri also makes selective use of the literature on the Holocaust and World War II, and even of quotes by Israeli and Zionist leaders, but he refrains from addressing the western historiography dealing with the various aspects he raises. In the introduction to his book *Zionism, Nazism, and the End of History*, al-Masiri explains his goal of conducting a comprehensive reassessment of Nazism and the Holocaust in order to undermine the prevailing Zionist approach to these issues. His primary conclusion is that Nazism is not a deviation or distortion of core western values and culture, as is usually argued by western scholarship, but rather a central and fundamental component of Western civilization and western modernity – as is Zionism. This, in his view, accounts for the great similarity between the two movements.

New Foci of Research beginning at the End of the 1990s

Beginning in the 1990s – as a result of the development of the new discourse in which Arab and North African academics, intellectuals, writers, and journalists living in the Middle East and the West took part – calls were also voiced for new original Arab studies on the Holocaust in order to better understand it as a historical phenomenon, or "in order to prove and corroborate the facts once and for all."[36] These calls have received only a partial response. In addition to Holocaust denial, the thrust of the research effort thus far has revolved around Arabs' attitudes toward the Holocaust and the connection between the collective Palestinian memory – memory of the Nakba, and the Holocaust, which plays a central role in the Jewish and Israeli collective memory. Only a few studies have dealt with the Holocaust itself or related aspects. Egyptian historian Ramsis 'Awad published a series of books on the Nazi extermination camps of Auschwitz, Treblinka, Dachau, and Ravensbrück; on the Roma during the Holocaust; and on the Holocaust in American literature.[37] His book *The Holocaust between Denial and Verification* consists of three sections: the first deals with Normal Finkelstein's book *The Holocaust Industry*, which was published in 2000; the second discusses Deborah Lipstadt's book on Holocaust denial; and the third surveys the trial in the case of Irving v. Lipstadt that took place in Britain.[38] Following al-Masiri's studies, his student Egyptian Haggag 'Ali (Abu Jabr) has continued exploring the question of modernity and the Holocaust and the relationship between al-Masiri's doctrine and Bauman's views. 'Ali also translated Bauman's book into Arabic and published a review of Yehuda Bauer's book *Rethinking the Holocaust*, which was published in 2001.[39] At the same time, Omar Kamil, an Egyptian scholar living in Germany, studied the Holocaust in Arab memory in an attempt to explain the reasons for the Arabs' attitudes toward it.[40]

The first in-depth attempt of an Arab intellectual to examine the Arab views of the Holocaust was made by former Israeli Knesset member Azmi Bishara in an article that was first presented in 1993 at a conference in Germany and that was later published in Hebrew.[41] The Arabs' connection to the history of the Holocaust is of a most indirect nature, explains Bishara, clarifying the still prevailing approach on the subject:

The scene of the disaster of the Holocaust was Europe, and the perpetrators of the extermination were Europeans. However, the "reparations" for it were paid first and foremost in the Middle East, by the Palestinians. Perhaps this is why it is the political implications of the Holocaust are under discussion in the Arab context, and not the event itself. The fundamental anti-Zionist position of the Arabs determined their position on the Holocaust, as well as their position on antisemitism – it is not the reason for the Arab-Israeli conflict but rather its consequence. Anti-Jewish texts have engaged in justification of the Holocaust and its denial as a Zionist hoax, and this rhetoric, among other things, has been an attempt to contend with the Zionist instrumentalization of the Holocaust.[42]

Although Bishara's claims were published at the beginning of the 1990s, they appear to continue to reflect the prevalent approaches in the Arab world toward the Holocaust as they had already emerged by the end of World War II.

Two additional books analyze the Arab approach to the Holocaust, albeit not on the level of Bishara's analysis, as part of their examination of the peace process. The authors harshly criticize the Arabs' alienation from the Holocaust and their lack of understanding of its significance not only for Israel and the Jews but for Post-World War II western culture as a whole. The books were authored by two well-known Lebanese journalists with two different points of departure, and both were published in Beirut. Joseph Samaha, who fiercely opposed peace with Israel but sought to separate the Holocaust from the conflict, published his book *Transitory Peace: Toward an Arab Solution of the 'Jewish Question'* in 1993; and Hazim Saghiya published his book *In Defense of Peace* in 1995, identifying a link between recognition of the Holocaust and peace with Israel. Another article written in a similar spirit, "The Nakba, Restarted?" by Lebanese journalist Samir Kasir, was published by a France-based Palestinian journal in French in 1998.[43]

It was more than a decade later that Gilbert Achcar's wide ranging academic study *The Arabs and the Holocaust: The Arab-Israeli War of Narratives*, based also on western literature, was published. Initially in French, the book was subsequently translated into a number of languages, including Arabic, and attracted significant interest in the Arab and western media.[44] One section of the book deals with the Arab responses to Nazism and antisemitism between 1933 and 1947 according to the ideological streams in the Arab world: liberal Westernizers,

Marxists, nationalists, and reactionary and/or Fundamentalist Pan-Islamists. The other section focuses on what he defines as "The Time of the Nakba," examining Arab attitudes to the Jews and the Holocaust by chronological period: Gamal Abdul Nasser's years in Egypt (1948-1967); "the PLO years" (1967-1988); and "the years of the Islamic resistances" (1988 to the beginning of the twenty-first century). Still, the book does not offer a systematic analysis of the Arabs' diverse responses to the Holocaust; moreover, Achcar rejects Litvak and Webman's presentation of these responses based on his critical view of Zionism and his understanding that they represent a "counter narrative" to the Zionist narrative on the Holocaust. He ascribes most of the blame for the development of the problematic Holocaust discourse in the Arab World to Zionism. Although he denounces the phenomenon of Holocaust denial in the Arab World, he minimizes its importance and prevalence and perceives it as an opportunistic response to and a form of protest against the Zionist exploitation of the memory of the Holocaust. It is not an expression of antisemitism, but rather an "anti-Zionism of fools" that serves the interests of Israel.[45] Achcar also deals with issues such as Arab leaders' collaboration with the Nazis and the views of liberal and left-wing circles on fascism and Nazism, overestimating the importance of the leftists' opposition to Nazism.

To this literature we can add Mehnaz Afridi's 2017 book *Shoah through Muslim Eyes*, which is an individual journey of learning about Jews, the Holocaust, and Judaism. Afridi, a Pakistani scholar who lives in the United States and directs the Holocaust, Genocide, and Interfaith Education Center at Manhattan College (a remarkable thing in itself), was motivated by her own desire to understand the 'other'. In light of existing antisemitism among Muslims and the spreading phenomena of Islamophobia, Afridi felt a need to present Muslims with a different point of view in order to deconstruct the erroneous conceptions of the Holocaust and the Jews in their midst, and to "help to create a dialogue about the pain and suffering of 'the other'."[46] In the process Afridi forges a close relationship with Holocaust survivors living in the United States, and, through their difficult experiences in the camps, she seeks to arouse empathy and understanding in her Muslim readers.

In addition to the literature on Arab responses to the Holocaust, a growing number of scholars, mostly Palestinians living inside and outside Israel, have dealt with the Holocaust from the Palestinian perspective. They have written articles, participated in academic conferences, and presented a clear narrative regarding the link between the Nakba and the Holocaust. For example, Nadim Rouhana, in conjunction with a number of other Muslims, took part in a conference on Third World perceptions of the Holocaust that was held in Boston in April 2001, and Palestinian activist Ata Qaymari presented an article on the Palestinian perspective on the Holocaust at a conference held in Cyprus in 2004. This conference, which was organized under the joint auspices of the Yakar Center for Social Concern, Panorama, the Palestinian Center for the Dissemination of Democracy and Community Development, and the Truman Center of the Hebrew University in Jerusalem, brought together 16 Israeli and Palestinian academics and journalists to discuss the joint history of both peoples. Palestinian scholar Saliba Sarsar, who is based in the United States, wrote an article on the Nakba in cooperation with Dan Bar-On.[47] Another series of encounters between Jewish and Palestinian citizens of Israel, conducted in 2008 under the auspices of the Van Leer Institute with the cooperation of the Heinrich Böll Foundation, yielded a book on the Holocaust and the Nakba.[48] This group of scholars set a goal of creating a joint discourse on the Holocaust but found itself engaged in a discussion of the Holocaust and the Nakba "as two formative traumatic pasts of the national identities of the Palestinians and the Jews in Palestine/Eretz Israel."[49] The authors of the book's various chapters recognize that although the historical events of the two tragedies are dissimilar in scope and character and "the connection between the two events is complex and not necessarily direct," they can nonetheless be compared in terms of their historization and the manner in which they establish a "dominant collective consciousness with elements of victimhood."[50]

The analogy between the tragedies that befell the Jews and the Arabs of Palestine has been a central theme of the Palestinian and Arab discourse on the Holocaust.[51] The comparison of the two tragedies seemed compelling from the Arab, and particularly the Palestinian, point of view, explains journalist Rami Khouri, as the Palestinians "have experienced many of the same historical pains that Jews have suffered over the past two and a half millennia."[52] Qaymari concedes that many Palestinians perceive the Holocaust directly through the prism of their own *Nakba*, "the counterpart of the Holocaust in Palestinian history, in which their whole social, economic and cultural fabric was destroyed and uprooted." For this reason, there is a great similarity between the ways in which the two communities relate to their tragedies in commemoration and in the historiography. Moreover, the Palestinians are trying, like the Jews in the past and present, to construct a collective memory that will preserve their social, cultural, and historical consciousness.[53] Rashid Khalidi, an American historian of Palestinian origins, went further, characterizing the Holocaust as "our benchmark for man's inhumanity to man," and maintaining that the Holocaust holds universal meaning: "It teaches that we should not be allowed to forget or forgive wrongs committed against a whole people."[54]

The sense of victimhood that has played and continues to play a decisive role in the representation of Jewish history and identity is also a major component of the Palestinian national narrative. Whereas in Israeli eyes the events of 1947-1948 – the partition of Mandate Palestine and the War of Independence – signify national rebirth after the Holocaust and "a cause for national celebration…for Palestinians, the same events are seen as an unmitigated disaster and are the focus of national mourning."[55] Approximately one decade before the publication of the above words, Palestinian-Israeli writer and Communist politician Emile Habibi addressed this point in an essay titled "Your Holocaust – Our Catastrophe." Although the suffering of the Palestinians cannot be compared to that of the Jews of Europe, he argued, the Palestinians were still suffering. In Arab eyes, the Holocaust is the "original sin" that enabled the Zionist movement to persuade millions of Jews that it was proposing the right solution. "Had it not been for your Holocaust and that of humanity as a whole in World War II, the tragedy that continues to befall my people would not have been possible."[56] Palestinian Israeli lawyer Khalid Kassab Mahamid expressed a similar view, arguing that the Palestinian Nakba was minor in scope relative to the horrible events of the Holocaust, but that the Palestinian people bore the brunt of its political ramifications. "The scope of the tragedy of the Palestinian People stems from the dimensions of the Holocaust; whereas Israel's problem is smaller than that of the Palestinians because it receives aid due to the Holocaust, the Palestinians are paying the price with their homeland and their difficult life."[57] In the Arab Holocaust museum that he opened in his office in Nazareth in April 2005, which closed its doors after only a short time due to opposition within the local population, Mahamid hung placards produced by Yad Vashem that reflected the atrocities of the Holocaust, as well as placards depicting the flight of Palestinian refugees during the 1948 War and symbols of the *Nakba* (such as the key). Mahamid appealed to the Palestinians and to all Arabs to learn about the Holocaust and to come to understand the Israelis' deep concern regarding security, based on the assumption that such an understanding would enable them to contend with the Israeli arguments and thereby help the Palestinians achieve their political goals.[58]

"The essence of the injustice that has been done to the Palestinians," maintains Mahamid, "lies not only in the loss of their homeland but also in the consistent refusal of the perpetrators of the crimes to compensate them or even recognize their responsibility for it."[59] From the Palestinians' perspective, their tragedy is hidden from sight, and "no one understands the full human price of the ethnic cleansing."[60] Rashid Khalidi also points to the "unremitting pressure from the Israeli side for more than 50 years to ignore, diminish and ideally to bury the whole question of the Palestinians made refugees in 1948," and asserts that "the key requirement for a solution is not so much compensation (important as it is) as acceptance of responsibility and some form of moral atonement."[61] Denial of the Palestinian tragedy is similar to the denial of the Holocaust, he concludes, "with all the allowances necessary when making comparisons between situations which are inherently dissimilar."[62]

Nadim Rouhana argues that Israel denies both the means it used to achieve the establishment of a Jewish state and its repercussions for the Palestinian People and that "in order to avoid the moral implications," it developed "a massive and sophisticated denial mechanism."[63] Both sides view themselves as having being victimized by the other. At the same time, there is an underlying fear that the acknowledgement of the tragedy of the 'other' will justify moral superiority and imply acceptance of their collective rationale. For the Palestinians, accepting the Jewish pain surrounding the Holocaust means accepting the moral ground for the creation of the State of Israel. For the Israeli Jews, accepting the pain of the 1948 Palestinian refugees means sharing responsibility for their plight and their right of return.[64]

Denial of the Palestinian catastrophe was also introduced by the Palestinians as a motivation for their denial of the Holocaust.[65] Joseph Massad, a professor of intellectual history of Palestinian origin at Columbia University, compares the "obscene number games on the part of Holocaust deniers" to Zionist denials of the Palestinian Nakba and the consistent tendency of the Zionists to play down the number of Palestinian refugees. "While the Nakba and the Holocaust are not equivalent in any sense," he contends, "the logic of denying them is indeed the same." The PLO and the majority of Palestinian intellectuals, he maintains, have, since the 1960s, expressed solidarity with the Jewish victims of the Holocaust and attacked its deniers, unlike official and unofficial Israel, which denies the expulsion of the Palestinians.[66]

The discussion of the Nakba and the Holocaust has also found expression in literary fiction. Two milestones in this writing have been Ghasan Kanafani's novel *Returning to Haifa* and Elias Khoury's *Bab al-Shams*. Written two years after the 1967 war, Kanafani's novel depicts an encounter between a Palestinian couple returning to their home in Haifa, which they abandoned when fleeing the war in 1948, and a Holocaust survivor who lives in the house along with the couple's son, who stayed behind during the flight.[67] Khoury's story, published in 1998, presents the Palestinian-Israeli conflict in broad perspective and engages in fundamental self-examination of the Arab position on the Holocaust, effectively reflecting the new approach to the Holocaust that developed during the same period.[68]

Another focus of new studies, which has no direct connection to the Holocaust and is therefore not discussed here, considers the Arab responses to fascism and Nazism during the 1930s and 1940s and is being pursued by Western, Arab, and Israeli scholars.[69] Studies by Mustafa Kabha and Mustafa Abbasi also deal with the Palestinians' attitudes toward and their participation in the civil war in Spain, and their enlistment in the British army in the war against the Nazis.[70] Concomitantly, a historiography has evolved on the legacy of the Mufti of Jerusalem, Hajj Amin al-Husayni, who spent most of the war years in Germany.

The Palestinians' official version of al-Husayni's legacy is elusive and is at least partially the product of the PLO leadership's desire to lower his status and to present itself as a counter-reaction to the leadership he represented. The eulogy that appeared in *Filastin al-Thawra* following his death on July 4, 1974, praised his support of the Iraqi nationalist movement in 1941 and his efforts on behalf of the Palestinian issue after arriving in Cairo in 1946, but it ignored his activity during the war. The Palestinian Encyclopedia briefly notes that al-Husayni resided in Europe for a period of four years, during which he established offices for the Arab national movement in Berlin and Rome and worked to advance Palestinian and Arab interests in diplomacy and propaganda. It also notes that the British, Yugoslav, and American governments sought to put him on trial for war crimes, but it does not specify the war crimes in question.[71] The official updated website of the Palestinian Authority makes no mention of al-Husayni, although it previously criticized the "reactionary" Arab circles that sided with Germany and conceded that al-Husayni "joined the Nazi Axis and promoted its aims." Nonetheless, it emphasizes that the Palestinian People did not respond to his call to rebel against the British.[72]

In the 1990s, on the other hand, the Palestinian Islamist historiography cleared al-Husayni's name, transforming him from a failed leader into a devoted leader who conducted a struggle against the Zionists from an Islamic perspective. Therefore, and because the Islamists pay much less attention to universal standards regarding the Nazis, they viewed al-Husayni's ties with Germany in a different way. Najib al-Ahmad praises al-Husayni's efforts to thwart Jewish immigration to Palestine from Europe during the war. Ahmad Nawfal and 'Awani Jadu' al-'Abidi go further by asserting that "he chose correctly" when he decided to collaborate with Germany. The Palestinian People, they explain, was unable to defend itself because the British had concealed their intention to give Palestine to the Jews, and no Arab leader aside from al-Husayni understood the situation. He therefore had no choice but to seek the assistance of a party that was stronger than Britain. Had Germany and Italy won the war, they conclude, "the fate of Palestine would have been much better than its current condition under Zionist rule."[73]

As a result of their unique historical circumstances, the countries of the Maghreb have not been part of this discussion. During World War II, they were subject to the control of the Axis countries and its allies, and in the early years of the development of the Arab discourse in the countries of the *Mashriq* (Egypt and the countries to its east) they were not yet independent states. It seems that during most of the period under review there was no connection between the discourse on the Holocaust in the Maghreb and in the Arab Middle East until the emergence of the alternative discourse, in which representatives of this region, particularly those living in the West, took part. Due to its nature, the Maghreb receives separate, comprehensive study.[74] Following Robert Satloff's research on the Muslim population's attitudes toward North Africa's Jews during the Holocaust – particularly those who rescued Jews – North African writers, scholars, and film directors have increasingly engaged in the examination of the local population's attitudes toward their Jewish neighbors during the war, and of Muslims who helped Jews.[75] For example, Mohammed Aïssaou, an Algerian writer living in France, wrote a book titled *The Yellow Star and the Crescent*,[76] which recounts the rescue efforts of Si Kaddour Benghabrit, the Imam of the Grand Mosque of Paris, who converted the mosque into a refuge for Jews.[77]

The first prose book to contend with the question of the Algerians' relations with the Nazis during the war was *The Village of the German, or the Diary of the Schiller Brothers* by Algerian writer Boualem Sansal, which was first published in French in January 2008 and was subsequently translated into Hebrew. The book tells the story of two brothers, sons of a German father who fled to Algeria after the war and an Algerian mother. Both brothers are sent to study in France: one becomes an Islamist activist, and the other, who is secular, investigates his father's past, exposing the story of the Holocaust.[78] A book edited by Aomar Boum and Sarah Abrevaya Stein examining the treatment of Jews in Libya, Tunisia, Algeria, and Morocco was published in 2019. The articles by Aomar Boum, a scholar of Moroccan origin living in the United States, and Muhammad Hatimi, a historian from Sidi Mohamed Ben Abdellah University in Fès–Saïss, on Jews' relations with their neighbors in the rural regions of Morocco during the war, reflect the growing interest in this topic among local scholars.[79]

A noteworthy new development contributing to the dissemination of reliable Arabic-language information on the Holocaust has been the activity of international organizations and the websites of government bodies and European newspapers. The websites of the United Nations, the US Holocaust Memorial Museum in Washington, the Israeli Foreign Ministry, Wikipedia in Arabic, and European newspapers such as *Deutsche Welle* publish entries and articles about the Holocaust, translate western literature into Arabic and into other Middle Eastern languages, and deal with various aspects related to the Holocaust, including its significance for Arab and Muslim immigrant communities in Europe. One of the first projects, "Project Aladdin," was established in Paris under the auspices of UNESCO, the French government, and the Mémorial de la Shoah. The Aladdin Project promotes knowledge of the history of the Holocaust in the Arab world for building bridges between Jews and Muslims. Among other things, it engages in the translation of a number of books into Arabic, including the diary of Anne Frank and Primo Levi's memoirs as a prisoner in Auschwitz. The project has also initiated meetings and conferences on the Holocaust in Cairo, Baghdad, Tunisia, Amman, Casablanca, and Nazareth.[80] This literature has the potential to reach those who are interested in the Holocaust, to balance out the prevailing information in the Arab discourse, and, perhaps, in time, to contribute to an Arab historiography of the Holocaust.

Various Arab websites and forums, such as Elaph, Sasapost, and Ashefaa, also publish articles on the Holocaust, some offering a more detailed picture of its events but continuing to engage in soft denial and raising ostensive doubts regarding the number of dead.[81] Of particular interest is the website of the Madar Center, an independent Palestinian center for Israel studies that was established in 2000 by Palestinian intellectuals and academics in Ramallah. The website maintains an encyclopedia of Israeli figures, places, organizations, and historical events. Among them there are short entries on the Holocaust, the Nazis, and the Nakba, which create a historiographical Palestinian outline of the Holocaust and its repercussions while reinforcing the linkage between the Holocaust, the establishment of the state of Israel, and the Palestinian Nakba. The entries describe the persecution of Jews in Germany following the Nazis' rise to power, clarify the meanings of the term "Holocaust" and the stages of the extermination, and highlight the Holocaust's impact on the acceleration of Jewish immigration to Palestine, the establishment of the state of Israel, and the collapse of Palestinian society that led to the Nakba.[82]

Why is there no Arabic historiography of the Holocaust?

In the summer of 2019, a student theatre group at Ain Shams University in Cairo staged a play titled *Sobibor* written by a young playwright named Muhammad Zaki. The play depicts the suffering of the Jews in this extermination camp and the escape of 200 Jewish prisoners with the assistance of a Russian officer. Apparently providing a reliable account of the fate of the Jews, the play caused art critic Omneya Talaat to question the reasons for Zaki's work on a topic "that serves the interests of our enemy." Instead of focusing on the Palestinian problem, which "is fundamentally a national, religious, and identity problem," and on the Zionists' massacres of Arabs, including Egyptians and Palestinians, Zaki stirs empathy for the Jews, who today cannot be separated from the Zionists in Israel, by emphasizing their extermination by the Nazis during World War II. "The truth is that international Zionism as embodied in the Zionist entity has exploited the story of the Holocaust for the sake of international achievements which they do not deserve," notes Talaat, reiterating one of the main arguments against Arab engagement in the Holocaust.[83]

Prevalent among politicians and intellectuals who shape Arab public opinion has been concern over the Holocaust's potential to arouse feelings of sympathy and to mobilize support not only in the West, and in Europe in particular, which has suffered from feelings of guilt since the scale of the atrocities were exposed, but also among the Arabs. This, it has been feared, would undermine sympathy for the Palestinian cause and weaken the struggle against Israel, which has become an integral part of the ethos of the national struggle of most Arab countries. The close linkage that was created between the Holocaust and the Jewish state turned any recognition of a Jewish right in Palestine that could stem from it into a threat to one of the foundations of state and society, deterring even those who had empathy for the Jews. It was therefore necessary to conceal the information about it, on the one hand, and to aim criticism at Israel and Zionism for its exploitation in an effort to mobilize the world's sympathy for materializing their goals, on the other hand.

Zionism and Israel were perceived as genuine threats to the emerging Arab states, and, as already noted, this sense of danger resulted in a diverse literature on Zionism, on the Jews and Judaism, and on the conflict and the Palestine problem, which incorporated references to the Holocaust. All engagement in the Holocaust alone was considered a distraction of public opinion away from the main issue – the struggle against Zionism. This understanding is unambiguous, explains Azmi Bishara, who argues that the Arabs' fundamental anti-Zionist position determined their views on the Holocaust and on antisemitism.[84] The deeper the awareness of the Holocaust took root in Israeli collective identity, especially after the Eichmann trial, the more its usage as one source of state legitimacy elicited a counter-reaction: its usage for delegitimizing the state. In fact, the centrality of the Holocaust has made it even more difficult for Arabs to acknowledge it, because doing so is perceived as lending a degree of legitimacy to Israeli identity. "Each side views itself as the only victim and completely rejects the victimhood of the other."[85] Recognizing the victimhood of the 'other', the enemy, is rare in any conflict, because it can be interpreted as justification for the enemy or recognition of its moral authority, and as undermining the victimized status of the denying side.

A concrete example of this attitude were the responses to the initiative of Christian Arab-Israeli educator Father Emile Shoufani (known as "Memory for Peace") to organize a trip to Auschwitz to learn about "the Jewish suffering" and "the sources of anxiety" that characterize the Israelis' attitudes toward the 'other', to share the pain, and, ultimately, to pave the way for better understanding and coexistence. Aware of the significance of the Holocaust in the Israeli psyche, he believed that the memory of the Holocaust "is the key to reopening dialogue" between the Palestinians and the Israelis, which grounded to a halt with the Second Intifada. After a period of joint learning about the Holocaust and after being presented with the personal experiences of Jewish survivors, a group of 250 Arabs and Jewish Israelis, and Muslims, Christians, and Jews from France, embarked upon a journey to the death camp of Auschwitz-Birkenau from May 26 through May 30, 2003. Although Shoufani had received the blessings of Egyptian and Palestinian government officials, including Yasser Arafat, criticism of the initiative quickly emerged, particularly from Arab Israelis, who viewed it as a betrayal of the Palestinian interest because it took place during a period of fighting between Israel and the Palestinians, and because it ignored the demand for parallel Jewish recognition of the tragedy of the Palestinians.[86]

The same dynamic was also manifested in the fierce opposition to allowing Holocaust studies in Palestinian schools in the Palestinian Authority and the rejection of every attempt by UNRWA to incorporate the study of the Holocaust into its school curriculum. Samira Aliyan studied the textbooks in use within the

Palestinian Authority and found that the Palestinian history books deal with all aspects of World War II: its background, the war itself, the loss of life and its economic and political repercussions, Nazi Germany and racial theory, and different forms of racism and ethnic cleansing. However, it makes no mention of the Holocaust in any of these contexts, even when enumerating their ramifications for the Palestinian People and the establishment of the state of Israel. "No book that was examined for the study made reference to the Holocaust or to the crimes committed by the Nazis. It is evident that the choice to skip this important chapter was intentional."[87] In Aliyan's view, ignoring the Holocaust "stems not from a denial of the Holocaust but rather from the current political situation."[88]

Indeed, when the issue of teaching the Holocaust was raised at a Jewish-Palestinian symposium on the subject of "how to strengthen peace through education" that was held in Cyprus in April 2000, it was rejected out of hand, but not due to Holocaust denial. "If the purpose is to express sympathy," noted Ziyad Abu 'Amr, chairman of the Political Committee of the Palestinian Legislative Council (PLC), "this is useless for us…What we need most is to learn our own heritage." Hatim 'Abd al-Qadir, another PLC member and a Fatah leader, went further by characterizing the teaching of the Holocaust as "a grave danger to the development of Palestinian mentality." If such a decision is made, it would undoubtedly destroy the Palestinian dream and Palestinian aspirations. It would completely erase the past, the present, and the future of the Palestinians."[89] In contrast, when Hamas spokespeople rejected UNRWA's 2009 attempts to incorporate Holocaust education into its schools for Palestinian refugees, they also denied the Holocaust as "a lie invented by the Zionists," and they characterized the subject's incorporation into the syllabus as "a war crime and an attempt to spread falsehoods" that serve to support the Zionists.[90] When the issue was again raised in August 2010 and October 2012 similar resistance was voiced. The UNRWA teachers committee in Jordan denounced the organization's proposal, which, it maintained, "equated the perpetrator with the victim," and demanded that instead of the Holocaust, subjects related to the Nakba and the life of the refugees be incorporated into the syllabus. According to the committee, teaching the Holocaust as part of the issue of human rights would harm the Palestinians' goal and could change the students' views on their true enemy.[91]

The lack of interest in the Holocaust may also reflect the Arab world's lack of general interest in the history and culture of other peoples or its engagement in these areas strictly through the prism of their repercussions, as manifested in the small number of Arabic translations from foreign languages. The United Nations' Arab Human Development Reports, which deal comparatively with levels of knowledge production in various countries, point to the limited scope of translations in Arab countries. For example, between 1970 and 1975, only 330 books were translated in the entire Arab world, approximately one-fifth of the number of books that were translated in Greece.[92] It can be assumed that this prevents literature on the Holocaust from reaching Arab book stores, even without considering the other hindering factors.

These points also explain the consistent Arab abstention from engaging in research on the Holocaust and the lack of Arab historiography of the Holocaust. Arab attitudes toward the Holocaust have been and continue to be influenced by developments in the Arab-Israeli conflict, and the discourse surrounding it develops as part of the conflict and serves as another means of reconstructing the image of the enemy – the 'other'. Joseph Massad agrees that the Arabs' views on the Holocaust are derived from the political situation but accuses Zionism of appropriating the Holocaust and its victims. "Israeli demands that Palestinians recognize the Holocaust are not about the Holocaust at all," he explains, "but rather about the other part of the package, namely recognizing and submitting to Israel's 'right to exist' as a colonial-settler racist state."[93] This package deal, Massad asserts, links acknowledgement of the Holocaust and recognition of Israel's right to exist, thereby pushing the Arabs in general, and the Palestinians in particular, to deny the Holocaust and to ignore it.

In contrast, Egyptian historian Omar Kamil attributes the narrow Arab view of the Holocaust to the different historical experiences and expectations that shaped collective memory in Europe and in the Arab World. Therefore, he argues, Arab readers face an epistemological barrier that impedes their intellectual ability to grasp the depth of the Holocaust's significance, and they internalize it through their colonial experience.[94] There is no doubt that the discourse on the Holocaust has been intertwined with the broader anticolonial discourse. Nonetheless, the epistemological barrier to understanding the

Holocaust is rooted not only in the Arab historical memory of colonialism but also in the deliberate rejection of the western and Jewish Holocaust scholarship and discourse, and the refraining from independent research on the subject. Simultaneously, free flow of information on the Holocaust had been disrupted, and the consumption of information by intellectual circles has been selective and unbalanced, creating fertile ground for widespread ignorance.

Endnotes

1　Hassan A. Barari, *Israelism: Arab Scholarship on Israel, a Critical Assessment* (Reading, UK, 2009, 2012), p. 16.

2　Meir Litvak and Esther Webman, *From Empathy to Denial: Arab Responses to the Holocaust* (London, 2009).

3　Ahmad Baha' al-Din, *Isra'iliyyat* (Cairo, 1965), pp. 95-96.

4　See, for example, the use of the term "Holocaust" to describe what happened in Gaza, Iraq, and other places in the Arab world. Nawaf al-Zaru, *Encyclopedia of the Ongoing Palestinian Holocaust: A Century of Terrorism and Zionist War Crimes in Palestine* (Amman, 2008) (Arabic); idem, *The Ongoing Palestinian Holocaust: Disagreement with Israel and the Policy of Ethnic Cleansing* (Amman, 2012) (Arabic); Majdi Kamil, *The Gaza Holocaust: The Hiroshima of the Twenty-First Century: Shocking Sights that the Camera Does Not Tolerate* (Damascus and Cairo, 2010) (Arabic).

5　For a discussion of the new approach, see Litvak and Webman, *From Empathy to Denial*, pp. 331-77.

6　See, for example, Muhammad Kamal Dessouki and 'Abd al-Tawwab Salman, *Zionism and Nazism: A Comparative Study* (Cairo, 1968) (Arabic); 'Isam Shurayh, *Zionism and Nazism* (Beirut, 1969) (Arabic); 'Abd al-Wahhab al-Masiri, *The End of History: Studies in the Foundations of Zionist Thinking* (Beirut, 1979) (Arabic); idem, "Hatred of the Jews between Reality and Facts," *Palestinian Affairs* 225-226 (December 1991-January 1992), pp. 82-92 (Arabic); idem, *Zionism, Nazism, and the End of History* (Cairo, 1997) (Arabic); Mahmud 'Abbas, *Zionism is the Twin of Nazism and the Jews Are Its First Victim, Palestinian Affairs* 112 (March 1981), pp. 3-7 (Arabic); Nizam 'Abbasi, *Zionist-Nazi Relations and Their Implications for Palestine and the Arab Liberation Movement, 1933-1945* (Kuwait, 1984) (Arabic); Rafiq Shakir Natshe, *Colonialism and Palestine: Israel, A Colonialist Project* (Amman, 1984) (Arabic).

7　See, for example, Mustafa al-Shihabi, *Lectures on Colonialism* (Cairo, 1955) (Arabic); Amin Sami al-Ghamrawi, *That Is Why I Hate the Jews* (Cairo, 1964) (Arabic); Sulayman Naji, *The Corrupt on Earth or the Political and Social Crimes of the Jews throughout History* (Damascus, 1969) (Arabic); 'Abduh al-Rajih, *The Israeli Personality* (Cairo, 1969) (Arabic); Sayyid Qutb, *Our Struggle with the Jews*, 2ⁿᵈ edition (Jedda, 1970) (Arabic); Muhammad Sayyid Tantawi, *The Children of Israel in the Qur'an and the Sunna* (Cairo, 1997) (Arabic).

8　See, for example, Ramadan Lawund, *World War II* (Beirut, 1965) (Arabic); Muhammad Kamal Dessouki, *World War II: A Colonialist Conflict* (Cairo, 1968) (Arabic).

9　For an extensive discussion of Holocaust denial in the Arab World see Litvak and Webman, *From Empathy to Denial*, pp. 155-193.

10 *Al-Hayat al-Jadida*, April 21, 2001 (Arabic).

11 Robert Faurisson, *The Historical Lie: Did six million really die?* translated by Majid Hillawi (Beirut, 1988) (Arabic).

12 Roger Garaudy, *The Founding Myths of Israeli Politics*, translated by Muhammad Hisham (Cairo, 1998) (Arabic).

13 Fred Leuchter, *The Leuchter Report: Or the End of the Myth of the Jews' Extermination by Gas*, translated by Iman 'Ali (Cairo, 2000) (Arabic); Norman D. Finkelstein, *The Holocaust Industry: Reflections on the Exploitation of Jewish Suffering*, translated by Sa'ud 'Atiyya (London, 2001) (Arabic).

14 *Al-Ahram al-'Arabi*, April 24, 1999, pp. 16-19; May 1, 1999, pp. 24-26 (Arabic).

15 *Yedioth Ahronoth*, February 23, 2001 (Hebrew); *al-Dustur*, March 28, 2001; April 3 and 8, 2001 (Arabic).

16 Mahmud 'Abbas, *The Other Side: The Secret Relationship between Nazism and Zionism* (Amman, 1984), introduction, pp. 2, 7 (Arabic). DeLorme was a Montreal television personality who ran as a Progressive Conservative Party candidate in a May 1977 provincial by-election and lost. DeLorme has publically doubted whether the number of Jewish victims exceeded one million. For an earlier text, see: Yahya Faris, *Zionist Relations with Nazi Germany* (Beirut, 1978).

17 Natshe, *Colonialism and Palestine*, pp. 147-148.

18 Ibid., pp. 147-151.

19 See Yasir Husayn, *Exonerating Hitler* (place of publication unspecified, 1995) (Arabic); Ramadan al-'Abbasi, *The Myth of the Nazi Gas Chambers* (Beirut, 1997) (Arabic); Muhammad Jarbu'a, *The Exoneration of Hitler from Blame for the Holocaust* (Beirut, 2002) (Arabic); Rif'at Sayyid Ahmad, *My Story with the Lie of the Holocaust* (Cairo, 2005) (Arabic).

20 Ibrahim Alloush, "Between Public Relations and Self-Alienation: Arab Intellectuals and the 'Holocaust'," *The Journal of Historical Review* 20(3) (May/June 2001), p. 7 (see http://www.ihr.org/jhr/v20/v20n3p-7_alloush.html).

21 Muhammad Nimr al-Madani, *Were the Jews burned in the gas chambers?* (Damascus, 2007) (Arabic). Al-Madani published another book in the same vein titled *The Forbidden Holocaust: The Holocaust and the Annihilation Philosophy of the Jews* (Damascus, 2007) (Arabic).

22 Al-Madani, *Were the Jews burned in the gas chambers?* pp. 151-152.

23 See, for example, *al-Ahram*, July 13, 1986 (Arabic); *al-'Arab al-Yawm*, April 27, 1998 (Arabic); *al-Quds al-'Arabi*, April 22, 1998 (Arabic); *al-Ahram Weekly*, September 24, 1998 (Arabic); *al-Hayat*, July 31, 1998 ; January 31, 2000 (Arabic);

Akhir Sa'a, May 24, 2001 (Arabic); *al-Liwa' al-Islami*, June 24, 2004; July 1, 2004 (Arabic); *al-'Arab al-Yawm*, April 12, 2007 (Arabic).

24　See Litvak and Webman, *From Empathy to Denial*, pp. 193-214 (on justification of the Holocaust in Arab discourse), pp. 215-42 (on the equation of Zionism with Nazism), and pp. 243-70 (on Zionist-Nazi collaboration).

25　Husayn Mu'nis, *October*, September 12, 1981 (Arabic). For similar views articulated by another senior Egyptian historian, see Ahmad al-Badawi, *al-Quds*, May 1984, quoted in Rivka Yadlin, *Arrogant and Exploitive Genius: Anti-Zionism as Anti-Judaism in Egypt* (Jerusalem, 1988), p. 106 (Hebrew). See also 'Abd al-Wahhab Zaytun, *Jewish or Zionist* (Beirut, 1991), p. 95 (Arabic).

26　Jarbu'a, *The Exoneration of Hitler*, pp. 8-9, 20, 54-55, 62, 65, 66, 72-73.

27　See, for example, Muhammad 'Ali al-Zu'bi, *The Depths of the Jewish Soul according to the Holy Scriptures: The Torah, the New Testament, the Qur'an, the History and Reality*, 3rd edition (Beirut, 1973) (Arabic); 'Abd al-Hadi Muhammad Mas'ud, *Hitler, Mussolini, and the Religions* (Cairo, 1951) (Arabic).

28　'Ali Imam 'Atiya, *World Zionism and the Promised Land* (Cairo, 1963), pp. 213-215 (Arabic).

29　Al-Tantawi, *The Children of Israel in the Quran and the Sunna*, pp. 623, 647-648, 651. For a similar description of the Jews, see Mahmud Mazru'a, *Studies in Judaism* (Cairo, 1987), pp. 131, 136-137 (Arabic); Ibrahim Khalil Ahmad, *Israel: A Sedition for Generations: Ancient Times* (Cairo, 1969), p. 19 (Arabic).

30　On the wide circulation of anti-Jewish writings in Egypt see Yadlin, *Arrogant and Exploitive Genius*; Raphael Israeli, *Peace Is in The Eyes of the Beholder* (New York, 1985). On the "silent agreement," see Fouad Ajami, *The Dream Palace of the Arabs: A Generation's Odyssey* (New York, 1999), see Chapter 5.

31　Bernard Lewis, *Semites and Anti-Semitism: An Inquiry into Conflict and Prejudice* (New York, 1987), p. 162-63.

32　See, for example, Nadia Sa'ad al-Din, *Zionism, Nazism, and Forms of Coexistence with the Other* (Amman, 2004) (Arabic). This book is based on the author's doctoral dissertation, which was approved by Al al-Bayt University in Jordan.

33　Baha' al-Din, *Isra'iliyyat*, p. 170

34　On these influences, see Haggag Ali, "Modernity in the discourse of Abdelwahab Elmessiri," *Intellectual Discourse*, 19 (2011), pp. 71-96.

35　Al-Masiri, *Zionism, Nazism, and the End of History*; 'Abd al-Wahhab al-Masiri, *Encyclopedia of the Jews, Judaism, and Zionism*, 8 vol. (Cairo, 1999) (Arabic). Also see note 4 and the extensive discussion of his views in Litvak and Webman, *From Empathy to Denial*, pp. 227-36.

36 See, for example, 'Abd al-Wahhab al-Masiri, "The Historians of the Holocaust… Exaggerated Numbers," *al-Ittihad*, April 8, 2006, https://www.alittihad.ae/wejhatarticle/19318 (Arabic) (accessed on September 10, 2019).

37 See, for example, Ramsis 'Awad, *The Holocaust in American Literature* (Cairo, 2001), (Arabic); idem, *The Gypsies between Massacre and Holocaust* (Cairo, 2007) (Arabic); idem, *The Most Well Known Nazi Detention Camp for Women: Ravensbrück, 1939-1945* (Cairo, 2007) (Arabic); idem, *Treblinka Detention Camp* (Cairo, 2012) (Arabic).

38 Ramsis 'Awad, *The Holocaust between Denial and Verification* (Cairo, 2000) (Arabic); Deborah Lipstadt, *Denying the Holocaust: The Growing Assault on Truth and Memory* (New York, 1993); idem, *History on Trial: My Day in Court With a Holocaust Denier* (New York, 2006).

39 See, for example, Haggag Abu Jabr, "Deconstructing the Sanctity of the Holocaust," *Wajhat Nazar* (September 2007), pp. 26-27 (Arabic); idem, "Modernism and the Holocaust," *Wajhat Nazar* (October 2010), pp. 71-71 (Arabic); idem, *A Critique of Secular Thinking: A Comparative Study on the Conceptions of Zygmunt Bauman and 'Abd al-Wahhad al-Masiri* (Cairo, 2017) (Arabic); Haggag Ali, "Modernity in the Discourse of Abdelwahab Elmessiri"; idem, *Mapping the Secular Mind: Modernity's Quest for a Godless Utopia* (London and Washington, 2013).

40 Omar Kamil, "Araber, Antisemitismus und Holocaust zur Rezeption der Shoah in der arabischen Welt" (parts 1 and 2), *Israel, Palästina und die deutsche Linke* 26-28 (March 2004), pp. 38-45; idem, *Der Holocaust im arabischen Gedächtnis: Eine Diskursgeschichte 1945-1967* (Göttingen, 2012)

41 Azmi Bishara, "The Arabs and the Holocaust: The Analysis of a Problematic Conjunctive Letter," *Zmanim* 53 (1995), pp. 54-71 (Hebrew). Bishara's article sparked bitter debate in Israel between Zionist Holocaust scholars and postmodernist and post-Zionist writers. See Dan Michman, "Arabs, Zionists, Bishara, and the Holocaust: Political Essay or Academic Study?" *Zmanim* 55 (1996), pp. 117-119 (Hebrew); Azmi Bishara, "On Nationalism and Universalism," *Zmanim* 55 (1996), pp. 102-105 (Hebrew); Moshe Zuckerman, "Who Owns Memory," *Zmanim* 55 (1996), pp. 106-107 (Hebrew); Dan Michman, "The Arabs and the Holocaust according to Azmi Bishara: Indeed, A Political Essay," *Zmanim* 56 (1996), pp. 113-118 (Hebrew).

42 Bishara, "The Arabs and the Holocaust: The Analysis of a Problematic Conjunctive Letter," p. 54.

43 Joseph Samaha, *Transitory Peace: Toward an Arab Solution of the 'Jewish Question'* (Beirut, 1993) (Arabic); Hazim Saghiya, *In Defense of Peace* (Beirut, 1997) (Arabic); Samir Kassir, "La Nakba recommencée?" *Palestiniennes d'Études Revue* 18(69) (Autumn 1998), pp. 59-65.

44 Gilbert Achcar, *The Arabs and the Holocaust: The Arab-Israeli War of Narratives* (London, 2010). See also Gilbert Achcar, "Eichmann in Cairo: The Eichmann Trial in Nasser's Egypt," *Arab Studies Journal* 20(1) (Spring 2012), pp. 74-103.

45 Gilbert Achcar, "Assessing Holocaust Denial in Western and Arab Contexts," *Journal of Palestine Studies* 41(1) (Autumn 2011), pp. 82-95.

46 Mehnaz M. Afridi, *Shoah through Muslim Eyes* (Boston, 2017), p. 210.

47 "Reflections on al-Nakba," *Journal of Palestine Studies* 28(1) (Autumn 1998), pp. 5-35; Nadim Rouhana, "The Holocaust and Psychological Dynamics of the Arab-Israeli Conflict," Paper submitted to the Third World Views of the Holocaust Conference, Boston, April 2001: http://www.northeastern.edu/brudnickcenter/past_conferences/third_world_views-2/transcriptions-of-presentations/nadim-rouhana-israelpalestine/ (accessed on September 7, 2019); Ata Qaymari, "The Holocaust in the Palestinian Perspective," in Paul Scham, Walid Salem, and Benjamin Pogrund (eds.), *Shared Histories: A Palestinian-Israeli Dialogue* (Jerusalem, 2005), pp. 148-153; Dan Bar-On and Saliba Sarsar, "Bridging the Unbridgeable: The Holocaust and Al- Nakba," *Palestine-Israel Journal* 11(1) (2004), pp. 63–70.

48 Bashir Bashir and Amos Goldberg (eds.), *The Holocaust and the Nakba: Memory, National Identity, and Jewish-Arab Partnership* (Jerusalem, 2015) (Hebrew).

49 Bashir and Goldberg, "Introduction: On the Possibility of Discussing the Holocaust and the Nakba Together," in ibid., p. 1.

50 Bashir and Goldberg, "Reflections on Memory, Trauma, and Nationalism in Israel/Palestine," in ibid., pp. 26-27.

51 On the Palestinian discourse on the Holocaust and the Nakba, see Litvak and Webman, *From Empathy to Denial*, pp. 309-29; Marzuk Halabi, "The Nakba and the Holocaust: Can that which divides also serve to connect?" in Bashir and Goldberg, *The Holocaust and the Nakba*, pp. 89-111; Antoine Shalhat, "On Life in the Shadow of the Holocaust and the Nakba," in ibid., pp. 112-133; Salman Natour, "The Memory of Death…And the Memory of Life: On the Non-Equivalence of the Holocaust and the Nakba," in ibid., pp. 134-146.

52 *Jordan Times*, May 15, 1998.

53 Qaymari, "The Holocaust in the Palestinian Perspective," p. 149

54 Rashid Khalidi, "Truth, Justice and Reconciliation: Elements of a Solution to the Palestinian Refugee Issue," in Ghada Karmi and Eugene Cotran (eds.), *The Palestinian Exodus, 1948–1998* (Reading, UK, 1999), p. 227.

55 "1948-1998 in the Eyes of Two Peoples. A Roundtable Discussion," *Palestine-Israel Journal of Politics, Economics and Culture* 5(2) (1998), p. 24; Khalidi, "Truth, Justice and Reconciliation," p. 224.

56 Emile Habibi, "Your Holocaust – Our Catastrophe," *Politica* 8 (June-July 1986), pp. 26-27 (Hebrew). See also the quote from the *Jerusalem Post*, April 28, 1989, in Ruth Linn and Ilan Gur-Ze'ev, "Holocaust as Metaphor: Arab and Israeli Use of the Same Symbol," *Metaphor and Symbolic Activity* 11(3) (1996), p. 200. This sentence was used repeatedly in different forms. See, for example, "Their Holocaust, Our Cemetery," *al-'Arab al-Yawm*, July 4, 1998 (Arabic).

57 Khalid Kassab Mahamid, *The Palestinians and the Holocaust State* (Umm al-Fahm, 2006), p. 11 (Arabic).

58 Ibid., pp. 8-12. On this museum, see *The Jerusalem Post*, March 18, 2005; *Haaretz*, February 24, 2006 (Hebrew).

59 Mahamid, *The Palestinians and the Holocaust State*, p. 201.

60 *Al-Ahram Weekly*, April 15, 1999; April 6, 2000.

61 Khalidi, "Truth, Justice and Reconciliation," pp. 221-222.

62 Ibid., pp. 225-226.

63 Rouhana, "The Holocaust and Psychological Dynamics of the Arab-Israeli Conflict." See also Nadim Rouhana, "Zionism's Encounter with the Palestinians: The Dynamics of Force, Fear, and Extremism," in Robert I. Rotberg (ed.), *Israeli and Palestinian Narratives of Conflict: History's Double Helix* (Indiana University Press, 2006), p. 115.

64 Bar-On and Sarsar, "Bridging the Unbridgeable," p. 67.

65 Mahamid, *The Palestinians and the Holocaust State*, p. 9.

66 Joseph Massad, "Semites and Anti-Semites: That is the Question," *al-Ahram Weekly*, December 9, 2004.

67 Mahmoud Kayyal, "*Returning to Haifa* by Ghasan Kanafani in Hebrew," in Hannan Hever and Mahmoud Kayyal (eds.), *An Arabic-Hebrew Literary Space* (Ra'anana, 2016), pp. 82-97 (Hebrew).

68 Elias Khoury, *Bab al-Shams*, translated by Moshe Hakham (Tel Aviv, 2002) (Hebrew). See the discussion of his work in Esther Webman, "The Limits of Holocaust Representation in the Arab World," in Aukje Kluge and Benn Williams (eds.), *Re-examining the Holocaust through Literature* (New Castle upon Tyne, 2009), pp. 61-108; Bashir Bashir and Amos Goldberg, "Deliberating the Holocaust and the Nakba: Disruptive Empathy and Binationalism in Israel/Palestine," *Journal of Genocide Research* 16(1) (2014), pp. 77-99.

69 See, for example, Mustafa Kabha, "My Enemy's Enemy – A Friend: The Palestinian Nationalist Movement's Attitude toward Fascism and Nazism, 1925-1945," *Zmanim* 67 (Summer 1999), pp. 79-86 (Hebrew); Gerhard Höpp, Peter Wien,

and René Wildangel (eds.), *Blind für die Geschichte? Arabische Begegnungen mit dem Nationalsozialismus* (Berlin, 2004); Peter Wien, *Iraq Arab Nationalism: Authoritarian, Totalitarian and Pro-Fascist Inclinations 1932-1941* (London, 2006); Israel Gershoni (ed.), *Arab Responses to Fascism and Nazism: Attraction and Repulsion* (University of Texas Press, 2014).

70 Mustafa Kabha, "The Spanish Civil War as Reflected in the Contemporary Palestinian Press," in Gershoni, *Arab Responses to Fascism and Nazism*, pp. 127-140; Mustafa 'Abbasi, "Palestinians Fighting the Nazis: The Story of the Palestinian Volunteers in World War II," *Cathedra* 171, April 2019, pp. 125-147 (Hebrew).

71 *Filastin al-Thawra*, July 10, 1974 and March 8, 1986 (Arabic); *The Palestinian Encyclopedia*, Vol. 4, p. 160 (Arabic). See also *al-Quds*, July 28, 2003, and *al-Hayat al-Jadida*, August 8, 2003 (Arabic).

72 http://www.plo.ps/ (Arabic) (accessed on December 15, 2019).

73 Najib al-Ahmad, *Palestine: History and Struggle* (Amman, 1985), pp. 295-298 (Arabic); Ahmad Nawfal and 'Awni Jadu' al-'Abidi, *Pages from the Life of Hajj Amin al-Husayni, the Grand Mufti of Palestine and Leader of the National Movement* (Zarqa, 1985), pp. 134-136 (Arabic); Husayn Ahmad Jarrar, *Hajj Amin al-Husayni: Pioneer of Jihad and Hero of a Cause* (Amman, 1987), pp. 213, 218-236 (Arabic).

74 See Michel Abitbol, *North African Jewry during World War II*, translated by Catherine Tihanyi Zentelis (Wayne State University Press, 1989); Michael M. Laskier, *The Jews of the Maghreb in the Shadow of Vichy and the Swastika* (Tel Aviv, 1992) (Hebrew); Special issue titled "The Jews and Spain and the Middle East during the Holocaust," *Pe'amim: Studies in Oriental Jewry* 28 (1986) (Hebrew); Robert Satloff, *Among the Righteous: Lost Stories from the Holocaust's Long Reach into Arab Lands* (New York, 2006).

75 This topic is also on the agenda in Iran and Turkey. On the activity of Abdol Hossein Sardari, the Iranian consul in Paris, see Fariborz Mokhtari, *In the Lion's Shadow: The Iranian Schindler and His Homeland in the Second World War* (Stroud, UK, 2011). In 2007, Iranian television broadcast an Iranian series on this issue titled *Zero Degree Turn*. In Turkey as well this topic has been dealt with in the films *Turkish Passport* (2000) and *Desperate Hours* (2011) and in books such as *Last Train to Istanbul* and *The Ambassador*. For a comprehensive study on Turkey's treatment of its Jews during World War II see Corry Guttstadt, *Turkey, the Jews, and the Holocaust* (Cambridge University Press, 2013).

76 Mohammed Aïssaoui, *L'Étoile jaune et le Croissant* (Paris, 2012).

77 A different version of this story, which penetrated the public consciousness, is represented by Ethan Katz, a researcher of North African Jewry. See "Did the Paris Mosque Save Jews?" *The Jewish Quarterly Review* 102(2) (Spring 2012), pp. 256-287.

78 Boualem Sansal, *The German Mujahid*, translated by Frank Wynne (New York, 2008).

79 Aomar Boum and Sarah Abrevaya Stein (eds.), *The Holocaust and North Africa* (Stanford University Press, 2019); Aomar Boum and Mohammed Hatimi, "Blessing of the Bled: Rural Moroccan Jewry During World War II," in ibid., pp. 113-131; Aomar Boum, "Eyewitness Djela: Daily Life in a Saharan Vichy Labor Camp," in ibid., pp. 149-167.

80 On the activities of this initiative, see http://www.projetaladin.org/en/the-aladdin-project.html.

81 See, for example, Sarkut Kamal ʿAli, "The Holocaust: Crime of the Era," Elaf blog site, May 1, 2019, https://www.sotaliraq.com/2019/05/02/%D8%A7%D9%84%D9%87%D9%88%D9%84%D9%88%D9%83%D9%88%D8%B3%D8%AA-%D8%AC%D8%B1%D9%8A%D9%85%D8%A9-%D8%A7%D9%84%D8%B9%D8%B5%D8%B1/(Arabic) (accessed on September 10, 2019); Fariq al-ʿAmal, "The Holocaust between Denial and Exaggeration," Sasapost website, February 4, 2014, https://www.sasapost.com/%D8%A7%D9%84%D9%87%D9%88%D9%84%D9%88%D9%83%D9%88%D8%B3%D8%AA-%D9%85%D8%A7-%D8%A8%D9%8A%D9%86-%D8%A7%D9%84%D8%A5%D9%86%D9%83%D8%A7%D8%B1-%D9%88%D8%A7%D9%84%D9%85%D8%A8%D8%A7%D9%84%D8%BA%D8%A9-2-4/(Arabic) (accessed on September 10, 2019).

82 See "The Jewish Holocaust" on the Madar website, https://www.madarcenter.org/%D9%85%D9%88%D8%B3%D9%88%D8%B9%D8%A9-%D8%A7%D9%84%D9%85%D8%B5%D8%B7%D9%84%D8%AD%D8%A7%D8%AA/1687-%D8%A7%D9%84%D9%83%D8%A7%D8%B1%D8%AB%D8%A9-%D8%A7%D9%84%D9%8A%D9%87%D9%88%D8%AF%D9%8A%D8%A9 (Arabic) (accessed on September 10, 2019).

83 Omneya Talaat, "Sobibor, a Play in Cairo at the Theater that Distorts History and Arouses Compassion for the Jews of the Holocaust," *al-Akhbar*, August 22, 2019, http://omneyatalaat.blogspot.com/2019/08/blog-post_22.html (Arabic) (accessed on August 22, 2019).

84 Bishara, "On Nationalism and Universalism"; Bishara, "The Arabs and the Holocaust: The Analysis of a Problematic Conjunctive Letter."

85 Samira Aliyan, "The Holocaust in Palestinian Textbooks in the Palestinian Authority and the State of Israel," in Bashir and Goldberg, *The Holocaust and the Nakba*, p. 243.

86 *Haaretz*, February 3, 5, 7 and May 27, 2003 (Hebrew); *al-Sinara*, February 7 and March 14, 2003; *Kul al-ʿArab*, February 7, June 5, 2003; *Panorama*, February 7, May 30, and June 11, 2003; *Fasl al-Maqal*, February 21 and 28, March 7, 2003; *al-Mashhad al-Israʾili*, May 2, 2003; *al-Sharq al-Awsat*, May 25, 2003; *Maariv*,

May 28, 2003; *Yedioth Aharonoth*, May 30, 2003. For a comprehensive account of Shoufani's worldview and initiative, see Jean Mouttapa, *Un Arabe Face à Auschwitz. La mémoire partagée* (Paris, 2004).

87 Aliyan, "The Holocaust in Palestinian Textbooks," p. 255.

88 Ibid., p. 256.

89 *Al-Risala*, April 13, 2000 (Arabic); *al-Istiqlal*, April 20, 2000 (Arabic). For a detailed report on the disagreements on this issue see *al-Quds al-ʿArabi*, April 11, 2000 (Arabic); *al-ʿArabi*, April 20, 2000 (Arabic); Memri, Dispatch No. 187, February 21, 2000.

90 The Meir Amit Intelligence and Terrorism Information Center at the Israeli Intelligence Heritage and Commemoration Center, "The Struggle over the Nature of Education in the Gaza Strip," September 6, 2009, https://www.terrorism-info.org.il/Data/pdf/PDF_09_247_1.pdf (Hebrew) (accessed on September 10, 2019).

91 The Meir Amit Intelligence and Terrorism Information Center at the Israeli Intelligence Heritage and Commemoration Center, "Hamas and Other Bodies Announce Their Resolute Opposition to Including Holocaust Studies in UNRWA Schools," October 24, 2012, http://www.terrorism-info.org.il/he/article/20408 (Hebrew) (accessed on September 10, 2019).

92 See *Arab Human Development Report 2003: Building a Knowledge Society*, pp. 67-68, http://www.arab-hdr.org/reports/2003/english/part2s2ch2-e2003..pdf?download (accessed on December 10, 2019).

93 Joseph Massad, "Palestinian and Jewish History: Recognition or Submission?" *Journal of Palestine Studies* 30(1) (Autumn 2000), p. 65.

94 Kamil, "Araber, Antisemitismus und Holocaust."

List of Contributors

Prof. Yehuda Bauer is an emeritus professor of Holocaust Studies at the Institute for Contemporary Jewry at the Hebrew University of Jerusalem. He is the academic advisor to Yad Vashem's International Institute for Holocaust Research, a member of the Israel Academy of Sciences and Humanities, and the Honorary Chairman of the Intergovernmental International Holocaust Remembrance Alliance. Bauer is the author of 22 books, most dealing with the Holocaust and genocide and the ways to prevent them, and approximately 100 articles published in anthologies, collections, and journals. He addressed the German Bundestag in 1988, the Stockholm International Forum on Holocaust Education in 2000 and Genocide Prevention in 2004, and the UN General Assembly in 2007. He has served as an advisor for numerous films, including Claud Lanzmann's *Shoah*, and he is a recipient of the Israel Prize (1998) and the Emet Prize (2017).

Prof. Judy Tydor Baumel-Schwartz, a Professor of Jewish History at Bar-Ilan University and director of the Arnold and Leona Finkler Institute of Holocaust Research, is the Abraham and Edita Spiegel Family Professor in Holocaust Research and the Rabbi Pynchas Brener Professor in Research on the Holocaust of European Jewry. She is the author and editor of numerous books and articles on subjects related to the Holocaust, particularly on women and gender, religious life and mutual assistance, and Holocaust commemoration in Israel. Her books include *Double Jeopardy: Gender and the Holocaust* (1998); *Perfect Heroes: The World War II Parachutists and the making of Collective Israeli Memory* (Heb.) (2004); *Never Look Back: The Jewish Refugee Children in Great Britain, 1938-1945* (2012); *Identity, Heroism and Religion in the Lives of Contemporary Jewish Women* (Peter Lang, 2013); *My Name is Frieda Sima: The American-Jewish Women's Immigrant Experience Through the Eyes of a Young Girl from the Bukovina* (2017); *A Very Special Life: The Bernice Chronicles* (2017) and *For the Love of Shirley: One Woman's Challenges and Choices in Postwar Jewish America* (2020).

Dr. Graciela Ben Dror has been the editor of *Yalkut Moreshet, The Journal for the Study of the Holocaust and Antisemitism*, since 2011. She has served as a researcher at the Stephen Roth Institute for the Study of Contemporary Antisemitism at

Tel-Aviv University and she is a former lecturer in the Departments of History and Jewish History at the University of Haifa. She was the director of Moreshet, Mordechai Anielevich Memorial, in Tel Aviv and Givat Haviva. Her recent books include: *The Catholic Church and the Jews: Argentina, 1933-1945* (2000) (Hebrew), which was awarded the Israeli Ministry of Culture's Sefer Habikurim Prize for the year 2000 and was also published in Spanish (2003) and English (2008); *La Iglesia Católica ante el Holocausto. España y América Latina 1933-1945* (2003); *Radical Socialist Zionism on the Banks of Rio de La Plata: The Mordechai Anielevich Movement in Uruguay, 1954-1976* (2016) in Hebrew (with Victor Ben Dror); and *Christianity without Mercy* (2018) (Hebrew), written with the support of the Claims Conference and the Elias Sourasky Chair of Iberian & Latin American Studies at Tel Aviv University.

Prof. Havi Dreifuss is a historian in the Department of Jewish History and head of the Institute for the History of Polish Jewry and Israel-Poland Relations at Tel Aviv University. She also heads the Center for Research on the Holocaust in Poland at Yad Vashem's International Institute for Holocaust Research. Her recent books include *Warsaw Ghetto: The End (April 1942-June 1943)* (2018) (Hebrew), which was awarded the Zalman Shazar Prize for 2017/18, and *Relations between Jews and Poles during the Holocaust: The Jewish Perspective* (2017). Recent articles include "Gerer Hasidic Youth during the Sho'ah: A Representative Blind Spot in Holocaust Research," *Polin* 33 (forthcoming in 2020); "Matys Gelman: nieznany przywódca nieznanego ruchu chasydzkiego w czasie Zagłady," *Zaglada Zydow* (forthcoming); and "In Favor of [the Conceptual Category of] Antisemitism in Holocaust Research," *Zion* (forthcoming) (Hebrew).

Prof. Aviva Halamish of the Open University is a scholar of Jewish history and the history of the Land of Israel in the twentieth century, with a focus on Jewish immigration, *Ha`apala*, the kibbutz, the Jewish Yishuv, and the State of Israel. She has authored and edited over a dozen books and numerous articles on her subjects of expertise, including *Exodus: The Real Story* (1990) (Hebrew); a biography of Meir Yaari (Vol. 1 in 2009; Vol. 2 in 2013) (Hebrew); *The Kibbutz: The First Hundred Years* (jointly edited with Zvi Zameret) (2010); *Holocaust and Antisemitism: Research and Public Discourse – Essays Presented in Honor of Dina*

Porat (jointly edited with Ronit Stauber and Esther Webman) (2015); *Israel, 1967-1977: Continuity and Change* (jointly edited with Ofer Schiff) (2017) (Hebrew).

Prof. Dan Michman is an emeritus professor in the Israel and Golda Koschitzky Department of Jewish History and Contemporary Jewry, a former head of the Arnold and Leona Finkler Institute of Holocaust Research, and the current holder of the Abraham and Edita Spiegel Family Chair in Holocaust Research at Bar-Ilan University. He also heads the International Institute for Holocaust Research and is the current holder of the John Najmann Chair of Holocaust Studies at Yad Vashem. His publications deal with a variety of aspects of the Holocaust itself, its representation in the historiography, and its influence on Israel, world Jewry, and the western world. He has written and edited numerous books, including: *Encyclopedia of Jewish Communities: The Netherlands* (1985) (Hebrew; an updated edition was subsequently published in Dutch); *Post-Zionism and the Holocaust I: The Role of the Holocaust in the Public Debate on Post-Zionism in Israel (1993-1996)* (1997) (Hebrew); *Post-Zionism and the Holocaust II: The Role of the Holocaust in the Public Debate on Post-Zionism in Israel, 1997-1998* (2007) (Hebrew); *The Holocaust and Holocaust Research: Conceptualization, Terminology and Basic Issues* (1998) (Hebrew; subsequently translated into French, German, English, Russian, and Hungarian); *Remembering the Holocaust in Germany, 1945-2000: German Strategies and Jewish Responses* (2002); *The Holocaust in Jewish History: Historiography, Consciousness, Interpretations* (2005) (Hebrew); *De la mémoire de la Shoah dans le monde juif* (2008); *The Jewish Ghettos during the Shoah: How and Why Did They Emerge?* (2008) (Hebrew; subsequently translated into English and German); *Adolf Hitler, the Decision-Making Process Leading to the "Final Solution of the Jewish Question," and the Grand Mufti of Jerusalem Hajj Amin al-Hussayni: The Current State of Research* (2017); and *l'Allemagne Nazie: Nouveaux regards* (2018).

Prof. Dalia Ofer (Emeritus) was recently awarded the Distinguished Achievement Award in Holocaust Studies by the Holocaust Educational Foundation of Northwestern University (2018). She was the Max and Rita Haber Professor of the Holocaust and Eastern European Jewry at the Avraham Hartman Institute of Contemporary Jewry and the Melton Center for Jewish Education at the Hebrew University of Jerusalem. She has served as head of the Institute of Contemporary

Jewry and the Vidal Sassoon International Center for the Study of Antisemitism at the Hebrew University. Prof. Ofer represented the Hebrew University on the Academic Committee of Yad Vashem and was a member of the Board of Yad Vashem's International Institute for Holocaust Research. As the representative of the Hebrew University of Jerusalem she headed the Board of Governors of Hebrew University High School, chaired the Israeli Ministry of Education's Professional Committee of History, and served on a number of committees of Israel's Council for Higher Education. Prof. Ofer has published widely in Hebrew and English on various subjects pertaining to the Holocaust, Jewish immigration to Eretz Israel, and the memory of the Holocaust in Israel. Her book *Derech Bayam: Illegal Immigration to Palestine during the Holocaust* received the Ben Zvi Award. Her books in English include *Escaping Holocaust: Illegal Immigration to the Land of Israel* (1990), winner of the Jewish Book Award; *Women in the Holocaust* (jointly edited with Lenore L. Weizman) (1998), finalist for the Jewish Book Award in the categories of Holocaust and Women in 1999; and *Jewish Women: A Comprehensive Historical Encyclopedia* (jointly edited with Paula Hayman) (2009).

Prof. Avinoam Patt holds the Doris and Simon Konover Chair of Judaic Studies and is the director of the Center for Judaic Studies and Contemporary Jewish Life at the University of Connecticut. He is the author of *Finding Home and Homeland: Jewish Youth and Zionism in the Aftermath of the Holocaust* (2009), and he is the co-editor (with Michael Berkowitz) of *We Are Here: New Approaches to the Study of Jewish Displaced Persons in Postwar Germany* (2010). He has been involved in a number of projects of the U.S. Holocaust Memorial Museum in Washington, including *Jewish Responses to Persecution, 1938-1940* (2011). Prof. Patt has co-edited an anthology of Jewish American literature titled *The New Diaspora: The Changing Landscape of American Jewish Fiction* (2015) and *The Joint Distribution Committee at 100: A Century of Humanitarianism* (2019). He is currently writing a new book about the Warsaw Ghetto Uprising, co-editing a forthcoming volume titled *Laughter After: Humor and the Holocaust* (2020), and co-editing a book on *Understanding and Teaching the Holocaust* (2020) with Laura Hilton.

Prof. Dina Porat has served as the head of Tel Aviv University's Chaim Rosenberg School of Jewish Studies and of the university's Jewish History Department, and head of the Stephen Roth Institute for the Study of Contemporary

Antisemitism and Racism, also at T.A.U. She currently holds the university's Alfred P. Slaner Chair for the Study of Racism and Antisemitism and is head of the Kantor Center for the Study of Contemporary European Jewry. In October 2011, she was appointed chief historian of Yad Vashem.

Porat was named Outstanding Lecturer of T.A.U.'s Faculty of the Humanities in 2004, and she was awarded the Raoul Wallenberg Centennial Medal in 2012. She has been named by *The Marker* as one of Israel's 50 sharpest minds and by *Forbes* as one of the 50 most influential women in Israel. She is the author of *Beyond the Corporeal: The Life and Times of Abba Kovner* (2000) (Hebrew), which was awarded the Zandman Prize by the International Organization of Fighters, Partisans, and Camp Prisoners and the Buchman Prize by Yad Vashem; *Smoke-Scented Morning Coffee: Essays on the Encounter of the Yishuv and Israeli Society with the Holocaust and its Survivors* (2011) (Hebrew), which was awarded the Agit Prize in 2011; and *Vengeance and Retribution are Mine: Community, the Holocaust, and Abba Kovner's Avengers* (2019) (Hebrew), recipient of the Bahat Prize.

Dr. Roni Stauber is the academic director of Tel Aviv University's Wiener Library for the Study of the Nazi Era and the Holocaust. He is a lecturer and a senior research fellow in the Department of Jewish History and the Kantor Center. His studies explore the memory of the Holocaust in Israel, particularly its influence on ideological and political discourse in the country and on Israel's international political activity. He recently concluded a broad study of Israel-West German relations, which will be published under the title *Diplomacy in the Shadow of Memory: Past and Present in Israel-West German relations, 1953-1965*. He is currently researching the cooperation between German prosecutors and Israeli legal officials and Jewish activists in bringing Nazi criminals to trial in West Germany, a topic that has received the support of the Israel Science Foundation. Among the books he has written and edited are: *Lessons for this Generation: Holocaust and Heroism in Israeli Public Discourse in the 1950s* (2007) (Hebrew); *The Holocaust in Israeli Public Debate in the 1950s: Ideology and Memory* (2007); *Laying The Foundations for Holocaust Research: The Impact of the Historian Philip Friedman* (2000); and *Collaborations with the Nazis: Collective Memory and Public Discourse* (2011).

Dr. Esther Webman is a senior research fellow at the Dayan Center for Middle Eastern and African Studies at Tel Aviv University and the academic advisor to the Program for the Study of Jews in the Middle East. Her research deals with Arab discourse on the Arab-Israeli conflict, particularly its antisemitic aspects and its perceptions of the Holocaust. Her doctoral dissertation focused on Egyptian public discourse regarding the Holocaust between 1945 and 1962 and was awarded a prize by the University of Haifa. She has been the guest of a number of research centers, including Yad Vashem in 2016-17. Her book *From Empathy to Denial: Reactions to the Holocaust in the Arab World* (2009), co-authored by Meir Litvak, was awarded the Washington Institute Book Prize. Webman has edited a number of books, the most recent being an Arabic-language collection of articles on antisemitism that was published in 2017.

Nikola Zimring is a Ph.D. student at New York University in the Department of Hebrew and Judaic studies and she specializes in Modern Jewish History and Israel Studies. Her thesis is under the guidance of Prof. David Engel. She holds a Master's degree in Jewish History from Tel Aviv University, Israel. She completed her MA theses under the guidance of Dr. Roni Stauber.

INSTRUCTIONS FOR CONTRIBUTORS

MORESHET, THE JOURNAL FOR THE STUDY OF THE HOLOCAUST AND ANTISEMITISM

1. Moreshet Journal, a **peer reviewed publication,** invites researchers to send us scholarly articles and/or review essays relating to topics dealing with the Holocaust and Antisemitism.

2. Articles have to be original, and not published in other publications.

3. Manuscripts should not exceed 12,000 words including notes, and including a short abstract of 150 words. The articles must be sent by email or on CD, must be typewritten, double-spaced, and all pages should be numbered consecutively. Two typewritten, double-spaced copies of the article on A4 paper should be sent to the address of the Moreshet Journal.

4. Details of the author's institutional affiliation, degree, short CV for the list of contributors (3-4 lines), address, phone number and email must be added.

5. To be accepted for publication the articles will pass both internal and external peer review and, if accepted, the author may be requested to make revisions.

6. Articles may be sent in English, French, German, Polish or Hebrew, but in some cases other languages will also be considered.

7. The author will receive 10 offprints of the article and a copy of the volume in which the article was published.

Please send the articles to the following address and e-mail:

Dr. Graciela Ben Dror, Editor

Moreshet, the Journal for the Study of the Holocaust and Antisemitism

Givat Haviva, Doar Na Menashe, 37850

Israel

graciela.moreshet@gmail.com

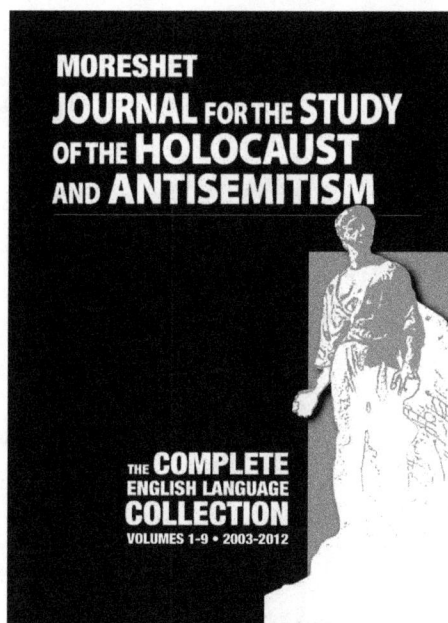

MORESHET

JOURNAL FOR THE STUDY OF THE HOLOCAUST AND ANTISEMITISM

14 2017

- Graciela Ben-Dror
- Yehuda Dvorkin
- Sharon Geva
- Aviva Halamish
- Liat Meirav
- Dalia Ofer
- Avinoam J. Patt
- Na'ama Seri-Levi
- Zipora Shehory-Rubin
- Ada Schein
- Bilha Shilo
- Yfaat Weiss
- Yechiel Weitzman

MORESHET

JOURNAL FOR THE STUDY OF THE HOLOCAUST AND ANTISEMITISM

15 2018

MORESHET

JOURNAL FOR THE STUDY OF THE HOLOCAUST AND ANTISEMITISM

16 2019

- Nava T. Barazani
- Tammy Bar- Joseph
- Graciela Ben-Dror
- Yaakov Borut
- Robert Cohen
- Sharon Geva
- Lior Inbar
- Nir Itzik
- Yvonne Kozlovsky-Golan
- Daniel Nadav
- Dina Porat
- Dov Schidorsky
- Margalit Shlain
- Eli Tzur
- Amit Varshizky

www.ingramcontent.com/pod-product-compliance
Lightning Source LLC
Chambersburg PA
CBHW062033090426
42740CB00016B/2892